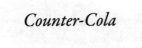

Counter-Cola

A multimedia companion to this book is available at http://scalar.usc.edu/works/counter-cola.

Counter-Cola

A MULTINATIONAL HISTORY OF THE GLOBAL CORPORATION

Amanda Ciafone

UNIVERSITY OF CALIFORNIA PRESS

University of California Press, one of the most distinguished university presses in the United States, enriches lives around the world by advancing scholarship in the humanities, social sciences, and natural sciences. Its activities are supported by the UC Press Foundation and by philanthropic contributions from individuals and institutions. For more information, visit www.ucpress.edu.

University of California Press
Oakland, California

Library of Congress Cataloging-in-Publication Data

Names: Ciafone, Amanda, author.
Title: Counter-cola : a multinational history of the global corporation / Amanda Ciafone.
Description: Oakland, California : University of California Press, [2019] | Includes bibliographical references and index. |
Identifiers: LCCN 2018039757 (print) | LCCN 2018042278 (ebook) | ISBN 9780520970946 | ISBN 9780520299016 (cloth : alk. paper) | ISBN 9780520299023 (pbk. : alk. paper)
Subjects: LCSH: Coca-Cola Company—History. | Globalization—Economic aspects. | Culture and globalization.
Classification: LCC HD9349.S634 (ebook) | LCC HD9349.S634 C6275 2019 (print) | DDC 338.7/66362—dc23
LC record available at https://lccn.loc.gov/2018039757

Manufactured in the United States of America

26 25 24 23 22 21 20 19
10 9 8 7 6 5 4 3 2 1

To my parents and Dan
for their labors and love

CONTENTS

ACKNOWLEDGMENTS

If I have learned anything in my years of schooling and living, and I think I have, it is that humankind's best work is collective, built on and shaped by the contributions of multiple people. The best of this work has been shaped by many. I am grateful to be able to begin to acknowledge them here.

This book emerged from a dissertation completed at Yale University, where Michael Denning was not just an advisor, but a model for the kind of committed scholar and teacher I will long hope to become. Now that I advise graduate students myself, I have an even deeper appreciation for Michael's generosity of time, spirit, and intellect, and I pledge to try to pay it forward. Matthew Frye Jacobson's enthusiasm and insights motivated me through the research and writing. Laura Wexler was a stalwart supporter from my first days at graduate school and gave me new theoretical perspectives for this work. Thank you to Seth Fein for being an interlocutor who excited new ideas and encouraged me to see them through. Many thanks also to Hazel Carby, Dana Frank, Lesley Gill, Gil Joseph, Jennifer Klein, George Lipsitz, Charles McGovern, Mai Ngai, and Vijay Prashad who generously offered key perspectives and interventions at just the right times.

This book came to fruition at the University of Illinois at Urbana-Champaign. Thank you to the Media and Cinema Studies Department, and colleagues across campus, including Sara Benson, Marcelo Bucheli, Anita Say Chan, C. L. Cole, Cliff Christians, Susmita Das, Susan Davis, Theresa Harris, James Hay, Kristin Hoganson, Derek Long, Cameron McCarthy, Isabel Molina-Guzmán, Jenny Oyallon-Koloski, Claudia Lagos Lira, Kathy Oberdeck, Fabian Prieto Ñañez, Ann Reisner, Jay Rosenstein, Dan Schiller, Antonio Sotomayor, Mark Steinberg, Inger Stole, Julie Turnock, Angharad Valdivia, and the faculty and staff of the Illinois Program for Research in the Humanities, the Unit for Criticism and Interpretive Theory, and the Center for Latin American and Caribbean Studies for working to create such a generative intellectual home. I feel so lucky that my path continues to cross with Naomi Paik's, as her intellect, determination, and commitment to justice inspire and challenge me. The students and collaborators in my global commodities and culture, history of capitalism, and transnational Latin American media and cultural studies courses at the University of Illinois and Macalester College pushed me to elaborate and clarify my ideas and helped me by offering their own. Thank you to my colleagues and friends at Macalester College, in International Studies, Media and Cultural Studies, and Latin American Studies, and beyond, including Ernesto Capello, Beth Cleary, Amy Damon, Susanna Drake, Olga Gónzalez, Lynn Hudson, Leola Johnson, David Chioni Moore, Nadya Nedelsky, Rachel Perlmeter, Peter Rachleff, Jane Rhodes, Ahmed Samatar, Scott Shoemaker, Clay Steinman, and James Von Geldern.

The members of the Yale Working Group on Globalization and Culture each contributed individually, and even more, collectively, to the ideas in this book which arose in conversation with them. Thank you to Amina El-Annan, Michael Denning, Rossen Djagalov, Daniel Gilbert, Sumanth Gopinath, Mandi Isaacs-Jackson, Myra Jones-Taylor, Nazima Kadir, Christina Moon, Bethany Moreton, Naomi Paik, Ariana Paulson, Olga Sooudi, Laura Trice, Van Truong, Charlie Veric, and Kirsten Weld. Thank you to other collectives that have fostered this work and have been central to my intellectual and political (not to mention social) formation in classrooms and picket lines: the Yale Graduate Employees and Students Organization, the Working Group on Marxism and Cultural Theory at Yale, the Photography and Memory Working Group at Yale, and the UIUC Campus Faculty Association.

My deep thanks to the archivists at the Manuscript, Archives & Rare Book Library at Emory University, the National Archives and Records Administration II, the National Security Archive, the Atlanta History Center, the Manuscripts Division and the Motion Picture, Broadcasting & Recorded Sound and Manuscript Divisions of the Library of Congress. Thank you especially to Kira Jones, Jonothan Lewis, Matthew Quallen, Erin Sexton, Kathleen Shoemaker, Josie Walters-Johnston, and Rachel Wisthuff for their indispensable assistance. Thank you to Ruth Caplan, Premal Dharia, and Barbara Stevens for the room, board, and excellent company during my long stints in Washington, DC.

A long list of people taught me about Colombia, even welcoming me into their lives and homes, especially Mary Bellman, Gerardo Cajamarca, Luis

Adolfo Cardona, Limberto Carranza, Javier Correa, Carlos Cruz, Campo Elias, Juan Carlos Espinosa, Juan Carlos Galvis, Lesley Gill, Efraín Guerrero, Beethoven Herrera Valencia, Dan Kovalik, Marco Llinás, Monica Lugo, Omar Martinez, William Mendoza, Ember Eduardo Ortiz, Edgar Páez, Luis Alejandro Pedraza, Ed Potter, Fabian Prieto Ñañez, Ray Rogers, Gimena Sánchez, Antonio Sotomayor, Abbey Steele, Hannah Stutzman, Efraín Surmay, John Jairo Tamayo, Jessye Weinstein, Euripides Yance, the Sinaltrainal members and non-affiliated Coca-Cola FEMSA workers I spoke with in Barrancabermeja, Barranquilla, Bucaramanga, Bogotá, Cali, Cartagena, Cúcuta, and Medellín, members of SICO, and other workers at Bebidas y Alimentos de Urabá, and some Coca-Cola executives and bottling plant managers who provided important insight. I was extremely fortunate to be named a Fellow at the Biblioteca Luis Angel Arango in Bogotá, where the archivists and other fellows helped me navigate their expansive collection of historical newspapers and provided me with much needed social breaks away from them. I also appreciate all the assistance from archivists at the Archivo General de la Nación in Bogotá, the Archivo Histórico de Medellín, and the Biblioteca Pública Piloto de Medellín para América Latina. The Asociación Nacional de Empresarios de Colombia (ANDI) subsidized my attendance to their Encuentro Internacional de Responsabilidad Social Empresarial, which provided me with a valuable entry into the world of corporate social responsibility in Colombia. Thank you to the editors and anonymous reviewers of *Historia y Sociedad* 34 (2018) (Universidad Nacional de Colombia, Medellín), which published an earlier version of chapter 1.

I had the farthest to go in my travels and learning on the history of Coca-Cola in India, and a number of people helped me along the way. Thank you to R. Ajayan, Vivek Bald, Miabi Chatterji, Susmita Das, Deepak Jolly, Sujith Koonan, MVRL Murthy, C. R. Neelakandan, Harry Ott, Rajendra Pandey, Ram Narayan Patel, Urmila Patel, Sujani Reddy, Ibrahim Hafeezur Rehman, C. Saratchandran, Kamlesh Kumar Sharma, Sridevi Shivarajan, Ajit Singh, Amit Srivastava, Daniel Vermeer, Manu Vimalassery, Urmila Vishwakarma, Kushal Yadav, Siyaram Yadav, Nandlal Master and the brothers and sisters of Lok Samiti, and the people of Mehdiganj, Plachimada, and Kala Dera who shared their Coca-Cola histories with me. I deeply appreciated the engagement of some Coca-Cola executives and plant managers in this research. Thank you to Raghvendra Upadhyay for his perspective and translation work and his wife Bunti and their family for welcoming me into their home. Archivists at the Nehru Memorial Library, the National Archives of India, and the Communist Party of India (Marxist) Archive helped me navigate their collections. The Banaras Hindu University Guest House in Varanasi provided me with a dramatically beautiful campus and wonderful meals at the end of hard days of research. Portions of chapter 6 originated as an article in *International Labor and Working Class History* 81 (Spring 2012) and a chapter in *The Sun Never Sets: South Asian Migrants in an Age of U.S. Power* (New York University Press, 2013); thank you to editors Vivek Bald, Miabi Chatterji, Mai Ngai, Mary Nolan, Sujani Reddy, and Manu Vimalassery, and the anonymous reviewers, for helping me hone my ideas, not to mention sharpen my writing.

This book would not have been possible without institutional and financial support from many sources. A fellowship at the John W. Kluge Center at the Library of Congress provided me with several months of residence at the most impressive library in the world; thank you to Mary Lou Reker, Jason Steinhauer, Travis Hensley, and my cohort of fellows. The University of Illinois's Research Board granted me time away from teaching to complete this book and funds for the large number of images within. I am grateful for the financial support for my research and writing as a graduate student from the John F. Enders Research Award and Robert M. Leylan Dissertation Fellowship. A committee of Yale faculty and staff from the MacMillan Center for International and Area Studies, the Law School, and the School of Management, with I believe a strong sense of irony, awarded me the Coca-Cola World Fund at Yale Grant (administered by Yale's MacMillan Center for International and Area Studies from a fund established by The Coca-Cola Company in 1992 to support research at the intersections of international law, business, and public policy, as a continuation of the Company's long-standing philanthropy around education, updated with a focus on global affairs for the neoliberal era). The $3,000 I received subsidized some of my travel expenses for preliminary research in Colombia and branded me just enough to be more palatable to some people with whom I spoke, and distasteful to others, which prompted productive interrogation of my research questions.

Comments and questions from respondents too numerous to name sent this work in fruitful directions; thank you to the Labor and Working Class History Association Section of the American Historical Association, the American Studies Association, the Tepoztlán Institute for Transnational History of the Americas, the South Asian Diaspora and the Piracy Working Groups at New York University, the International Association for Media and

Communications Research, the National Communication Association, the Union for Democratic Communications, the Global Studies Association, the American Studies Department at Purdue University, the History and Society Division at Babson College, the History of Capitalism Summer Camp at Cornell University, and the History Department at the University of Illinois at Urbana-Champaign. The New Americanists Working Group at Notre Dame—my friends and colleagues, Aaron Carico, Dan Gilbert, Sarah Haley, Naomi Paik, Shana Redmond, and especially Jason Ruiz—provided this project with the best kind of criticism: smart, incisive, and motivated by a feeling of mutual responsibility. Thank you to my friends, colleagues and comrades, including Adam Arenson, Kathleen Belew, Rebecca Berne, Gerry Cadava, Aaron Carico, Brenda Carter, Sonali Chakravarti, Premal Dharia, Andy and Krista Gaedtke, Sarah Haley, Mandi Isaacs-Jackson, Amanda Izzo, Prema Katari, Seth Kertzer, Mark Krasovic, Jana Lipman, Ben Looker, James Lundberg, Monica Muñoz Martinez, Rebecca McKenna, Uri McMillan, Bethany Moreton, Bob and Haley Morrissey, Naomi Paik, Ariana Paulson, Lisa Pinley-Covert, Shana Redmond, Mary Reynolds, Jason Ruiz, Theresa Runstedtler, Annemarie Strassel, Helen Veit, Madeleine Weil, Aaron Wong, and Erin Wood. Thank you to all of those I am unintentionally forgetting, but to whom I am nevertheless indebted: please come collect.

A number of people shepherded this book toward production, improving it at every stage. The reviewers for the University of California Press provided rigorous comments, generative questions, and words of encouragement that I repeatedly returned to for direction and motivation. Thank you to the editorial team at UC Press, including Niels Hooper, Elena Bellaart, Bradley Depew, Cindy Fulton, Robin Manley, Gabriela Ramirez-Chavez, and those who helped the book take its final shape, leaving their indelible marks, including Peter Dreyer, Cathy Hannabach, and Dave Ivy, and Ryan Sherwood.

Betty and Edwin Vetog and Elvera and Frank Ciafone taught me to learn from people's histories and empowered me to make my own. My life and work has been enriched by new family who have provided patient support and welcome distraction through the long years of this project: thank you, Peggy, Tom, Carrie, Andrew and Carl Gilbert, Ben Douglas, and Matthew Lindsay. My parents, Judy and Russ, and my sisters, Joanna and C.C., are my home. They gave me unfettered love, even when this research regularly took me away and I returned back exhausted and in need of more. I feel so thankful, every day, to have lucked into our family. Thank you to Milo Ciafone-

Gilbert for opening up my world and reminding me what's at stake for everyone in its future. This "line in my acknowledgements" cannot begin to thank Dan Gilbert, who is my partner in everything. The best ideas herein have been shaped most of all by him; the worst ones he has gently encouraged me to change. I am most grateful that I will have more time to thank him fully.

Introduction

COCA-COLA IS AN ICON OF GLOBALIZATION. Few things are more closely identified with global capitalism than "The Real Thing," as one of The Coca-Cola Company's memorable advertising campaigns branded the drink. But precisely *how* is Coke global? Coca-Cola is the single most widely distributed branded commodity on the planet. More nation-states have Coca-Cola products than are members of the United Nations.[1] Nearly three-quarters of The Coca-Cola Company's revenue comes from international sales.[2] Since Interbrand started ranking the most valuable brands in the world in 2000, Coca-Cola has topped the list twelve times.[3] And, perhaps most relevant in gauging its popular significance, "Coca-Cola" is the second most widely known word on earth, trailing only "OK." Second-place status being unacceptable to a company accustomed to being at the top, in 1996, CEO Roberto Goizueta assured investors that Coca-Cola has "the trademark rights to [OK] in many markets, too . . ."[4]

But the global significance of Coca-Cola emerges from a history far more complicated than its ubiquitous branded bottles and cans. Indeed, precisely because of how the commodity has become a material and symbolic presence in global daily life, people from all over the planet have narrated global capitalism through it, redeploying Coca-Cola to create disruptions and alternatives to the world figured in Goizueta's report to his investors. The histories of the corporation and the struggles that have represented, resisted, and remade the brand of globalization that Coca-Cola signifies are constitutive of the corporation's "world." The history of *this* world, the subject of *Counter-Cola,* suggests that "The Real Thing" is something quite different.

Studying a single corporation, The Coca-Cola Company, over time reveals transnational connections of economic, political, social, and cultural power as it attempts to configure and participate in global capitalism.[5] A Coca-Cola world system internationally interconnects people and places, linked through relationships with the corporation, its capital, commodities and raw materials, and representational texts. The Coca-Cola Company itself conceives of the corporate network comprised of the underlying company, its bottlers, and vendors as "the Coca-Cola System."[6] Of course, no corporation is a world system entirely of its own making; it participates in, influences and is shaped by the international economics and politics that link markets, states, labor, consumers, and resources. But a corporation as large and transnational as The Coca-Cola Company has "a social system. . . that has boundaries, structures, member groups, rules of legitimation, and coherence."[7] These mostly overlap . with those of the larger international capitalist world system, but sometimes slightly vary: the Coca-Cola System has some of its own centers of power, governing structures, and justifying logics, which reveal with greater specificity the workings of global capitalism and the ways in which it is also shaped at its margins.[8]

Two international systems of corporate production constitute this Coca-Cola System.[9] The first is the material production of soft drinks by the Company and its bottlers. The Coca-Cola Company sells drink concentrates to bottlers around the world, who manufacture and distribute the final product. Second, as these bottled drinks are produced as much by ideas, associations, and business plans—their secret formulas, brands, and business and financial strategies—as by sugar and water and fizz, the Coca-Cola world system is constructed through the production and managed dissemination of immaterial products. As Peter Drucker, the "father of modern management theory," noted, The Coca-Cola Company is fundamentally "an advertiser with tremendous access to a distribution system."[10] Addressing a group of bottlers, a Coca-Cola executive reportedly explained the success of this immaterial production of the brand through advertising, and their almost secondary status relative to it, with this hypothetical: if the Company were to lose all its bottling plants, equipment, staff, and inventory in a fire or cataclysmic disaster overnight, the next morning an executive could walk into a major bank anywhere in the world and get a loan to rebuild it all based solely on the security of the value of the brand, the goodwill accrued to its trademark.[11] The true business of Coca-Cola is the symbolic system of production, the construction of brands through texts that represent and distinguish its material products, and everything else about its business could be rebuilt on that immaterial foundation.[12]

But this is not just about advertising and marketing. The Coca-Cola Company's creation, management, and investment in the system of bottling production is central to its immaterial production. In fact, The Coca-Cola Company is not in the business of selling soft drinks, but in the business of selling the selling of soft drinks: the franchising of bottling production. The Company sells bottlers the business model of Coca-Cola production itself, and the Company and its stockholders make money through transactional and financial relationships between the underlying corporation and these franchise bottlers. The Coca-Cola Company charges them, not only for soft-drink concentrates, but for the right to use trademarks, business strategies, technical services, and marketing materials. Additional profits are derived from financial machinations such as the setting of prices for these materials and services, hedging against changes in foreign exchange and interest rates, and investing in franchise bottlers. The Company thus displays elements of the immaterial turn in global capitalism that characterized the final decades of the twentieth century, as the commodification of culture, the commercialization of knowledge and information as intellectual property, and financialization emerged as defining features of the world economy.

The Coca-Cola Company has employed two very different business strategies to develop these two systems of production, material and immaterial. Coca-Cola globalized by externalizing material production, franchising soft-drink manufacturing to independently owned bottlers. Through this franchise model, the Company grew quickly, while minimizing the risks and responsibilities of direct investment and employment in overseas markets. Over the course of the twentieth century, bottling companies extended this externalizing logic even further, increasingly hiring subcontracted and temporary workers, for example, and externalizing the social, environmental, and health costs of its business model. Outsourcing material production through franchising also required managing the potential loss of control over production and representation of its commodities. While decentralizing material production, the Company centralized its immaterial production, since it was both the driver of its revenue and the means of asserting power in the Coca-Cola system. It produced intellectual property such as formulas, trademarks, marketing, and business plans over which it had monopoly control and upon which bottlers relied. It developed legal and economic strategies to manage bottlers, including restrictive bottling contracts, interlocking boards, and strategic investment in the bottling industry. And the Company strove to produce social and cultural associations, orientations, and practices through corporate relations, communications, and events to generate cooperation among its bottlers and, of course, consumers and the public at large.

I use "the Company" as shorthand for The Coca-Cola Company throughout this book, both for narrative ease and to distinguish the work's main corporate subject from other companies. The Coca-Cola Company also refers to itself as the Company with a capital *C*. I also capitalize the *T* in "The Coca-Cola Company," since that is its legal title. In 1919, *the* Coca-Cola Company, known then as now for its Atlanta "home," was reincorporated and renamed in Delaware, establishing a legal address with little more than a mailbox. Delaware is one of the world's most notorious tax havens, allowing companies to both dramatically reduce state taxes and obscure profits made in other countries, while offering business-friendly case law and state courts. And Delaware does not tax revenue from "intangible assets" like trademarks, patents, and copyrights—in other words, the Company's immaterial production.[13] So, *the* Coca-Cola Company became *The* Coca-Cola Company.

Over the century since its Delaware reincorporation, the Company has continued to hide profits from US and international taxation. As a US-based multinational corporation, The Coca-Cola Company is required to pay US federal taxes on profits earned around the world, minus a tax credit equal to whatever taxes the Company paid to foreign governments. But those taxes on foreign income become due only when profits are repatriated to the United States. So, the Company shields income generated in foreign jurisdictions by keeping it in the hands of international subsidiaries incorporated in low-tax locations. The Company's immaterial system of production enables such economic manipulations: the bulk of the Company's profits are generated from licensing intangible property—brands, services, and intellectual property such as formulas—to foreign subsidiaries who in turn charge bottlers for the right to manufacture, distribute, market, and advertise Coca-Cola products. These deals, governed by agreements between the subsidiaries and the parent company and involving payments for intangible assets with no market equivalent or documented value, take place in secrecy within the Coca-Cola world system. As a result, such transactions can be priced to effectively transfer profits to countries with lower tax rates. This is what the IRS accused The Coca-

Cola Company of doing, when in 2015 it handed the Company a $3.3 billion tax bill for underreporting 2007–9 income and threatened to readjust the Company's tax liabilities by reevaluating how it prices intangible assets. The Coca-Cola Company had allegedly given subsidiaries in Ireland, Swaziland, Brazil, Mexico, Chile, Costa Rica, and Egypt discounts totaling $9.4 billion in licensing rights so as to leave more of its profits in those low-tax nations.[14] At the end of 2017, The Coca-Cola Company's international subsidiaries were holding $42 billion in offshore profits, shielding them from taxation in the United States.[15] Much of this profit is held by subsidiaries incorporated in tax havens, which do business in various countries, but avoid paying taxes by bringing their profits home to the extremely low-tax nations in which they are "based." The Coca-Cola Company has three subsidiaries in the Cayman Islands, for example, which are not there to serve the exceptionally small local soda-drinking population.[16]

The Coca-Cola Company's "genius, its secret formula in many ways, was staying out of the business of making stuff," Bartow Elmore argues in his 2015 study *Citizen Coke*,[17] a compelling study of the Company's relationship to raw materials, state support, and environmental impact. This characterization mistakes the Company's genius, however, since its lack of vertical integration of raw materials like sugar, water, and aluminum was not that rare in the history of US capitalism. Its externalization of the production of its final products of bottled and canned drinks was, however. But then what becomes important for analysis is how the Company made stuff while staying out of the business of making stuff, in other words, without owning the majority of its bottling operations. The Company wielded significant power over "independent" bottlers through mechanisms that included monopoly power over its brands and formulas upon which bottlers depended, restrictive contracts that required exclusive manufacture of Coca-Cola products, and the strategic buying up of large stock positions in bottlers, enabling it to influence mergers and acquisitions. The Coca-Cola Company even bought up bottlers outright, when it was in its interest; in 2015, it directly owned and operated bottling operations in nineteen countries—25 percent of its global system volume.[18] Even more important, saying that the Company does not "make stuff" ignores its principal commodities—the brands, advertising, formulas, business strategies, and financial investments—which the Company produced more successfully than nearly any other corporation in history. It neglects the ways in which the Company's ownership of this immaterial production is used to manage the material bottling of Cokes. Writing it off as "immaterial" (i.e., inconsequential) obscures how immaterial and material systems of production have worked together in this corporate system, and the ways in which this nineteenth-century corporation prefigured the power of cultural and financial capitalism in the externalization of material production that has defined the political economy of the twenty-first century.

A PEOPLE'S HISTORY OF THE COCA-COLA COMPANY

These two interrelated systems of production—one material, the other immaterial—have established The Coca-Cola Company as a global business and icon, but its corporate practices have given rise to a body of lived experience that belies its own global imaginary. Through consumption practices, popular media and culture, and protest and political action, people throughout the world have instilled their own meanings into Coca-Cola's business, products, and branding. The Coca-Cola Company has responded to such interpretations by countering them, constraining them, and at the same time, and perhaps most surprisingly, incorporating elements of their critiques to remake its version of capitalism and reassert its products' role in daily life. Popular culture and social movements thus represent an additional system of production that shapes and propels the Company's meaning, commodities, and history.[19] *Counter-Cola* builds on studies of the "anti-globalization" movements of the post–Cold War era, when free-market reforms were taking hold around the world. These movements constituted "counter-global networks," to use David Featherstone's terms, and imaginaries, often drawing on corporations' financial relationships, production, and cultural representations to map interdependencies and potential solidarities and use corporations' own systems of global power against them.[20]

In considering Coca-Cola as a global system, this book narrates the history of the Company from perspectives external to the United States. Its focus emanates from two nodes of this system, Colombia and India, arguing that events that unfolded in these seemingly "peripheral" regions were in fact central to the multinational corporation's development. By the 1950s, more than a third of the Company's profits came from outside the United States,[21] by the 1970s, more than half,[22] and by 2000, almost three-quarters.[23] In this sense, the majority of the corporation's business is conducted outside the United States and more of the lived history of this iconic global corporation has unfolded in places like Colombia and India than in Atlanta offices.

FIGURE 1. "All over the World Coca-Cola Brings Refreshment," 1947.

Focusing on these two locations reveals both the Company's universalizing capitalist tendencies and the specificity of local contexts that challenged it and obliged it to respond. Moreover, the particularities of the Colombian and Indian cases make them central chapters in the corporation's larger history. Struggles over water privatization in India and labor rights in Colombia, for example, reverberated throughout Coca-Cola's global system.

These challenges to The Coca-Cola Company were the product of Company efforts to make its products materially and symbolically central to daily life. The Coca-Cola Company strove to locate its products always "within arm's length of desire"[24] anywhere in the world, and produced this desire by associating itself with sources of social, cultural, and emotional meaning in people's lives (fig. 1). In turn, the corporation, its commodities, and brand images became vehicles through which challenges to the injustices of daily life under capitalism were articulated. Struggles like those in Colombia and India have both resisted and depended on the Company's multinational material and immaterial systems. Based on common exposure to the Company's soft drinks, branding lexicon, and business practices, activists were able to form local, national, and even transnational interrelationships among consumers, workers, and communities. Since Coca-Cola is a pervasive element of global popular culture, social movements could mobilize this transnational collective language and experience to organize against the exploitation and dislocation endemic to global capitalism and foster alternative solidarities and politics. These multinational manifestations of Colombian and Indian struggles changed both the course of Coca-Cola's history and their communities. They exemplify both the power and the pitfalls of organizing around single corporations or brands.

The Company has reacted by attempting to reestablish capitalist hegemony. It has co-opted criticisms, calls for justice, and commitments to the common good in minor but visible adjustments to business practices for the sake of public relations. Even more insidiously, it has assimilated elements of critical resistance to ideologically legitimize itself, while further extending its power. Drawing on the work of the sociologists Luc Boltanski and Eve Chiapello, *Counter-Cola* traces this dynamic of corporate strategy and popular resistance in the history of Coca-Cola,[25] interrogating the ways in which critique is a "powerful motor" that compels capitalism to justify itself through the values articulated by its challengers.[26]

Few histories of companies and capitalism are told this way. Much of the history of corporations and capitalist forms of organization are written as if these entities acted on their own, without human agency. When people are included, business histories risk becoming hagiographies, or even when critical, focused on individual executives and decision-making. Most studies of multinational corporations situate their analysis at the perceived "center," or, when attempting to provide global perspective, they do so from an aerial viewpoint, overlooking local specificity and historical context—how capitalism plays out "on the ground." *Counter-Cola* is grounded in methods of archival and textual historical and cultural analysis, but has also been heavily influenced by anthropologists' rich, people-centered studies of multinational capitalism, local understanding and practices, and the interplay of power and resistance.[27] Complicating narratives of corporate decision-making through attention to popular meaning and challenges, this book identifies the interrelationship of Atlanta boardrooms, Colombian bottling plants, and Indian villages to begin to construct a "people's history of The Coca-Cola Company."

DOING CORPORATE CULTURAL STUDIES

In mapping Coca-Cola's global system, *Counter-Cola* places the corporation more squarely at the center of critical studies of the history and culture of global capitalism. Exciting new work on multinationals has emerged outside management studies and business history,[28] but despite the fact that they play increasingly powerful roles in international politics, economics, and culture, corporations remain underresearched. Perhaps this relative lack of critical scholarship can be attributed to the fact that these complex institutions cross the national and disciplinary boundaries that demarcate the modern academy. Given the methodological and logistical challenges to reconstructing corporate history, the diverse approaches taken in this book arose as much out of necessity as from commitments to interdisciplinarity.

Corporate history is proprietary history. With company records owned and guarded by corporations, if archived at all, researchers and the broader public alike lack access to crucial historical documents. In addition, the same corporate organization that structures The Coca-Cola Company (the system of subsidiaries and franchises, mergers and acquisitions, etc.) also structures the versions of history available. For example, the multiple corporate entities involved in this study claimed varied degrees of ownership or distance from the historical record following a complex line of mergers and buyouts. Corporations have brands and investors to protect, and they value a profitable future more highly than a clear historical past, especially when the details of the latter have the potential to affect the economics of the former. The Mexico-based Latin American mega-bottler Coca-Cola FEMSA, which by the beginning of the millennium owned all but a few of Colombia's

Coca-Cola bottling plants, protected its reputation by not delving into the history of previous plant owners, as was made clear in my correspondence with its representatives and lawyers.[29] Thus the bottling company refuses access to proprietary history by defining that history as not "its own," a stance only possible because of its very ownership thereof.

It is easier to write the history of The Coca-Cola Company than many other multinationals, I suspect, because of the type of corporation it is. The Company and its executives have had a strong sense of their own importance, archiving their business, advertising, and personal papers in multiple locations, which are more publicly accessible than many corporate historical records. I am also indebted to the invaluable published studies of the Company by Mark Pendergrast, Bartow Elmore, Robert Foster, Frederick Allen, Constance Hays, and Michael Blanding, some of whom have also made their research materials available for future study in archives of primary documents.[30] Because the Company is so visible in its size, consumer products, marketing, and public stock, its activities have received more attention than other more nebulous, inconspicuous, or even covert corporate forms. But, for the same reason, because of the value of the Company's brand, it is extremely protective of its history and resistant to research on its actions. And the critical popular, political, and legal attention that activists have brought to bear on the Company in both Colombia and India has exacerbated the corporation's defensiveness. As part of the Company's recent focus on corporate social responsibility, executives in charge of environmental, labor, and health policy and public relations have engaged with some researchers and activists, but in a highly instrumental fashion, limiting their discussions to current or future projects rather than dwelling on history.

I have thus constructed this cultural history of The Coca-Cola Company and its struggles from diverse sources—archival executive correspondence and notes, company publications, newspaper reports, interviews with workers, community members, executives and activists, and corporate, popular, and protest texts. Even with unrestricted access to proprietary corporate records, the diverse sources examined in this study must be considered essential documents of the Coca-Cola world system. Indeed, even as multinationals like Coca-Cola help constitute modern global life, few people read their official memos or see into their boardrooms. As such, "unofficial" sources reveal the history of the lived experiences and meaning of the Company, from the floors of bottling plants to kitchen tables to the front lines of activists' mobilizations.

It is no accident that activists are drawn to defetishizing The Coca-Cola Company's commodities to think through political economic relations—you can begin to map the capitalist world system by following a trail of Coke bottles. Indeed, Coca-Cola also presents an ideal entry point into interrogating twentieth-century global economic transformations: the shifts from liberal developmentalism to national developmentalism to neoliberalism. As both a key corporate actor *in* and pervasive symbolic representation *of* these shifts, Coca-Cola exemplifies the evolving economic logic and ideologies of modern capitalism. Tracking key changes in the two dynamic relationships that structure the Coca-Cola world system—the interrelated structures of material and immaterial production, on the one hand, and the interrelated actions and imaginaries of corporate and critical actors, on the other—sheds new light on the history of modern global capitalism.

Coca-Cola's expansion reproduced the geography of US imperialism, as it first expanded across US empire and countries with elites espousing liberal developmentalist goals aligned with US economic and political interests, like Colombia, as well as the markets of traditional trading partners. It then followed the US military during World War II to farther reaches like India. But as Colombia and the newly independent nation of India both turned to more national developmentalist thinking around the middle of the twentieth century, the Company emphasized an operational and discursive project of localization, promoting its system of franchise bottlers and drawing on the discourse of modernization to proclaim itself a multinational developer of local and national economies. The Company simultaneously represented its soft drinks in these international markets through a system of pattern advertising that representationally echoed the localization discourse of import-substitution industrialization, while actually maintaining the Company's centralized control of the production of its brand images.

The 1970s saw a key shift, emblematic of the Company's neoliberal trajectory, as the immaterial and material production of the Coca-Cola world system came to be defined by the emerging logic of free-market globalization. Assimilating cultural referents from the period's social and cultural critiques, and offering a competing imaginary to postcolonial nationalisms in the global south, Coca-Cola set the symbolic stage for neoliberalism by framing its global commodities and their consumption in universal, utopian terms of freedom and liberation. The Company adopted a globally consolidated advertising strategy, defined by "one sight–one sound" representations of a new multicultural generation of liberated consumers. As the global advertising campaigns heralded a single world market, neoliberal reforms in countries around the world—including Colombia and India—enabled The Coca-Cola Company to expand and restructure its world system, consolidating its much-lauded local franchise bottlers into multinational anchor mega-bottlers in the 1980s and 1990s.

As new social movements assailed neoliberal globalization, often taking on Coca-Cola, Company executives recommitted the Company to a strategy of localizing its self-representation. International advertising campaigns portrayed Coca-Cola as a locally embedded commodity and brand, obscuring the increasingly consolidated ownership of its material production. However, Colombian and Indian social movements continued to unmask the Company's political economy, denouncing the forms of dispossession that defined it and using the Coca-Cola world system to exert transnational pressure on the corporation. The power of these challenges was reflected in the response of the Company, which introduced new "corporate social responsibility" (CSR) practices aimed at ameliorating the worst effects of its corporate practices and ensuring long-term profitability by contributing to the social good with private, voluntary solutions to public problems. Through CSR, the Company reasserted its legitimacy, ideologically justifying its centrality to daily life and the necessity of capitalism itself.

Coke's near global ubiquity resulted from one of the world's first and most successful examples of international corporate franchising. The Coca-Cola Company's material production was structured through contracting the manufacture of soft drinks out to "local, independent" bottlers. The Company sold concentrates and the rights to use its trademarked brands to franchise bottlers who would locally produce and sell bottled soft drinks in designated geographic areas around the world. Chapter 1, "The Coca-Cola Bottling System and the Logics of the Franchise," narrates the establishment of franchise bottlers in Colombia and India from the 1920s through the 1940s. The franchise system enabled international expansion without large corporate growth or direct local employment, allowing the Company to externalize liability and financial risk. The franchise also helped the Company situate and integrate Coca-Cola's production within international contexts, conscripting local elites, workers, and consumers into relationships with its industry. Thus, there were social and cultural logics to the franchise system that partnered with its economic motivations and impacts.[31] The franchise organized social relations, proposed engagements, and built commitments between people in various parts of the world. While it externalized production, it structured and inspired international interconnection among those involved in Coca-Cola production and consumption. Coca-Cola's franchise system also had cultural logics, or aesthetic features, communicative strategies, and modes of representation, most prominently portrayed in advertising and Company cultural production, but also in popular representations of Coca-Cola. These social and cultural logics were articulated through different terms to meet the ideological demands of different eras, but were the means through which the Company attempted to construct its industry, products, and brands as simultaneously global and local at various historical moments. As described in the first chapter, at the earliest moment of the Company's globalization, these logics framed the US multinational as a purveyor of international modernity through a local franchise, representing Coca-Cola as a new, innovative and stylish alternative to traditional and local beverages and businesses in countries including Colombia since the late 1920s. Asserting its franchise bottlers as both "local" and conduits to international capitalist modernity, Coca-Cola sold its industry, products, and brand by alluding to their international popularity and profitability.

Chapter 2, "Mediating Coca-Colonization: Negotiating National Development and Difference in Coca-Cola's Postwar Internationalization," examines Coca-Cola's massive expansion of its international business after World War II in Colombia, the newly independent nation of India, and other countries around the world. In the United States, Coca-Cola represented itself as a commodity ambassador for the "American Century." But in the postwar decades, many nations turned to more nationalist development economics, including Keynesian and import-substitution industrialization models, and a popular critique of economic and cultural "coca-colonization" emerged. The Company celebrated the cultural differences of the locales where Coca-Cola was drunk to exemplify its local acceptance and the universal adaptability of consumer capitalism. Critically, Coca-Cola mobilized new social and cultural logics of the franchise with the language of import substitution to frame its franchise bottlers as modernizing developers of local economies because of, not despite, their relationships with the multinational corporation, trumpeting what I call a "multinational developmentalism." While such claims of local ownership often contained some truth, as in the case of the Indian-owned bottling company Pure Drinks, the US-controlled Colombian bottling company Panamco, to cite another example, was in reality neither local nor independent.

The expansion of the Coca-Cola system's material production of soft drinks was possible only because of the Company's investment in the immaterial production of advertising; promoting its soft drink brands and imbuing them with meaning turned bubbly drinks into Coca-Colas or Sprites and sold them to consumers around the world. For decades the Company's "pattern advertising," in which texts were produced centrally, then disseminated to international markets for modification (achieving a degree of localization), reflected US racial and cultural hierarchization and promotion of consumer culture. The 1960s "social revolutions," as a Coca-Cola executive called them, posed significant social and cultural threats to the Company, even attacking its business practices and using Coca-Cola as a symbol of global capitalism's exploitation and consumer culture's homogenization. Chapter 3, "'I'd Like to Buy the World a Coke': The 'Real Thing' and the Revolutions of the 1960s," considers these threats against The Coca-Cola Company, from direct challenges to its business operations to artistic and cultural expressions that made use of its brand image, to argue that the Company attempted to representationally assimilate the feeling of the era and contain its critiques. Some of the Company's first international TV campaigns incorporated cultural elements of these revolutions, using race, gender, nationality, and cultural difference to signify authenticity and rebellion, and attempted to represent itself with the utopian, liberatory social values of a perceived global youth culture. With iconic advertising like "I'd Like to Buy the World a Coke," the Company prefigured neoliberalism in its corporate globalist image of a new, more integrative and unified free market—one world liberated through consumption of a global commodity, Coke.

In 1977, adopting a new stance toward foreign corporations, the Indian state dramatically evicted The Coca-Cola Company from the country. Chapter 4, "Indianize or Quit India: Nationalist Challenges to Coca-Cola in Postcolonial India," elucidates the political, economic, and cultural forces that drove one of the greatest challenges to the Coca-Cola world system— the threat of nationalization of its foreign nodes of business. The Coca-Cola Company's departure from India in the late 1970s reflected a broader phenomenon: the reverberation of the political economic critique from dependency theory and concerns about neocolonialism through the global south. The Indian government pointed out the dependency structured into the franchise system, arguing that the Company was draining the country of necessary financial resources by repatriating its profits in foreign currency to the United States. Why should a multinational be making such large profits selling a nonessential product like soft drinks? Indian industry could surely produce bubbly drinks on its own, the government reasoned. India's Foreign Exchange Regulation Act of 1973 (FERA) required that Coca-Cola "Indianize" its operations in the country—divest at least 60 percent of the ownership of its Indian subsidiary to Indian shareholders and transfer technological "know-how" to Indian employees—in a national challenge to two fundamental systems of property in global capitalism, financial and intellectual capital. Claiming a defense of its "secret formula" as intellectual property, the Company refused a larger Indian role in its Indian subsidiary while launching a campaign to rebrand itself in the discourse of "Indianization," before dramatically pulling out of the country entirely.

Chapter 5, "A Man in Every Bottle: Labor and Neoliberal Violence in Colombian Coca-Cola Bottling," examines the bottling system's reconfiguration in the 1990s and 2000s as a result of consolidation, restructuring, and financialization, and the organizing of the Colombian food and beverage workers' union, the Sindicato Nacional de Trabajadores del Sistema Agroalimentario, or Sinaltrainal, in the face of resulting labor precarity. This "precarization," as they termed the process of livelihoods and lives being made insecure, was enabled in large part by the Colombian state's outsourcing of violence to paramilitaries who targeted not only guerrilla fighters, but also leftists and perceived threats to the social order, resulting in the assassination and persecution of Sinaltrainal members. At the same time, the Company capitalized on the neoliberal shift in Latin America to consolidate a Latin American mega-bottler and node in the Coca-Cola world system, while significantly decreasing local labor power. In this context, work at Colombian Coca-Cola bottling plants was downsized, "flexibilized," and subcontracted, challenging Coca-Cola workers' abilities to support themselves and their labor organizations. In the midst of this ongoing armed conflict, and after protracted labor struggles, repeated acts of violence, and the loss of union membership, Sinaltrainal members denounced The Coca-Cola Company's labor model and complicity in violence and joined with US-based solidarity activists to challenge the Company through work actions, a boycott of its soft drinks, and a US lawsuit. Together these activists built arguably the most significant transnational labor campaign of the 2000s. But international calls to action did not easily translate into solidarity in different economic and political contexts: the US and European labor movements offered limited support, student activists were often hemmed into actions that defined them as consumers, and organizers often indulged in oversimplified human-rights discourses, which at times elided the workers' more trenchant calls for radical change. Through the franchise system, the Company externalized the human costs of its labor practices and shielded itself from legal responsibility. But Colombian workers insisted on their own centrality to the Company, together with international allies creating an alternative network of pressure on the corporation by remapping the Coca-Cola world system.

As economic liberalization opened up new international markets to foreign corporations in the 1990s, The Coca-Cola Company invested heavily in the "vast markets that were closed or underdeveloped for decades," in its words, including India.[32] The Company burst back into India in 1993 after a sixteen-year absence, buying up the largest Indian soft-drink company, Parle, and appropriating Indian popular culture in advertising in an attempt to localize its products and construct Coke as a constitutive part of contemporary "Indianness." While making these efforts to portray Coke as Indian, Atlanta in fact directly controlled more Indian Coca-Cola bottling than ever before. Coca-Cola's sudden reappearance made it a highly visible and tangible representation of India's liberalization. Thus neoliberal privatization, underregulation, and underinvestment by the state, as well as widening economic inequality, evoked powerful responses from consumers and communities, including two environmental challenges to the Company addressed in chapter 6, "Water for Life, Not for Coca-Cola: Commodification, Consumption, and Environmental Challenges in Neoliberal India." First, an NGO revealed the pesticide contamination of Coca-Cola and other bottled drinks, resulting in a middle-class crisis of consumer confidence in the quality of commodities produced by global corporations and calls for greater regulation of food safety and investment in water infrastructure. Second, villagers living around bottling plants challenged the Company over its privatization and pollution of the common water resources upon which their rural agricultural communities depended. This "environmentalism of the poor"[33] and its critique of neoliberalism's "accumulation by dispossession"[34] galvanized international pressure against Coca-Cola.

Such critiques have challenged the Coca-Cola world system's economics, politics, and cultures, requiring the corporation to continually justify its place in society. This dialectical process of corporate power, social confrontation, and efforts to reestablish capitalist hegemony defined the history of the Company—and, indeed, capitalism itself—in the twentieth century. At the beginning of the twenty-first century, confronted by Indian peasants, Colombian workers, and consumers and public health advocates concerned about the link between soda consumption and unprecedented obesity and diabetes rates, The Coca-Cola Company framed justifications for itself through the discourse and practice of "corporate social responsibility." As with all Coca-Cola products, CSR has been as much symbolic as material and thus part of a larger effort to rebrand the global corporation. The concluding chapter of *Counter-Cola*, "CSR: Corporate Social Responsibility and Continued Social Resistance, A Nonconclusion," argues that the Company's leadership in the field of CSR is part of a neoliberal shift in the relationship between states, corporations, and the public. These CSR initiatives are intended to maximize long-term profit by contributing to the common good through private voluntary solutions to public problems, thus managing social risks to brands and forestalling governmental regulation. Coca-Cola's high-profile CSR initiatives around the world—organizing the private sector to address poverty and violence in Colombia, pledging to become globally "water neutral" by conserving water reserves and creating alternative water sources in locations including India, and addressing growing obesity by encouraging exercise and marketing healthy drinks—simultaneously attempt to ameliorate the worst effects of capitalism while seeking to further legitimize the corporation's prominent place in the world order. Not only do they help The Coca-Cola Company continue to sell soft drinks, they sell the ideology that the market will provide solutions to society's problems; that there is no future without capitalism.

But capitalism creates more problems than it solves, and struggles will continue to arise. The Coca-Cola Company has been formed by these struggles; its bottled drinks, brands, and business were produced by the corporation, but always in concert and conflict with the consumers, communities, and workers who make it a "real thing." At its broadest level, this book argues that the power to both shape and represent global capitalism is contested, and that the process of contestation is itself the central dynamic of modern history.

ONE

The Coca-Cola Bottling System and the Logics of the Franchise

COCA-COLA'S EARLIEST WORLD SYSTEM, which took shape in the final two decades of the nineteenth century, considered territories outside the United States almost exclusively as sites of extraction of raw materials. From transnational markets the Company had to acquire key ingredients like sugar from the Caribbean, caffeine from tea leaves from Asia, extract of coca leaf from Latin America, and kola nut powder from Africa.[1] At the same time, international peoples and their locales were central to the cultural imaginary that Coca-Cola produced for US consumers from the beginning, even if non-US subjects were not yet themselves consumers of its products. Coca-Cola's inventor, John Pemberton, originally marketed it in 1886 as a temperance drink, a "Brain Tonic and a cure for all nervous affections—Sick Head-Ache, Neuralgia, Hysteria, Melancholy, Etc."[2] According to its advertisements, Coca-Cola derived its potency from exotic Latin American coca leaves and African kola nuts. Like rival patent medicines promising remedies from hitherto untapped natural sources, the discoveries of marvelous healers, or the secret knowledge of remote communities,[3] Coca-Cola was alleged to relieve the ailments of a population facing urbanization, technological change, social fragmentation, and the division of labors between overtaxed assembly-line and desk workers. And no doubt they did feel restored by the bubbly drink, compounded of caffeine (from the kola nut and tea leaves; the original formula had about four times as much as today's Cokes), coca extract (until 1903 when the Company began using "decocainized coca leaves" for flavor and to protect its copyrighted name), and lots and lots of sugar.[4]

But in the first decades of the twentieth century, Coca-Cola began to see the rest of the world not only as a source of raw materials, but as a consumer market, and to develop strategies to deliver and promote its product to it. The

Company looked first to potential consumers in the United States' imperial possessions, neocolonies, and trading partners. Coca-Cola established its first international bottling ventures in Cuba and Panama in 1906, followed quickly by others in Puerto Rico, Hawaii, the Philippines, and Guam. By 1928, the list included Antigua, Bermuda, Colombia, the Dominican Republic, Guatemala, Haiti, Honduras, Mexico, and Venezuela in the Caribbean and Latin America, as well as France, Belgium, Italy, Holland, and Spain in Europe, and Burma and China in Asia.[5] According to the Company's advertising and promotional materials, the central, heroic actor in its US and international expansion was the "local, independent" franchise bottler: the enterprising small businessman who brought the modern drink, Coca-Cola, and its business model to his hometown.

FRANCHISE CAPITALISM

By organizing its production through bottling franchises, the Company expanded quickly and affordably, getting access to new markets while externalizing production costs and acquiring capital to invest in promotion for further growth. Franchise contracts granted bottlers monopoly rights to buy soft-drink syrups and concentrates, manufacture the drinks, promote them using registered trademarks, and sell them to retailers in a designated territory. In exchange, The Coca-Cola Company in Atlanta profited from sales of drink bases, franchise rights, technical and promotional services, and advertising materials to bottlers, while retaining the right to control essential production and marketing details, violations of which could jeopardize a bottler's contract. Franchising bottling thus gave the Company control without ownership.

In its own corporate histories, The Coca-Cola Company humbly narrates the birth of its bottling business as a haphazard accident.[6] In fact, it was the first step in developing one of the most powerful business models of the twentieth century: the franchise. As Company lore has it, in 1899, two Tennessee attorneys walked into the office of Coke's principal owner, Asa Griggs Candler, with what in hindsight seems an obvious proposition: to bottle and sell Coca-Cola. Candler had already made the product a household name, if not yet a drink consumed at home, through soda fountain sales. Reluctant to go into the capital- and labor-intensive bottling business himself, Candler granted the men the right in perpetuity to buy the syrup at $1 a gallon, manufacture the soft drink, and sell it in nearly the entire US market using the familiar Spencerian-script trademark. Concerned about maintaining the soft drink's reputation, however, Candler retained extensive rights to dictate the terms of its production and marketing. The Company would regret the terms of this original deal, spending millions of dollars and engaging in strong-arm maneuvers in the coming decades to amend its bottling contracts with respect to price, duration, and territory size. By the time it established its network of international bottlers, Coca-Cola lawyers had succeeded in rewriting its franchise contracts with more favorable terms. So started one of the earliest and most successful franchise systems in global history. As Coca-Cola expanded internationally, and faced the challenges of doing business in different economic, political, social, and cultural contexts, the franchise system enabled it to externalize the risks and costs of its globalization.

Beginning in the 1920s, The Coca-Cola Company began concertedly reproducing this franchise business model around the world. From the perspective of Atlanta executives, franchising trimmed expenses. Producing drinks closer to their point of sale dramatically reduced transport and quality-loss costs. At the turn of the century, before the Company established bottlers in distant markets, it shipped syrup or full bottles of the drink to international soda fountains and retailers. But there were few soda fountains outside the United States, and shipping bulky crates of fragile glass bottles by steamship or rail was expensive and inefficient, and breakage and spoilage might harm the Company's product and reputation. The Company could have established its own bottling factories abroad, as did other early internationalizing food manufacturers like Swift and Heinz, directly investing in foreign processing plants to be closer to potential markets and avoid such transportation and spoilage costs, as well as tariffs on imported ingredients.[7] But building bottling plants all over the world would mean slow, costly investment in physical infrastructure, expenditures on inputs like clean water and price-volatile sugar, and management of a local workforce, all with their resulting responsibilities and liabilities.

The Coca-Cola Company instead grew quickly and cheaply by adopting a version of globalization that reduced the costs and risks of internationalizing by externalizing production itself. Although it was not the first corporation to embark on franchising, its early franchising of *production* was exceptional. Producers of goods that required special handling (like fresh fruit or beer) or expert service (such as technologies like sewing machines or harvesters) had previously contracted with agents to serve as independent dealers in their products. But these were franchises of retailers; the underlying corporations manufactured products and shipped them to these outlets to be promoted, sold, and serviced. The Coca-Cola Company's realization was that it not only saved transport and quality-loss costs by having its soft drinks produced closer to consumer markets, but that it didn't actually have to produce them itself at all. The startup, labor, and production costs of international bottling plants, as well as the complexities of navigating foreign markets and associated liabilities, could all be outsourced to franchisees. Even ingredient-sourcing costs could be externalized, especially for ingredients that were hard to come by in developing markets, like the largest input, safe drinking water, or those with fluctuating prices, like sugar. Early failed forays into international bottling during the market disruptions of World War I convinced Coca-Cola executives that it was far cheaper and less risky to produce concentrate without sugar and have bottlers source and pay for it themselves, and, overall, to license bottling plants overseas rather than invest in direct ownership.[8]

The history of the English term "franchise" reveals much about corporate history. As the business historian Thomas S. Dicke explains, as early as the Middle Ages, the word, meaning roughly "endowing with a freedom," was applied in economic contexts as when governments granted special privileges "in exchange for some service, like tax collection or road construction, that the state subcontracted to private individuals." In the nineteenth and twentieth centuries, the term was associated with state grants of incorporation according special privileges such as limited liability or monopoly rights to a group of incorporating individuals in exchange for "the private performance of public services." The corporation existed only by the will of the state, enabling individuals to pool large amounts of capital through incorporation to undertake a costly enterprise in the public interest, which constituted much of the legal justification for the entity's existence.[9]

The contemporary use of "franchise" did not enter the business lexicon until the 1950s, a development that suggests how corporate rights were being redefined in US culture and law. By the mid-twentieth century, a corporation's franchise rights and freedoms were defined not by contractual service to the state and public, but instead by subcontractual rights and freedoms granted by one corporate entity to another. Franchising became a method of organizing a large-scale enterprise by distributing products and production through relationships between two legally (if not practically) independent corporations. In fact, in many cases, franchises were far from independent firms because their economic ties to the underlying corporations (through dependency in the purchasing of goods, requirements of exclusive dealing, dictation of business policies, representation on corporate boards, ownership of shares or debt, etc.) were tighter than the contractual ones and hardly free market.[10]

THE SOCIAL AND CULTURAL LOGICS
OF THE FRANCHISE

The franchise did not just have economic motivations and repercussions; it also had social and cultural logics that distinguished it from other types of international business organization. The franchise was a different model of capitalist internationalization than international trade or even the establishment of foreign subsidiaries, for example, and this was reflected in the social relations and cultural forms it produced. Socially, the franchise simultaneously structured independence and interdependence between the bottler and the Company, resulting in the negotiation of power and cooperation between them. It manifested in cultural representation and modes of communication that represented Coca-Cola's operations and products as simultaneously local and global and thus was central to the discursive strategies for negotiating social and cultural difference across Coca-Cola's world system. The multinational cast its bottlers as localizing agents by having them advertise Coca-Cola in local media, connect it to potential local vendors and consumers, and embed its business in the local context. In its first wave of international expansion, from the 1920s to the 1940s, advertising made a point of informing consumers of local bottling franchises producing its drinks, framing them as local, independent businesses that tied Coca-Cola to a place but also linked it to a distant modernity represented by the transnational brand.

A franchise model of globalization could, of course, mean a loss of control. Indeed, Company executives worried that independent, often "foreign," bottlers could not be entrusted with expanding the business, maintaining production standards, and marketing products profitably on their own. The Company's bottling contracts and monopoly power were legal and economic structures for asserting control in the franchise system. The bottling contract granted franchisees the rights to purchase concentrates, produce soft drinks, market them with trademarks, and sell them in a designated geographical area, but also granted the Company the right to strictly dictate production, advertising, and sales practices. In a 1927 international bottling contract, for example, the agreement was heavily weighted in favor of the US multinational: the contract required that bottlers invest in production and distribution at levels "satisfactory to the Company . . . [and] conform at all times to the high standards set by the Company"; "encourage and push the sale of the beverage within the territory at all times in a proper and vigorous manner"; submit any bottler-created advertising for Company approval; purchase goods and supplies only from Company-authorized manufacturers; and not deal in any beverage perceived as a "substitute for or an imitation of" Company brands. The bottler would be in breach of contract if it did not "meet and satisfy every demand for the beverage within the territory," as determined by the Company.[11] Coca-Cola was not the first bottled beverage, either in the United States or elsewhere.[12] When it first appeared, it was one of thousands of locally produced and distributed beverages—bottled beers, alcoholic drinks, patent medicines, fruit juices, sodas, and other soft drinks. Over the course of the twentieth century, The Coca-Cola Company (and later Pepsi-Cola Co.) consolidated power in the market through acquisition and expansion, advertising, trademark litigation, protection of trade secrets, and such restrictive franchise bottler contracts. Because franchisees were contractually limited to producing Coca-Cola products and required to invest in them to meet the Company's standards, they were typically forced to cease production of their own previously developed soft drinks.

The Coca-Cola Company took great care in granting its bottling franchises so that such contractual power might never need to be invoked. This was easier after mid-century when the Company had built a reputation that allowed it to be more selective in choosing franchisees who actively sought them out. As a 1950 *Time* magazine cover story described the process and power dynamic: "Choosing a bottler from among the applicants (at the moment, Coca-Cola is weighing more than 1,000 applications from all over the world), the Coca-Cola Export Corp. acts approximately like a fairy-tale king choosing a proper husband for his daughter." But even at the earliest moment of its globalization, the prospective bottler had first and foremost to demonstrate the ability to amass enough capital to produce, distribute, and market Coca-Cola beverages at the standards demanded by the multinational. The bottler's own business interests must align with those of the Company, or at least not infringe upon the Company's profit motives, and they must be faithfully committed to the Company's market growth. "But the suitor must also measure up in character and honor and local reputation," such that the bottling company would be able to embed the Coca-Cola industry in the local economic, political, and social context.[13] Of course, the selection of bottlers came with risks aplenty. The model of franchise globalization relied on outsiders—who were not in Coca-Cola's direct employ, and often thousands of miles away, with different interests, perspectives, and societies—to represent and grow its business.

The Coca-Cola Company thus developed several social and cultural strategies for structuring international business relations with its bottlers. In 1926, the Company created a Foreign Department, inspired by the State Department,[14] to establish new franchises, oversee and assist international bottlers in production and marketing, and lobby the US state and international governments. In 1930, the Company converted this department into the Coca-Cola Export Corporation, a subsidiary based in New York City, and committed more financial and personnel resources to international expansion. The Export Corporation established regional and national offices and subsidiaries around the world to sell (and in some cases also produce) concentrate, localize marketing messages, and support, influence, and monitor bottlers' operations. The Coca-Cola "field men" who peopled these offices had often worked at Coca-Cola's US headquarters or in bottling before joining Export, where they would receive weeks of training in New York and Atlanta, as well as several more weeks rotating through production jobs at various US plants. This training was designed to ensure that Company representatives knew the ins and outs of the industry before being stationed in their different divisions around the world, where their "pupils, ready & waiting for instruction, [were] the foreign bottlers."[15] Export field men would provide a wide range of startup services for bottlers, from helping choose the bottler's plant site, providing layout instructions, advising on what machinery to buy, checking production quality, approving advertising, to training sales and deliverymen. After World War II, key Export and bottling employees attended an eighteen-week training course that, in Coca-Cola Export's words, would "turn out men well indoctrinated in all phases of 'Coca-Cola,'"[16] transforming Coca-Cola's central Production School in Atlanta into "a minor university" by mid-century.[17] To turn them into Coca-Cola men, by the 1950s, Export and bottling managers in international markets would be brought to the United States for an eight-month training course in bottling-plant work, sales promotion, and advertising strategies, with extensive educational and morale-building presentations in various languages.[18]

In addition to field visits and training sessions, the Export Corporation cultivated other means of maintaining relationships with far-flung franchise bottlers. Annual bottlers' conventions feted franchisees with banquets, celebrity appearances, and elaborate stage performances (that were also performances of Company ideology).[19] Company magazines such as *The Red Barrel* (published from the 1920s to the 1940s), *The Refresher* (1950s–80s), *The Coca-Cola Bottler* (1920s–80s; a magazine of the Coca-Cola Bottlers' Association but edited and controlled by The Coca-Cola Company), *T.O. Digest* (for Coca-Cola workers embedded with US troops during World War II), and *Coca-Cola Overseas* and its Spanish-language edition, *Coca-Cola Mundial* (1940s–70s; Coca-Cola Export magazines) provided news about the business, reported and editorialized on contemporary politics related (and unrelated) to the industry, informed bottlers of new manufacturing and marketing developments, advertised Company-approved equipment and suppliers, and relayed Company perspectives.

As one of the first globally successful franchise systems, the Company shifted conceptions of property and ownership to maintain independence from its bottlers while asserting control over their products. The franchise system created an additional level of legal and economic protection for the US corporation and its investors as The Coca-Cola Company did not own its bottling plants. Under US corporate law, Coca-Cola's stock investors enjoyed limited liability (protection from any liability over the amount invested), while franchise bottlers' separate corporations further shielded the Company and its investors from the costs, risks, and liabilities of labor and production.

While The Coca-Cola Company avoided ownership by franchising, it asserted new forms of ownership by defining and defending its trademarks and formulas as intellectual property as they were franchised out. The Company's ownership over these immaterial products of intellectual property structured relations between the Company and its bottlers. As the Company had monopoly power over this intellectual property, bottling companies paid money and deference to the Company in order to make and market its products. Without the Company's agreement, bottlers could produce colas, sure, but they could not make trademarked Cokes. At the same time, the Company pledged to its bottlers a flow of intellectual property—product formulas, marketing materials, and business services—that would enable their profitability and mutual financial futures.

Like most of the tonics and elixirs that were referred to as "patent medicines," Coca-Cola was not patented. A patent would be protected from copying for a period of time but then expire, allowing others to use or further develop the patented process or device and profit from it. Instead, The Coca-Cola Company never patented its "secret formulas" for Coca-Cola and other beverages, instead guarding them as trade secrets that would never enter the public domain. The concentrates produced from the formulas have only ever been manufactured by a handful of Company-owned factories, each supplying a large region of bottlers. The Company's macro-level division of labor meant that the secret formulas (and creative and technological development of soft drinks and brands) would remain centralized in The Coca-Cola Company, while the manual work of bottling would be done by franchise bottlers around the world.

The Company's trademarks, which over time would become more valuable than its "secret formulas" themselves, would also be closely overseen by The Coca-Cola Company. Coca-Cola came of age in the late nineteenth and early twentieth centuries, the golden age of trademarks. These communicative signifiers (words, symbols, images, etc.) marked and marketed products, generating demand and a mass market of consumers. A company used its trademark to differentiate itself from competitors and the broader field of unmarked generic goods. The trademark identified the commercial source or origin of a product, promising consumers consistent, standardized quality wherever it was purchased across a growing corporate geography. Companies deployed their trademarks to assuage Progressive Era reformers concerned about the standards, safety, and sanitariness of goods and manufacturing, contending that the brand names ensured quality and accountability.[20] And a trademark label was good for business, producers believed, as it generated "the favorable consideration of customers that derived from a company's reputation."[21] In a series of court cases in the late nineteenth century, corporations established the legal status of non-material assets such as consumer goodwill and expected earning power as "intangible but legally salable" forms of immaterial property, facilitating the growth of the corporate form.[22] In fact, the definition of property changed so rapidly at this time that there was legal confusion and several court reversals pertaining to trademarks until Congress passed clarifying federal legislation in 1905.[23] Once established as property, trademarks were soon licensed out to other producers for the sale of products legally treated as deriving from a single source but in fact manufactured by different, distant licensees, as in the case of Coca-Cola's franchisees.

The Coca-Cola Company's prodigious corpus of trademark infringement lawsuits and injunctions, and the tenacity of its early twentieth-century trademark lawyer Harold Hirsch, "virtually created modern American trademark law."[24] Recognizing the growing value of Coca-Cola's image, both in attracting consumers and warding off competitors, executives expanded the definition and scope of the trademark by registering not only the Company's name and logos, but also bottle size and shape, and label designs, and aggressively pursuing litigation against those who arguably infringed on these new property rights. Hirsch filed on average one case per week, suing colas that dared to use a script logo, a diamond-shaped label (like Coca-Cola's at the time), red barrels, or even a dark caramel color, all of which he argued should be proprietarily Coca-Cola's alone.[25] Coca-Cola oversaw the "burials" of over seven thousand "copy-cat" competitors by 1926, a reporter estimated at the time.[26] In a trademark infringement case in 1920,[27] the US Supreme Court sided with The Coca-Cola Company, ruling: "It [Coca-Cola] means a single thing coming from a single source, and well known to the community. It hardly would be too much to say that the drink characterizes the name as much as the name the drink."[28] "Coca-Cola" was now more than the sum of its ingredients (which included little coca or kola), but a single thing in its own right. And while anyone was free to make a drink from such ingredients, only a trademarked drink was a Coca-Cola. Coca-Cola would be protected from producers using similar signification, even if it represented what was actually in their products, as infringers on Coca-Cola's name and goodwill. The Company preemptively registered trademarks in prospective international markets and aggressively sued competitors and "imitators," establishing key precedents in international intellectual property law in the process.

For a globalizing firm like Coca-Cola, the trademark was also a means to control its expansion and business relationships. Coca-Cola directly oversaw production of most trademarked content, and allowed bottlers to produce branded materials only under strict guidelines or upon review, to maintain a consistent, high-quality brand image from the Company's perspective. Yet the Company wanted bottlers to advertise heavily and successfully to market its product in distinct international markets. Ensuring they did so while maintaining corporate control of cultural production was no straightforward enterprise, since franchise bottlers often acted out of different interests and perspectives than those of the Export Corporation. Slippages in the representation of Coca-Cola products abroad reveal the challenges to a globalizing corporation in the first half of the twentieth century.

INTRODUCING COCA-COLA IN THE LAND
OF COFFEE CAPITALISM

While the Company portrayed its franchise system of bottlers as a constella-
tion of small business owners, the reality often reflected established political
and economic power rather than entrepreneurial spirit, with franchises being
granted to well-established business interests, such as the Philippine brewery
La Fábrica de Cerveza de San Miguel, the Mexican brewery and bottler
Cervecería Cuauhtémoc Moctezuma (which would become the Fomento
Económico Mexicano, or FEMSA), and the Colombian bottler Posada y
Tobón, the latter two corporations playing a prominent role in the history of
bottling in Colombia and Latin America. When the Company partnered
with entities new to the bottling business, it preferred local business and
industrial elites who met the baseline requirement of deep pockets, enabling
them to invest in production, distribution, and marketing. Prospective franchisees needed to demonstrate their ability to provide the "necessary investment" and "ample capital," two oft-repeated phrases in Export's internal
magazine for international bottlers, *Coca-Cola Overseas:* "None of our bottlers overseas can start business without the necessary investment. The
Company just won't approve an application where there isn't the capital in
hand to aggressively and uniformly develop a territory from the day a plant
opens."[29] Prospective bottlers were also expected to bring political and economic connections, or at least be members of the rising capitalist class. Such
investors would embed the Company with the local elite, and, in return, get
the prestige and profitability of a multinational US product and business.
Thousands of businessmen around the world took a vested interest in The
Coca-Cola Company through franchise ownership, and as a result the
Company often avoided the charge of imperialism and the threat of nationalization faced by other highly visible transnationals in Latin America like
Standard Oil and the United Fruit Company.[30]

Even while The Coca-Cola Company touted its independent, locally
owned franchise bottlers, its entrance into its first international markets was
a constitutive part of US empire. Coca-Cola frequently contracted with US
interests (individual, corporate, and even military) operating in an area. Coca-
Cola bottling was sometimes franchised to US corporations with extraordinary economic and political influence in host countries, like the United Fruit
Company in Honduras and Guatemala, and the Illinois-based Sparks Milling
Company in the Dominican Republic, Haiti, and Puerto Rico.[31] US military

interventions and occupations in the first decade of the twentieth century facilitated Coca-Cola's international expansion, opening up markets to foreign investment and bringing armies of thirsty US servicemen as consumers, as was the case in the Philippines and Panama, which would become important bases for the Company's development in Asia and Latin America.

The Company granted franchises to proven US bottlers and Company men, who sometimes partnered with local elites and capital. Coca-Cola bottling in Colombia, and a large swathe of Latin America, would be dominated by the Statons, a Coca-Cola Company family. At crucial moments, the Company played a heavy hand in the development of its bottlers, pairing bottlers with investment capital or investing in them itself, often to the point of holding a near-controlling interest or buying them out entirely. Through such investment Coca-Cola supported the growth of its preferred bottlers by providing expansion capital. Alternatively, the corporation kept problematic bottlers in check by taking a large position in their stock, installing executives on their corporate boards, encouraging acquisition by other bottlers, recruiting new franchisees, or challenging bottling contracts.[32]

Coca-Cola first came to Latin America by ship in fragile bottles, and Coca-Cola syrup was delivered to a small number of tourist and expatriate-oriented eateries. The taste of Coke existed for only a small minority of people in Colombia before it was actually bottled there. In 1927, The Coca-Cola Company contracted its first Colombian bottler, Postobón (at the time Posada y Tobón), which manufactured and distributed the drink from its Medellín, Pereira, and Bogotá plants.[33] Postobón had just begun to expand its production to multiple plants, but would become the largest and best-known Colombian soft drink company and Coca-Cola's main competitor. Olarte Valerio Tobón, a young pharmacist, and Gabriel Posada Villa, a prominent businessman, founded Postobón in 1904 to manufacture a product emulating imported carbonated soft drinks.[34] They began bottling their *bebidas gaseosas* for the urbanizing and industrializing population of Medellín—history much like that of Coca-Cola's pharmacist entrepreneur Asa Candler and the marketing innovator Frank Robinson supplying Coca-Cola to the rising "New South" city of Atlanta beginning in the 1880s.[35] Known for its interrelated corporate structures and early market capitalization, Medellín was a center of business and industrialization with disproportionate national economic importance.[36]

Medellín's dramatic economic growth at the end of the nineteenth century was well-timed for the emergence of a bottled drinks business, inasmuch as the city was becoming a commercial center providing both imported and domestic foodstuff and merchandise to the surrounding booming coffee-growing and gold-mining regions, further contributing to fortunes for *paisa* merchants.[37] The city's merchants invested in manufacturing, most notably of textiles, but also in coffee-packing plants, cigarette factories, chocolate companies, and breweries and bottling plants.[38] Urbanization accelerated dramatically after the 1930s, when high levels of rural violence and the lack of educational and economic opportunities drove struggling young *campesinos* to the city. There, Medellín's urban economy and industrial waged work constructed working and middle-classes who labored, shopped, ate, and drank, constituting a market for mass consumer goods like Coca-Cola.[39]

Bottled beverages were among the most global mass-produced consumer goods of the first quarter of the twentieth century, both in terms of the emergence of bottling industries around the world, as well as the globalization of brands like Coca-Cola. Postobón's contributions to this boom included Cola-Champaña (a cola introduced in 1904), Freskola/Popular (a cola introduced in 1918), fruit-flavored carbonated beverages, and Agua Cristal (filtered water, introduced in 1917). Thus, when Postobón introduced Coca-Cola into the Colombian market in 1927, there were a number of competing products, including its own. Coca-Cola had to contend with a wide field of potables in Colombian drinking culture: other carbonated soft drinks (including those of Gaseosas Lux and Gaseosas Colombiana, many of which would be acquired by Postobón or Coca-Cola), beers (produced by a number of economically influential breweries like Cervecería Bavaria), imported liquors and indigenous alcoholic drinks like *aguardiente* (anise flavored sugarcane brandy), rum, and *chicha* (fermented maize, yucca, or other grains or fruits), fresh fruit juices (sold by street vendors and restaurants) and *guarapo* (sugarcane juice), *chocolate santafareño* (rich hot chocolate), and Colombia's largest export: coffee. Colombia's economic reliance on this competitive drink, coffee, and the resulting ideologies of free trade and collaboration with US capitalist interests, set the stage for Coca-Cola's arrival.

Coca-Cola entered Colombia in the 1920s, when laissez-faire tenets dominated economic policy and the United States extended its power through financial and commercial investment abroad.[40] Such economic practice was central to the ideology of liberal developmentalism,[41] which championed economic development and modernization through liberal economic relations with developed nations like the United States. There was particular openness to trade with the United States in Colombia, where the agrarian elite who wanted free markets for their coffee crops wielded more power than the nascent class of industrialists who favored protection of their fledgling industries. Colombia had dramatically felt the impact of US power when it lost an economically and strategically important piece of territory—what would become Panama—to the United States in 1903, and its subsequent relations with the United States reflected both US hegemony in Latin America, and an assumption by Colombian elites that the goals of economic development and modernization required collaboration with the United States. The Colombian government designed policies to attract US investment in the country and invited US economic experts to advise on the direction of Colombia's development. Like their international counterparts, Colombia's political and economic elite subscribed to developmentalist assumptions socially as well as economically. They justified stark social inequalities as products of inherent racial, ethnic, and class difference, but close contact with more "developed" foreign states, industries, and privileged social groups was assumed to help lift their nation out of isolation and "backwardness."[42] By the 1920s, Colombia's president Marco Fidel Suárez represented the country's doctrine of aligning its foreign policy and economic interests with those of the United States with the Latin phrase *respice polum,* or "Follow the North Star."[43]

Given its economic and political history, 1920s Colombia would not have been an obvious choice for foreign investment. Through the first boom of economic globalization in the nineteenth century, which saw a host of new trade links forged throughout the region, Colombia was arguably Latin America's least-favored international market. It had poor transportation infrastructure and a complex and rocky political as well as geographical terrain, making it not very accessible to foreign capital.[44] In its first century of national independence, Colombia experienced three military coups, two international wars, and nine civil wars, one of which, the War of a Thousand Days, had ended as recently as 1902. The Colombian government was left deeply in debt and collecting little income through taxes.

But in the 1920s, US capital, and soon Coca-Cola concentrate, was arriving in quantity in Colombia. In 1919, the United States successfully negotiated a peace treaty between itself, Colombia, and Panama, the isthmus-cum-colony on which the United States built and occupied a transcontinental canal providing the shortest and quickest route for ships between the Atlantic and Pacific oceans. With the peace treaty, the United States agreed to pay Colombia a $25 million indemnity for its loss of territory. Colombia needed capital so badly that it capitulated to the treaty even with the US government's refusal to include language expressing regret over instigating Panama's "inde-pendence." The United States further pressured Colombia out of proclaiming national control over its subsoil, which would have prevented oil exploration and exploitation by US companies.[45]

US banks also swelled Colombian coffers, lending approximately $200 million to federal, departmental, and municipal governments in the 1920s alone.[46] A Princeton University economist, Edward Kemmerer, called the "Money-Doctor," served as a "one-man International Monetary Fund" in Colombia on stabilization missions to overhaul the government's financial and fiscal systems (reprised throughout Andean Latin America and parts of Africa, Eastern Europe, and East Asia).[47] With the goal of making the coun-try more attractive to foreign lending and investment, the Colombian gov-ernment employed Kemmerer to create a Colombian central bank, pin the Colombian currency to the gold standard, and set the Colombian economy on a course of liberal developmentalism, patterning the country on the United States, while deepening its dependence on US-dominated interna-tional trade and finance networks.[48] Much of what the United States had enforced through coercion in Central America and the Caribbean was repli-cated in Colombia through consent and claims to economic science.[49]

US financiers, fiscal advisors, and corporate executives employed "capital investment imperialism" to grow profits abroad where the US economy was saturated at home, serving as "financial missionaries" spreading the word of capitalism in Latin America.[50] At the end of the 1920s, Colombian wealth was calculated at just $500 per capita, with consumers' purchasing power estimated at one-twentieth of that of US citizens. Economic growth rarely trickled down from the top 10 percent of Colombian society.[51] US-based investments in Colombia grew from capitalists' interests in improving Colombian consumer capacity for purchasing US goods. "If we can bring the remaining 90 per cent into the market we shall enormously increase our sales in those countries," a US Department of Commerce representative noted in 1929. "That is why the United States, even for the most selfish commercial reasons, is desirous of helping the peoples of Latin America to attain a greater degree of prosperity. Our hopes for future increased trade with Latin America are based upon the rise of the masses, and not upon the purchases of the present wealthy ruling classes."[52] This motivation drove large-scale lending to Colombia, so that by the end of the 1920s, every level of public administration, as well as the banks, agricultural sector, and burgeoning industrialist class had accrued significant capital and debt, in a process

Colombians came to call *prosperidad al debe* (debt prosperity).[53] Colombian coffee capitalism had fully taken root, with production increasing annually and its price rising steadily, flooding capital into the producing regions.[54] Although Colombians controlled most coffee production, they financed this expansion through credit obtained from mortgage banks floating bonds in the US market.[55] Foreign debt further financed public works projects like transportation and communications infrastructure to ensure the smooth movement of commodities.[56] These entanglements with the US economy, and the institutions and practices Colombia adopted in response, would reverberate during the global depression of the following decade. But in the 1920s, Colombians were enjoying the "Dance of the Millions" to the tune of the US-Panama indemnity payment, bank loans, and coffee earnings. What with urbanization and a growing retail sector, for the first time in Colombian history, there was an expanding market for consumer nondurable goods— textiles, packaged foods, and of course, bottled drinks.[57]

COCA-COLA AND THE TASTE OF CAPITALIST MODERNITY

The Coca-Cola Company's earliest advertising in Colombia in the late 1920s and early 1930s demonstrates the complex representational politics of an international product being introduced by both a growing multinational corporation and local franchises in Latin America. Advertising in *El Heraldo de Antioquia,* the leading Medellín daily newspaper,[58] represented Coca-Cola as a sign of modern business and culture. Latin Americans had long purchased imported goods from Europe, which were associated with modernity, quality, and style.[59] In the 1920s and 1930s, US products were relatively new to the Colombian marketplace, and their local reception was negatively impacted by what were perceived as bullying US assertions of power, including US lenders cutting off credit to the country in 1928 in disapproval of government spending and legislation protecting national oil reserves.[60] It was also resented when, under a threat of US military intervention to protect corporate interests, the Colombian army colluded with the United Fruit Company to massacre striking banana workers in Santa Marta in 1928, and was dispatched to Barrancabermeja to defend the Tropical Oil Company in 1927 and 1929. Strategically, then, Postobón's first Coca-Cola advertisements emphasized the drink's global popularity, rather than its North

Para deleitar su paladar y refrescar
su espíritu, tome Coca-Cola

Hoy día es la preferida en el mundo
entero. Su incomparable sabor seduce a
las personas de más experto paladar y
la convierte en la bebida preferida
cuando se ha tomado dos veces. ¡Prué-
bela hoy mismo!

Coca-Cola

Marca registrada

FIGURE 2. "To delight your palate and refresh your spirit,
drink Coca-Cola," *El Heraldo de Antioquia,* Medellín,
January 21, 1931.

American identity, figuring it as an international marker of modern taste and
class status.

According to the ads, Coca-Cola was the "preferred drink the world over."
Coca-Cola ads celebrated the "discerning palate[s]" of men and women
dressed in urbane, modern attire in sophisticated settings (fig. 2). "This drink
quenches the thirst of thirty European countries," Postobón advertised—
Europe being Colombian elites' model of taste and culture.[61] Advertising
directly addressed the issue of the cross-cultural acceptance of the product,
calling for Coca-Cola to be accepted in Colombia as it had already been
"everywhere" by society's crème de la crème.

The advertisement reproduced in figure 3, "Buena Compañía" ("Good
Company"), with its double play on the word company—signifying both the

FIGURE 3. "Here it is—At five centavos—Good Company," *El Heraldo de Antioquia,* Medellín, October 27, 1930.

company of the fashionable international youth who drink it and the company that manufactures it—implies that Coke pairs well with both social life and capitalist modernization. "On the terràces of the casinos, clubs, ballrooms, cafes, everywhere, Coca-Cola is the drink chosen by elegant youth. No other drink, in the entire world, has had the same acceptance."[62] The repeated figure of the Coca-Cola vendor streaming out from the English-language billboard suggests the unceasing diffusion of Coca-Cola's business, products, and advertising, manifest in the newspaper advertisement itself. This image of inexorable corporate growth, portrayed in an ad partially in English, strikes us today as an uncomfortable assertion of US corporate clout, but to contemporaries in Colombia in 1930 it may have evoked the pleasures of modernity offered by mechanical reproduction in both the exactitude of copies of the image of the Coca-Cola salesman and the implicit quality of his industrially-produced wares.[63]

FIGURE 4. "When the demand exists," *El Heraldo de Antioquia,*
Medellín, July 14, 1930.

Postobón advertised to prospective merchants as well as consumers, selling Coca-Cola's "good company" business model along with its product. The
advertisement "Cuando existe la demanda" ("When the demand exists")
(fig. 4), stresses the ease with which a vendor will be able to sell Coca-Cola
because of the "demand created by quality and advertising." The Coca-Cola
trademark, endowed with meaning through reputational goodwill by

¡He aquí...
La Reina de las bebidas!

La Coca-Cola ha merecido la aprobación de
innumerables paladares. Usted encontrará en
ella el refresco ideal y la pronunciará su
bebida favorita.

Coca-Cola

Marca registrada

Latin-American Division—Coca-Cola
Mexico City—1930—No. 4

Coca Cola—9435—He aquí—3½ x 5

Set By KING | First Proof | 1040D | 7.25 | g122 | C2

FIGURE 5. "Behold...
The Queen of Drinks!" *El Heraldo
de Antioquia,* Medellín, January
17, 1931.

consumers, and even more powerfully through promotional advertising produced by the multinational corporation, "eases the work of the retailer and gives him moreover, doubly superior profits" over "cheap imitations." 'Imitators and substitutors' were a threat to pricier Coca-Colas, since vendors often offered consumers cheaper alternatives, and such ads attempted to sell vendors on the profitability of a more expensive, better advertised product, while also suggesting that Coca-Cola was worth imitation. As the ad asserted, "When the demand exists it is easy to sell large quantities of a product with good benefits," suggesting both assets to the consumer and profits for the seller.[64]

The regular identification of Postobón as the sole authorized franchise bottler at the bottom of ads asserted the role of the Colombian company in the production of Coca-Cola and capitalist modernity. Articulated in Company publications as well as in public advertising, the cultural logic of the franchise in The Coca-Cola Company's earliest globalization framed the franchise bottler as a handpicked, trusted industrial elite, serving as conduit to the modern forms of production and consumption in the north.

But elements of these advertisements betrayed the infancy of the Coca-Cola bottling and marketing systems in Colombia, and the limits to the Company's representational power in distant geographic, cultural, and linguistic markets when the brand was primarily produced in the United States. In the advertisement reproduced in figure 5, "¡He aquí . . . La Reina de las bebidas!" ("Behold . . . The Queen of Drinks!"), internal details (everything below the first black line) were accidentally published with the ad, identifying Coca-Cola's Latin American Division in Mexico City as its source and specifying how it should be reproduced in print for the public. One of the earliest print ads in Colombia was reproduced exactly as it was used in the US market without translation into Spanish. The ad, "Stop at the Red Sign," justified Coca-Cola's presence in the country by saying, "It had to be good to get where it is." Playing on the signification of red STOP signs, the ad directed readers to stop for a Coca-Cola whenever they saw red signage. Common in turn of the century advertising, the strategy was to associate Coca-Colas with "arrows" and "signs"—other ads suggested "whenever you see an arrow, think of Coca-Cola"—to trigger automatic consumer reactions to the increasingly prevalent symbols in modern daily life. But even if such psychological associations could be established, the advertisement's own signification took on unintended and confused meanings through its publication in English, a foreign language that only a small percentage of the population could read.[65]

As early as 1929, The Coca-Cola Company bragged in its magazine for bottlers, The Red Barrel, that "Coca-Cola' is already a well-known product to a large part of the Colombian public,"[66] and in The Coca-Cola Bottler, the organ of the Bottlers' Association, that the drink was being bottled in "about ten Coca-Cola plants in the little country of Colombia."[67] Historical photos show horse-drawn carts delivering Coca-Colas, man-powered pushcarts selling Coca-Cola on streets, and signs on restaurants and storefronts in Medellín, Cali, and Bogotá in the late 1920s.[68] Images of the June 1929 anti-government protests in Bogotá show students and banana workers marching through plazas and streets backed by Coca-Cola billboards and "Tome Coca-Cola" signs on storefronts, evidencing that the brand had already become part of the visual culture of major Colombian cities.[69]

Despite its message to other bottlers, the Company was frustrated with its market growth under Postobón, suspending its franchise in 1936. The Company surmised that Postobón had courted Coca-Cola to protect its existing soft drink business and restrain the multinational's expansion in the country.[70] Coca-Cola's new bottler would later assert that Postobón had effectively stopped producing Coca-Cola products before this point and that its "franchise was suspended for factors of product quality."[71] There would have been ulterior motives in representing the fallout as a failure of quality, since Postobón would become the largest national soft drink company and Coca-Cola's main competitor in Colombia. Moving forward in Colombia, the Export Corporation preferred franchises that principally produced Coca-Cola products and thus, the Atlanta company hoped, shared a commitment to its brands and interests.

Colombian soda producers wasted little time in positioning their competing drink brands, often marketing them as authentically regional or national, to confront the return of Coca-Cola on Colombian soil. Postobón responded to the loss of the Coca-Cola franchise by investing more in its cola drink, Freskola/Popular, and launching an additional competitor, King Cola. Postobón represented Freskola as part of traditional Colombian celebrations, like the advertisement depicting a 1904 Christmas celebration, which suggested that three generations of Antioqueños—residents of the Colombian department where Medellín is located—had chosen Freskola ever since (an imagined nostalgia, because the drink wouldn't be introduced until 1918)[72] Postobón's 1940s advertising for another of its drink brands, Popular, drew on nationalism, calling it simply: "The drink of Colombians." Another major competitor, Gaseosas Colombianas, which featured the national symbol of an Andean Condor on its drink logos, launched a new cola, Kol-Cana, and continued to promote a "cola champagne" flavor, Colombiana, using the country's tricolor flag and even more overt nationalism, celebrating it as a "national product."[73]

The Coca-Cola Company planned to establish new franchises in Colombia, however, and in preparation it aggressively asserted claims to its intellectual property at the end of the 1930s. Coca-Cola was as concerned with the production (and protection) of trademarks as it was with the manufacturing of soft drinks. Colombian companies had marketed tonics and remedies derived from kola nuts and coca long before Coca-Cola arrived in the country.[74] An affidavit by the Harvard law professor Stephen Ladas, the Company's mid-century expert in international trademark law, describes the trademark infringement cases The Coca-Cola Company had brought against competitive drinks in Colombia since its early 1912 trademark registration in the country. Targeting the use of the term "cola," beginning in 1939, the Company won trademark infringement cases against Pepsi-Cola, King-Cola, Café Cola, Kinkola, CheroKola, CherKola, ChirKola, ChorKola, ChurKola, CharKola, Lime Cola, Rika-Cola, Posto-Kola, and Freskola/Popular, the Postobón drink produced since 1918, well before the bottling of Coca-Cola in Colombia.[75] The Company also contested the use of the term "coca," notwithstanding that coca cultivation and consumption were indigenous to Colombia. Not all the legal decisions would stand, but these lawsuits were meant to dissuade potential competitors, and Coca-Cola's legal fixer Roy Stubbs served on retainer and on assignment in Colombia and across Latin America in the 1940s and 1950s at the ready to pursue further litigation.[76]

LOCAL MODERNITY THROUGH THE MULTINATIONAL CORPORATION: COCA-COLA BOTTLING IN COLOMBIA

The Coca-Cola Company expanded its bid for market supremacy in Colombia in the 1940s by cultivating new franchise bottlers who would produce only Coca-Cola products, particularly in the country's growing inland and coastal cities. In 1940, it granted a new franchise to five Antioqueños, José Gutiérrez Gómez, Daniel Peláez, Alberto Mejía, Jesús Mora, and Hernando Duque, whose limited liability corporation, Industrial de Gaseosas Ltda. (INDEGA), established its first bottling plant in Medellín.[77] Gutiérrez Gómez went on to become president of the Asociación Nacional de Industriales (ANDI), the country's most powerful group of industrialists, formed in 1944, and later Colombia's ambassador to the United States, mayor of Medellín, president of the Permanent Council of the Organization of American States, and one of the most powerful Colombian financial leaders, heading some of Colombia's most important financial institutions and representing the country in international economic meetings of the World Bank and IMF.[78] While also president of the franchise of a major US multinational, as president of ANDI at mid-century, Gutiérrez Gómez would promote national industry and economic protection of Colombian industries, asserting that their particular economic interests were also in the best interest of Colombia and its peoples.[79] In search of additional capital to expand its bottling operations to Bogotá in

1941 and Cali in 1944, INDEGA subsequently became a joint-stock company.[80]

The Coca-Cola Company did not rely on the INDEGA franchise alone to grow its business in Colombia. In 1939, Coca-Cola had granted a contract to Robert W. Young and five other North Americans to open a plant called Embotelladora Tropical Ltda. in the port city of Barranquilla.[81] Located on the Caribbean coast at the mouth of the Magdalena River, one of the few freight transport routes into the interior of Colombia, and accessible to international trade and communications of the Atlantic, Barranquilla was the country's chief port. This geographic position made it an economic and industrial hub, a center for agriculture and livestock trade,[82] and a destination for migrants (mostly from within Colombia, but also international), hence ripe for the sale of mass consumables like bottled soft drinks. It also facilitated the importation from the United States of the ingredients and materials to produce Coca-Cola, with the exception of sugar, which retirees remember being purchased from Colombia's large sugar mill, Manuelita, in which Mr. Young's wife was an investor.[83] Over the subsequent decades coastal bottling would grow, consolidating through mergers and acquisitions under a handful of bottling companies, before being absorbed by the corporate owner of INDEGA (by then Panamco, see below) in 1970. INDEGA-Panamco thereafter monopolized Coca-Cola bottling in Colombia, aside from a few independent single-plant franchises.

Although INDEGA would dominate the Coca-Cola industry in Colombia, its growth was neither instantaneous nor smooth. Postobón and the large Colombian breweries controlled most of the bottled drinks business. And, according to INDEGA's own internal history, the young company lacked experience and was beset by "the constant pressure of the competition and import difficulties."[84] The Coca-Cola bottling business required large capital expenditures in advertising to promote the drink in a young market. Moreover, through the 1940s, the Colombian Coca-Cola business depended heavily on imports. "To manufacture the product in those early years," an INDEGA company publication recorded, "the bottling company had to import the concentrate, which was brought weekly to Medellín on a DC3 plane from Colón, Panamá, where Coca-Cola Export kept its deposits to serve various Latin American countries." But that was just the start, according to INDEGA, which "likewise, imported from the United States bottles, cases, crown tops, and advertising," as well as carbonic gas and production machinery.[85]

INDEGA's early growth unfolded against a political backdrop of growing calls for economic reform. In the late 1930s, the Colombian Left demanded that a larger swathe of society share in the fruits of capitalist modernization. Responding to a wave of labor militancy and federation, the Colombian government passed new labor legislation, facilitating the creation of trade unions.[86] Backed by labor and rural voters, the Liberal Party leader Alfonso López Pumarejo was elected to the presidency twice, in 1934 and 1942, on a platform of social and political reforms, under the slogan "Revolution on the March." López's populism and cooperation with the small but vocal Communist Party were threatening to Colombia's industrial elite, including soft-drink executives. Colombian industrialists were able to neutralize some of the labor critique by using patriotic nationalism to conscript the Colombian state and citizenry into a shared commitment to the growth of Colombian industry. They pushed for increased protectionism to grow their businesses, putting them in conflict with coffee-growing exporters and their free-trade orientation. While the Colombian government and marketplace was open to foreign investment and brands, the global depression of the 1930s fueled critiques of the nation's dependency on the United States. The Colombian government passed a 1936 constitutional amendment that gave the state the right to expropriate private property "for motives of public utility and social interest," both of which worried US multinationals (especially the oil companies).[87] The threat of expropriation never truly materialized, as López's reforms were derailed by World War II, as well as by domestic political conflict, including a failed coup, presidential resignation, and large-scale political violence in the late 1940s and 1950s. Despite lobbying by Colombian manufacturing interests, López never fully endorsed protectionism, viewing tariff barriers as "a tax on many to benefit the few," which increased the prices of foreign goods, fomented monopolies, and depressed wages in protected sectors, thus hurting the working class, while enriching company owners.[88] Colombia maintained its free-trade orientation throughout the 1930s, including signing a trade agreement with the United States in 1935 that reduced tariffs and eliminated taxes for over two hundred US products, and in exchange, Colombian coffee and bananas saw neither tariffs nor taxes in the United States.[89] The country's powerful export-oriented agricultural interests, especially producers of coffee, seen as the basis of the Colombian economy, were persistent advocates of free trade. But Colombian industry grew as US imports were restrained by the disruption of World War II, and Colombia's manufacturing elite continued to promote the view that the country's future was industrial and in need of state subsidy and protection.[90]

For The Coca-Cola Company, this political terrain was complicated. As early as 1930, a competing product—Ko-Kana—attacked Coca-Cola's vulnerable otherness, heralding future challenges to the multinational cast in conceptions of nationalist economic development. In contrast to Coca-Cola's appeals to universal aspirations to international modernity, Ko-Kana's Depression-era advertising emphasized that it was a "national industry" in every link of its commodity chain: "it is notable how many Colombians this great industry employs: Its corona tops: Colombian; Its carbonic gas: Colombian; Its labeling: Colombian; Its sugar: Colombian; Its bottles: Colombian; Its advertising: Colombian. Its Business: Colombian," an advertisement in *El Heraldo de Antioquia* proclaimed. Produced by the "Colombian spirit," Ko-Kana had been embraced by Colombians in a true example of "Colombian Protection."[91]

Against such threats, The Coca-Cola Company cast itself as simultaneously an international commodity representative of the modernity of developed countries *and* a local product enabling Colombian industry and consumers to develop and modernize. The often-repeated tagline "Safety . . . Hygienically Manufactured Security," represented Coca-Cola in relation to other local beverages, bottled or otherwise, which did not boast such modern claims. Emphasizing "quality," "purity" and "attention and care in its preparation" by INDEGA, "under contract with The Coca-Cola Company," such ads suggested Coca-Cola was safer than juices made on the street, fermented indigenous drinks, or "less modern" bottled soft drinks in Colombia.[92]

The Company and its advertising agency were also beginning to apply the modern theory of market segmentation, constructing "homemakers," "workers," and the "youth market," as distinct social categories. In the elite Conservative Party–oriented newspaper *El Colombiano,* advertisements paired modern middle-class leisure with Coca-Colas. Such ads promised not just thirst-quenching refreshment, but consumption and recreation as self-defining activities opened up by capitalist modernity. Produced by Coca-Cola Export and adapted from US campaigns, the ads often contained characters with (lightly) darkened features and generic Spanish translation. Many advertisements demonstrated attempts by Coca-Cola Export representatives and INDEGA to identify images among the offerings from Coca-Cola's international marketing provisions that might be more relevant to Colombian culture and context. For example, the Company's "Drink Coca-Cola—Ice Cold" campaign emphasized thirst-quenching refreshment through images of universal modern bourgeois leisure, such as lounging by a swimming pool,[93] and sports gaining popularity in

Colombia like swimming, jai alai (from Spain),[94] and baseball (from the United States).[95]

With Colombian newspapers lauding US military valor against fascism in World War II, editorializing in favor of US Good Neighbor policies, and giving space to anti-communist screeds, Coca-Cola's association with the United States linked it to the ascent of democratic capitalism. Nonetheless, an effort was made in advertising to assert the local production of Coca-Cola products as conduit to capitalist modernity. Each advertisement ended with "Bottled Under Contract With The Coca-Cola Co. by . . ." and space for the local bottler to fill in its company name (e.g., "Industrial de Gaseosas S.A."). INDEGA's sponsorship of the 1944 Exposición Nacional de Medellín, a celebration of Medellín's industrial prowess, provided an opportunity for the bottling company to support the promotion of local industry, and to assert itself as a member. In a series of advertisements, Coca-Cola invited guests to the exposition, as an implicit host,[96] and both simultaneously "the favorite drink of the Americas" and a "product of National Industry."[97] From the US perspective, as provided by a reporter from *Women's Wear* sent to cover Medellín's booming textile industry at the exposition, Coca-Cola's presence was a sign of the city's emergence into modernity: "It has all the entertainment features of our own fairs . . . 'Coca-Cola' is especially conspicuous and popular."[98]

Fluctuations in the wartime economy posed special challenges for INDEGA's balancing act. At the beginning of the 1940s, it was selling a crate of Coca-Colas at ninety centavos, so that retailers could sell to consumers at five centavos a bottle, and according to the company, "while the product sustained this competitive price level, its sales were good."[99] But in 1944, it found it "necessary for profitability" to raise the price of a crate to COP$1.60, an increase of 100 percent to the consumer when the retailer sold each bottle at ten centavos. Postobón and Lux were able to maintain their lower prices, COP$0.45 for a dozen. Coca-Cola sales plunged, and INDEGA considered taking Coke off the market entirely. To "defend" itself financially, the company "had to resort to competing in price with the competition" by putting out a new, cheaper product, Club Soda, and acquiring the brand Kist and its more affordable orange, grape, and "red" drinks.[100] INDEGA reintroduced Kist with mysterious newspaper ads and posters around Medellín featuring question marks and the Kist trademark. A viral marketing campaign invited people to tell everyone they saw: "Kist arrives on Monday!" with the possibility of receiving COP$20 from INDEGA employees planted around town waiting to hear that greeting.[101] A short paid "news" story (early twentieth century's "native advertising") on Kist simultaneously emphasized INDEGA's embeddedness in local industry and society and its international cultural connections, declaring that Kist would "surely find general acceptance" as yet "another pleasing effort from a company linked to *antioqueño* progress" and "'Coca-Cola,' the drink with endless international prestige." Attempting to draft Colombians into consumption as an act of national civic duty,[102] the article concluded: "Our votes, not just as friends but as Colombians, are for 'KIST' to achieve the renown it deserves and be as widely drunk as its delicious flavor merits."[103] Not mentioned was that INDEGA licensed KIST from Citrus Products Co. of Chicago, IL.[104]

There were increasing signs that developmentalism was beginning to lose some of its free market liberalism in Colombia. Colombian industrialists were becoming more powerful, and more threatened by what they saw as economic policies that benefited import-export interests to the detriment of Colombian manufacturing while empowering a growing labor movement that threatened their control over their factories. INDEGA's Gutiérrez Gómez, or in this case more importantly the Asociación Nacional de Industriales' Gutiérrez Gómez, as INDEGA still relied heavily on imports of various kinds, promoted protectionism, and industrialists like him were not the only ones to do so. Support for government planning—from the multiple and often divergent motivations of developing national industries, empowering a national bourgeoisie, "modernizing" the Colombian economy and society, and protecting workers—was beginning to take root. But the Depression and World War II limited US exports and shielded emerging Colombian industries, so a protectionist program would not be seriously considered until the end of the war amid growing fears that foreign goods would inundate the Colombian economy.[105]

COCA-COLA GOES TO WAR

By the beginning of the 1940s, The Coca-Cola Company had established dozens of international bottling franchises. But its globalization was still nascent—Coca-Cola had plants in only a small number of countries—and the outbreak of World War II brought both increased costs of inputs like sugar and reduced consumer confidence. Despite this insecurity, Coca-Cola saw the war as an opportunity for international expansion, cultivating US servicemen as a generation of consumers and reaping the benefits of the

US state's promotion of corporate capitalism. With support from the US government, which saw corporate advertising of the modern industrial products of capitalist democracy as a weapon in the war of hemispheric public opinion, the Company more than tripled its advertising expenditures in Latin America during the early years of the conflict. It proudly reported its advertising payouts to Nelson Rockefeller's Office of Inter-American Affairs (OIAA), which incentivized US companies to increase their advertising spending to make good neighbors out of Latin American media outlets which had seen 40 percent drops in advertising revenue from US firms during the war.[106] With encouragement from OIAA and sensing a market opportunity, Coca-Cola more than doubled its spending on advertising in Latin America from 1941 to 1942, from $150,000 to $350,000, and then by another 50 percent again in 1943 to $523,000, putting its reported advertising spending fourth among 110 firms. Coca-Cola Export was quick to point out that the actual spending on advertising placement was almost twice this amount, since bottlers were also required to buy advertising. And Coca-Cola Export had full authority over the content of that advertising: "any advertising done in the territories is entirely and completely under our control."[107]

US government reports noted the cultural impact of wartime Coca-Cola advertising in Colombia. Colombian bottlers received a modest US$5,200 from Coca-Cola Export to advertise, but it went a long way in promoting the brand in "publications," "radio," "outside displays," "artwork & inside display," "walls & bulletins," "trams & bus displays," "cinema," and "posters."[108] Coca-Cola also sponsored a Sunday night broadcast of Spanish and Italian symphonic music performed by the "45-piece Coca-Cola orchestra" from Bogotá's 3,500-seat Teatro Colombia. OIAA's director of radio operations in Colombia reported that the broadcast had "fairly close to one-hundred per cent of Bogotá's listening audience" and was relayed via radio network to the country's major cities.[109]

The Coca-Cola Company increased its advertising spending in Latin America as part of the US war effort, but its wartime advertising stressed pan-American, rather than US, cultural referents. Ads featured the Coca-Cola red disc with a map of the Americas North and South inside it and the tagline "United today. United Always." Advertisements such as "The Universal Invitation...Let's Have a Coke!" emphasized that Coca-Cola consumption was universally shared across modern Latin America; a modernity portrayed as emerging from a shared relationship to indigeneity that was venerable but decidedly in the "past." A "modern" Guatemalan couple picnic alongside an ancient Mayan monolith sharing Coca-Colas, while in the background indigenous Guatemalan women carry pots of water on their heads contrastingly representing the "pre-modern" surpassed through the likes of Coca-Cola. Even though the Company avoided waving the US flag in its advertising, it served US interests by promoting the products of capitalist modernity with images of consumption, leisure, and abundance.[110]

While the Company attributes its rapid mid-century growth to marketplace success, the history of Coca-Cola in World War II clarifies the pivotal role of the state in corporate expansion. For decades prior to the war, the Company and other producers of sweet drinks and foodstuffs had benefited from US state intervention through tariff protection and bounty programs that encouraged sugar production and refining, and produced economies of scale that resulted in a glut of cheap sugar in a far from "free market."[111] But in the run-up to World War II, Company executives were fixated on the negative ramifications of government involvement in commodity markets, recalling World War I sugar rationing that had imposed a tax on syrup sales and limited the Company's sugar use.[112] In fact, heavy lobbying from Coca-Cola executives had kept the Company's sugar allotments relatively stable through the course of that war. The US government's price controls enabled the Company to buy sugar cheaply, garnering record profits by 1919 as the government removed purchasing restrictions but kept prices low.[113] It was not until wartime price controls were lifted and the Company was exposed to the freer market and its commodity speculators that it saw a looming crisis over sugar.[114]

Such exposure to a volatile commodity market motivated Coca-Cola executives to make key changes to the Company's franchise model of globalization after World War I. By the 1920s, bottlers accounted for 40 percent of syrup sales, with signs that this would soon overtake the Company's long-standing soda fountain business.[115] Company President Ernest Woodruff moved to insulate the corporation from fluctuations in sugar prices by abolishing the US bottlers' perpetual contracts with fixed prices for syrup, which had meant that, depending on the cost of raw materials like sugar, the Company sometimes sold syrup at a cost.[116] US bottlers sued the Company, and after a legal battle, the courts approved of modifications to the bottling contract, which set a base cost per gallon of syrup but allowed for the Company to charge an additional six cents for every one-cent increase in the price of sugar.[117] But as the international bottling system was only just being established, the Company had more leeway in establishing the terms of its business and externalizing the cost of the sweetener. In 1926, concurrent with the establishment of its Foreign Department, the

Company developed a sugarless concentrate to sell to international bottlers, who would then have to purchase and add sugar to produce the finished drink.[118] By removing the sugar, Coca-Cola capitalized on the logics of franchise globalization to not only avoid fluctuations in the cost of sugar and cut transportation costs, but also take advantage of sugar tariff protection enacted by different national governments. Even after off-loading the risks of sugar acquisition to bottlers, the Company remained concerned about sugar markets. Expensive inputs might lead bottlers to raise prices on their drinks, which could deter consumers from purchasing their product, in turn affecting the Company's sales of concentrate. As a result, The Coca-Cola Company continued to lobby governments around the world to create and maintain markets in cheap and plentiful sweeteners.[119]

At the outbreak of World War II, Coca-Cola feared both disruption of sugar markets and the impact of government restrictions on consumer demand. Its US syrup manufacturing benefited from government intervention through price controls in the short term, but by 1942, the US government limited soft-drink producers to 70 percent of their 1941 sugar use.[120] Coca-Cola's lobbyist in Washington, DC, Ben Oehlert, set out on a public relations campaign to establish Coca-Cola's image as a good corporate citizen. He proposed that Coca-Cola sell thousands of pounds of sugar inventories to the US government at below market cost.[121] The Company expected some benefit in return and successfully lobbied to dismiss a proposed national sales tax on soft drinks that had been part of the Roosevelt administration's wartime excess-profits tax plan.[122]

A larger concern of the Company's was the US government's classification of Coca-Cola as a nonessential luxury item that consumed large amounts of a staple commodity, sugar, exposing it to severe wartime rationing. In ingenious maneuvering, the Company asserted that Coca-Cola's high sugar composition made it a wartime necessity essential to the war effort. Such decisions were made by the US government's sugar-rationing board, to which Coca-Cola's politicking had succeeded in getting one of its top executives, Ed Forio, appointed.[123] Forio described his work as "an untiring effort . . . to point out the tremendous part that soft drinks play in the ordinary everyday lives of average people to those highest in authority in government," crowned by a report that remarkably quantified that "a minimum of 65 per cent of the products of this industry was necessary to the maintenance of civilian morale."[124] This strategy was further articulated in a memo entitled "Soft Drinks in War" by Coca-Cola Export Vice President Ralph Hayes,[125] which argued that soldiers would be expending large amounts of energy, and drinking sodas with high sugar content could provide both a momentary break for rest and a cheap, delicious supply of calories.[126] Lobbyist Oehlert and the D'Arcy advertising agency took the argument to Washington with a lobbying pamphlet on the "Importance of the Rest-Pause in Maximum War Effort," which drew on contemporary theories of industrial management and the Company's pseudo-scientific health claims about the "refreshing" benefits derived from sugar and caffeine to argue for the necessity of periodic breaks for both soldiers and factory workers. "Men work better refreshed.... In times like these Coca-Cola is doing a necessary job for workers," it asserted.[127]

Company lobbyists and executives succeeded in convincing the US government that Coke was vital to the morale and productivity of the troops. By the beginning of 1942, the US government had exempted Coca-Cola and its bottling plants from sugar rationing for drinks it sold to the military or retailers serving military forces. The rest of the US soft-drink industry languished under heavy sugar restrictions, with Coca-Cola's competitors suffering from an 80 percent sugar-use quota, while its own dropped as low as 50 percent, and only for those domestic US bottlers who did not have any military bases nearby to justify a sugar exemption.[128]

Getting Coke to servicemen and -women deployed internationally would be a different matter, though, and would require significant costs as well as additional subsidization. A day after the United States declared war on Germany and Italy, Coca-Cola President Robert W. Woodruff issued a statement of support, adding that the Company "will see that every man in uniform gets a bottle of Coca-Cola for five cents, wherever he is and no matter what the cost."[129] Supplying Coca-Colas to the troops at home and abroad would mean putting short-term profits on hold, but could come with potential long-term gains: the brand loyalty it would produce in soldiers, exposure to new international consumer markets, and goodwill from the US government. As a Company memo described:

> A proper attitude toward supplying Coca-Cola to those troops wherever they go can do us more good, both domestically and abroad, than could a generation of effort and millions spent in advertising and merchandising.... When the troops come back they will spend the rest of their lives in conscious or unconscious contemplation of their lives and experiences in the armed forces abroad. Simultaneously, the widespread use of Coca-Cola by those troops abroad will place the product and its trade-mark in an unprecedented position with the civilian population of the countries ... [130]

The Company's assertions that it could boost morale of military personnel in the various theaters of war were bolstered by letters from troops requesting Coke to remind them of home.

The government was persuaded to subsidize the bottling of Coca-Cola where US troops were stationed, "in six active theaters of war ... a part of every major campaign in Africa, Asia, Europe, India, the Pacific, and the South Atlantic."[131] Coca-Cola established sixty-four bottling plants, largely at government expense, serving approximately three billion Cokes over the course of the war. The 248 Company employees stationed with troops were given a "simulated military rank" of "Technical Observers" (TOs), and nick-named "Coca-Cola Colonels."[132] This military-soda industrial complex, financed through government funds, spread the drink's production to new locales in Europe, Africa and Asia, including India.

This collaboration with the US military launched the second stage of the Company's globalization and brought Coca-Cola production to new international markets, especially in Africa and Asia, including India. By the start of 1944, TOs had established Indian wartime bottling plants in Calcutta, Delhi, and Chabua and Ledo in Assam.[133] Nearly 6,000 bottles of Coke were sold each day in India alone during the war, while shortages of glass bottles limited production and demand outmatched supply, necessitating an "honor system" whereby each US service member was "entitled to one bottle of Coca-Cola per day."[134] TOs reported their entrepreneurialism in working with mobile bottling plants, converting former food and drink factories to Coca-Cola, sourcing needed materials through barter as well as payment, managing foreign workforces without speaking the local language, and relying on the cooperation of Army personnel assigned to their plants.

Although they were rarely in combat danger, the work of a TO supplying Coca-Cola to US troops was challenging, and their reports evoked military and colonial exploits. Writing from India, one Sydney W. McCabe made light of the difficulties: "[We] are still holding out in India. I am rather doubtful that we can hold out long. The chances of survival over here are very slim. It is not a case so much of disease, but the fact that the whiskey is poison and the people drive on the wrong side of the street. I have had a chance to do some hunting. I have so far gotten a nice buck with a fair set of antlers."[135] The tone of their communications could be more serious, as was the dispatch from New Delhi by Turk Beard, who asked that the other Coca-Cola men "pardon my eleven-month delay in writing, but the first six were hardly worth reporting on as so many complications arose to prevent our getting into stride. The last several have been more than busy. We are learning ... that there are some places hotter than Texas."[136] Beard died just two months later in a plane crash in India,[137] one of three TOs to die in air accidents while traveling between Coca-Cola facilities they oversaw during the war.[138]

TOs often wrote of the racial and cultural difference of the local people they encountered as both workers and potential consumers, relaying their powerful assumptions that their industry was bettering the existing local ways of life. In Tunis, a TO reported of the improvements in hygiene forced upon the local workforce: "You would get a kick out of seeing some of the workers here in the plant. They are Arabs and come in dressed like some of the doormen of some of the New York night clubs. Every once in a while I give them a bar of soap and have the water hose turned on them. Otherwise they start to smell like that well known goat."[139] A TO stationed in New Guinea expressed the typical condescension to peoples the Company would soon rely on as consumers: "A Fuzzy-Wuzzy native was passing by the plant ... I offered him a drink of 'Coca-Cola.' At first he was a little skeptical and reluctant but after a little persuasion he sniffed at it, stuck his tongue in it and then drank it down rather fast. Then the fun began. He belched, the gas went up his nose and brought tears to his eyes. He was a scared native for a few minutes. So now it can be said that we have sampled and opened up a new outlet—the Fuzzy-Wuzzy market."[140] Less than a month later one of his TO partners in New Guinea was confident that they were successfully opening up a new market on the island after providing Cokes to a ship full of war refugees: "I'm sure that many of the smaller children had never tasted 'Coca-Cola' before but they'll certainly be steady customers from now on."[141] The Company hoped the effect was similar in India, where the war brought Coca-Cola and would help establish a new postwar market. A US Army lieutenant happily wrote to *The Red Barrel* that Coca-Colas had arrived to his base and that his unit had "adopted a little Indian boy" who emulated everything the US GIs did. "He brushes his teeth three or four times a day and takes showers regularly. They told him that if he washes frequently he will become white like us, and he certainly tries hard. . . . He does everything we do," including, presumably, drink Coca-Cola.[142]

The corporation's wartime contributions and the resulting global distribution of its products became fodder for the Company's domestic US advertising during the latter stages of the war. The "The Global High-Sign" campaign featured US troops sharing Coca-Colas with locals in exotic lands (fig. 6), telling US consumers that the Company was boosting US troops' morale and spreading Coca-Cola and all it "signified" around the world. Some thirty lushly illustrated ads for Coca-Cola on the back covers of *National Geographic* and *Life* projected an image of benevolent US military and corporate power being cheerfully received internationally. The ads cast Coca-Cola as a means of communication across difference, to signal a moment of relaxation in the midst of the conflict. For US audiences, the advertisements were an introduction to Coca-Cola's international identity, instructing them that Coca-Cola was simultaneously deeply American (no less than a soft-drink division of the armed forces embedded with America's fighting boys) and in the process of becoming global through its universal appeal.[143]

Coca-Cola's red disc logo during this time period became a visual representation of the kind of localization Coca-Cola imagined. Transformed into a globe, it rotated to show the geographic region portrayed in each of the ads. The ads were each captioned with a rendering of "Have a Coca-Cola" into a local phrase that was not a direct translation at all, but instead one that suggested friendship and connection. To the wartime US consumer who saw these advertisements, Coca-Cola appeared as literally in service to the military, helping soldiers make friends around the world. These moments of friendship in the advertisements were everyday and frequently "domestic," with soldiers doing their chores (bathing, cleaning) or at leisure in their camps (playing sports, eating and drinking). Such advertising arose from a longer visual history of sentimental images of "domesticity" and the everyday in distant locales used to suggest the naturalness and benevolence of imperialism and capitalist expansion, while erasing the violence and conflicts of these encounters.[144]

To assert Coke's universality necessitated the assertion of the "otherness" of the various international peoples who now also enjoyed it. Coca-Cola ads contrasted essentialized depictions of such peoples with representations of the physical and industrial fitness of the white male soldiers and the technologies of the United States. Images of soldiers as clean-shaven young men alongside quietly resting military machinery projected fantasies of US power abroad. In many of the images, US military personnel appeared to be introducing capitalist modernity as well as Coca-Cola to the less civilized, demonstrating modern technologies, Western conceptions of leisure, and modern consumer culture. In the ad reproduced in figure 6, the slower pace of underdeveloped Latin America represented by a chubby, middle-aged Panamanian man and a young boy on a mule is contrasted with the US soldiers in their physical prime and the boats speeding through the US-built Panama Canal. In another,

Have a Coca-Cola = ¿Qué Hay, Amigo?
(WHAT GIVES, PAL?)

...or making pals in Panama

Down Panama way, American ideas of friend-liness and good neighborliness are nothing new. Folks there understand and like our love of sports, our humor and our everyday customs. *Have a "Coke"*, says the American soldier, and the natives know he is saying *We are friends* ... the same friendly invitation as when you offer Coca-Cola from your own refrigerator at home. Everywhere Coca-Cola stands for *the pause that refreshes,*—has become the high-sign of kindly-minded people the world over.

* * *

In news stories, books and magazines, you read how much our fighting men cherish Coca-Cola whenever they get it. Yes, more than just a delicious and refreshing drink, "Coke" reminds them of happy times at home. Luckily, they find Coca-Cola —bottled on the spot—in over 35 allied and neutral countries 'round the globe.

It's natural for popular names to acquire friendly abbrevia-tions. That's why you hear Coca-Cola called "Coke".

COPYRIGHT 1944, THE COCA-COLA COMPANY

FIGURE 6. "Have a Coca-Cola = ¿Qué Hay Amigo?" *Life,* April 3, 1944, and *National Geographic Magazine,* April 1944.

shirtless US soldiers demonstrate the workings of their military radio to shirtless, primitive Maori men who gape in amazement. In such representa-tions, international "others" were similar yet so different, with Coca-Cola a modernizing force that was universally accepted, capable of making "them" a little more like "us," while not erasing their difference entirely. Such concep-tions of a US "us" were all the more powerful in the context of wartime nationalism, but were also in the process of being refigured for an "American Century" in which the United States was more internationally engaged, with US corporations profiting from and propelling its ascendancy.

In these images Coca-Cola's globalization is represented not as the conscious work of executives or even its wartime TOs, but instead as the organic process of men sharing a beloved commodity as an act of friendship with the diverse peoples they encounter who readily accept Coca-Cola. In the postwar period, Coca-Cola would extend the cultural projections first created during the war, repeatedly using images of Coca-Colas in the hands of exotic others to celebrate the brand's reach and suggest the universality of US models of corporate and consumer capitalism. This narrative not only appeared in Coca-Cola advertisements, it emerged again and again in internal publications. Coca-Cola suggested that its "postwar business that blossomed and burgeoned from both the physical and visual sampling of 'Coca-Cola' in supplying the military services" amounted to "imitation . . . the sincerest form of flattery."[145]

The story of one of the most popular and salacious songs of the 1940s suggests there were more complex feelings about the presence of US GIs and their associated commodities, both in the locales occupied by US troops and in the United States. The Trinidadian musician Lord Invader's catchy calypso tune, "Drinkin' Rum and Coca-Cola," was a biting social critique of the stationed US soldiers and their power—economic, military, and sexual: "Since the Yankees came to Trinidad / They have the young girls going mad / The young girls say they treat them nice / And they give them a better price / They buy rum and Coca-Cola / Go down Point Koomhana / Both mother and daughter / Workin' for the Yankee dollar." But when a slightly sanitized version of "Rum and Coca-Cola" was recorded by the white swing songstresses the Andrews Sisters, it became a number one hit in the United States and was so heavily requested by the troops that it received the moniker the "National Anthem of the GI Camps."[146] The song's reference to sex work, US soldiers' exploits with Trinidadian women, and racial miscegenation in the metaphor of mixing of rum and Coca-Cola (Coke is black to rum's white; Coke is United States to rum's Caribbean), speaks to both a Trinidadian critique of US military presence and prurient American interest in the multiple manifestations of US power internationally. "Rum and Coca-Cola" also demonstrated the ways in which Coca-Cola was imbued with meaning through popular consumption and symbolic culture beyond the Company's control.

For three years after the end of the war, TOs would stay on in their international locations converting the wartime operations into civilian, long-term businesses, and one Company publication, *T.O. Digest*, would transition to another, *Coca-Cola Overseas*.[147] The Company's World War II maneuvers—collaborating with the government to ensure its access to raw materials, shielding itself from taxation, and spreading its business to new shores—positioned it to capitalize after the war on the United States' rising international economic power, launching the second stage of Coca-Cola's globalization after 1945.

NO LONGER LOCAL, INDEPENDENT: CAPITALIST MODERNITY'S DRIVE TO GROW THE FRANCHISE

To a degree, both US government officials and Coca-Cola executives expressed strategic support for an emerging national developmentalist thinking about the modernization of international economies, especially in Latin America. Policies that promoted national industrialization and social welfare programs as solutions to poverty and economic disparity might grow international consumer markets, prevent social revolutions, and protect capitalism in the long term. In 1939, Sumner Welles, architect of the "Good Neighbor" policy, had articulated the US government's position of offering the assistance of private banks and US government agencies "to cooperate with all other American republics in such efforts of each to develop the resources of its country along sound economic and noncompetitive lines." Quoting this intention, US agencies undertook a study of Colombia to determine what kind of commercial and industrial policies might be beneficial to the country's development, while also serving US national interests. The resulting 1941 report conveyed the US government's acceptance of potential import substitution industrialization policies as a necessary means of expanding Colombia's manufacturing sector, and recommended government investments aimed at both initiating industries and improving transportation and infrastructure to support existing Colombian manufacturers. With a larger manufacturing sector and waged working class, the report argued, the "home market" of Colombian consumers could be expanded beyond the small upper class. Better-paid industrial workers could purchase the products coming off their very own production lines.[148]

The US government's 1941 report on Colombia's economic prospects noted that the nation's "small-scale industries" in areas such as soft drinks "have thrived in local hands," as in the case of Postobón. But expectations should not be raised too quickly about Colombian industrialization, inasmuch as "a number of foreign specialties ... will continue to be imported even over tariff walls and other barriers," as with the syrups of Coca-Cola and Pepsi. Hopes for an export market for Colombian manufactured products were not very high, according to the report, with just a few exceptions, including notably, soft drinks. Not only could the soft-drink industry produce for national consumption, it also had the potential to export. Colombia could create a "coffee-cola drink" for export, which would merit government support; "should a coffee-cola drink be developed worthy of an attempt to explore the American market, some official encouragement might be forthcoming," presumably from the United States as well as Colombian government, the report hypothesized.[149] But no such drink was developed, leaving more of the Colombian market available for Coca-Cola's growth.

As INDEGA and Coca-Cola were concertedly characterizing the franchise as a Colombian industry to appeal to Colombian national development goals, the company's ownership and leadership were about to become more North American and demonstrative of the powerful role of the US multinational in the operations of its "independent" franchise bottlers. Dependent on imported packaging, advertising, and machinery, as well as concentrate from Coca-Cola Export, and given the vagaries of the wartime sugar market, Colombian investors in the business bore the burden of high and unpredictable costs, and "these enormous demands on the company made the directors think about the urgent necessity of looking for good refinancing."[150] The Coca-Cola Company itself had weathered the effects of economic depression and wartime austerity on its business. But with many of its international franchises in vulnerable economic positions, the Company seized the opportunity to exert its influence with an eye to expansion. With the encouragement of Coca-Cola Export, in 1945, INDEGA's shareholders commissioned two of their directors, José Gutiérrez Gómez and Daniel Peláez, to travel to Export's New York headquarters to negotiate the sale of interest in the company to Albert H. Staton and his budding Latin American bottling company, Refrescos, S.A. of Panama (incorporated as Panamerican Beverages, known as Panamco, after 1954).

Albert H. Staton was already a Coca-Cola Company man, employed since 1924 after graduating with superlatives from Georgia Tech. He went on to a similarly successful career with Coca-Cola in Connecticut, Canada, Europe, and Asia, rising the ranks to vice president of the Pan American Division of Coca-Cola Export, which had brought him to Colombia in 1938 to seek out potential franchisees, when he contracted Robert Young as the bottler in Barranquilla.[151] From this position managing Coca-Cola Export's business throughout Latin America, Staton not only promoted existing bottling businesses but also surveyed the field for opportunities to expand the market and his own profits. Staton had owned bottling plants in the United States, and in 1941 he and a group of investors acquired Coca-Cola bottling operations in Mexico.[152] Returned from World War II service and presented with the opportunity by Gutiérrez Gómez and Peláez, in 1944 Staton invested in and assumed management of INDEGA but kept all the local signage, advertising, and corporate identification of the Colombian subsidiary. The following year he would again transnationally expand his Coca-Cola bottling holding company, purchasing his first franchise in Brazil. In 1945, Staton traveled for the first time to Medellín, the city in which he would make his home when not overseeing his investments elsewhere.[153]

Albert Staton's long history with Coca-Cola Export enhanced the growing bottling company's ties to the multinational, which realized the possibility for expansion under a trusted member of the Coca-Cola family. Staton's brother John became vice president of Coca-Cola Export in charge of sales in South America (fortuitously, just as his brother's franchises were getting their start in Colombia, Mexico, and Brazil), and would later rise to a vice presidency of The Coca-Cola Company in Atlanta.[154] Albert Staton brought with him technicians and consultants to revamp the business in Colombia. As a good Coca-Cola man of his era, he quickly sold off the recently acquired Kist franchise to Postobón, keeping only Coca-Cola and Club Soda, so that more attention and capital could be focused on the Coca-Cola brand.[155] With this plan to expand its business in the country, Coca-Cola Export established a wholly owned subsidiary, Coca-Cola de Colombia to produce concentrate and oversee the marketing and production of Panamco and other Colombian franchise bottlers.[156] Coca-Cola Export managers and members of its sales promotion force instructed bottlers and local salesmen in modern marketing techniques. Under Staton's direction, his large capital infusion, and support from Coca-Cola corporate headquarters, Coca-Cola Export collaborated with Panamco to launch new advertising and promotional campaigns, including popular bottle cap promotions offering miniature bottles, yo-yos (Coca-Cola credits itself with introducing the yo-yo to

Colombia),[157] Disney toys, and other treats, marketing the drinks to Colombian children. Panamco bottlers made "weekly visits to schools, factories, and stores" to give out free samples and promotional materials, "which immediately resulted in an increase in sales."[158]

Albert Staton publicly praised his Colombian business partners, especially José Gutiérrez Gómez and Daniel Peláez, as was the common practice of Coca-Cola businessmen to assert the local rootedness and leadership of their franchises.[159] But retirees from the Colombian plants and Coca-Cola executives remember Staton himself as the dominant force in the expansion and management of the bottling system in Colombia and throughout much of Latin America. The influence of the "true helmsman of the business"[160] was spelled out in a 1976 company magazine for its intended readership of workers: "With the arrival of Mr. Staton, a complete reorganization of the three plants was made, and a new phase began; the experiences, new techniques and the dynamic organization of this moment began the dizzying race that has not stopped to this day and has converted our business in one of the strongest, most prestigious and united in Colombia."[161] In contrast, in the long obituaries and tributes recording the extensive public and private employment of José Gutiérrez Gómez, his presidency of INDEGA does not get a mention, although he was strategically maintained as president of the bottling corporation through the 1960s, even while among other things serving as Colombian ambassador to the United States.[162]

Staton pushed The Coca-Cola Company to rethink its stated preference for local bottlers, following the Company's own model of monopoly capitalism. Seeking to expand from existing bottling plants in Medellín, Cali, and Bogotá to include a new plant in Pereira, in the foothills of the Andes, he argued that meeting the challenges of creating a Coca-Cola distribution system in this poor, rural, mountainous region required a single, large company. Staton's INDEGA could make a poor region profitable through economies of scale: it had the equipment, trucks, the sugar, and the carbonic gas, "all of which are extremely difficult to get under present conditions," and the capital to expand its territory. INDEGA's advertising already "blankets the area, and if INDEGA puts up the money for these programs, it seems that they should be allowed to reap the benefits," he asserted. Staton countered criticism of "chain bottlers" at The Coca-Cola Company, which feared the concentration of manufacturing power in the hands of a few large bottling company owners who could then demand more in contract negotiations with the Company or overextend themselves and jeopardize a region's profitability. Staton insisted that he was not himself such a bottler, being just one of multiple investors in his plants. He argued, however, that the concentration of capital and resources—financial, human, material, and political—was necessary to grow the business: a larger bottler had "the advantage of capital, ability to employ good men, pooled experience, a longer view and far better ability to handle raw material and political problems than the average or even exceptional small bottler." In fact, according to Staton, "the only real chain bottler I know of, outside the US" was the Texan H. H. Fleishman's Mexican bottling company, "possibly the best foreign bottler." Newer, small local bottling firms could not be trusted to expand the Coca-Cola industry reliably, because they looked on the relationship with suspicion: established bottlers "know and admire" the Company, "whereas many of your smaller bottlers know it only as another foreign firm, to beware of."[163] While in signage and representation bottling plants continued to look "local, independent," this argument about the profitability and security of big bottling business won out; Staton's Panamco would be a Latin American bottling empire by the end of the twentieth century.

If the social and cultural logics of the franchise in The Coca-Cola Company's earliest globalization framed the franchise bottler as a local conduit to capitalist modernity, it also conflicted with the imperatives of capitalist growth itself. The "local, independent" bottler's profit motive, and pressures from the underlying corporation in Atlanta for market growth, drove an expanded definition of locality and independence, broadening the franchise's geographical market and deepening its relationships with the Company. But local, independent bottlers would still be essential to Coca-Cola's self-representation internationally. The Coca-Cola Company negotiated the shift from liberal developmentalism in the first half of the twentieth century to more protectionist developmental politics at mid-century by advocating for local bottlers as agents of national modernization.

TWO

Mediating Coca-Colonization

NEGOTIATING NATIONAL DEVELOPMENT AND DIFFERENCE IN COCA-COLA'S POSTWAR INTERNATIONALIZATION

VIRTUALLY UNTOUCHED BY THE DESTRUCTION OF WORLD WAR II, unlike much of Europe and Asia, the United States was well positioned to lead the postwar world. The Coca-Cola Company, a US corporation seeking international markets, was similarly poised for global power. When representatives of fifty countries met in San Francisco in July 1945 to charter the United Nations, the supranational institution they hoped would maintain the peace of this new world order, Coca-Cola Export Chairman James Aloysius "Jim" Farley took up residence in the delegates' hotel.[1] With an unlimited budget "to wine, Coca-Cola, and dine," he hosted luncheons and parties for heads of state, foreign ministers, and delegates.[2] It would have taken him "two years of round-the-world traveling" to meet so many world leaders, he said,[3] a statement all the more significant coming from someone who was now accustomed to regular world tours for Coca-Cola Export. "The relationships I established," Farley modestly reported, "might be helpful in our efforts to establish Coca-Cola bottling companies" in parts of the world not yet penetrated by the soft drink company.[4]

What better symbol of the economic and social modernity achieved in the United States and applicable around the world than Coca-Cola? At least so argued the Company's executives on such trips abroad. On his frequent international tours, Farley—a former chairman of the Democratic Party's national committee, Roosevelt postmaster general, and presidential candidate himself—was received as much as a political emissary as a corporate executive. "Big Jim," as he was touted in the press both for his physical size and political power, met with government leaders and was regularly asked if he was on "mission for the President," or, if he planned on running for the office himself. Coca-Cola Company President Robert W. Woodruff explained Farley's assets to an internationalizing business: "Farley's quite a fellow. I don't care where he goes—Spain, England, wherever, he's entertained by the government. He still keeps up all those political connections."[5] Over the course of his career, US presidents would claim him as a friend and "emissary" abroad,[6] a businessman building US soft power internationally. In his speeches, Farley spoke in the Good Neighbor discourse of political and economic "cooperation," emphasizing the role of international trade and businesses for development, especially Coca-Cola's franchised bottling industry, which he argued would bring modern employment and social progress.[7]

In 1941, Farley traveled through Latin America with Albert H. Staton, then chief of the Company's Pan American Division and soon to be head of INDEGA-Panamco, inspecting and promoting Coca-Cola's Latin American bottling business; he would return to visit Staton's Coca-Cola franchises on subsequent trips.[8] Major and minor international newspapers participated in the fanfare around Farley's arrivals in different cities, but concern about the economic and political power he represented also crept into the coverage. A caricature of Farley's 1941 arrival in Ecuador portrayed him as a modern colossus of Rhodes, as the reach of British colonialism in Africa had been satirized in the late nineteenth century, with a remarkably realistic, but mammoth likeness of Farley imperially striding from north to south while a cartoonishly tiny, dark Latin American man waves "Bienvenido a Sud-America" from a palm-treed island.[9]

Farley and other Coca-Cola Export executives found plenty of reason for international travel in the postwar period. The Company expanded dramatically in the first postwar decade, riding the wave of the rise of the United States to global power and embodying its "market empire," as Victoria De Grazia has called the "insatiable ambitions of its leading corporations for global markets"[10] and the imposition of the US model of free enterprise and mass consumption through both consent and coercion. The latter was primarily enacted by aggressively prying open international markets, but often took place through military force as well. The Coca-Cola Company had survived the economic challenges of the Depression and World War II through its franchise business model and US government sugar-rationing exemptions. It was now solidifying its influence in existing international markets, like Colombia, and with its penetration into new foreign locales through its wartime collaboration with the US military, beginning its second wave of globalization to more distant markets, like those of India. To speak to its growing cadre of representatives and bottlers around the world, in 1948, Coca-Cola

FIGURE 7. *Time*, May 15, 1950.

Export launched *Coca-Cola Overseas,* its magazine on the Company's international business. In its inaugural edition, Export President J. F. Curtis announced the Company's unprecedented internationalization: "Coca-Cola already has the distinction of dealing in more countries at one time and on a larger scale than any other trader in world history."[11]

Coca-Cola's internationalization captured the American popular imagination in representations like the 1950 cover of *Time* magazine featuring a personified Coca-Cola trademark nursing an infantilized earth from its famous bottle, with the legend "World & Friend" (fig. 7). Despite that title, it was a rather discomforting illustration—a smiling face peering out from behind the earth, gripping it with its long, thin fingers. The corresponding *Time* article, "The Sun Never Sets on Cacoola,"[12] also walked the line between celebration and critique of what it characterized as "Coke's peaceful near-conquest of the world." The title likened Coca-Cola's world system to other imperial projects, like Spain's in the late sixteenth century and Britain's in the early twentieth. Company executives had also used that phrase, "The Sun Never Sets on Coca-Cola," to describe their global reach, betraying the fact that they had not studied the rise and fall of empires.[13] Now, at mid-century, looking out on unfolding decolonizing revolutions, the Company sought to maintain its reach while avoiding the label and fate of colonialism.

The *Time* article asserted that Coca-Cola was "on the march" in a "Battle for Europe," with those who challenged the product's advance characterized as the "resistance" and markets that had been won over by Coca-Cola as "fallen" to the Company. In Egypt, where Coca-Cola was popularly known as "Cacoola," the drink was "flooding … like a second life-giving Nile" of "350 million cokes a year," sold to consumers who used to buy "sickly sweet, dirty concoctions of street vendors." However, the Hungarian-born Pathy brothers who bottled the drink, whom the article called "Egypt's shrewdest businessmen," would flee to North America just two years later after Gamel Abdel Nasser came to power and enacted a wave of nationalizations[14] (although Coca-Cola's Egyptian franchises would be safe, for now).

The Coca-Cola business modernized economies and peoples, the article suggested, transforming traditional societies and developing them along the path of consumer capitalism. Coca-Cola's business model kept its products "'always within an arm's length of desire.' And where there is no desire for it, Coke creates desire," with advertising that manufactured "new appetites and thirsts." It "brought refrigeration to sweltering one-ox towns without plumbing." And "transformed men one generation removed from jungle barter into American salesmen," inculcating them in capitalist ideology and comportment. US commodities around the world were ambassadors of the "American Century," and demonstrative of the success of the United States' shift from isolationism to an embrace of its international political, economic, and cultural leadership as called for by *Time*'s own Henry Luce. "To find something as thoroughly native American hawked in half a hundred languages on all the world's crossroads … is still strangely anomalous. … But it is reassuring. It is also simpler, sharper evidence than the Marshall Plan or a Voice of America broadcast that the US has gone out into the world to stay," the author mused.[15]

Time credited Coca-Cola's international success to its innovation of forms of immaterial production and the externalization of material manufacturing.

Unlike the steel and automobile manufacturing industries emblematic of the modern economy, the article asserted, the Company profited through information and intellectual property (market research, secret formulas, and trademarked images), advertising, and financial investment, while outsourcing production and retailing. Its business model and cultural representation was the product itself, not bottles of Coke. And its success "rests on such intangibles as a market analysis, sales training, advertising and financial decentralization" that take root around the world through "local, independent franchises" in "one of U.S. industry's miracles of organization."[16]

Any concern about US imperial reach was tempered by insistence that the decentralization of Coca-Cola's outsourced production model had allowed it to become part of local cultures, rather than reproducing them in the exact image of the United States. "In most places Coke has blended into the local scene as if the brown-green of its bottles and the fire-brigade red of its advertising were some kind of protective coloring. In Brazil, it has become part of the language: buses are known as Coca-Colas (because the fare is nearly the price of a Coke); in British Guiana, schoolchildren get a free Coke on Empire Day; in the Middle East, Coke bottles have become accepted missiles with which to punish unjust umpires at soccer games."[17]

The Coca-Cola Company was culturally adaptive, the article asserted, because it was not on a mission for America, but for capitalism: Coca-Cola "is not a missionary in the sense, for example, that the Voice of America is. Except in the sense that it is for free trade everywhere it is not specifically trying to spread the American way of life. Its chief and boundlessly healthy interest is in the liras and the piasters, the tickeys and the centavos." Coca-Cola was interested in making money in whatever language and could justify that profit because "Coca-Cola's 270-odd foreign bottlers and 3,000-odd foreign retail dealers grossed roughly $150 million.... Coca-Cola is in the business of creating business wherever it goes." Inasmuch as Coca-Cola capitalists around the world profited, marketing Coke "did not constitute American exploitation, as the Reds bellow."[18]

As The Coca-Cola Company undertook a dramatic postwar expansion, it mobilized the franchise as a specific mode of capitalist internationalization, different from international trade or even the establishment of foreign subsidiaries. This franchised capitalism had social and cultural logics at midcentury that emerged from the friction between the multinational's profit motives, the interests of national elites, and critiques of US capitalist expansion. Although Coca-Cola benefited from its association with the United

States, the Company often distanced itself representationally from its metropole. In its symbolic strategy in this period, Coca-Cola portrayed its system as comprised of independent, locally owned bottlers, and thus a national industry everywhere in the world. Governments' import substitution and Keynesian economic policies, the Left's concern about the rise of US hegemony and capitalism, and postcolonial nationalisms in what was beginning to be called the Third World all led the Company to promote itself as a national industry. As countries turned to national developmentalism, Coca-Cola promoted a multinational developmentalism through its "local, independent" franchises as drivers of the development of national economies around the world. This history, then, contradicts perceptions of the so-called American Century as a smooth ascendance of US economic, political, and cultural hegemony. In fact, US corporations like The Coca-Cola Company had to negotiate their expansion with national developmentalists in the Third World, even if only temporarily and symbolically. Much of the world was sold capitalism with promises of local development, with "local" constructed as a sense of shared interests and benefits to those in a specific geographic area and "development" defined as modernization and increased production and consumption, rather than shared prosperity, happiness, sustainability, or ownership of the means of production.[19]

Coca-Cola's strategy of promoting multinational developmentalism came about because, as the *Time* article suggested, the Reds were bellowing, quite loudly, along with national political elites, international industrial competitors, workers, and consumers, whose interests tenuously converged into a politics of national economic development.

COCA-COLONIZATION AND ITS DISCONTENTS

In the postwar period, many areas of the world responded negatively to The Coca-Cola Company's international expansion, and expressed critiques of US market empire generally through distaste for Coca-Cola. Soviet bloc countries refused the Company entry, and the Chinese Communist Party nationalized all mainland bottling plants and cut off the Company's supply of one of its "secret" ingredients, cassia, or Chinese cinnamon.[20] But Coca-Cola's postwar growth also provoked opposition across much of western Europe and in various locales in the global south. Communist parties and leftists in general were concerned about the expansion of a monopolistic "American trust,"[21] the march of consumer capitalism, Coca-Cola's profit-extractive business model, and the Company's connection with US state interests. Government leaders suspected that foreign investment by US multinational corporations would not benefit national economies but instead exacerbate balance of payments deficits and the loss of reserves of dollars to the United States. National beverage interests, which sometimes produced traditional drinks, saw a proven competitive threat to their businesses and heritage drinking cultures. As US economic assistance programs opened up regions to free trade and US corporations, many saw Coca-Cola as a symbol of US hegemony, and in the deepening Cold War climate, NATO, the Korean War, US strategic military bases in Asia, and a US-backed coup in Guatemala were all perceived as losses of national self-determination and the consolidation of the capitalist bloc. Others worried about the impact of US products, commercialism, and corporate practices on national social and cultural values.

The conflict was perhaps most fierce and best documented in France, where a convergence of odd bedfellows including French communists, wine producers, middle-class consumers, and intellectuals campaigned against Coca-Cola through protests, lawsuits, regulations, and biting cultural critique. The Left decried the Company as the reification of US capitalism,[22] demanding to know, "Will we be [coca-colonized] *coca-colonisés?*"[23] Press coverage of the conflict spread the question internationally: coca-colonization would become shorthand for Americanization.

While the Company characterized the problems in France as the connivances of "Reds" and winemakers, it was not just the party faithful and competitive interests who challenged Coca-Cola's entrance to France. By 1950, five separate ministries of the French government were investigating Coca-Cola, customs authorities had suspended the Company's import license, the police had brought criminal fraud charges against Coca-Cola's bottlers in Paris and Algiers, and Coca-Cola executives believed they were being followed by the secret police.[24] Communists and beverage interests leveraged popular concern about potential deleterious health effects into government investigations, multiple lawsuits, and eventually legislation allowing the banning of nonalcoholic drinks found to be injurious to public health.[25] Health ministries were avenues for pursuing oversight over the Company, as regulatory agencies that had governmental power as well as general public support. And Coca-Cola was an easy target for such focus, as a drink that contained sugar, caffeine, and phosphoric acid, among its known ingredients, and its avid guarding of the drink's "secret formula" made it all the more inscrutable and suspicious to international governments like France, accustomed to regulatory oversight of mass consumables and a history of traditional beverages. As a foreign commodity, and one that is ingested, Coca-Cola was perceived as a potential threat to bodies as well as the national body politic.

If public health concerns gained the most purchase in popular imagination and political wrangling, they were as much a gauge of worries about the fitness of the national economy and culture as physical health. The French Ministry of Finance denied the Company a license for foreign investment, arguing that its investments were small and its bottling contracts "draconian," guaranteeing the US multinational ultimate control and most of the profits.[26] Prince Alexander Makinsky, a worldly Russian white émigré aristocrat and anti-communist who had worked as a political operative with ties to US intelligence before becoming Coca-Cola's man in Paris, confided to executives: "the trouble is . . . our investments are negligible."[27] French cultural critics decried the commercialism and superficiality of Coca-Cola advertising papering streets and public spaces in France. They argued that mass production of commodities and the commercialization of culture would produce social conformity determined by the market, replacing existing French social and cultural values. To appeal to and placate French consumers, Coca-Cola moved its French advertising account from the US firm McCann-Erickson (which had a Paris office) to a French agency.[28]

Coca-Cola sent instructions from the United States to spend whatever amount was necessary to enlist as many "soldiers"—lawyers, scientists, and the well-connected—to sway the French government.[29] Jim Farley railed in the US press against French ungratefulness, given the United States' role in the country's liberation from German occupation and accused the government of acquiescence to Communist pressure. US newspapers even called for retaliation against French products. The Company also enlisted the US State Department, which warned that legislation "prejudicial to legitimate American interests" could result in "possible serious repercussions, while the French ambassador in Washington reported that banning Coca-Cola would be "a sign of hostility toward the US" that could endanger economic aid to France.[30] Faced with this threat, French Prime Minister Georges Bidault assured the US ambassador that he would thwart Health Ministry actions against the Company.[31]

But the Company's parallel strategy was to establish as many French bottlers as quickly as possible. As Coca-Cola's international legal fixer wrote of the plan in 1950, "when Frenchmen place their millions into plants and factories and trucks, etc., they will see to it through their deputies and friends that any interference with their business is avoided." By signing bottling contracts with existing French beverage interests, the Company would "bore into the enemy from within."[32]

Coca-Cola's problems in France made news around the world, as far away as Colombia and India.[33] Coca-Cola, which to French youth already represented modern American popular culture, now had the additional cachet of mysterious and potentially risky secret ingredients. Contrasted with traditional European beverages, it represented "emancipation" from parental authority, Makinsky happily reported from France.[34] But, in general, France continued to resist Coca-Cola's postwar expansion; a 1953 poll "reported that only 17 percent of the French liked Coca-Cola either 'well enough' or 'a lot' while 61 percent said 'not at all.'"[35] Well into the late twentieth century, French consumption trailed other western European markets and Coca-Cola remained a symbol of "Americanization."[36]

FRANCHISING THE ESSENCE OF CAPITALISM: MULTINATIONAL DEVELOPMENTALISM

At the Company's first international convention in Atlantic City in 1948, which brought many of new postwar overseas franchises together, including Colombian and Indian bottlers, a placard pronounced: "When we think of Communists, we think of the Iron Curtain. BUT when THEY think of democracy, they think of Coca-Cola."[37] The linkage between Coca-Cola and the larger project of capitalist democracy gave the Company's postwar rhetoric a missionary zeal; at the convention, an executive led the group in prayer: "May Providence give us the faith ... to serve those two billion customers who are only waiting for us to bring our product to them."[38] Executives regularly equated consumer choice with democracy and figured wherever Coca-Cola could be freely chosen, both capitalism and democracy would take hold. Coca-Cola President Robert W. Woodruff, who oversaw the Company's rapid mid-century internationalization, explained that Coca-Cola received the ire of the Left because it was the "essence of capitalism."[39] "With every Coca-Cola, every shopkeeper makes a profit and becomes a member of the bourgeoisie. That's why the Commies are anti-Coke," J. Paul Austin, who would take the helm of the Company in the early 1960s, further explained.[40] Coca-Cola was offering more than fizzy drinks; it offered to franchise capitalism as a form of multinational development.

In speeches with titles like "Trademarks: America's Goodwill Ambassador," "Brand Names: A Basis for Unity, Our Greatest Hope of Expanding World Trade," and "Advertising as a World Force," in the late 1940s and early 1950s, Coca-Cola Export Chairman Farley celebrated the work done by US brands in building the cultural hegemony of capitalist democracy. There was a "close parallel between the brand names system and some of the basic fundamentals of our system of government." Brand-named products were "ambassadors" of the capitalist values of competitive enterprise and the free exercise of individual choice.[41] Brands also had the potential to build "unity" and "bind together" diverse segments of global society, as they "cut across national and ideological barriers." This branded unity was all the more important because it could combat communism, the enemy of "our way of life" that "permits no difference of ideas, no competition, no freedom of choice ... an insidious unity of Godless fanaticism ... based on hatred and maintained by compulsion." "When we speak to a man in another country of democracy ... the idea may be beyond his comprehension." But brand-named goods, as commodities one could hold, consume, and experience, were more persuasive representatives of capitalist democracy than any ideas or words could ever be. "The more people we expose to American products and American ways of business ... the better off both they and we will be." Branded products were not "monopolistic," as "those who would like to tear down our system claim," but rather the bulwarks of an increasingly international system of economic and political relations. Threats to the brand-name system—including proposed consumer protection reforms like labeling regulations—were "thinly disguised socialistic measures," that "take away from our public the right to pick and choose," Farley declared.[42]

But by the end of the 1950s, Farley tempered his position, lecturing US businessmen that multinationals dealing with developing countries must accept some government intervention. He justified this as an interim strategy in the fight against communism, arguing that the increase in the developing world's consumption as a result of import-substitution industrialization would eventually lead to increased international trade. In industrializing economies, workers would be better paid and develop more modern tastes, making them better future consumers of US exports and the products of US multinationals. There were large potential markets in the developing world, but for now, they did not have the money to buy imports, and countries were looking to develop their own industries and increase employment. "The underdeveloped countries want to industrialize," Farley argued, but the majority world lacked the social and economic conditions to develop. He admitted the neocolonialism of the global economy, although not in those terms, in which global south nations were sources of raw resource extraction to the global north, leaving them dependent on US and European economies, while paying high costs for imported goods often manufactured from their own resources. Industrializing the developing world would require importing foreign manufacturing technology that it could not afford, and this was where US multinationals could come in, Farley argued. They should promote direct foreign investment as a development strategy if governments adopted import-substitution industrialization policies. "The next best thing to having a motor car company of your own, which is difficult without capital, is to have a foreign motor car company build and operate a plant in your country," Farley articulated his vision of multinational developmentalism.[43]

If developing nations became more productive, they would have capital to pay down their international debts and purchase US exports. In a win-win for global capitalism, "wherever any of us can assist a country to produce manufactured goods in its own region we have helped them and have helped ourselves." Then Farley said something he knew to be controversial: rather than insist on true free markets, multinationals must work with the government-planned economies taking shape around the world. Governments worldwide were pushing to play a heavier role in their economies, while still receiving US foreign-aid assistance, Farley explained, and multinationals "ought to support" this. Acknowledging that he was risking being tried for "heresy," he pointed out that the US government also intervened in markets to the benefit of US industry: establishing import quotas to protect the US oil industry, for example, and stabilizing sugar prices to the Company's great benefit. If US industry "will not risk a free market economy why should you expect that the European . . . or the Brazilian . . . industry will accept a free market?" He told the audience, "you and I may not like this planned economy movement," but had to "face facts" and "live in a world that does exist instead of crying because the 19th Century came to an end nearly sixty years ago."[44]

MULTI-NATION-AL: COCA-COLA PITCHES ITSELF AS NATIONAL ECONOMIC DEVELOPMENT

Farley was right: it was the twentieth century. And after global depression, runaway wartime government spending, and postwar currency stabilization, many national governments were adopting import substitution, Keynesian monetary policies, and government planning to stimulate national economies at mid-century. At the same time, many nations of the global south had recently gained independence, and postcolonial nationalisms and leftist struggles identified the continued yoke of multinational corporations' economic, political, and cultural power which they would soon term "neocolonialism." Countries countered US economic hegemony by protecting their national markets. Washington pushed to pry open these markets, and some US multinationals explored models of foreign direct investment and externalization to justify their business ventures as multinational developmentalism, while maintaining both control and profits.[45]

Throughout the 1950s, Coca-Cola executives stressed that its bottlers were "local, independent" businesses; "everywhere you find Coke, you find it is a local enterprise," Coca-Cola's president H. B. Nicholson claimed in 1953.[46] This became all the more imperative as Coca-Cola's international business grew rapidly and governments questioned the desirability of allowing a giant multinational to monopolize production of nonessential consumer goods. When calls for government intervention in the market or expressions of economic nationalism resulted, Coca-Cola was depicted as a national industry— Philippine, Egyptian, or Colombian, not American. Such "decentralization," the Company claimed, "not only promotes efficiency, but enhances the good will accruing to the product and the product organization throughout the world."[47] Nicholson portrayed franchised production in terms of economic benefit to developing economies:

> When Coke goes on sale anywhere, the business contributes fairly and squarely to the economic welfare of the people there. . . . Coca-Cola has been a pioneer in creating new markets over the world and in organizing local groups that prosper by supplying them. Such prosperity means purchasing power. It means business activity. It means education in the ways of a free competitive market. In a very real sense, the export of Coca-Cola service, organization and know-how is the export of effective capital to foreign countries, and it is more important than the export of dollars.[48]

The Coca-Cola Company thus justified its drive for global growth with claims that its franchises simultaneously benefited from the business strategy, technological experience, and marketing power of the multinational corporation, on the one hand, but also hired local workers, purchased local goods and services, and embedded themselves in the local business community, on the other. The growing size of corporations worried critics, but through its franchises Coca-Cola asserted it was doing big business through small businesses, and thus ameliorated concerns about the monopolistic threat of corporate capitalism.[49] The multinational's stimulation of capitalism—the "education in the ways of a free competitive market" it offered—was more helpful to the developing world than aid, Coca-Cola asserted.

In developing nations, foreign direct investment and local franchises did seem to address major concerns: increasing employment, building industrial capacity (not just exporting primary resources), and substituting imports so as to keep money in-country (although not true of the Coca-Cola industry specifically). A range of texts in the emerging development paradigm, from US President Harry Truman's 1949 inaugural address to the final communiqué from the Bandung Conference in 1955, articulated the need for private, corporate investment of foreign capital and technology to industrialize the global south. They assumed "development" to be determined and defined by economic production and growth.[50] Elided by both business and political discourse at the time was the potential effect of multinationals' foreign direct investment and franchising on the balance of payments through repatriation, royalties, and imports that drained reserves of foreign currency and maintained a dependent relationship between the franchisee and its underlying corporation. And Coca-Cola did not so much substitute imports as replace the products of national industries.

While The Coca-Cola Company and its bottlers had regularly emphasized the social justification of the transnational enterprise by identifying its drinks as products of local franchises, the developmentalism of the logic was made more direct when countries considered protectionist policies. In Egypt, for example, Coca-Cola was vulnerable to growing nationalism, anti-imperialist critique, and calls for the nationalization of Western interests in the context of a brewing revolution and the Company's close ties to Egypt's (soon to be dethroned) King Farouk I.[51] Coca-Cola's Egyptian ads, which had typically focused on recreation and sociality, now juxtaposed a thirsty crowd at a soccer game or attractive beachgoers sipping Cokes with the legend "Friendly Moments ... Create Jobs for Egyptians."[52] The ad "Employment for Thousands of Egyptians" stressed Coca-Cola plants' direct employment of Egyptian workers and benefit to the Egyptian economy, depicting a line of workers heading into a plant. Another ad, "Tens of Thousands of Egyptian Dealers," asserted that "Coca-Cola is an Egyptian industry" that "now occupies a prominent place in the economy of this country."[53] "Yes! Coca-Cola opens new working areas of real business with satisfactory wages for the efficient workers in modern Egypt," an ad titled "Modern Egypt" exclaimed, albeit with an image depicting a large, complex bottle-making machine and only half of an Egyptian worker visible.[54]

Coca-Cola similarly endeavored to reframe its business as a constituent part of, rather than a gringo threat to, the "Mexican Miracle," the country's economic growth through import substitution, state promotion of Mexican industry, and a nationalist consumption ethos. Coca-Cola ran a series of ads highlighting its local production and materials sourcing,[55] even suggesting its peppy product was contributing to the overall productivity of Mexican workers. "From this close interrelationship between the local Coca-Cola industry and other local industries, its importance to our national economy is clear. That's because Coca-Cola REFLECTS INDUSTRIAL UNITY . . . for the good of Mexico."[56] Hitting home the assertion that Coca-Colas were produced locally for the benefit of Mexican consumers and workers alike, another set of ads asked Mexican readers if they recognized actual Coca-Cola plant workers in their communities. A photo of "one of the most modern plants in the Republic," ran alongside a portrait of a formally attired man and the question to readers: "Do you know this man from Tuxpan? It's your good friend and neighbor, Hermenegildo Santisteben, Jr., manager of Embotelladora Tuxpan, S.A., your Coca-Cola bottling plant. For years he has been making friends in Mexico, especially in the Tuxpan region . . . [and] is an exemplary citizen and a true credit to the community where he lives together with your loved ones."[57]

DEVELOPING THE COCA-COLA
INDUSTRY IN POSTCOLONIAL INDIA

If The Coca-Cola Company's Colombian operations typify the first stage of its international expansion, the Company's history in India characterizes its next stage. The Coca-Cola Export Corporation had been considering expansion into India before World War II, when future Colombian bottling president Albert Staton reviewed the Indian market on a 1940 tour of Asia. Staton had little positive to say about India: "I saw quite a lot of Calcutta traveling about, but not enough to want to go back in this lifetime . . . the city has absolutely nothing in the way of interest, and the sights on the streets just chill your blood." He described the train to Madras (now Chennai) as "nothing but an unending succession of monotonous landscapes. . . . The occasional miserable hut is mud covered and thatched, the natives either stark or half naked and looking like Gandhi in the last stages of a hunger strike. It is hard to imagine anything more uninteresting." But India's "business prospects" were "boundless, each new territory being a potential gold field, just waiting to be mined."[58]

Coca-Cola began makeshift bottling operations in India during World War II, when Coca-Cola Technical Observers bottled it for US troops stationed on the Indian subcontinent. After the war, the Company made efforts to establish itself permanently in the newly independent nation. In 1947, Export chairman Farley traveled to India on his postwar world tour of operations, and found "great interest on the part of businessmen in introducing Coca-Cola in that market," finalizing negotiations for "large bottling operations in that country." Far-sighted, with his eyes focused on long-range profitability, Farley lacked perspective on the widespread sectarian violence between Hindus, Sikhs, and Muslims following the partition of India, instead bemoaning that although he had "every confidence from what [he] saw there that the Indian people will work out a satisfactory and sound democratic basis for their future . . . the present unrest has affected economic conditions."[59]

Other US Coca-Cola men sent to India were not so positive in their characterizations. At mid-century, these high-level representatives were white, well-off Americans, who traveled internationally with the Company, but were overcome by the economic, social, and cultural differences they encountered, framing India and Indians in terms of inscrutable, radical otherness. For Ted Duffield, who had traveled much of the world for Export, India and its people were incomprehensible. The country and its people's underdevelopment was essentially determined by geography and cultural inferiority, he surmised, due to the likes of climate and irrational religious belief:

In a day's time my eyes swept over scenes appalling. Death was to the right of me, to the left of me and swooping down from the sky. . . . Nature and religion have been most unkind to these people. Water, more than enlightened Christianity, and penicillin would be "First Aid" in this land. Here, in a country where there are more cattle than on the plains of the southwest, they cannot feed a starving nation. Instead, these cattle wander aimlessly as "Sacred Cows" along the highways and byways of the land. They dare not be molested because one of them might be their great-great grandfather. . . . Hinduism and all its branches, so rife with multitudinous taboos, seemed slowly but surely to be reducing India to "ashes" for the Ganges. . . . Here was a city and a people impossible for a western mind to comprehend.[60]

Having neither water systems nor penicillin to offer, Duffield promoted Coca-Cola as a commodified solution to what he saw as a modernity gap.

Coca-Cola's collaboration with the US Army also introduced the Company to its first permanent Indian bottlers. Sardar Mohan Singh ran a successful Delhi-based furniture business that outfitted the homes of US officers stationed in India, who first introduced him to the idea of bottling Coca-Cola. As in the case of Colombia and elsewhere, in India the Company identified future bottlers from among the local political and economic elite. It was the Punjabi Sikh Mohan Singh family and their new Coca-Cola bottling franchise Pure Drinks that rooted Coca-Cola economically, politically, and socially in India. To a member of Export's Sales Promotion team, Mohan Singh "looked to me like the best that India could produce."[61] For their Coca-Cola bottling business, the Singhs received financing from their "dear friend" the Maharaja Yadavindra Singh of Patiala, Chancellor of the Chamber of Princes, one of the country's largest citrus growers, India's delegate to the United Nations in the 1950s, and ambassador to two European nations in the 1960s and early 1970s (who also fostered a Sikh communalist politics in his northern state, and then had to address its repercussions of bloody communal violence against Muslims during Partition).[62] Yadavindra Singh's princely wealth and lifestyle astounded Export executives, who recounted his ornate palace, golf course, tennis courts, four swimming pools, gardens, lakes, game preserve, and hundreds of servants, as well as the stark contrast with the rest of India: "His jewels have been estimated at one hundred million dollars . . . [but] outside the palace walls and so on for three thousand miles is the worst squalor and filth and poverty in the world."[63] From furniture, the Mohan Singhs had entered the construction business, building stately embassies and residences for Indian and foreign dignitaries in New Delhi. The family soon entered the top echelons of the Delhi political elite themselves, with one son (Daljit Singh) serving as the vice president of the Delhi Municipal Corporation and another (Charanjit Singh) representing Delhi as a member of the Congress Party in the Indian parliament. This proximity to power was physically manifest on Delhi's geography: the family's Coca-Cola franchise was the only industry granted permission to establish a manufacturing plant among the radial roads emanating from Connaught Place in the heart of central New Delhi, the capital of the newly independent nation.[64]

The Company and its Indian bottlers envisaged a central role for Coca-Cola in the economic modernization and development of the new nation. In 1950, Pure Drinks hosted more than two thousand guests at the lavish grand opening of Coca-Cola's first Indian-franchised bottling plant in New Delhi. Alluding to India's need of reserves of international currency and its goal of industrialization, Mohan Singh lauded Coca-Cola as "a beverage of international name and fame," whose production would both earn foreign currency and "stimulate the growth of other sister industries" employing "skilled and unskilled artisans . . . [and] supplying a livelihood for over 2,000 families."[65] He failed to mention that significant foreign currency in dollars would also have to be paid out to the Company for the use of its concentrate and brand.

Hare Krishna Mahtab, India's minister of industries and supplies, officiated at the New Delhi plant's opening ceremony, and Prime Minister Jawaharlal Nehru himself had a seat of honor in the audience and posed for photographs sipping from a bottle of Coca-Cola.[66] Mahtab's remarks, as reported by a Coca-Cola executive, emphasized that the Company was there at India's behest, inasmuch as "Americans had rendered all assistance in establishing the plant in response to the appeal by the Prime Minister," no less. Although it was negotiated on India's terms, the Company seemed to see its Indian expansion as an affirmation of its international power. At the Delhi plant's grand opening, a three-dimensional sculpture of the cartoon of the Coca-Cola trademark bottle-feeding the world—the image on the May 15, 1950, cover of *Time* magazine—was unabashedly displayed. "[Coca-Cola's] inauguration was truly an impressive affair, and it is said that New Delhi has not seen such a function since the visit to India of King George V [in 1911]," *Coca-Cola Overseas* boasted, unwittingly predicting future Indian critiques of coca-colonization and corporate neocolonialism.[67]

Coca-Cola and Pure Drinks presented their business as "a model of industry, illustrating the possibilities to others, and thus [improving] living standards and working conditions." Pure Drinks' Bombay plant was "one of the most beautiful and modern establishments" in the city, with multiple buildings containing two bottling production lines, executive offices, training rooms, sugar and water treatment facilities, a laboratory, stock rooms, sugar storage, a service garage for fifty trucks, staff quarters, a guest apartment, a dispensary with a registered nurse, a canteen, a reading room equipped to show "educational and entertaining films," tennis and badminton courts, plans for a pool, and surrounding gardens to attract youthful customers, making the Pure Drinks plant "a show place of Bombay," according to *Coca-Cola Overseas*. "The plant rose from a rubble field to an efficient self-contained unit," with its own 100,000 gallon water storage tank and 500 horsepower generator:[68] a drop of capitalist modernization in a sea of underdevelopment, from the Company's perspective. As an American Coca-Cola executive remarked, "there is nothing else like it in Bombay, I am told . . . perfectly gorgeous." But outside the plant he saw, in contrast, "a seething, boiling mass of humanity striving to survive from one day to the next."[69]

Coca-Cola was industrially manufactured, by a US multinational business, from a proprietary chemical formula, all attributes the Company typically promoted. But in India, as in many other new markets at mid-century, the Company and its Indian franchisee had to construct it as safe and appropriate for local consumers. In his grand opening speech at Pure Drinks' Delhi plant, Minister of Industries and Supplies Mahtab assured the assembled guests that Coca-Cola was pure, wholesome, and hygienic, even expressing hope that it would "prove more attractive than other drinks that were in vogue in India."[70] His implicit criticism of these other drinks reflected the developmentalist state's preference for modern industrial drinks as opposed to traditional beverages, religious and caste-based disdain for alcohol production and consumption, and a nationalist critique of the ongoing presence of British colonial drinks. As with the Colombia example explored in the previous chapter, when Coca-Cola was introduced in India, a rich commercial drinking culture already existed there, supplying both bottled drinks and, more significantly for the vast majority of the Indian population, the beverages of the large informal sector. This latter group included *nimbu-pani* (lemon/limeade) wallahs, sugarcane juice vendors, *jal-jeera* (cumin-spiced lemonade) carts, juice and sherbet sellers, and the nearly ubiquitous chai stalls, which were affordable and accessible, and served beverages made from indigenous ingredients if not always safe drinking water. Advertisements for industrially bottled drinks often questioned the "quality" and "hygienic preparation" of such street beverages. Upper-middle-class Indians had begun to consume bottled soft drinks well before the arrival of Coca-Cola, and attitudes to beverages were closely tied to socioeconomic position.

Coca-Cola entered a beverage field in India in which claims of foreignness or nationality were constructed in the context of colonialism. In nineteenth-century colonial India, the only bottled soft drinks were those imported from England, which were expensive and available mostly in British colonial centers. Few Indians drank them. But in 1837, well before John Pemberton concocted Coca-Cola's formula, the British chemist Henry Rogers began making "soda water" in his small laboratory and soon opened a factory producing a range of carbonated drinks in Bombay.[71] Around 1915, Rogers sold his firm to four "Parsi gentlemen" (Indian Zoroastrians), who sold it to new Indian owners in

1945. The Rogers company would sell more than any other soft drinks bottler until the end of the 1940s, when Coca-Cola entered the Indian market.[72]

As in Colombia and much of the rest of the world, the initial history of the Indian soft drinks industry arose from transnational cultural exchange and colonial influence, although the makers of many drink brands articulated nationalist sentiments, even in the industry's early stages. Hajoori & Sons was founded by an enterprising Dawoodi Bohra (a subsect of Ismaili Shia Islam), Abbas Abdul Rahim Hajoori, who in his teens began selling the British soft drinks that dominated the Indian market. When in the 1920s Hajoori created his own soda, he marketed it as wholly Indian beverage, in reply to Gandhi's call for *swadeshi*, or the boycott of foreign-made goods to challenge British colonialism. Hajoori had good anticolonial business sense. The drink's name, "Whisky No," simultaneously signaled its daring alcoholic taste while affirming it as nonalcoholic (and non-British) in a climate of growing nationalism. But the national "purity" of even this drink was debatable, inasmuch as it was produced on soda-making machines from London, and when the company changed the brand's name to "Sosyo" in 1960, it derived its new moniker from the drink's "essence," which came from Italy and the Latin word *socius* to suggest a "social drink."[73] Ethno-religious minorities (like the producers of Rogers, Hajoori, Dukes, Pallonji, and other drink brands) were at the center of the development of the soft drink industry in India, as the Hindu merchant "bania community felt that making a profit from selling water was not right,"[74] and the regionalism of the large Indian subcontinent produced different popular brands, revealing the constructedness of any assertion of a drink brand as singularly "Indian."

But as the newly independent India was negotiating a national identity amid this complexity and diversity, soft drinks marketing continued a long Indian history of nationalism framed in contrast to foreign goods. Coca-Cola's history with commodities linked to Indian national identity has been most intertwined, from the very beginning, with one particular company: Parle (see chapters 4 and 7). The year before Pure Drinks opened its first Coca-Cola plant, the successful biscuit and sweets company Parle began to manufacture soft drinks. In 1949, Parle introduced Gluco-Cola, which claimed the title and slogan "India's First Cola." An ingenious front-page newspaper ad introduced the drink with the image of a hand holding a bottle of Gluco-Cola punching through a (fake) story about alcohol prohibition in Bombay. Playing on Parle's knowledge of local conditions and contexts, the ad called out its foreign competitor: "A Cola Drink has always been America's most popular soft drink but it never caught on in India because *Tastes Differ!* Now, who could know more about Tastes than Parles," maker of India's most popular cookies and treats.[75] A series of ads in 1951 organized around comic "moral" lessons were veiled attacks on Coca-Cola's foreignness. One ad featured a shapely, barely clothed foreign wife who impoverishes then divorces an Indian prince ending with a "MORAL: Had the Raja married one of his kind—a respectable Indian lady with identical tastes—he would have lived happily ever after" and the tagline "Gluco-Cola . . . The Right Taste Appeal for India."[76] Another ad told of a race between "Khaki Babu" riding a tortoise and "Jockey White" aloft a hare, who "collapsed" when he "reached tropical regions." The tortoise's "special shield" protected him, leading him to victory "in grand style to become a national favorite." The "MORAL": "always select what is made specially to suit local conditions."[77] Yet another ad seemingly taunts the new Indian owners of the Coca-Cola franchise, telling of a man who bought an expensive buffalo hoping to "reap a fortune selling milk to his neighbors." But, alas, the buffalo "cost more to maintain" than could be made selling the milk, and he was forced to quit the milk business altogether. Extending the financial analogy to its consumers, Gluco-Cola, the ad took care to note, "comes in *larger* bottles, giving you more for your money."[78]

While Parle took shots at Coca-Cola in its advertising, a larger conflict was playing out behind the scenes. Coca-Cola had filed a trademark infringement dispute against the company, arguing that Gluco-Cola was too close to its own brand both in look and name, which would confuse consumers and merchants and allow the upstart cola to profit from its popularity and reputation.[79] Although Coca-Cola's Pure Drinks plants would not open until a year after Gluco-Cola came on the market, the Export Corporation had already filed its trademark in India. Gluco-Cola's brand name used the familiar cursive lettering and did sound similar, but the possessive "Parle's" was prominently featured on the trademark and bottle. And ads almost always played on the brand's comparative "Indianness," distinguishing it from the other cola. When the Registrar of Trade Marks decided for Coca-Cola, Parle briefly produced a new drink "Parle Cola" before conceding the cola market to the US brand and focusing on its fruit-flavored sodas.[80]

In the first half of the twentieth century, several Indian soft drink companies entered the market: Parle, Duke, Turf, Brandon, Premier, and Pallonji were started in Bombay, Ferrinni in Calcutta, Spencer, Kali, and Vincent in Madras, and Hajoori & Sons in Surat, Gujarat, among other regional small- and mid-sized bottling businesses. But in the decades following 1950, "the year

Coca-Cola invaded India," a *Times of India* retrospective in 1977 lamented, "most of these companies ... [were] slowly pushed out of existence."[81] The market for soft drinks in a poor, rural population that had little money for such expenditures was tiny, and the Singh family's Coca-Cola franchise continued to grow. From Pure Drinks' first plants in New Delhi (1950), Bombay (1951), Calcutta (1953), and Kanpur (1954), it expanded to a total of eight bottling plants in the 1970s—covering the largest geographic area of any independent bottler in the entire Coca-Cola world system at the time.

"COCA-COLA MATA TINTO": COCA-COLA ENCOUNTERS COLOMBIAN ECONOMIC NATIONALISM

There is a popular saying in Colombia: "Coca-Cola mata tinto." It directly translates as "Coca-Cola kills coffee," but suggests, really, that Coca-Cola is stronger than or superior to coffee.[82] If you have a long trip tomorrow and you are planning on taking a crowded bus, but then your friend offers you a ride in her new car, well, "Coca-Cola mata tinto," and you happily accept the ride. In a country known for raw exports (oil, bananas, cocaine), arguably no single product has been more linked to Colombian national identity than coffee. So, for it to be "killed" by Coca-Cola in the popular imagination evidences the impact of the Company. The history of coffee capitalism's free-trade orientation actually helped Coca-Cola, as did the legacy of US neocolonial intervention, inflows of capital from US loans and foreign investment, and outflows of commodities, which had for decades made Colombia open to multinational corporations and foreign trade. But negotiating Coca-Cola's relationship to Colombian nationhood, making it a *Coca-Cola* as well as a coffee country, challenged the Company and its franchises at mid-century. Multinationals in Colombia sensed increasing threats to their businesses from growing national developmentalism: protectionist tariff and trade policies to encourage import substitution industrialization, interventionist monetary policy to stimulate investment in industry, legislation allowing the expropriation of foreign assets, and the establishment of labor unions, requiring new social justifications for their businesses.

Through the 1930s and 1940s, a class critique of large corporations and multinationals grew in Colombia. In these decades, the Colombian labor movement had gained some ground, creating federations and winning concessions from companies and reforms from the government.[83] Socialist and communist parties grew until they were suppressed by official and paramilitary forces in the 1950s.[84] The populist leader Jorge Eliécer Gaitán condemned elites and monopoly capitalism, appealing for the rights of workers and consumers, before his assassination in 1948, which set off a decade of brutal conflict known as *La Violencia*.

On the other side of the class spectrum, the growing Colombian industrial elite, to ensure their growth and oligopolistic dominance, pressed for protectionist policies that limited imports or enacted high tariffs on goods that threatened to flood the market at cheaper prices. Led by the powerful Medellín textile manufacturers, but with support from producers of packaged foods, bottled drinks, metals and machinery, chemicals and pharmaceuticals, industrialists utilized political connections, the popular press, and their recently constituted Asociación Nacional de Industriales (ANDI) (headed by José Gutiérrez Gómez, Coca-Cola INDEGA president, co-founder, and minority investor) to launch a vigorous campaign for the protection of the budding Colombian industrial sector. The new industrial bourgeoisie driving this economic nationalism was not the model for "progressivism" in political, economic, or social terms. It was committed to repressing leftist and independent trade unionism, determined to maintain its oligarchic control of the domestic marketplace, and aligned itself with the country's political and military dictatorships when it served its interests to do so.[85] This national bourgeoisie, as with industrial elites elsewhere in the world, mobilized a discourse of economic nationalism, with national economic development to be achieved through privately held industry, asserting that its own economic interests were also in the best interest of Colombia and its peoples.[86] This protectionist industrial class vied with the large landholding elite, especially coffee-growers, who sought free trade to ensure that their exports had access to US markets, and fought them in escalating political conflict to assert its political and economic influence.

To avoid the threats to their businesses from growing national developmentalism and Colombian labor unions, some multinationals shifted to forms of indirect control over the production and extraction of resources in the country. Even the United Fruit Company, with its historically extreme vertical integration—from ownership of banana plantations, processors, cargo ships, to the distribution and marketing of bananas internationally—began to divest ownership of banana plantations to Colombians in the 1950s, while still maintaining indirect control through technical oversight, strict contracts, and monopoly power.[87] Of course, this innovation was already The

Coca-Cola Company's long-standing business practice in Colombia and around the world.

Both the United States government and The Coca-Cola Company tolerated Colombia's more active role in the development of its economy to a degree, even as they pushed for free trade. Modernization of Latin American economies through state promotion of national industries, import substitution, and Keynesian monetary intervention, might relieve widespread poverty and economic disparity, expand potential future consumer markets, and prevent social revolutions around the world, they reasoned.[88] As the INDEGA-Panamco bottler Albert Staton explained to *Coca-Cola Overseas* in 1949, Colombia fielded requests for over $1 billion worth of imports, when only $250 million was earned from exports, so "some control is necessary to prevent devaluation of the peso, and consequent economic upheaval within the country."[89] When the United States compelled many nations around the world to accept free trade after World War II, Colombia leveraged its status as a staunch ally with shared anti-communist ideology into US acceptance of some protectionist economic policies. In trade negotiations in the 1950s, Colombia freed itself from previous free trade provisions, allowing the country to enact tariffs on US imports to shield its infant industries. In return, the United States won guarantees of more secure conditions for US foreign direct investment in Colombia—promises that US businesses would not be expropriated and their profits would be safely remitted to the United States.[90]

The result was a "golden age of Colombian industry,"[91] encouraged by the Colombian state's protection and promotion of national industries and government investment in infrastructure. Further stimulating investments in Colombian industry were profits from burgeoning coffee production, along with historically high coffee prices and the country's financial relations with the booming US economy.[92] In the decade of the 1950s, Colombian industry grew by an astounding 89.5 percent, with the vast majority coming from consumer goods (like Coca-Cola).[93] But it was also a "golden age of power and influence," the labor historian Miguel Urrutia notes.[94]

As it turned out, the expansion of capitalism in Colombia was not accompanied by the growth of democracy, however much Coca-Cola executives, Colombian industrialists, and US diplomats seemed to profess it. During this era, Colombians were experiencing large-scale social unrest and the dissolution of democratic society in the protracted bloody struggle between Liberals and Conservatives called *La Violencia,* which killed some two hundred thousand people. As the historian Mary Roldán notes, *La Violencia* made for a "surreal" life: some Colombians formed armed groups, others were displaced by the violence raging in the countryside, and José Gutiérrez Gómez, president of both ANDI and Coca-Cola INDEGA, "coolly declare[d] that Colombia's economy had never been better."[95]

Urbanization rapidly increased at mid-century: more than half of the country's once rural population were living in cities by 1960.[96] Rural Colombians fled the violence to the cities. Landless agricultural laborers and impoverished small landholders were additionally displaced when agricultural commercialization, mechanization, and population growth exacerbated the already vast inequities produced by the concentration of land in the hands of a few.[97] The country's industrial growth also pulled these previously rural Colombians to cities with the lure of modern work and consumption. These massive social changes disrupted traditional ways of living and livelihoods as large swaths of the Colombian populace were absorbed into the urban economy. And the affluent urban classes in Colombia consumed its products in unprecedented amounts. Nationally, consumption increased at an annual rate of 6.2 percent from 1945 to 1953, with new chain stores like Ley and Tía selling mass-produced Colombian and imported goods.[98]

While Colombia embraced aspects of government intervention in the economy, the country remained closely tied to the US state and capital. Colombia was the only Latin American country to actively participate in the Korean War,[99] which ensured continued US economic and military aid. Such resources were increasingly tied to the United States' agenda of fighting communism, which aligned with the interests of the Colombian elite.[100] The US government celebrated Colombian presidents Laureano Gómez and Gustavo Rojas Pinilla as democrats and sent them aid, but they had more in common with Latin American dictators (whom the United States also supported when in its interest). Gómez had Fascist and Falangist affinities, and Rojas Pinilla honed his anti-communist ideology as a Korean War general. Neither was democratically elected and both ruled by decree.[101] With the goal of transforming the Colombian military into the most powerful on the continent, Rojas Pinilla convinced the US government that Liberal Party, communist, and peasant uprisings were a large-scale communist insurgency that threatened the nation.[102] He "unleashed military forces in campaigns of merciless repression" during *La Violencia,* knowing that the United States would overlook such actions "as long as they were conducted against alleged Communists."[103] Such Cold War strategies were regularly validated by the United States' own military and CIA incursions into Latin America. The

United States provided military aid and hardware to Colombia, and its army helped train Colombian forces in counterinsurgency techniques in the newly established Escuela de Lanceros.[104]

Financial loans and aid from the United States and international lending authorities aimed to develop Colombia's economy by investing in infrastructure and exacting fiscal responsibility. Colombia became one of the World Bank's "favorite clients"; by 1963, it had lent the country more money for highway construction than any other.[105] Such transportation investments would expedite international trade, and the Bank recommended that the country stimulate industry through monetary policy and the financing of industries, but limit spending on broad social programs, including public works and agrarian reform.[106] In the 1960s, the United States sought to make Colombia the showpiece of the Alliance for Progress in Latin America, lending over US$1,000,000 (11 percent of total Alliance funding), together with international banks and agencies, to encourage development projects in the hopes of easing poverty and deterring communist insurgency.[107]

But even as US political and financial hegemony won the consent of elite Colombian interests, Colombian national developmentalism frustrated US Coca-Cola capitalist Staton. Colombian tariff and duty policies, although less protectionist than those of many Latin American governments, limited the importation of ingredients and materials into the country. As Staton wrote to Coca-Cola President Woodruff, "Life is never dull in these latitudes, if it is not machinery breaking down, it is the government trying to put you out of business."[108] His letters complained of a shortage of dollars to pay for foreign imports, and the difficulty of getting sugar, carbonic gas, bottles, and Coca-Cola concentrate due to cost and government restrictions.[109] As a franchisee negotiating his relationship with the Company, Staton emphasized his adeptness at working with government regulators, commenting "permits for the importation of raw materials are granted with fair liberality" to his franchise,[110] while also pressing the need for Company assistance by reducing the cost of imported supplies and establishing a Colombian concentrate factory. Even with government protectionism, Staton's INDEGA franchise was able to prosper and profit—its 1949 sales were six times those of 1945 (the year he joined the business).[111] But this was not true of all franchises of US soft drink multinationals. The US consulate in Barranquilla sent back worried reports on the effect of protectionism: the Coca-Cola franchise, Embotelladora del Tropical, complained that the "stiff duties on imported syrup" pushed the bottler "near the breaking point," so that the plant was only running two or three days a week. The Pepsi Cola bottler, the consulate reported, might actually close its doors. But the Colombian bottler in the city, Postobón, was profiting and even increasing production, and it seemed "unlikely under foreseeable conditions that these [US] firms can compete with those using domestic syrup."[112]

Although Colombia generally accepted US capital investment and businesses, Coca-Cola had to tread carefully with its self-representation in the context of increased economic nationalism. When the US embassy in Bogotá encouraged INDEGA and Coca-Cola Export to participate in the large US pavilion at the 1955 Colombian International Trade Fair, they chose instead to pay for a separate exhibit of Coca-Cola's own. They "wish to be considered as [a] Colombian enterprise," the US embassy reported, one of a handful of US multinational corporations operating through subsidiaries or offices in Colombia that "did not wish to be identified as American firms" at the fair.[113]

Despite Colombian economic protectionism, Coca-Cola was still on its way to "killing coffee," as the colloquialism goes. Perhaps the most compelling evidence was the image of the 1957 coffee queen at the annual Feria del Café waving to spectators lining the parade route in Manizales, in the heart of Colombia's coffee region, from atop the Coca-Cola bottler's float.[114] Coca-Cola's success came neither really by "killing coffee" nor by wiping out the local and national contexts in which it did business, but by using them for Coca-Cola's own promotion.

FULL PRODUCTION, FULL CONSUMPTION: A
MULTINATIONAL BRAND FOR NATIONAL
DEVELOPMENT

The Company's global postwar advertising frequently featured images of seemingly endless gleaming, uniform bottles of Coca-Cola rolling off of the production lines of modern plants (fig. 8). With taglines like "Continuous Quality Is Quality You Trust" and "Always the same Quality, Always the Same Taste," such ads suggested to consumers that the standardization of production and product, both hygienic and modern, was guaranteed by Coca-Cola plants and trademarks. Such production-oriented messages complemented the consumption-focused ads showing happy people sipping Cokes. These advertising visions drew on the promise of a Fordist "virtuous cycle," a consumer capitalist economic model in which mass production paired with mass consumption by the same industrial workers who would both make and

FIGURE 8. "Continuous Quality is Quality You Trust," *National Geographic,* October 1947, back cover.

consume its products, and meshed with Keynesian economics' theories of demand-driven economic growth and stability. The mass dissemination of these branded images promised that consumer demand would be spurred along by advertising, driving capitalism continuously into a future spared the past crises of overaccumulation and underconsumption.[115] The Coca-Cola Company had to convince the Third World, as well as capitalist First World economies burned by the Depression, that it played a developmental role in future economic stability. Coca-Cola benefited from mid-century liberal economic theories that attributed the economic crisis to "a shortage of consumption rather than any fundamental problem of capitalism itself."[116] In the 1958 lectures that became his influential *Stages of Economic Growth: A Non-Communist Manifesto* (1960), W. W. Rostow argued that all "underdeveloped" countries might evolve into modern ones through stages of colonialism, international trade in agricultural commodities, and private investment, industrialization, and technological advances, with economic growth determining the qualities of a "mature," developed society. Even nationalism had a place in the process, in which a sense of shared economic interest motivated a national elite to entrepreneurial activity and investment. Such Coca-Cola ads were like visual representations of the promise of Rostow's "age of high mass consumption." Demand-side economics promised capitalist stability, and modernization theory sold countries on US capitalist development. [117]

In both presence and content, such advertisements asserted that advertising and branded products could stabilize consumer economies. Advertising offered capitalists "a blueprint for 'manufacturing' consumers to the specifications of mass production,"[118] promoting consumption as a driver of production. Coca-Cola executives regularly asserted that advertising drove economic growth for both individual franchises and whole national economies. Export Chairman Farley quoted US President Harry S. Truman, who praised ad men's role in stimulating consumption and hence postwar employment of discharged US troops: "This will require the complete mobilization, the thorough training, and the effective work of the millions of our people engaged in the processes of advertising and selling. I am confident that American business can and will do this."[119] Farley employed the language that the advertising industry had used since its professionalization in the 1920s to justify its work both economically and socially: product marketing served not only the economy, but the public, by producing greater understanding of products and consumer choice.

And consumer choice, according to Coca-Cola execs, was a fundamental value of capitalist democracy. *Coca-Cola Overseas* launched in 1948 with an editorial directly linking consumer choice with democracy: "Wherever, whenever people buy Coca-Cola, they are registering a vote of confidence for Coca-Cola in all its aspects. Maintaining this confidence assures an ever-growing electorate—free to choose the refreshing thing to do North, South, East, West."[120] Just a few pages later, an article titled "Democracy and Trademarks" contended that brands meant "democracy for the public who can rely on the sign or trademark as the means of making a free choice between competing merchants" and thus were the "essence of free competition and free choice for the consuming public." Countering concerns that multinationals would monopolize markets, crowding out and buying up local products in an anti-competitive and anti-democratic manner, this argument made the brand the starting point for market competition, which it equated with the "democratic right of free choice."[121] Coca-Cola's mid-century advertising promoted not only its products but this logic of consumer democracy.[122]

While Coca-Cola suggested its model of consumer capitalism modernized public life, its advertising targeted homemakers with images of consumption as the modernization of private, domestic life. Ads featured smiling, well-dressed kids asking for and receiving Coca-Cola bottles from their mothers, and guests gratefully enjoying Coke in glasses on a nicely set table. Female consumers were understood to have a gendered responsibility to provision a household, while needing a justification to spend on nonessential commodities. Ads themed around the "home market" told homemakers that Coca-Cola met the demands of their kids, who desired the new and best, while "hospitality" themed ads assured them that Coca-Cola demonstrated to their guests their "good taste" both in cultural competency and generous hospitality. And as a benefit to the woman doing the domestic labor of serving these groups, Coca-Cola was a packaged product that required little work on her part (unlike making juices and mixing drinks). In Latin American publications, advertorials like "*De Compras con* Nancy Sasser [Shopping with Nancy Sasser]," paid advertisements posing as advice columns, promoted US products Coca-Cola, Flan Royal box flan mix, Camel cigarettes, and Tampax tampons for the "modern" "Spanish American woman." Ms. Sasser explained that "distinguished homes serve Coca-Cola" as it was "simple" to serve but "'speaks loudly' of its good taste."[123] Coca-Cola's 1950s slogan of "Signo de buen gusto" ("Sign of Good Taste") played on the era's excitement about consumption and promoted the drink as a standard for modern good living. While the bulk of this Coca-Cola campaign's ads portrayed consumers comfortably at leisure, this mode of address to women reveals that their work made such modern consumption possible.

In the postwar period, building on its wartime health claims of providing high caloric "refreshing pauses" from exertion, Coca-Cola promoted its fueling of an industrial working class. Coca-Cola salesmen sold managers on putting coolers and eventually vending machines in their workplaces, pitching Coke's stimulating effect, which when drunk at lunches and breaks made workers far more productive than when under the effects of less "modern," hygienically-prepared or alcoholic drinks, they claimed. Coca-Cola was a popular "proletarian hunger-killer"—Sidney Mintz's term for "sugar and other drug-foods."[124] It provided a quick metabolic sensation of fullness that was perfectly calibrated to the "availability of wages *and* to the constraints of industrial capitalism's new workday," in which wage earners had capital to spend and the need for rapidly consumed energy, fitting the model of consumption and production prescribed for the working class around the world.[125] Coca-Cola was also "symbolically powerful"[126] suggesting the possibility for a moment of leisure in the middle of the work day, or a payoff in the cultural capital of "good taste" for a day's labor. In urbanizing and industrializing 1950s Colombia, Coca-Cola advertisements promoted the modern work and consumption of secretaries, engineers, businessmen, and industrial workers. In appealing to workers, Coca-Cola ads sometimes adopted a surprisingly proletarian aesthetic. Muscular forearms passed bottles between workers, as if in an act of solidarity; a Coke raised high like a militant fist celebrated modern labor's power and consumption.

Consumer culture in the 1950s is often characterized as hedonistic, even in Colombia where the developing economy and outbreaks of violence limited the sale of commodities. But such ads remind us that, as Jackson Lears argues, consumer culture "was less a riot of hedonism than a new way of ordering the existing balance of tensions between control and release" in society. The culture of consumption was a central element of the "system of tradeoffs between labor and management" in which labor discipline and political passivity came in exchange for regularized, higher wages to be put to the consumption of the commodities produced by that labor.[127] In the United States and much of the Western world (including Colombia),[128] labor negotiated away other demands, like control over the means of production or fewer working hours, in return for higher wages. These concessions for a share of the fruits of industrial productivity were all the easier for capitalists to win from workers in the midst of anti-communist crackdowns, in Colombia through violent political repression. Consumption, at breaks determined by time clocks and factory whistles or during leisure time increasingly made "productive" by industries eager for their workers to be consumers in their off hours, was the payoff for workers subscribing to the labor discipline of modern industry and fulfilling Colombian industrialists' desire for a less radical proletariat.[129] In fact, it was an essential part of the Keynesian model and social compact: "a balanced economy—full production—full consumption."[130]

Modern workers and consumers would be made in Coca-Cola plants, through exposure to the quality standards, labor discipline, technology, and business culture inside, the Company claimed. In Farley's postwar speeches, he portrayed "sparkling white . . . modern Coca-Cola manufacturing plant[s]" opening up amid mud huts where "natives are shabbily dressed" and the "children mostly wear no clothes at all." Following the same script in such speeches, but varying the setting of the story to different developing countries including the Philippines and Egypt depending on the audience, Coca-Cola workers wore freshly laundered uniforms, had access to a factory doctor's office, and took mandatory showers. Farley quoted unnamed public health officials who said "that the influence of Coke on sanitation would be one of the most effective factors in promoting health that had ever reached this country.... 'Coca-Cola is worth its weight in gold as education in cleanliness.'"[131]

Coca-Cola Export and franchisees constructed the opening of bottling plants as events of major economic, political, and cultural import to a locale. The 1946 inauguration of a plant in Cartagena, Colombia, for example, involved the elite of the city and broad exposure to the rest of its populace. "The Big Day" began with full-page announcements in all local newspapers. A fourteen-piece band headed two parades through the city featuring the city elite's "daughters, wives and sweethearts," all wearing "red skirts, white blouses, and facsimile Coca-Cola crowns." "The Mayor's charming daughter reigned in the first float, proudly standing next to an eight-foot high Coca-Cola bottle peeping from a bed of simulated ice." The parade terminated at the plant, where five hundred guests, including representatives of the city's government, media, and social organizations, were treated to speeches by the governor and the president of the Chamber of Commerce, a blessing of the plant by the archbishop, the national anthem, and performance by a full orchestra, all broadcast on the radio for the widest possible audience. Tours of the plant and a ball at the city's toniest hotel entertained the city's elite through the night. Colombia's president was unable to attend, but his congratulatory message was published in all the local newspapers.[132]

Coca-Cola's frequent use of the image of plants in its mid-century advertising emphasized not only the superiority of the modern production reflected in its products, but the role of its industry in national economic development.[133] These ads reified production itself as a commodity of the Company, simultaneously offering it up as available and observable to local consumers while also mystifying Coca-Cola manufacturing as a complex and technical process that resulted in products of unprecedented "quality" and "purity." Such ads were adapted from Export's pattern campaigns for announcing new plants, which could be modified for the addition of different bottlers' details. Advertisements featured illustrations or photos of building exteriors and images of Coca-Cola production lines, highlighting the modern machinery and the local employees at work as visual tours of plants for host communities that might be suspicious of this new, foreign company.[134] They often portrayed families or schoolchildren on visits to the plant to assuage potential consumers' fears, while deferring

"Miren! ...allí trabaja papito..."

Datos interesantes sobre la industria Coca-Cola

- Coca-Cola, primera en calidad por más de 65 años.
- Se embotella en más de 80 países, por embotelladores locales independientes.
- Coca-Cola llena los más altos requisitos de pureza e higiene.
- Y más de 50.000.000 de personas al día gozan tomando Coca-Cola.

FIGURE 9. "Look! ... that's where Daddy works ...," *Selecciones del Reader's Digest,* November 1954, 199.

any need for them to actually visit the plant.[135] But ads sometimes offered invitations with copy like "Come on over, Friends,"[136] and even a special grand opening day of tours.[137] An Argentine ad demonstrates the construction of Coca-Cola production as both transparent and visibly local, reading: "At Paraguay 550 [the plant's address in the city of Rosario] Coca-Cola is bottled in the sight of all."[138]

Colombian Coca-Cola plants reproduced Export's multi-page brochure to explain Coca-Cola manufacturing to the communities that hosted them. Captioned "Pura como la luz del sol" ("Pure as Sunlight"), the cover images combine symbols of nature and industry to suggest both the product's purity and the transparency of Coca-Cola manufacturing. On the back cover is that oft repeated image of an interminable line of "continuously quality" Coca-Cola's streaming off a production line. Below, a line of cartoon people from around the world—distinguished by their traditional dress—excitedly watch Coca-Cola production. Inside the brochure, a multiple-page flow chart portrays each step of the production process with smiley-faced stick men working alongside contrastingly realistic, complex drawings of machinery.[139] This representation suggested that Coca-Cola's quality derived from the uniformly high standards of the Company's management and technology, not the workforce, whose lack of local identifiers meant this message could be deployed anywhere in the world much like the Company's industrial model.

ADVERTISING DEVELOPMENT

The Coca-Cola Company promoted its contributions to national development in advertising in Colombian periodicals and US-produced Spanish-language publications such as *Selecciones del Reader's Digest* and *Life en Español,* which were delivered by subscription and sold in major Latin American cities.[140] Coca-Cola ads featured whitewashed Latin Americans in vignettes illustrating the local benefits of its industry.[141]

The Company repeatedly used images of a prototypical "national family" whose livelihood was linked to the Coca-Cola industry, to suggest the modernization offered by its plants, both in employment and technology, and its contributions to national and familial economies. Multiple ads used the trope of the son proudly pointing to the work of his father at a Coca-Cola plant to assert that it was a modern employer, compensating workers with good wages, fulfilling technological work, and respect for their leisure time. As in figure 9, a well-dressed young family strolls on the father's day off. Passing by the Coca-Cola plant, the young son, "full of the pride the whole family feels," points, exclaiming, "Look! My daddy works there!" "Juanito" is "right" to feel this pride, the ad continues, because his father's job "is well-remunerated and interesting, as with the many other people who are occupied in the manufacture, bottling, and distribution of Coca-Cola."[142] Another used the perspective of a child excitedly pointing to his father working as an inspector of bottles emerging "shiny and sterilized from the powerful automatic washer" to comment: "Many are the good jobs that the

Coca-Cola industry offers, which means economic well-being that supports families." And the economic benefit extended to the community and even the nation, as "every Coca-Cola bottler is an independent business that contributes to the prosperity of the businesses in a locality, buying the goods and services that it needs. In this way, the manufacture, bottling, and distribution of Coca-Cola contribute to the progress of the country."[143]

Bottling company owners and their new Coca-Cola franchises were represented as "pillars of progress in their native communit[ies]" in the 1954 ad "This Is How a New Business Is Born," featuring an entrepreneur, "Don Pedro," who launches a Coca-Cola plant in his town. He proposed the idea at a regular meeting with associates at their social club, the ad emphasizes, suggesting to readers that Coca-Cola's international expansion was a local, organic process. Don Pedro, encapsulating the bottling "men of business, alert and visionary," points proudly to the modern plant as a credit and benefit to the local community: "Thanks also to the cooperation of a great number of people, as workers directly employed in the preparation of this quality drink, or those who sell it in their own corner shops, our bottler is today an important factor in the economy of this community and the livelihoods of many of its families."[144] Engagement with Coca-Cola ushered in the future for both individuals and nations as the dramatically entitled "First Step To Tomorrow" suggested in the image of a young, professional man being hired by a Coca-Cola bottler and the text: "Those that work in the local Coca-Cola bottling plant become a part of an entity that links large and small industries: sugar, glass, textiles, cork, wood, machines . . . All so important for constant progress! An ice-cold bottle of Coca-Cola is a global symbol of pleasure and progress."[145]

Numerous ads promoted Coca-Cola as a generator of local employment secondary to the actual bottling of the drink. One featured a friendly, older couple, "Juan & Maria," whose corner store is "growing and growing" thanks to sales of Coca-Cola, as well as the other products Coke drinkers buy while in their store.[146] In another, working-class "Juan & José" enjoy the "double pleasure" of a Coca-Cola break from the "well-paid" work of hanging Coca-Cola billboards.[147] Another ad points out the "man who is everywhere"—the legion of standardized Coca-Cola vendors who seem omnipresent and interchangeable as they serve and, even more important, create, the demand for the popular drink, while also making an income for themselves.[148]

The Coca-Cola industry's positive effects on tributary industries were celebrated in these advertisements, going so far as to assert that "perhaps more people derive at least a part of their income directly or indirectly from Coca-

Cola than any other individual product."[149] Such ads implied that Coca-Cola bottlers sourced goods and services locally. In one ad, a glassmaker proudly holds up a Coca-Cola bottle, a product of his manufacture "famous all around the world." In another, the description of the "buzzing" of saws clearing a mountain forest for lumber is celebrated as a sign of development. The owner of the sawmill points to Coca-Cola as one of his "best clients," as the local bottler purchases wood for Coca-Cola crates, billboards, and expansions to his plant.[150] "Every time you enjoy drinking Coca-Cola," another ad argued, workers in local industries prospered: bottling workers, glass makers, bottle-cap producers, carpenters, truckers, manufacturers of coolers, and vendors. It was "difficult to cite all those that benefit from the Coca-Cola industry."[151]

By the end of the 1950s, Coca-Cola advertising in Latin America often focused explicitly on national development, promoting economic and social modernization and linking them to the Coca-Cola brand. Such ads presented themselves as public service announcements that "the Coca-Cola Bottler in your community dedicates to you [the reader] in tribute to" the professions that were modernizing Latin American nations, in hope of "inspiring," "orienting," and "encouraging" youth to participate in such modernization. They celebrated professionals with the technical skills to rationalize and civilize both environment and society to create the preconditions for development. An architect designs an urban building complex,[152] a hydroelectric engineer harnesses the power of a giant river dam,[153] a chemist creates formulas that change lives,[154] a teacher shapes children into productive workers and citizens,[155] an engineer clears a jungle for a highway, and even a traditional Latin American profession like cattle ranching is celebrated for its modernization of animal breeding through the application of genetic science.[156] Each ad concluded with a suggestion that young people should consider such careers "to contribute to the progress of their country, and live a prosperous life."[157] And at the bottom of the page was the reminder that Coca-Cola was bottled in a seemingly ever-increasing number of countries—eighty in 1956 and a hundred in 1957—"by independent bottlers."[158]

THE LIMITS TO COCA-COLA'S MULTINATIONAL DEVELOPMENTALISM

Although the Company's self-promotion at mid-century suggested that national economic development was a central goal of Coca-Cola's business, executives did not accept the politics of postwar economic self-determination and national developmentalism's protectionism without reservations. It embraced its language, when expedient, only as long as it could promote itself as a national industry and only to the degree that it protected the Company and capitalism's growth from more radical critiques. Meanwhile, the Company took advantage of opportunities to advocate for free trade when possible. Production of Coca-Cola was fundamentally transnational, dependent on the importation of concentrates and materials and the repatriation of profits to the United States, so the multinational's growth required ongoing advocacy for free markets. Farley told the 1957 National Foreign Trade Convention that "national sovereignty, when pressed to its extreme limit is an enemy of progress, peace and mutual understanding." According to Farley, the idea of "national sovereignty" was being used by nations as a license to impose new regulations and taxes, restrict multinationals' growth, limit the repatriation of profits to corporate home nations, even nationalize industries. Foreign investment was contingent on developing countries' "morality" and "maturity," he said, speaking of them as if they were schoolchildren. As guidance, Farley proposed a list of "conditions conducive to the flow of private investment capital": foreign operations of US corporations should be exempted from US laws, US corporations should not have to pay taxes on profits earned abroad, and, ironic given his critique of state protectionism, host countries should protect "long-established foreign capital investments" from new foreign investments in their sectors.[159]

Although Coca-Cola Export strenuously emphasized its stimulation of national economies, much of the capital generated from its business in Colombia in fact remained in US hands. The subsidiary industries supplying Coca-Cola were a far cry from the local producers celebrated in advertising. The most expensive, complex equipment was sourced from US-based companies and overseen by US professionals. The Colombian and Indian bottling franchises purchased expensive US machinery to fill, cap, and wash bottles.[160] US companies that manufactured both machinery and materials—like Liquid Carbonic Corporation, Electronic Assistance Corporation, and the Barry-Wehmiller Machinery Company—established offices in Australia, Brazil, Cuba, England, Mexico, New Zealand, Trinidad, and Venezuela, as well as Colombia, to service international franchises.[161] When international bottlers needed to fill managerial and technical positions, they placed want ads in Company publications looking for "experienced" candidates with expertise on US machinery. In 1948, a Colombian bottler, most likely Albert

Staton, advertised positions in his expanding franchises. Making clear that Colombia was in South America, the ads sought experts familiar with US bottling equipment, and with some knowledge of Spanish, for short- or long-term contracts, noting that although the work was difficult, there was the possibility of participation in a growing business. Travel expenses would be paid, the climate was ideal, living conditions were good, and taxes were low.[162]

The tributary industries in Colombia did not look like those celebrated in Coca-Cola's developmentalist advertising. Through the 1950s the bulk of trademarked Coca-Cola materials (bottles, tops, printed materials, etc.) were still imported from the United States through Panama.[163] According to US government reviews of Colombian industry in 1953 and 1957, Coca-Cola's Colombian competitors Postobón and Gaseosas Colombianas had their own bottle-top plants but all of the soda companies still had to import bottles.[164] To avoid tariffs and address the lack of existing Colombian manufacturers, Staton financed and managed businesses to supply his Coca-Cola operations with bottles, crown tops, delivery crates, carbonic acid gas, and signs, as well as producing refrigerated coolers and lithographic printing in-house.[165] Coca-Cola touted these examples of foreign direct investment as "catalysts for Latin America's industrialization."[166] By employing Colombian workers and resources, manufacturing in Colombia arguably contributed more to economic growth than imports from abroad, but the profits remained primarily in the hands of US investors and a small segment of the established Colombian business elite. And when direct control of these tributary industries was no longer deemed necessary or profitable, Coca-Cola investors moved their business to familiar corporations like Liquid Carbonic or Owens Illinois Glass Company, themselves growing multinationals that expanded to Colombia under local subsidiary names.[167]

Albert Staton, who dominated the Coca-Cola bottling industry in Colombia, was not the "local, independent bottler" celebrated in Coke advertising. Leaving Georgia, he had worked for Coca-Cola around the world, managing several bottling franchises internationally before rising to the vice presidency of Export's Pan American Division. From that perspective on Coca-Cola's Latin American business, he acquired INDEGA in Colombia, and other bottling franchises in Mexico and Brazil in the 1940s, when his brother was conveniently Coca-Cola's vice president in charge of export sales in South America. Staton grew the bottling business in those three countries to over a dozen plants. Staton's sons Albert Jr. and Woods and his executive successors would follow in his path, acquiring additional bottling plants in Colombia, Mexico, and Brazil before expanding into a Latin American bottling empire across Brazil, Colombia, Costa Rica, Guatemala, Mexico, Nicaragua, Panama, and Venezuela after economic liberalization in the 1990s—making it the largest soft-drink bottling corporation in Latin America and the second largest in the entire Coca-Cola global system at the end of the century.[168] Staton's grandson Woods W. Staton, born in Medellín, would work in the family business and serve on the board of Panamco while also developing another major US multinational in Latin America: McDonald's. Woods W. Staton would become president of McDonald's South America Division before, like his grandfather, going into the franchise side of a multinational with his holding company, Arcos Dorados [Golden Arches]. Arcos Dorados grew to own over 1,800 locations across twenty countries in Latin America and the Caribbean, becoming McDonald's largest franchisee in the world. In 2012, although he had lived for decades in Buenos Aires, he was named the third wealthiest Colombian on the *Forbes* list of global billionaires.[169] And so the familial as well as business histories of these two powerful multinationals were closely related. McDonald's is The Coca-Cola Company's largest customer and Woods W. Staton would be chairman of the boards of the largest Latin American franchises of both at the turn of the twenty-first century.[170] Clearly, the Statons were not the "Don Pedros" of the Coca-Cola ads.

This is not just a twenty-first century critique with the benefit of hindsight on the resulting decades of international economic inequality perpetuated by the multinational corporation. The Coca-Cola Company's claim that its bottling plants stimulated the economies of other nations did not fully persuade everyone, including the US government, even in the mid-twentieth century. Coca-Cola Export applied twice to US agencies for assistance in expanding its business internationally in the name of aiding in international development. In 1948, Export applied to the US Economic Cooperation Administration (ECA) which oversaw the Marshall Plan's post–World War II economic recovery program for Europe, requesting guarantees of the convertibility to US dollars of profits from new investments in Europe and French colonial North Africa. Coca-Cola's application sought guarantees of $7,362,500 for spending on bottling machinery, trucks, autos, cases, bottles, and crown tops for prospective international bottling plants; syrup and concentrate to be supplied to bottlers; laboratory equipment for the testing of ingredients and products; equipment and construction costs; the provision of ingredients and sugar for the making of concentrate and syrup; the renovation and furnishing of branch offices; and the vague and very costly "technical services and promotion and development expense," which presumably paid for the force of Coca-Cola Export men supervising production efficiency, quality control, and sales promotion.[171]

Coca-Cola Export framed its application in terms of the multinational developmentalism of the franchise, saying that "local independently owned bottle operations in each country would participate importantly in the project both financially and managerially," to which the ECA reviewer remarked in handwritten notes: "Good!"[172] And while the Company explained that its primary function was selling concentrate and syrup to international bottlers, it suggested that its secondary purpose was practically international development: the Company supplied "expert chemical, engineering, technical, production and merchandising advice and know-how to the foreign bottling establishments," promoted the expansion of "tributary" manufacturing industries, and encouraged the merchandising of products "by methods and ways ensuring the most extensive distribution of income."[173]

But ECA administrators found the Company's description of the economic benefits of its business disingenuous. One took issue with the Company's flowery narrative of Cairo street vendors who sold Coca-Cola to "thirsty people" from "cooler[s] on their backs" so that "at the end of a day these formerly destitute people have a small income which permits them to buy food for their children, clothes for their wives and shoes for themselves," resulting in the "growth of the market for food, clothes and shoes." One reviewer commented in the margins: "this must have been written by the company's bright young advertising copy writers!"[174]

In fact, ECA administrators were concerned that Coca-Cola would actually hurt European economic recovery. For them, the numbers didn't add up. "The Coca-Cola Company makes the rather disingenuous assertion that the project will not affect the foreign exchange situation of the particular countries," an ECA reviewer noted. "As a matter of fact . . . the projects will in the end adversely affect the foreign exchange situation of these countries in that it will require the application of resources to the manufacture and distribution of a product which can hardly be called essential and which is not designed for sale abroad [as a European export]."[175]

The ECA also doubted Coca-Cola's claims that its investments would benefit countries through the "stimulation of employment and the stimulation of a number of industries which cater to the domestic market." Coca-Cola's business model would in fact siphon off critical raw materials to

produce a nonessential commodity, undercutting domestic beverage industries, like European wine, which employed many people and generated substantial exports, which Coca-Cola would not do. Moreover, foreign currency
would be needed to buy concentrate and equipment and pay Coca-Cola
Export's high fees for its technical, sales, and marketing services. European
countries were already at risk of a foreign exchange crisis, in large part due to
a flood of imports from booming US industries, and unable to defend their
currencies.[176] "I imagine that a considerable amount of opposition would be
caused if it became known that in effect the ECA proposed to grant assistance to countries for the purpose of enabling its citizens to drink coca-cola
[sic]," a reviewer observed, concluding: "I strongly advise against" granting
guarantees to the Company.[177] In its response to the Company, the ECA
explained that its objectives did not align with Coca-Cola's business proposal, as it sought to fulfill "the basic needs" of European and North African
countries, none of which "have even suggested that funds be allotted for
items such as soft drinks."[178]

A decade later the US government remained unconvinced by Coca-Cola
Export's claim that its international business assisted foreign economies. In
1957, the Company sought guarantees of the dollar convertibility of rupees
earned on new investments in India, applying to the International
Cooperation Administration (ICA), which was tasked with providing foreign assistance to hasten international economic development. Coca-Cola
proposed building a wholly owned concentrate plant in India for $250,000,
which would eliminate the cost of importing concentrate from abroad at
£120,000 Australian pounds a year. Coca-Cola even pledged to defer the
earnings on the concentrate plant for three years, at which time it would
repatriate the annual profits plus 25 percent of the past three years' accumulation of profits. The annual expected profits were to begin at $62,500 (plus the
$46,878 owed from the previous years), but might quickly increase, since
Coca-Cola planned on establishing over a dozen new bottling plants through
Indian partnerships with US capital investors. The Indian government
expressed concerns about the foreign exchange implications of the multinational's expansion in its country, worried that the profits Coca-Cola repatriated to the United States would quickly outweigh the level of investment in
the Indian concentrate plant. Such was the price of doing business with a
valuable brand and franchise business model, the Company responded. "The
problem is that GOI [Government of India] considers the profit-capital
investment ratio too high," a US government investment advisor reported.

"Coca-Cola maintains that such earnings are justified since these result from years of research in soft drink manufacture and marketing and world-wide advertising which has to be paid for."[179] The ICA disagreed,[180] concluding: "this appears to be very bad business for the Indian Government."[181]

"ALL OVER THE WORLD . . . SIGN OF GOOD TASTE": VISIONS OF CORPORATE GLOBALISM AT MID-CENTURY

As US companies' power grew in the postwar period, expanding the US market empire, Americans saw repeated images of Coca-Cola's comfortable international presence.[182] Coca-Cola expressed its corporate globalism, its drive to be and represent the global, while insisting on its localness everywhere around the world. These portrayals of the Company's ability to supply its offerings and win over consumers in diverse settings suggested the inherent appeal and adaptability of US consumer capitalism. Images of international peoples enjoying US commodities seemed further assuaging evidence that the American Century was under way and warmly accepted. This was not the United States imposing itself globally, these texts implied, but rather a demonstration that Coca-Cola and capitalism were universally appealing across international differences.

Coca-Cola ads conveying this message appeared in privileged positions on the back covers of the principal US mass market magazines including *National Geographic, Life,* and *The Saturday Evening Post.* The "Sign of Good Taste" campaign featured images of Coca-Cola consumed in international markets including Bermuda, Belgium, Brazil, Cuba, India, Italy, Japan, and Mexico. The ads invited Americans—specifically white Americans who were always conspicuously visible in frame—to travel the world, since no matter how distant the destination, they would find Coca-Cola there. It was an appreciated and adaptive participant in world cultures: "Through more than 100 countries... more than 58 million times each day... the invitation, *Have a Coke,* has a welcome meaning and acceptance all its own," the Rio de Janeiro ad explained. The ads produced a pleasure of looking at "others" enjoying Coca-Cola just like "Americans"—enjoying free enterprise and its consumer goods—while maintaining their exotic "otherness." This was another mark of the superiority of US capitalist hegemony: it allowed for difference. In fact, per these ads, the persistence of such differences, around

Coca-Cola consumption and capitalist expansion, demonstrated the global appeal of both.

One ad's image of Coca-Cola's consumption at "a Maharaja's Palace in far-off India," inspired by Coke franchise investor the Maharaja of Patiala, portrayed Coca-Cola integrated into the highest order of stereotypically exotic worlds, with princely men in turbans, demure sari-clad women, and grand palaces.[183] This otherness is made even more consumable to US viewers through the easy presence of fashionable white and Indian people, and their shared good taste in Coca-Cola. An elegant white woman and presumably the maharaja himself invitingly gaze back at the viewer as if just interrupted from their natural chatting and sipping Cokes. The image's familiar impressionistic style and the use of perspective, which positioned the maharaja in middle ground, further mediated reality and his imposing six foot five height to a more consumable degree.[184]

The Company also produced documentary-style promotional films celebrating Coca-Cola's appreciation of the world and the world's appreciation of it, which were shown in schools, social and business clubs, theaters and anywhere else bottlers could screen them. In *Pearl of the Orient* (1954), for example, the subject is the duality of the "traditional" and "modern" in the Philippines of the 1950s. Scenes of customary dances, dress, food, and rural life are mixed with factories, cities, and western-clothed young people, all of which are comfortable pairings for Coca-Cola, which has become a custom of its own. Whether knee deep in rice fields or in a bustling city, Filipinos are shown choosing Coca-Cola for sociability, taste, and quality, just like people in the United States. For Filipino viewers and others needing to be convinced of Coca-Cola's embeddedness, the film's narrator calls the Philippines "this beautiful land of ours" and asserts that Coca-Cola is a "member of the family . . . a trusted, old friend" that "naturally belongs," as a "partner in progress." Coca-Cola bottling plants where "modern equipment and trained people work as a team" work in conjunction with exotic means of local delivery—*banca* boats, horse-drawn *caretelas*, and the tops of women's heads. Coca-Cola is "made in the Philippines, by the people of the Philippines, for the people of the Philippines," the film insists, showcasing Philippine tributary industries, down to the manufacture of glass bottles from Philippine sand.

Wonderful World (1959), opens in the United States before touching down in twenty-five locales to "portray . . . how Coca-Cola fits graciously and naturally" across six continents.[185] The film suggested human universality across cultural difference by emphasizing the "universal ideals," "uniting force[s]," "common desires," and "parallel pursuits of happiness" of "people everywhere." The social mores of "boy meeting girl," national sports, and dances, are portrayed as exotically diverse yet motivated by common impulses, like the universality of Coca-Cola consumption across differences.[186] The Company translated the film into nine languages and produced over two thousand prints for distribution to US and international bottlers.[187] Wherever it was viewed, the film's argument for the universal applicability of the Coca-Cola business was communicated through the social and cultural logics of the franchise that produced the multinational corporation as local, with the credits explaining that it "has come to you through the courtesy of your friendly neighbor who bottles Coca-Cola."

Coca-Cola continued to articulate its mid-century corporate globalism by building a lavish version of *Wonderful World* transposed into "life-sized diaramas [sic]" for the 1964 World's Fair, turning down a proposal from Walt Disney to design a pavilion entitled "One Nation Under God" with a theme of US unity focused around an animatronic Abraham Lincoln. Instead, millions of visitors passed from a Chinese hotel room to the streets of Hong Kong, where "the fragrance of sandalwood was in the air and you heard the chatter of a Chinaman in the market," to the Taj Mahal awash with moonlight and jasmine, then on to a Swiss ski lodge, set amid fir and pine trees, and "a rain forest alive with the sound of birds and the essence of fragrant flowers" at Angkor Wat in Cambodia, before finding themselves looking out from the "deck of a pleasure cruiser anchored off Rio de Janeiro." Finally, visitors ended up in a room filled with Company drink brands. Next to the pavilion, the Company built a very visible "hidden persuader," a tower housing the largest carillon in the world to play the Coca-Cola theme song in bells every hour to remind guests, if only subliminally, to visit the pavilion or have a Coke at any one of the stalls around the fair.[188]

By the end of the 1950s, the emphasis on the multinational developmentalism of Coca-Cola's franchise model of globalization was central to the Company's narration of its business history and future. "In Europe, Africa, Asia and the far islands of the Pacific—in the neighboring countries of Latin America, the business of Coca-Cola is everywhere accepted as a local enterprise," Roy S. Jones, vice president of the Export Corporation, proclaimed in 1959.[189] Coca-Cola's business "has grown so phenomenally throughout the free world because it has put in practice for so many years the enduring principle that 'healthy world economy is dependent on healthy local economy everywhere.' ... This means more jobs, of course, for more local inhabitants—and definitely strengthens the reputation of Coca-Cola as an honest contributor to the economic well-being of that country." Soon markets everywhere would be open to Coke, the Coca-Cola Export executive predicted: "In these times of dwindling trade restrictions, and the promise of greater prosperity in the areas of freedom, the business of Coca-Cola everywhere is decidedly geared to the future."[190]

THREE

"I'd Like to Buy the World a Coke"

THE "REAL THING" AND
THE REVOLUTIONS OF THE 1960S

THE COCA-COLA COMPANY VIEWED the new social movements, countercultures, and postcolonial challenges of the 1960s and 1970s as a threat to the geopolitical order and expansion of transnational capital, but very much wanted to have its drinks in the hands of the young people leading them. Responding to the era's "social revolutions," as executives called them, the Company produced global advertising—notably the "The Real Thing" campaign—for radio and television in the United States and its foreign markets, assimilating elements of the styles and values of its critics to recast an international youth generation as liberated consumers of its product. In the iconic ad of the campaign, "I'd Like to Buy the World a Coke," the Company responded to the radical social and cultural movements of the time by offering a competing imaginary that incorporated some of their impulses and modes of representation, marketing itself through countercultural values and a multiracial cast in an attempt to construct a utopian vision of international friendship in a diverse-yet-harmonious world. But this harmony derived from an imagined unity in the universal freedom of consumption of the global commodity, and thus came at a price: bottles of Coke and capitalist markets. Projecting "corporate globalism," a portrayal of itself as a global corporation everywhere in the world and representing it, the Company not only marketed itself through international advertising like "I'd Like to Buy the World a Coke," but wishfully prefigured a free global market for Coke.

The Coca-Cola Company had already developed one of the earliest and "most ambitious"[1] models for the production and dissemination of transnational branded communications. What came to be called "pattern advertising" aimed at representing Coca-Cola internationally in a systematic way, with Coca-Cola Export supplying prototype advertising materials and detailed strategies for releasing advertising campaigns in international markets. Pattern advertising allowed for choice between slightly different versions of advertisements within a campaign, as well as the subtle adaptation of advertising for local consumers, but often resulted in the direct translation and replication of advertising produced by Coca-Cola Export and its international advertising agency. Like its material system of production, The Coca-Cola Company's symbolic system of advertising was also structured around its franchise bottling system. Before multinational advertising agencies or even local advertising companies operated in many parts of the world to facilitate country-specific advertising campaigns, the Company used its own international system to distribute, translate (linguistically and sometimes culturally), and locate its advertising to reach local consumers. Pattern advertising was thus the structure by which the cultural logic of the franchise was communicated. Through its system of international subsidiaries and franchises, the Company constructed its business as simultaneously local and global, as seen in the histories of Coca-Cola in Colombia and India in the previous chapters. Pattern advertising, like the franchising of the material system of production by workers in international markets, demonstrated the clear hierarchies of power and divisions of labor in the representation of what the Company and its products meant. This earliest advertising system kept the majority of cultural production centralized in Atlanta and New York, while exploiting international bottlers and subsidiaries' local knowledge by giving them limited autonomy to choose among pattern-advertising materials, modify them as needed, and identify the best media outlets or locations to reach potential consumers.

The Company's pattern advertising insisted on uniformity, although allowing for slight local variations. With pattern advertising, Coca-Cola Export and its international advertising agency, McCann Erickson, developed newspaper and magazine advertising campaigns (and later radio and television) with what they perceived to be "universal" themes around the world, like "Coca-Cola with food," "hospitality" that targeted "the house-wife," or "sports" and recreation for the "youth market." They would then create various versions of the original prototype ads for a few large cultural-linguistic markets (produced by McCann Erickson's Mexico City-based Latin American Division, for example), as well as provide instructions for their modification by international offices and bottlers, which would be sent out in annual "pattern books." As McCann Erickson described it in 1964, pattern advertising sought to identify themes with universal appeal that could be approached from various international perspectives through slight modification. The aim was to achieve "a family look for a company's world-wide advertising and still fulfill local needs." Prototype ads in "an easily varied basic format" included large headlines, illustration panels, and sales copy. These could be modified to fit local contexts, but offices were asked to adhere strictly to the format and theme. Of the resulting final advertising produced around the world, the advertising agency reported, "some are exact copies of the prototypes; others show variations."[2] More rarely, and only if the market was important enough in terms of potential profits, or it was deemed to have cultural differences significant enough to necessitate unique advertis-ing, and the bottlers were powerful enough to demand it, did Coca-Cola Export develop nation- or smaller region-specific campaigns.

Coca-Cola bottlers could also produce their own advertising, and they sometimes did. But they were required to stay within the strict parameters dictated by the Company—precise representation of the trademark, fidelity to the spirit of the product, high-quality aesthetics and materials—and to submit all advertising to Coca-Cola Export for approval before use.[3] The extent to which bottlers produced local advertising was dependent on their own cost-benefit analysis and ability to pay for it. Since franchise bottlers already paid the Company for advertising and received a steady flow of pat-tern-advertising texts, these were widely used. In most of the world, Coca-Cola's advertising was modeled on prototypes produced in the United States for international markets. And, as a result, US cultural assumptions of quality and taste, and hierarchies of race, class, and ways of life, were patterned in the "universalizing and homogenizing"[4] tendencies of Coca-Cola advertising.

A Coca-Cola Company film, *Community of the World,* assured viewers at a 1961 national convention of US bottlers—who had a stake in protecting the brand from being tarnished by unscrupulous international franchisees—that the Company's pattern-advertising strategy maintained uniform quality and messaging across diverse markets, allowing for local variations to maximize profitability. "Of course, our problems are multiplied by over 110 different countries and 57 different languages. Therefore we must work for flexibility," Joseph Rintelen, the head of Export's Advertising Department explained. To do so, Export distributed a yearly "pattern book" with advertising that could "be adapted to suit the customs of many countries." An illustrated pattern advertisement developed in the United States around the theme "Coke and food" that featured a glistening bottle of Coke next to a sandwich would be locally modified for different international markets: "In Mexico, the idea remains the same but the food changes. Instead of liverwurst we see tacos." In markets like Germany or Italy, advertisements might only translate the language and otherwise be exact copies of the prototypes produced in New York, even when photography was used, "since the models are typical of many European nations." But for markets like the Philippines, Hong Kong, or Brazil, the film explained, the visuals had to be reshot with local models and dress. Export executives did not admit, or could not see, that such images still did not reflect the diversity of local populations, however, and embodied racial and cultural hierarchies through markers such as skin tone, phenotype, class, and demonstrations of "modernity." In their eyes, this pattern advertising system was able "to provide prototype advertising that lends itself to direct and easy adaptation to the local need for traditional Coca-Cola advertising; to provide advertising that fits into the environment of local foreign media as if it belongs there."[5]

Marketing also required insistence on uniformity while allowing adaptation for different contexts; Coca-Cola Export's head of sales and merchandising explained that significant energy was invested in conveying "the basic principles of merchandizing" through the "same uniform training methods" across its diverse markets all over the world. "The Coca-Cola business, as we all know, is truly a local business everywhere. Consequently, the training must be tailored to local needs. Yet, it must be uniform." One of the principal tools was the "Treasure Chest," a cabinet in each of the international offices filled with manuals, brochures, slide presentations, and films of US marketing programs, including over twenty volumes with detailed instructions on everything from promotional giveaways to management of salesmen's truck routes. There was also a "Sales Shelf" with twenty-one volumes cataloguing international merchandizing activities. This material was then "translated, adapted, and taken out by our regional field men to over 550 bottling plants" for training "some 10,000 salesman for the purpose of increasing sales in nearly 2 million outlets . . . in more than 110 different countries." Such training employed "chalk talks," described as "simple line drawings, neutral in story treatment, that remain the same for any country or language." "Intentionally simple and basic," with as much cultural content as possible removed, the drawings portrayed "Customer, Dealer, Salesman . . . as symbolic universal characters recognizable to any audience of sales personnel, anywhere in the world." Where necessary, Export subsidiaries commissioned local photographs, patterned on sketches sent from New York, to capture the "local atmosphere and color."

PATTERNING SAMENESS, MANAGING DIFFERENCE

The international pattern-advertising system encapsulated Coca-Cola's mid-century model of globalization, visually asserting a universality in which US consumer capitalism served as a prototype that could be modified for application around the world through subtle, manageable differences in representation, while adhering to a common theme, style, and standards. Coca-Cola Export directives told international offices to "follow the advertisements in the [pattern-advertising] book as faithfully as is practicable," since it was "the belief of the Home Office that a close adherence to the principles set down in the 1957 Pattern Campaign will do much to strengthen and unify the quality image for Coca-Cola all over the world."[6] Variations, if any, from the original illustrated pattern advertisements were often slight. Consumers in markets as varied as Australia, Lebanon, and the Congo read different advertising copy in their own languages, with promotion of local bottlers, but saw the same pattern-advertising illustration for the Company's "Friendly Hospitality" campaign, reproduced without modification. A woman serves Coca-Cola bottles to two seated female friends. All three are in Western clothing and phenotypically white, as was the bias of the Company's advertisements.[7]

Although variations were subtle, their significance may have been meaningful in localizing images. Among the options sent by Coca-Cola Export, international offices and bottlers strategically identified those ads they felt would be most culturally appropriate for their region of consumers, sometimes slightly modifying them to enhance their local appeal. Whereas in Europe and Latin America, a common "hospitality-themed" advertisement featured a woman serving Coca-Colas to a man and woman in her home, in the Arabic-language Egyptian market the same Cokes are served to the same couple, who retain the Western style and features of the prototype ad, but by a turbaned servant, who culturally contextualizes the hospitality of the wealthy in North Africa.[8] As another example, of the many 1950s sports-themed print advertisements, both Moroccan and Colombian subsidiaries used images of soccer players enjoying Cokes. In addition to modifications to the advertising copy in translation (Arabic and Spanish), there were also slight variations in facial features and hairstyles.[9]

The Coca-Cola Export Corporation's international offices and bottlers also drew on specific cultural referents and national symbols in the localization of pattern advertising and the creation of market-specific targeted advertising. Such advertising often suggested that an internationally originated, industrially produced drink went well with the local culture. Advertising in predominantly Muslim countries sold Coca-Cola as the perfect drink after a Ramadan fast and, implicitly, as appropriate to a nation that was both traditional and modern. Egyptian ads from the 1950s, for example, showed a well-off family breaking fast in their apartment, with the city skyline of traditional Islamic architecture and modern office buildings behind them.[10] Or men in Egyptian military uniforms enjoying Coca-Colas and a hookah at the end of a fast day.[11] Coca-Cola's print advertising in Egypt in the 1950s repeatedly featured Egyptian men in army and air force uniforms, aligning its product with constructions of Arab modernity and nationalism.

The female form was also a terrain for Coca-Cola to map out positions of traditional cultural acceptability and modern appeal. In an Egyptian ad, a smiling woman in a headscarf holds a Coca-Cola as she stands next to a turbaned man smoking a hookah, with modern and traditional consumables paired for the "Total Refreshment" promised in the ad's tagline.[12] Demonstrative of mid-century Egyptian liberalism, the ad "Pure as a Summer Sky" shows a smiling woman lounging by a stylish pool in a bathing suit, drawn with accentuated breasts, waist, and hips.[13] "Coca-Cola girl" ads were common in the United States, of course, where young women were depicted as girl-next-door pinups, sexualized, but clothed in socially acceptable bathing suits or dresses, drinking Coca-Cola, smilingly offering a bottle, or accepting one from an outstretched hand, with the suggestive text simply saying: "Yes."[14] Coca-Cola's Egyptian versions of such ads were tamer, and associated the "pure" and "wholesome" beverage with the unsullied beauty of young Egyptian women, depicted smiling sweetly and holding Coca-Cola bottles close to their mouths, with just a hint of sexuality.[15]

As the use of photography in advertising increased in international markets, the politics of representation in pattern advertising became more complicated.[16] Moving from illustrations to photos meant having to reshoot advertising cam-

FIGURE 10. Pattern advertisement comparison, *Coca-Cola Overseas,* October 1956, 21.

paigns rather than just modifying print prototypes. The mimetic capacity of photographic advertising increased the promise, and viewers' expectation, of realistic and locally appropriate characters and situations, represented through ethno-racial signifiers, dress, settings, and sociocultural contexts. Under the heading "NATIVE SITUATIONS," the 1957 pattern book insisted that both illustrations and photographic ads could "be easily adapted to the needs of countries where different races must be featured."[17] The local version depicted "the same general situation [as the pattern prototype] but features a Chinese instead of a Caucasian," *Coca-Cola Overseas* wrote of the photographic adaptation for the Hong Kong market (fig. 10). "To make the change, the agency simply furnishes a local photographer with the original illustration as a guide and has him photograph a native model."[18]

Even when they were recreated for distinct international markets, ads were based on US prototypes and generally passed on their biases and assumptions, representing people with whiter features and in contexts consistent with Western definitions of economic, social, and cultural development. The standards of beauty, class, and modernity of illustrated pattern advertisements carried over to the new medium of photographic advertising through the casting of models and art direction. The photographic image was, of course, a construction, but its persuasive realism meant that advertising became an even more compelling representation of the "realities" to which the consumers of the developing world should aspire.

Coca-Cola's 1958 hospitality-themed ad of a woman serving female friends in her well-appointed parlor illustrates the choices and adaptations made by international advertising managers and bottlers. The photographic prototype used in Italy, illustration prototype used in Iraq, and finally, the reshoot for the Philippines, show almost identical character types, positioning, dress and hairstyles, and setting (down to the window, buffet, bowl, and plant in each background). The Italian ad used Coca-Cola Export's prototype with white US models, but this would have been overtly foreign in the Iraq and Philippine markets. For the Philippines, the ad was reshot with racially representative models. In Iraq it reproduced the prototype illustration with Western-dressed, but racially vague, line-drawn characters. Racial representation may have been a secondary consideration in markets like Iraq, where photographic reshoots might have been prohibitively expensive, or, as the pattern book warned, local newspapers and magazines lacked the print technology to reproduce half-tone photographic images. From the perspective of Coca-Cola Export, such threats to advertising quality, and thus to Coca-Cola's brand image, made simple line conversion drawings preferable to photography in many contexts.[19] Each of these ads, through their different modes of representing potential local consumers, conveyed the powerful association of Coca-Cola with modern housewives who had the means and leisure to play cards in a well-appointed home. Coca-Cola's advertising directed at the "domestic" or "housewife" market, as executives referred to it, regularly played on themes of hospitality and service, pairing Cokes with home-cooked meals, and providing desirable beverages to kids, constructing gender roles as well as sales of drinks.[20]

Throughout the 1950s and early 1960s, well-dressed, white, wholesome-looking upper-middle-class families and young people populated Coca-Cola advertising in the United States, which was the standard upon which the Company's international advertising was patterned. The Company explained to bottlers in its introduction of the 1955 advertising campaign, "You will notice that the models are definitely among the higher social and economic levels (in some instances in the highest social and economic and cultural group). This is no mistaken 'snob appeal.' It capitalizes upon the well established psychological fact that people enjoy looking at situations in which they can project themselves even though it be sometimes only in their dreams." Advertisements would emphasize that "50 million [Cokes were] consumed every day," making it the "most widely consumed soft drink in the world." But, at the same time, the copy and images did not strive to be overly inclusive or "commonplace," according to Coca-Cola's advertising department, but instead worked to retain "a little exclusivity which encourages everyone *to want to be* a member of our particular group which, after all, does not take in everybody."[21]

Even when modification of pattern advertisements attempted to adjust their content to the contexts of consumers in different parts of the world, the ads retained powerful assertions of the drink brand's association with capitalist modernity. As with most US advertising of the time, Coca-Cola ads projected and played upon Americans' postwar aspirations to peace, stability, and economic prosperity. The postwar period was the golden age of US capitalism, and Americans saw an unprecedented increase in their standard of living. Mass consumption was encouraged alongside mass production to drive economic growth. This was epitomized by the growth of homogeneous suburbs where white, middle-class American families could buy into the American Way through the private consumption of goods and products to fill their homes and create comfortable, safe, and orderly environments and lifestyles for their nuclear families.[22] Postwar consumer culture thus contributed to social conformity, promoting a sense that a person's identity could be defined by the consumption of goods produced by capitalism, and that one could differentiate oneself, however slightly, with and through its products. The pattern-advertising system, with its allowance for slight variation, while demanding ultimate uniformity, was a representation of and a conduit for these socially conservative values as they were relayed around the world.

BROADCASTING MODERN CONSUMPTION

The medium that relayed advertising was itself an assertion of Coca-Cola's association with the modern. To align itself with the shifting modes of representing the modern, the Company had to negotiate the complications of transitioning the pattern-advertising strategy to new forms of media, from print to radio (and later TV). The beverage industry was an early radio advertiser. In the United States, the Company started radio advertising in 1927, and went on to sponsor a serial drama, sports shows, and several musical/variety programs through the 1950s.[23] In this era of single-sponsor broadcast media, the whole show had the potential for commercial promotion. But there was scope for more direct sells. Coca-Cola's radio programming was packaged in segments, with an orchestral waltz known as "The Coca-Cola

Signature," direct appeals from the announcer or star host, short vignettes highlighting Coca-Cola slogans, and reminders to listeners that the show was brought to them by "your friendly neighbor who bottles Coca-Cola."

As seen in the Colombian example in chapter 1, Coca-Cola Export and international bottlers often sponsored orchestral or sports broadcasts on local or national radio networks. But Coca-Cola Export also centrally produced radio programming for use internationally, such as the 1940s *Ronda Musical de Las Americas* (Musical Roundup of the Americas), broadcast in at least thirty-five different bottling regions in Latin America,[24] which Coca-Cola imagined as a cultural-linguistic market with shared musical tastes. In large national markets, like Brazil and Mexico, Coca-Cola repackaged similar material in a slightly more targeted manner with *Um milhão de melodias* (A Million Melodies) and *Estampas musicales* (Musical Snapshots), which were sponsored by "your bottler of Coca-Cola." All three of these popular shows followed the same formula, combining poetic descriptions of Latin American scenes and performers with samples of music from around the region. Interwoven with the Latin American music was "The Coca-Cola Signature," with a reinterpreted overture featuring additional horns and guitars, and advertising copy read in Spanish or Portuguese by the male host.

In the 1950s and early 1960s, The Coca-Cola Company linked its brand to a series of jingles that reminded listeners to "Bring Home the Coke," that "King Size Coke Has More for You," and that they could "Be Really Refreshed." The catchy tunes combined music with lyrics that emphasized rhythm, rhyme, and repetition, as well as concision to make their advertising messages eminently memorable. These "earworms," which wriggled into listeners' brains from repeated exposure through the radio (and soon TV), were designed to stick with the listener and be sung, whistled, or hummed, sometimes even unknowingly long after the commercial had ended. Contagious limericks and "ditties" circulated well before the advent of broadcasting—as far back as 1896, we find: "Stronger! Stronger! Grow they all, / who for Coca-Cola call. / Brighter! Brighter! Thinkers think, / when they Coca-Cola drink."[25] Read on printed marketing materials, such sing-song lines were intended to be catchy, "heard" in one's head or repeated out loud, and to this end corporate lyrics were often inserted into popular or traditional tunes.[26] But with the mass adoption of radio and its commercial structure in many countries around the world, advertising jingles reached new heights and distances. Just as print advertising used trademarks and visual signs to incorporate products and potential purchasers into a larger whole of consumer and brand identity, jingles were aural logos for companies and their products that used music as a "tool for the creation or consolidation of a community, of a totality."[27] The catchy capitalist sound of jingles became a significant part of international soundscapes.[28] The jingle form itself was modern, with its highly structured time, rhyme, and repetition. Through the 1950s and into the 1960s, Coca-Cola's jingle commercials frequently featured the McGuire Sisters, a singing group of three midwestern sisters whose palatable, white-bread swing and wholesomely sweet harmonies typified middle-class pop music and represented the Company on US radio and TV.

The themes and subjects of this Coca-Cola advertising imagined and constructed a modern consumer market. Coca-Cola radio advertising frequently employed the realism of the radio medium to produce the sound effects of modern life and consumer society—factory whistles, typewriters, trains and car horns, refrigerator doors, and even the radio itself—to draw the listener's attention and associate Coke with the modern:

[Sound of kitchen door opening.]

KID: Did you bring home the Coke, Mom?

MOM: Uh-huh. A whole bottle full.

KID: Oh, only one bottle? [Concerned. Opens fridge] Wow, it's a giant!

ANNOUNCER: It's Coca-Cola the new, big-big family size. Same lively Coke you love in the standard size. Same real great taste. And enough Coke to put the whole family at its sparkling best. So,

SUNG JINGLE: Bring home the Coke!

ANNOUNCER: Now in standard size and new big-big family size too.[29]

Such ads targeted broad groups of prospective consumers: the housewife and her kids, industrial and office workers on their breaks, the young person at leisure with some recreation and sport. The Company's emphasis on advertising with a universal thrust merged with new marketing strategies to exploit consumer segmentation. But these appeals were simultaneously broad and conforming compared to the niches the Company would target by the end of the 1960s as a result of critiques of the homogenizing nature of generalized consumer marketing like "Work Refreshed," "Coke in your home," "Family Size," "Coca-Cola with food," and the "Youth Market," although the last of these would increasingly construct the postwar baby boom generation as the consumptive drivers of both the soft drink industry and contemporary popular culture.

With television's rise in the 1950s, Coca-Cola expanded its advertising to the new medium, sponsoring popular musical variety shows to appeal to modern teens. By the end of the decade, US TV broadcasters had adopted the magazine advertising model. Commercials appeared in "breaks" between programming segments to maximize advertising revenue, while minimizing sponsors' influence over programming content. Coca-Cola Export distributed US-produced TV commercials alongside pattern radio ads. Where local production was necessary, advertising managers had scripts, recorded sound and music, and the original ads to remake the commercial for their market.

Television commercials were even more difficult to pattern than radio, with the expectation of visuals of locally appropriate settings and characters, but Export included storyboards, sheet music or recordings, "plus full instructions to assist our overseas managers in producing uniform high quality television and motion picture advertising." So, as the head of Export's Advertising Department explained, "Mexican bottlers get a Mexican version of the McGuire sisters, produced in Mexico." In one such ad, these "Mexican McGuire sisters," with their girl-next-door sensuality, appeared as young secretaries dancing around a mod office singing that "Coca-Cola Grande" gave you "mucho más" for your money to the tune of the "Be Really Refreshed" jingle.[30]

STICKY SIGNIFIERS: THE CAPITAL OF AMERICAN CULTURE AT MID-CENTURY

The Coca-Cola Company's advertising helped make its products "mean" to its potential consumers, branding them. Like words in a language, brands are signifiers that do not have essential meanings on their own, nor are their meanings derived from the essence of the products themselves. Rather, brands are imbued with meaning through the shifting relationships and interactions within systems of meanings, in relation to other ideas, cultural texts, events, competitors in a field of products, people (consumers, workers, regulators, etc.), and of course, the conscious efforts of advertisers to make them mean. The change in the signification of a brand like Coca-Cola, exemplified by its histories in Colombia, France, and India in chapter 2, show it to be a "floating signifier," not fixed in its inner nature, but open to recharacterization and interpretation, the making of associations and the projections of desires. Advertisers contribute to this flexibility of meaning by constantly trying to construct it as a popular symbol, to address new market imperatives, contexts, and ideologies, to align it with the popular. But brands don't float completely freely—traces of their histories and past significances remain. And, of course, their meaning is defined by forces beyond the control of the companies, marketers, and advertisers who claim ownership of the brand and seek to shape it to their benefit. Competitors, consumers, workers, activists, and cultural producers who make use of the brand both draw on its existing meaning and reshape it through their use. As the Company marketed its products in new areas of the world, it relied on this lack of fixity of meaning to modify its brands' meanings for local markets. But there were elements of the brand's signification that were *stickier* than others, that stayed with it.

Through most of the twentieth century, even while emphasizing global expansion, decentralization in production, and adaptation in advertising, The Coca-Cola Company "stuck" its advertising with American ideologies. Many of these were intended, like the celebration of consumption and youth. But Coca-Cola advertising carried the values of those that had the most powerful hand in its production: ethnocentrism and white supremacism, cultural hierarchies and definitions of modernity, and the assumed practicability and acceptability of the communicative "patterning" of texts emanating from the corporation's core to the majority of the world, perceived to be at the periphery. Even when the Company made efforts to localize its advertising, the consumerist ideology of the Company's advertisements had an American accent.

Coca-Cola advertising was not heard/seen in isolation, but rather consumed intertextually alongside other media representations of Coca-Cola's "Americanness." With the goal of making its product a feature of daily life, the Company's brand was a visible presence on billboards, store signage, vending machines, and point-of-sale advertising, as well as in restaurants, clubs, theaters, homes, and even schools across the United States. After decades of concerted efforts in advertising and marketing, the Company had successfully linked its product to an understanding of the "American Way of Life"—which the Company had itself contributed to defining through advertising that put Coca-Colas in the hands of Norman Rockwell stock characters, national sports heroes, soldiers, girl-next-door pinups, celebrities, and Santa (whose coat became permanently red in the public's mind because of his role in advertising Coca-Cola).[31] Such powerful cultural associations and the drink's ubiquity in social life in the United States resulted in the use of Coca-Cola both as a backdrop for and signifier of American life in popular culture, especially in Hollywood movies, which were themselves growing international markets. To spur this along, the Company opened a Los Angeles office in the 1960s to attempt to encourage and manage Hollywood's brand references.[32]

Coca-Cola was a self-proclaimed product of modern industry and associated itself with the high standards of living portrayed in US popular culture. As the Colombian economy grew in the 1950s and 1960s, the more affluent classes saw rising incomes and plenty of images showing them how to spend their money. This new consumer culture was encapsulated by the teenagers of the middle and upper classes who were increasingly identifying with and consuming like their international counterparts. Colombia's explosive population growth and urbanization meant that youth culture was more powerful and visible than ever before: in the early 1960s, nearly half of all Colombians were under fifteen years of age.[33] In the hope of dissuading them from alcohol consumption, schools and parents would throw their teenagers parties popularly called *coca-cola bailables* for their soft drinks and dance music, often played by live *cumbia* bands. Colombian Coca-Cola bottlers happily encouraged this identification, providing the soft drinks and sponsoring pop-up "a-go-go" nightclubs in places like the Sears showroom in the city of Cali.[34]

For their taste in things representing the new and their cultivation of a generational style that increasingly rejected Colombian middle-class social and cultural mores and authorities in their consumption and self-expression, these teenagers were referred to in common parlance, somewhat derisively, as *cocacolos*.[35] The cocacolos and their female counterparts, the *kolkanitas,* had a strong sense of themselves and were not waiting for definition, the Bogotá magazine *Semana* remarked in 1954 while trying itself to define the generational subculture anyway. "One enters into *cocacolismo* at 13 years old and leaves it at 20," wears the signal attire of blue jeans, sweaters and moccasins and speaks in the key slang of youth. They must dance well and to "only the mambo, bolero, cumbia and blues (all imported dances with the exception of the cumbia)" and "cultivate at least five of the following tastes: comics, interplanetary adventure books, US music, ice-cold soft drinks, movies, the radio, sports, chewing gum, hot-rods,"[36] sharing many generational affinities and styles with US teenagers.

The cocacolos may seem tame and their interests superficial. But their expressions of a generational subculture, their resistance to conforming to existing social and cultural standards, and even their consumption of goods marketed to them as a distinct demographic would become the roots of various bohemian experimentations, avant-garde cultural and literary movements, social movements, and a general sense of youth rebellion in the decade that followed. The cultural critic Antonio Cruz Cárdenas noted that *antico-cacolista* Colombian elders portrayed them as a "calamity that terrifies." But they were no more foolish than other generations, rather products of their time and poised to remake it, just as the youth culture of previous generations had brought cultural, social, and political revolutions to Colombia. The coca-colo, he argued, came into being in one of the most "difficult and contradictory periods" of national culture and "the rapid transformations in national and global life . . . separated him completely from the past. He is the son of the jet, the movies, comic books and television."[37] It was "not all mambo, chewing gum and interplanetary phenomena within coca-colismo," Cruz Cárdenas insisted. "Cocacolo youth" had recently produced "events as serious as those of June 8th and 9th in Bogotá," when university students protested General Rojas Pinilla's repressive dictatorship, and were confronted by a Colombian military battalion (recently returned from Korea) who shot and killed ten. The ensuing student declarations and protests, "serious and thoughtful" statements "that proposed a transformation of custom for Colombia, a revolution of behavior,"[38] would begin to turn the tide against that military regime (although another would follow). According to Cruz Cárdenas these youth were not unlike the country's founding fathers: "coca-colos of the 1800s who changed the course of national history."[39]

The poets of the major Colombian literary movement of the late 1950s and 1960s, *Nadaísmo* (Nothing-ism), who much like the US Beats irreverently and iconoclastically criticized contemporary society, but with more existential, even nihilistic overtones, having witnessed the brutality of *La Violencia* in the 1940s and 1950s, embraced the cocacolos as their own. The "First Nadaísta Manifesto," written in 1958 by the poet Gonzalo Arango on a roll of toilet paper (before being published widely in both a less delicate and coarse medium) included several sheets portraying the cocacolos as a generation on the brink of historical agency. Cocacolo youth, already rebelling against previous generations in their preoccupation with popular culture, consumption, free-thinking, and sensuality, were on the verge of becoming a revolutionary force against the "military tyranny" and "spiritual and cultural order of the country": "The Cocacolos thus form a generation that I call from now on: The Generation of the Threat."[40] The anti-ideology of the Nadaistas captured the imagination of Colombian society, and while the cocacolo generation's disaffection with the establishment grew, an empowered youth culture continued to be engendered by Coca-Cola advertising and broader consumer culture.

The national economic development promised by capitalists was failing the majority of Colombians in the 1960s. A slowdown in the growth of import-substitution industrialization, low coffee prices, increasing public debt, inflation, wage stagnation, and unemployment were felt by most Colombians.[41] In 1965, Colombia's income inequality was the second worst of major Latin American nations; 45 percent of people were considered poor; infant mortality was eight times that of advanced nations; and only half of people in the countryside had potable water, although all the Coke plants did, from either public water systems or their own private wells.[42] While the discourse of national development was powerful, the reality was weak: the Colombian state played a relatively small role in the economy, especially when compared with the statist or interventionist economic policies and extensive investment in the public sector taking place elsewhere in the world. Liberal and Conservative parties occupied the presidency alternately in the National Front between 1958 and 1974, which brought relative peace to Colombia, but also constructed an undemocratic political center that was largely ineffective in addressing agrarian reform, labor rights, and poverty reduction, and further radicalized others away from electoral politics.

Students radicalized by the Cuban revolution, and the combination of communism and liberation theology modeled by the priest and university professor Camilo Torres Restrepo joined the Ejército de Liberación Nacional (ELN) guerillas in the 1960s. In those same years, the Fuerzas Armadas Revolucionarias de Colombia (FARC) formed its even larger Marxist peasant army in the countryside. Both would target Coca-Cola plants and delivery trucks for bombings, thefts, and extortion in the following decades. Only a small minority of Colombians took up arms, but an additional swath of the populace would be influenced by their political economic critique, as well as the countercultural *hippismo* of the 1960s and 1970s. This middle-class youth rebellion expressed its subcultural defiance in part through a challenge to The Coca-Cola Company and its brand, even as they played a part in propagating a sense of the generation's cultural agency.[43] Capitalism had brought mass culture to Colombia, and young urban Colombians now shared many of the commodities, interests, and ideas of their counterparts in other parts of the world. That culture now included criticism of those very commodities.

During the "long" 1960s, a period not precisely bounded by the decade itself, young people fueled liberation, decolonization, and revolutionary movements across various parts of the world. Since decades of globalization and the ubiquity of its advertising had made it an iconic representation of US corporate capitalism, The Coca-Cola Company would become a target of some of these struggles, with movements and countercultural expression challenging its business and representational practices. The Company was accused of promoting a stultifying and impoverishing consumer capitalism, repatriating profits from the poorest countries to the richest, partnering with local elites complicit in repressive political and economic systems, and being a representative of US international political and economic power.

James Farley, Coca-Cola Export Corporation Board chairman until his retirement in 1973, and a staunch Cold Warrior, saw attacks on Coca-Cola as the work of "trained operators—from student agitators to professional terror squads," directed by the Kremlin, one more case of the "Communist python . . . throwing its coils" around "helpless free peoples."[44] In fact, challenges were coming at the Company from various directions, uncoordinated, making them perhaps even more threatening. Socialist and revolutionary governments, those of Chile, Cuba, and Egypt among them, nationalized or shuttered Coca-Cola plants as exemplars of economic and cultural neocolonialism, and India and other nations in the global south regularly threatened to do so as well, as described in the following chapter.

In the 1960s and 1970s, intellectuals of the emerging school of dependency theory such as Raúl Prebisch, André Gunder Frank, Fernando Henrique Cardoso, and Samir Amin attacked the international economic order, and US corporate neocolonialism in particular, for having reduced the global south to dependent status.[45] Paul Baran and Paul Sweezy's neo-Marxist analysis in *Monopoly Capital* (1966) argued that oligopolistic big businesses controlled the market and generated wasteful economic surpluses, resulting in unemployment, inequality, and a neglect of socially useful goods and services. They saw capitalists acting in their class interest, underutilizing productive capacity and resisting redistributive spending, leading to stagnation and crisis. Corporations sought to increase demand by investing profits in advertising and sales, while supporting US imperial expansion to absorb surplus capital and goods. Baran and Sweezy called attention to the irrationality of a world capitalist system that would produce revolutionary challenges from the exploited in the global south and people of color in the north.[46] Richard Barnet and Ronald Miller's *Global Reach* (1974) specifically accused The Coca-Cola Company of economic exploitation by draining international economies and causing "commerciogenic malnutrition" with marketing "globaloney" that exhorted people in the developing world to embrace consumerism and spend money on Cokes rather than needed nutrients.[47]

Coca-Cola plants and personnel became targets of armed revolutionary movements opposed to this economic exploitation and the political dictatorships seen to be colluding with US capital. Some revolutionary groups used threats of violence to improve pay or working conditions, while others funded their struggles by extorting corporations with threats against places of business or by kidnapping corporate executives. In Guerrero, Mexico, in 1971, a millionaire Coca-Cola bottling company owner was kidnapped by rural guerrillas demanding the release of political prisoners to Cuba and the payment of a $200,000 ransom. In Argentina, the left-wing Peronist Montoneros bombed US corporate locations, including Coca-Cola, and the Company was forced to pay out large ransoms to the Fuerzas Armadas de Liberación (FAL) and other guerrilla groups for the safe return of Coca-Cola managers after a series of kidnappings.[48] In addition to working with US and Argentine state forces, including employing army intelligence officers involved in the detention, torture, and killing of leftists, the Company dispatched its own anticommunist covert operations specialist who received international press after reportedly publicly informing the kidnappers, "We will kill you. We'll go after your wife. We'll kill her."[49] Coca-Cola was accused of complicity with governments where it did business, legitimizing their policies and strengthening their economies. Some states developed similar politics; in 1968, Arab League nations instituted the Arab Boycott of several corporations doing business in Israel, including The Coca-Cola Company, severely limiting the Company's business across the Middle East and North Africa.

The Company regularly battled labor militancy flaring up in various parts of the world in this period. In 1971, when a bottling plant in Italy declared bankruptcy rather than recognize the demands of a strong union, the workers took over the plant. In Uruguay in 1972, bottling workers revolted and occupied the plant when two co-workers were arrested for involvement in a leftist revolutionary movement.[50] In the Company's Minute Maid Florida citrus fields, César Chávez organized the primarily African American migrant workforce to fight for better pay, housing, medical care, and working conditions, which had been described as "near slavery conditions,"[51] drawing public attention to the Company's labor practices.[52] Operation Breadbasket, an Atlanta organization of ministers, targeted Coca-Cola with a "selective buying campaign" (i.e., boycott) because of racist employment practices, demanding that it hire black workers for its production lines and do away with segregated employee bathrooms and locker rooms.[53]

Coca-Cola was under attack by the anti-racist, consumer, and environmental movements of the 1960s and 1970s. The Congress of Racial Equality leveled a thinly veiled boycott threat at the Company over the lack of representation of African Americans in its advertising. (Coca-Cola appeased the group with a few integrated advertisements and increasing its advertising spending in African American media markets.) The Federal Trade Commission filed complaints against the Company for misleading advertising and antitrust violations, charging that its contracts with franchise bottlers effectively produced local monopolies that reduced competition and led to increased prices.[54] Speaking before Senator George McGovern's Select Committee on Nutrition and Human Needs, the consumer advocate Ralph Nader accused the Company of selling a drink with "absolutely no vitamins or proteins."[55] As the first Earth Day approached in 1970, Coca-Cola CEO J. Paul Austin was especially concerned about the environmental movement, which saw the Company as "littering the landscape" with nonreturnable bottles, fleets of delivery trucks, and a countryside speckled with billboards, making it an "ideal target" for protest, as he put it.[56] In a series of personal memos in 1969, Austin lamented that "anti-establishmentarianism is here to stay ... the American business community is in for a period of prolonged harassment by radical elements." He predicted class action lawsuits and activism by minority shareholders and asked Coca-Cola lawyers to ensure that he was shielded from personal liability.[57] The Company, Austin argued, had to recognize "the phenomenal influence ... the 'new left' has over public opinion in this country today."[58]

HEGEMONIC COUNTERCULTURE

The New Left did have influence, and it rose on a larger current of cultural discontent in US popular discourse leading up to the 1960s. Academics and journalists decried the corporate culture produced by Fordism and consumer capitalism. David Riesman's *The Lonely Crowd* (1950) suggested that the prosperity of postwar America and its institutions (like the modern corporation) and its social and cultural arrangements (like suburbia and mass consumption) privileged an "other-directed" man who looked to those around him for guidance and approval. William Whyte's *The Organization Man* (1956) argued that corporate bureaucracy valued conformity and loyalty over creativity and individuality. John K. Galbraith's *The Affluent Society* (1958) argued that treating the economy's production of private goods as the measure of a society's prosperity overlooked the public good and social and individual well-being, a state of affairs exacerbated by the consumer economy's dependence on the creation of new consumer desires and needs through advertising.[59]

Remarkably, critiques of the hierarchies, conformity and alienation of corporations (if not their structural role in an exploitative economy) appealed to some in the business community, especially younger members, who sought to revivify corporate capitalism from the inside.[60] Douglas McGregor's influential *The Human Side of Enterprise* (1960) called for replacing the dominant management model, which coerced workers through standardization, authoritative control, and corporate hierarchies, with one that empowered productivity by recognizing worker creativity and individuality. Robert Townsend's *Up the Organization* (1970) went even further, denouncing "monster corporations" that "made slaves" of employees, invoking Gandhi, Martin Luther King Jr., and even Ho Chi Minh as models for business.[61]

Advertising was also criticized even as, or perhaps because, consumer capitalism intensified at mid-century. At first this was just a "casually cynical perception" of the advertising industry, represented in popular culture by skits like *I Love Lucy*'s "Vitameatavegamin" episode and exposés like Roy Norr's "Cancer by the Carton" article in *Reader's Digest* (both appearing in 1952).[62] But by the 1960s, advertising was seen by some with outright suspicion as a result of Vance Packard's best-selling exposé *The Hidden Persuaders* (1957), which detailed the industry's use of "motivation research" by social scientists and self-proclaimed experts in human behavior "to channel our unthinking habits, our purchasing decisions, and our thought processes . . . to manipulate our habits and choices in their favor."[63] Coca-Cola had boasted to its bottlers that its 1955 advertising campaign was exactly the work of such experts in "the new technique of 'motivation research' . . . 'clinical psychologists,' 'psychiatrists,' and 'social anthropologists'" attempting "to determine how Coca-Cola fitted into the consciousness (or even sub-consciousness) of our consumers."[64] Researchers argued that the color red,[65] marketing verbiage ("BRIGHT, BRACING . . . DELICIOUS, REFRESHING, WHOLESOME, QUALITY"), and aspirational "dream" models and settings[66] provoked particular psychological responses in consumers. Coca-Cola became central to public concern about the potential manipulation of advertising after one of Packard's "motivational researchers" announced that sales of the drink had increased by 18.1 percent after the words "Drink Coca-Cola" flashed surreptitiously on the screen during a movie. Public outrage led all the way to a congressional investigation and resulted in the major TV networks establishing a policy against "subliminal messages." The experiment failed upon an attempt at replication, and the uproar died down, but a distrust of the ethics of the advertising industry remained. And Packard's larger critique, that the advertising industry perceived the public as docile and manipulable, creating "packaged soul . . . packaged communities," was not so easily dismissed.[67]

Many young advertising "creatives" identified with the sixties' youth generation and sympathized with the criticisms of the advertising industry's treatment of consumers as a homogeneous, obedient mass, and the phoniness and conformism of the ads it produced. Seeing economic potential in this emerging cultural critique and an opportunity to regenerate capitalism with a dose of countercultural style and values, they turned to some of the very "social engineering" approaches Packard had identified, such as "depth" studies of a consumer group's motivations and constructing a brand "personality," for example, to develop new strategies to communicate to narrower markets. To create more subtle, targeted pitches, the advertising industry embraced what it called "market segmentation." Suddenly, the carving out of a youth market presented a dynamic new field for advertising innovation and corporate competition, with the potential for both an accelerated turnover of styles and increased consumption.[68]

ADVERTISING DIFFERENCE

In the early 1960s, an era of unprecedented prosperity, The Coca-Cola Company's advertising was failing to capitalize on the emerging liberatory youth culture of the generation that was coming of age in the United States. Print ads featured "aspirational" images of all-white, upper-middle-class picture-perfect families and wholesome young people. Radio vignettes of mothers offering their teenage sons refreshing Cokes after baseball practice or young women chatting about what food would best go with "family-sized" Coca-Colas at their next party seemed hokey and contrived. And the jingles like "Be Really Refreshed" that invited listeners to "work and play at your best, enjoy the refreshing-est," sung sweetly and repetitively by the McGuire Sisters, sounded cloying and rang false in the ears of 1960s youth.[69]

Pepsi was doing a better job of capturing the younger generation's attention. Pepsi ads directly addressed the young as fellow up-and-comers and even rebellious upstarts. It was the drink "For Those Who Think Young," its 1961–63 advertising campaign proclaimed, and by the end of the decade they were "the Pepsi Generation." In Pepsi TV ads, a quiet setting would be broken by the sound of excitement, like the vroom of a motorcycle or a roller coaster, and California teenager-types would embark on a frenetic, almost anarchic adventure. The form matched the youthful content, using camera work that broke the "rules" of conventional cinematography with swirling arc shots circling around characters and even rotating 360 degrees filming upside down, shots from the inside of soda machines, reflecting off of mirrors or framed by the body parts of characters, dramatic panoramic aerial shots, and intimate extreme close-ups, shot with handheld cameras for a New Wave style, with a soundtrack of lively music and a voice-over urging young consumers to "Come Alive! Come Alive! You're in the Pepsi Generation."[70] Pepsi would meet youth culture wherever it was, the company insisted. In one television spot, a helicopter drops a Pepsi soda machine to a cool young couple on a mountain pass, with the voice-over: "Pepsi belongs to your generation. Why else would Pepsi try so hard to be where you are?"[71] By directly addressing young people as a powerful consumer group with their own tastes, interests, and needs, such advertising encouraged generational identity formation, countercultural style, and the construction of a new consumer market segment in the process.[72]

Some cultural critics have suggested that such advertising prefigured and even spawned the "sixties generation." "Pepsi's fictional liberated generation . . . anticipated the actual youth movement of the 1960s," Thomas Frank claims in *The Conquest of Cool* (1998).[73] It is true that such advertising hailed and empowered young people as a group, but this was only possible because advertising professionals were able to see (and in some cases already themselves embodied) the kinds of cultural, social, and political rebellion going on around them.[74] The genius of the advertisers was to identify the likes of soda brands with youth culture and direct the decade's energetic countercultural celebration of liberation and rejection of the disempowering confines of mass culture towards expressions of freedom of product choice and perceived empowerment through the market. Over the course of a decade, advertisers had succeeded in mobilizing youth culture to change Sloan Wilson's man in the gray flannel suit into "bluejeans capitalism,"[75] enlisting the values of freedom and liberation to provide new social and cultural justifications for the generation's consent to capitalist hegemony.

The Coca-Cola Company feared it might be missing the boat on this vibrant youth-oriented capitalism and, heaven forbid, the "Pepsi Generation": it wanted to be where the kids were, which meant new forms of advertising, international markets, and a hipper connotation. But the Company's long-time advertising agency in the United States, the St. Louis-based D'Arcy agency, seemed out of step with the growing multinational and its goals for growing markets. In 1956, the Company moved its account to McCann Erickson, which boasted a more aggressive outlook on radio advertising and the new medium of television, as well as numerous overseas satellite offices and operations.[76] The Coca-Cola Company wanted to be seen and heard by youth consumers and be central to their culture, which meant being on radio and TV. While D'Arcy had struggled to expand Coca-Cola's branding beyond the single sponsorship of radio and television programs,[77] the year after Coca-Cola moved its account, McCann Erickson became the first agency in the United States, and by implication the world, to bill more than $100 million in television and radio. McCann especially touted its experience in broadcast media in Latin America,[78] where Coca-Cola hoped to grow its market.

The Coca-Cola Company had already worked with McCann Erickson for more than a decade on its international advertising. McCann Erickson had expanded internationally since the 1920s, driven by multinational clients including Standard Oil, General Motors, Gillette, Nestlé, Goodyear, and of course, Coca-Cola, and had twenty-four offices in fifteen countries by 1956.[79] The international side of McCann Erickson's business "mushroomed during the 1960s": by the end of the decade the agency would be doing more business outside the United States than in it, and by the start of the 1970s, it did more international business than any agency in the world.[80] It was not McCann Erickson's international perspective and embrace of broadcast media alone that drew The Coca-Cola Company to the agency, but rather what they suggested in combination: youthful difference in mode of representation. McCann Erickson would be "a symbol of hipness and difference by the late 1960s."[81]

Coca-Cola was in the midst of its major postwar expansion—by 1959 it would be selling drinks in 120 countries around the world.[82] In light of this, the Company's president, William E. Robinson, moved to integrate its international and domestic advertising in a more coordinated global strategy with the multinational McCann Erickson agency. Before the 1950s, the Company had only a $2 million deal with McCann Erickson, spread out over international accounts in various nations, which the agency estimated was 40 percent of the total Coca-Cola Export spent on advertising outside of the United States. Now Coca-Cola became McCann's largest and arguably most important account (second perhaps only to GM's Buick brand), producing all of the Company's US, much of its European, and most of its Latin American and general prototype Export advertising. As a result, Coca-Cola received focused attention from McCann Erickson's dedicated Coca-Cola group, an exclusive "task force" of 121 full-time staff, including creatives from various international offices.[83]

By the mid-1960s, The Coca-Cola Company had become one of the world's "most ambitious practitioners" of the emerging field of global advertising, with its team at McCann Erickson "devoted to discussing the coordination of global marketing strategies." McCann Erickson devised Coca-Cola's advertising on the "one sight, one sound" principle, seeking both to make it cohesive all over the world and to "interrelate advertising in all media, whether visually or aurally." And as the media landscape broadened to include not only print but radio and then television, the advertising aimed to seem intrinsically connected regardless of the medium. "'One Sight' indicates that wherever an advertisement for Coca-Cola appears, it will bear a strong 'family' resemblance to every other advertisement for Coca-Cola," a McCann Erickson newsletter explained. "Each [ad] varies as the requirements of a particular medium dictate, but all are related by certain basic and universally repeated elements. . . . The 'One Sound' concept assures that advertising for Coca-Cola will have a familiar ring no matter where it meets the ear."[84]

McCann Erickson conceived of this as a shift from previous approaches to international advertising. Whereas earlier campaigns had assumed that "what's good for the US is good for the world," simply transplanting advertising that was originally designed for the US market to other parts of the world, with "one sight, one sound" pattern-advertising McCann Erickson and Coca-Cola Export endeavored to conceive of campaigns with "universal" themes that might appeal across international markets. Content was thus created centrally, but with international consumers consciously in mind from the start, further allowing for modifications in different locations, a director for Coca-Cola international advertising at McCann Erickson said in hindsight in 1987, describing it as a "franchised" advertising system.[85] But in the actual power structure of communication, there may have been little difference between these two models of international advertising. In the latter, even if the agency was actively trying to understand and appeal to international audiences and authorized international offices to create their own versions based on prototypes, Coca-Cola's advertising was still conceptualized in New York with an aspiration to the applicability of assumed universal themes. Interviewed again in 2008, the same McCann executive admitted that this model's "think globally, act locally" ideal still led, in practice, to centralized control of the brand's image by McCann and Coca-Cola even as they tried to integrate international perspectives.[86] This was multinational Coca-Cola and McCann Erickson's challenge: to produce prototypes that achieved "standardization and diversity at the same time ... [in a form that] mediated the emerging imperatives of global capital and the cultural particularities of local terrains."[87]

THE CHILDREN OF MARX AND COCA-COLA

A famous intertitle in Jean-Luc Godard's 1966 New Wave film *Masculin féminin* calls the generation that came of age in the 1960s "the children of Marx and Coca-Cola" ("Les Enfants de Marx et de Coca-Cola"). Attempting to keep up with the ongoing social and cultural changes of the 1960s and their unruly "children," The Coca-Cola Company mobilized the representation of both countercultural and minority difference in global advertising that capitalized on youthful cultural rebellion and assertions of minority power, in what Roderick Ferguson has called "an emergent system of hegemonic possibility."[88]

As the Company applied more of its advertising energies to attracting attention from the powerful consumer demographic of post-war baby boomers, McCann Erickson creatives pushed a somewhat reluctant Coca-Cola to take on a new look and sound that would speak their language. McCann Erickson's creative director Bill Backer pointed out that it mattered how the Company addressed 1960s youth—commercials directly targeting the "youth market" would actually repel them. However, by changing the form and style of the advertising, young people could be brought to see it as their own.[89] The Company and its advertising executives accordingly came up with a new spin on the "Things Go Better With Coca-Cola" campaign with a song about all the everyday activities that were better with a Coke in hand, sung by a popular folk-revival group. This "revolutionized jingles forever," *Advertising Age* wrote—because it wasn't a jingle, but rather the "first 'song-form' commercial, geared to the Top 40 radio and rock 'n' roll market."[90] Experimenting with this new form of advertising, the campaign offered thirty-, sixty-, and even ninety-second "songs" of this kind, produced and recorded like the other popular music of the day, in which the lyrics were mostly not about the product being sold, but rather about the things that went better with Coke. The ads sounded like the pop songs heard on the radio, but with references to Coca-Cola slipped in, suggesting that the drink was a natural part of the youth experience. No matter how long the buildup, each song climaxed with the chorus "Things go better with Coca-Cola / Things go better with Coke."

With the songs of "Things Go Better with Coca-Cola," the Company incorporated youth popular culture and the racially diverse performers who were making "authentic" 1960s sounds. For the first time in its advertising history in the United States, the Company hired black and Latino as well as white musicians: R&B and soul musicians The Supremes, Aretha Franklin, Marvin Gaye, Ray Charles, the Shirelles, and Gladys Knight and the Pips, as well as the Mexican *nueva ola* (new wave) rocker Manolo Muñoz and the Nuyorican boogaloo drummer Joe Cuba, in ads targeted at Spanish-language audiences. Rock artists ranged from pop to psychedelic with the Moody Blues, The Who, The Four Seasons, Jay and the Americans, Jan and Dean, the Everly Brothers, Roy Orbison, the Bee Gees, The Mindbenders, The Troggs, as well as pop songstresses Petula Clark, Lesley Gore, and Lulu. International artists like South African Miriam Makeba (a popular singer, but also an exiled anti-apartheid activist who would marry Stokely Carmichael, leader of SNCC and the black power movement), and beat rockers from Argentina (La Joven Guardia), Spain (Los Bravos), and Japan (The Four Leaves), as well as various local talents were hired for international markets.[91]

Coca-Cola's next advertising slogan released in 1969, "It's the Real Thing," epitomized the Company's attempts to harness the cultural and political turn of 1960s youth. To represent Coke as "the real thing," to a generation of consumers who had grown up with as much exposure to Pepsi and were being told they were members of the "Pepsi Generation," was to assert that Coke was the original, authentic cola, an early salvo in a corporate image battle that was becoming known as "The Cola Wars."[92] But it also suggested an acknowledgement of a shift in cultural values. The idea "grew out of listening to pleas of the sixties. 'Take us away from the plastics to basics,'" the McCann Erickson creative Bill Backer said.[93] "The Real Thing" campaign asserted "the genuine, the basic and the authentic qualities of Coke," a Company magazine explained.[94] Over any "real" as in actual attribute of the product—like its taste, refreshment, size, or packaging, which had all previously been highlighted and now seemed superficial—it was a *feeling of realness* and an appeal to notions of authenticity that was being advertised. "If American capitalism can be said to have spent the 1950s dealing in conformity and consumer fakery, during the decade that followed, it would offer the public authenticity, individuality, difference, rebellion," Thomas Frank argues, and there were few more blatant attempts by advertisers than the Coca-Cola slogan "The Real Thing."[95]

To assert Coca-Cola as "the real thing," in a symbolic order of advertising images now criticized as phony but in large part produced by The Coca-Cola Company itself, the Company used race and countercultural aesthetics as signifiers of authenticity and hipness to the changing times. For its history up until the 1960s, the Company's US advertising had been virtually whites-only. There had been only a handful of ads featuring African American athletes (like Jesse Owens or the Harlem Globetrotters) and versions of pattern advertisements with black characters for *Ebony* and the "negro market." And there was a de facto rule against "integrated" advertising.[96] In the few instances when black people had appeared, they were portrayed in subservient roles to whites, as servants and mammy characters.[97] The new visibility of black people in US advertising in this era began to address years of cultural erasure and signal to African American consumers their previously denied cultural and economic power. But the "representation" offered by such images was limited to its service to the market and the profitability of African Americans as paying consumers, leaving actual political, economic, and social issues to other realms. This representational shift was not so much a progressive push for social change as a realization that marketing difference was not only profitable—industry research showed that in the mid-1960s while only 11 percent of the population, African Americans consumed 17 percent of all soft drinks[98]—but that difference was also commodifiable as authentically "real," raw, and countercultural, which the Company marketed to youth consumers of all races.

With the 1969 "Real Thing" campaign, for the first time the Company put out true integrated advertising with black and white characters in the same scene interacting with each other as equals. Its first integrated TV commercial opened in Manhattan with a multiracial group of teenagers playing basketball together, before visuals swept across America, with shots of dirt roads, log cabins, an American flag, to the beaches of California.[99] And the print advertisement "Boys on a Bench" pictured teenaged boys, black and white, sitting shoulder-to-shoulder on a park bench, all the more symbolic because it might have been legally segregated just five years earlier.[100]

FIGURE 11. "Every moment is colored, with Coca-Cola," Hindi advertisement, 1971.

"Real Thing" ads in the United States and across the Company's international markets used popular music and countercultural aesthetics as signifiers of a youth insurgency against what had come before. The Company and McCann Erickson expanded their strategy of seeking out popular music groups to sing ads, avoiding jingles and staged dramatic dialogue, which now sounded phony.[101] Coca-Cola songs performed by the "Godfather of Soul" James Brown tried to capture the sounds of funk's spontaneity and urgency, while the Moody Blues and the 5th Dimension projected Coca-Cola into spacey psychedelic rock and soul.[102] Such advertising played on the otherness of racialized artists and countercultural rock stars, whose sounds and styles seemed implicitly to challenge normative middle-class culture, and suggest

El sabor de lo auténtico,
el sabor real que pide la vida.
Coca-Cola lo tiene.

La chispa de la vida

FIGURE 12. "The spark of life," Latin American advertisement, 1971.

the raw, "real thing," with which Coca-Cola was trying to associate itself. Print advertising featured young people in bell bottoms and holding guitars and even sometimes mimicked the psychedelic style of contemporary concert posters, with their planes of vivid, solid colors and wild, unrestrained images that attempted to make Coke seem rebellious, even hallucinogenic. The Indian ad shown in Figure 11 reflected not just the global hippie aesthetic, which borrowed heavily from South Asian culture, but also its Bollywood reappropriation and reinterpretation in movies like Dev Anand's *Hare Rama Hare Krishna* (1971).[103]

The Company's international pattern campaign for "It's the Real Thing" banked on a global youth culture. The idea that there was a shared generational culture was exciting to a company that was eager to build both new market segments and international markets, but was still wedded to a mostly centralized production of advertising materials. The "Real Thing" campaign proved extremely successful, with translations that played for years in most international markets, including the fiery Spanish language translation "La Chispa de la Vida" ("The Spark of Life") (see fig. 12).[104] The Argentine version of the radio commercial was so popular it was commercially released by RCA and sold 20,000 copies in its first fourteen days on sale in Buenos Aires alone.[105] Although the direct reference to Coca-Cola was removed from the song, after the advertising blitz that preceded it, anyone who heard it would recognize the sound of Coca-Cola.

"The Real Thing" campaign inadvertently articulated in essence a major shift in capitalism's relationship to culture. In the 1960s, advertising went from selling the functional value of products—their attributes and uses—to promoting *brands*. With markets full of relatively standardized quality goods, products competed with each other not by comparing use values but by associating emotional, cultural, and even social connections and desires with the sign value of a brand. To claim a product was "the real thing," while paying little attention to the product itself begs for treatment by theorists of postmodernity, who "projected a vision of commodity culture in which the code of marketing signs did not just take priority over or precede commodities, but subsumed the distinction between object and representation altogether."[106] Freed from having to refer to anything "real" about products, while selling "realness" as the commodity, highly mediated advertising sold constructed brands as self-referential signs. Brands, their images and connotations, began to give value to their products, not the other way around. For a consumer goods company like Coca-Cola that hoped to produce demand through the meanings of its brands, they became the principal site of investment and source of value.[107] Brand Coca-Cola became the Company's most valuable asset.

By the late twentieth century, "commodified forms of cultural representation" saturated daily life becoming "constitutive of the 'cultures'" of much of the developed world.[108] While corporations fiercely defended these commodified forms as their proprietary intellectual property, they also promoted their wide circulation and relied on the collaborative involvement of consumers and other cultural producers to endow them with meanings and associations (memories of your first date at the soda shop or references in Hollywood movies, for example).[109] Brands thus became part of the popular lexicon and public culture, and people began to lay claim to them for their own meaning-making. Coca-Cola's persistence in asserting its presence in everyday life nearly everywhere, made it a shared cultural resource for people around the world. It thus constituted one of the few true examples of global popular culture, and its presence and power made it a signifier that could be used and misused to communicate counterhegemonic cultural politics.

The use of Coca-Cola in expressions of popular discontent exemplified the broader "cultural turn" of the social movements and social theory of the long 1960s. The cultural sphere formed the shared bases for mobilizing groups of people toward social struggle in movements as varied as civil rights to student activism to national liberation. It was a field of social struggle itself, challenging the ruling class, institutions, norms, and codes of behavior and expression. Culture could also be a mode of attack, with organizers and allied cultural producers using forms of cultural expression to draw attention to issues, radicalize populations, develop new ways of seeing and thinking about the present. Such cultural interventions leveraged dominant culture for *détournement* (French for derailment, hijacking, or misappropriation, i.e., the semiotic jiu-jitsu of using the overwhelming power of hegemonic culture against itself) and created alternative cultural formations and styles of life.[110] Finally, as movements and their students tried to understand these new positions and strategies, the theoretical approaches of cultural studies, like that of Gramscian cultural hegemony itself, developed the idea of the cultural as political—the means by which the existing power structure was justified and by which it could be changed.

The political and economic struggles of the long 1960s were thus also waged on the symbolic front, as artists and cultural producers questioned consumer capitalism, the massification of culture, and US imperialism, many through the almost globally ubiquitous commodity sign of Coca-Cola. The final lines of Gil Scott-Heron's poem "The Revolution Will Not Be Televised" (1970) demonstrate the growing critique of the racial and economic politics of American mediated culture and consumer society, in which Coca-Cola and its jingles had made themselves iconic:

> The revolution will not be right back after a message
> about a white tornado, white lightning, or white people.
> You will not have to worry about a dove in your
> bedroom, a tiger in your tank, or the giant in your toilet bowl.
> The revolution will not go better with Coke.
> The revolution will not fight the germs that may cause bad breath.
> The revolution will put you in the driver's seat.

The revolution will not be televised, will not be televised,
will not be televised, will not be televised.
The revolution will be no re-run brothers;
The revolution will be live.[111]

Iconic movies of the time seized Coca-Cola as a symbol of corporate power
and the massification of culture, often displaying a violent desire to rebel
against it, usually ending badly for the Cokes—Coca-Cola vending machines
were shot at in *Dr. Strangelove, or, How I Stopped Worrying and Learned to
Love the Bomb* (1963) and blown up in the Monkees' psychedelic *Head* (1968).

In the graphic arts, pop artists regularly used the brand's trademark script
and hobble-skirt bottle to make overt the ubiquity of the commodity sign,
and comment on and contribute to the fracturing of distinctions between
high and mass culture. Andy Warhol explored the vast reproducibility of the
commodity in his early 1960s Coca-Cola series, as well as in his 1966 screen-
test film that paired Lou Reed of the Velvet Underground with Coke. The
reproduction and recoding of trademarks emerged as a postmodern practice
of meaning-making, sometimes challenging corporate omnipresence, and
making use of a shared semiotic language. While poststructuralist thought
deconstructed capitalist ideologies of authorship, originality, and distinction,
cultural producers made use of corporate intellectual property as common
language.[112] The Coca-Cola Company, however, maintained its reputation
for assiduously policing the use of its trademarks. When, in 1970, the New
York printer Gemini Rising started producing "Enjoy Cocaine" posters using
the brand's distinctive script, colors, and recent advertising slogan (but with
"Raid-Mark" in place of "Trade-Mark"), the multinational shut it down with
a trademark infringement suit.[113] In the age of the brand and postmodern
protest, trademark suits were no longer just about competitive copycats. Now
they revealed corporate desires and fears about brand culture—Coca-Cola
wanted people to connect with its brands, imbue them with meaning, and
disseminate them to other potential consumers, but it also feared the loss of
control of this popularization of meaning.

Coca-Cola became a common motif in critical contemporary Latin
American art in the 1960s and 1970s.[114] In Mexico, Rubén Gámez's 1964
surrealistic film *La fórmula secreta, o Coca-Cola en la sangre (The Secret
Formula, or Coca-Cola in the Blood)*, which won several prizes at the country's first experimental film festival, directly parodied the pop sensibilities of
early 1960s TV commercials and represented Mexican passivity to US imperialism with the image of a patient receiving an intravenous transfusion of

FIGURE 13. *Insertions into Ideological Circuits: Coca-Cola Project,* 1970 © Cildo Meireles
Courtesy Galerie Lelong & Co., New York.

Coca-Cola. The Colombian conceptual artist Antonio Caro repeatedly
painted the country's name in Coca-Cola's trademark Spencerian script and
even inserted it into the red band of its national flag in a series of works he
entitled, simply, *Colombia* (1976), suggesting the entanglement of the state
and global capitalism.[115] The Brazilian Cildo Meireles's "Interçóes em circuitos ideológicos: Projeto Coca-Cola" ("Insertions into Ideological Circuits:
Coca-Cola Project"; 1970), a work of radical performance as well as visual art,
attempted to short circuit the Coca-Cola system by adding political statements onto actual Coca-Cola bottles and returning them into circulation
(fig. 13). While almost invisible when the bottles were empty, once refilled
with the dark Coke as background, they read "Yankees Go Home" or offered
instructions for turning the bottle into a Molotov cocktail. As guerrilla

challenges to US imperialism and the Brazilian dictatorship, Meireles transformed Coke bottles into ideological weapons by turning their material and symbolic ubiquity against themselves in the hope that they might tear at the corporate system as they circulated through it, like malware, and instigate a critical consumption in those that encountered them. The work didn't need a soundtrack, but it could have had one with radical Brazilian composer Gilberto Mendes's 1966 choral composition "Beba Coca-Cola" ("Drink Coca-Cola"). With lyrics taken from Décio Pignatari's anti-jingle poem by the same name, the chorus chants permutations of the sales pitch until the drink becomes *cloaca,* or cesspool, in a disorienting cacophony of voices punctuated by a soloist's loud belch.

A "NEW FORCE FOR PEACE" OR TARGET OF NEW "SOCIAL REVOLUTIONS"

So concerned were the Company's executives about this context of challenges to the Coca-Cola system that in 1970 they held a series of conferences on the subject of "revolution." The first was a three-day special conference on the "youth revolution." Vice presidents, brand managers, planners, researchers, and executives from the Company's advertising agencies heard specialists in anthropology, psychology, journalism, and popular culture, and a Harvard university student discuss "topics including youth tastes, styles, beliefs and identification, young peoples' attitudes toward family and society, dissent and restraint, revolution, reform and disillusionment, and communications for the changing scene."[116]

The next conference was the more forbiddingly titled, "How To Survive in a Social Revolution."[117] In his invitation letter to a potential speaker, Coca-Cola President J. Paul Austin explained the conference's intention by narrating the rise and fall of "great civilizations" from those on the Tigris and Euphrates to the British empire, ending ominously on the image of Rockefeller Center and American capitalism:

[We] must look at the developing challenges for any multinational company, especially an American based one. The relative decline in American military, technical, political, and economic ascendancy will inevitably affect an American business, especially such a symbol of the American way as Coca-Cola. The revolutionary changes in so many attitudes and life styles in the United States affect the world and the world's attitude toward us. And, the exploding power and self-consciousness of other societies from Japan to Russia to Western Europe to the newest developing nation are enormously influencing everyone else, including Coca-Cola. This is our focus . . . change, a forecast of events, movements and influences on the total world stage and a discussion of their meaning to a multinational American based company.[118]

Austin also pondered power shifts within The Coca-Cola Company itself. By the early 1970s almost half of all of the Company's soft drinks were being sold outside the United States, and with executives of "many nationalities," Austin noted, the Company's management itself was becoming more "decentralized." But it was a target of "revolutionary changes in . . . attitudes and life styles" as well as "political and economic changes" that led to criticism of US imperialism and corporate power. Austin considered extreme measures to adapt to those changes, inviting "questions about where we should be based (some neutral nation, perhaps), about our ownership and our organization as well as our products and our social and economic responsibilities. You will find us open to any thoughtful point of view."[119]

Those final lines reveal growing doubt in what had been the Coca-Cola president's extreme confidence in the power of consumer capitalism to bring the world together. In the 1960s, in a speech entitled "A New Force for Peace," Austin had preached about the "miracle of economic growth and change" through international trade and marketing, portraying governments as inflexible, restrictive, and belligerent, in contrast to innovative, liberating internationalist corporations and the free market. Foreshadowing discourses of neoliberal globalization, he argued that corporations and the free market would empower a global citizen-consumer, overturning the old notion of the citizen-producer who needed state protections that impeded the growth of multinationals and international trade and who were then beholden to the dictates of intransigent governments. This partnership between the empowered global consumer and the multinational corporation would drive internationalization, break down barriers to the demand for goods and services, and necessitate cooperation between nations. Austin saw a world beyond Cold War dualism, a new "polycentrism" with "dynamic forces in a number of places" and "the liberation of new and uncommitted nations from a need to join either the Eastern or the Western Bloc." US multinationals were "equipped to cope with that transformation in world alliances" because they had demonstrated "flexibility" and "innovation" in overcoming the "problems raised by nationalism and trade protectionism" through business structures like international "sourcing" as well as "licensing, the granting of franchises, [and] the formation of joint ventures." Now they had the potential to realize their "hope for a 'free world common market.'" Their success would have dramatic social impact as "greater opportunities for free trade mean greater assurance of world-wide peace!" Austin exclaimed, insisting that by encouraging consumer interest in their brands and ensuring international free markets, multinationals like Coca-Cola would be a "new force for peace" around the world.[120]

"TEACH THE WORLD TO SING": ENVISIONING CORPORATE GLOBALISM

The Coca-Cola Company responded to the "social revolutions" of the 1960s, not with material changes to its structure or politics as suggested by the proposal of Austin's conference, but with his vision of Coca-Cola consumption as a "new force for peace" reflected in an ad. The Company pushed "The Real Thing" campaign further, using it as a vehicle not only to advertise globally, but to represent itself as the real global utopic imaginary amid the radical ruptures of the long 1960s in the 1971 addition, "I'd Like to Buy the World a Coke." McCann Erickson creative director Bill Backer was inspired to create "I'd Like to Buy the World a Coke" by the events of the times and the sense that "especially young people, felt a need and a desire for anything that might promote better understanding between various peoples of the world." The idea struck Backer in 1971 when he was flying to London to record Coca-Cola "Real Thing" radio commercials and his transatlantic flight was rerouted to Ireland. Tired and angry, the passengers were forced to spend the night together. But the next morning Backer saw the most combative of them cheerfully sharing Coca-Colas: "it was ten or twelve ounces of commonality between diverse peoples. . . . That was the basic idea: to see Coke not as it was originally designed to be—a liquid refresh[ment]—but as a tiny bit of commonality between all peoples, a universally liked formula that would help them keep each other company for a few minutes." And he had the realization that "this idea's appeal might go beyond the United States, that it could be worldwide."[121]

Backer credits the ad's vision to the diversity of the McCann Erickson creative team. He himself came from a "silver spoon" background of early American settlers and statesmen. His love of Tin Pan Alley songs had inspired him to become a songwriter, a background he would draw upon in creating singing commercials for Coca-Cola. Also on the writing team were

Roger Cook, a rebel white middle-class British songwriter who had created hits for rock-and-roll bands, and Billy Davis, an African American songwriter and producer who had toured the South as one of the Four Tops in the 1950s and worked for Motown Records and Chess Records before advertising executives "cajoled" him into the business.[122]

The process of creating an advertising anthem of global unity was marked by tensions based on these differences, as well as some participants' suspicions about the sincerity and applicability of such a message coming from a corporation. Even in The Coca-Cola Company's recounting of the story, Davis was skeptical of the central premise, saying: "Well, if I could do something for everybody in the world, it would not be to buy them a Coke." Instead, he would "buy everyone a home first and share with them in peace and love."[123] Backer suggests that it was Davis's background that gave him this insight—having a roof over their heads had never been an issue for the other two writers. They started off with the lyric, "I'd like to buy the world a home." But Davis asked: "How many people can afford to *buy* someone a home? We don't want to be just for the rich. How about 'I'd like to *build* the world a home?'"[124] For the TV commercial version, however, the Company went with "buy" and the consumer agency it implied:

> I'd like to buy the world a home and furnish it with love.
> Grow apple trees and honey bees and snow white turtle doves.
> I'd like to teach the world to sing in perfect harmony.
> Sing with me.
> I'd like to buy the world a Coke and keep it company.
> That's the real thing. What the world wants today.
> I'd like to teach the world to sing in perfect harmony
> I'd like to buy the world a Coke and keep it company.
> It's the real thing. Coca-Cola. What the world wants today. It's the real thing.
> Coca-Cola. It's the real thing.

This question of voice, who would be doing this wishing and buying, and its double meaning for a song that required both a perspectival voice and a singing voice, was a repeated concern in the development of a commercial coming from a major multinational corporation. "Without the right tone of voice, 'Buy the World' would become unbelievable—even a joke; a piece of communication that had no validity at all," Backer worried. "Was 'Buy the World' the voice of Coca-Cola, or a much bigger voice—a voice of the times in which we were living, and of which Coke was a very natural part?"

Suggesting the advertising creative's hope that corporate interests could converge with larger social interests of the day, Backer continued: "I decided it was a voice of the time in which Coke would join believably because it was natural that [T]he Coca-Cola Company would wish for an ideal world where consumers could enjoy its product and where the product could play—in a minor way—an active part." "Sure, Coca-Cola is a profit-making corporation," Backer admitted, "but . . . [i]t would try to be the voice of the times— the end of the sixties . . . peace groups are parading in front of the nation's capital, flower children are calling for more understanding among peoples, the time is rapidly ripening for the fruit of this idea to be plucked."[125]

The "fruit of this idea" might be ready to be "plucked" by a corporation like Coca-Cola, but it would only be persuasively consumed by audiences if the song could be sold as sincere. Backer admits to being strategic on this front; cognizant that the commercial was on "thin ice," he "resolved to have the song sung with as much emotion as if it were a true hit folk song of the day—or even a hymn . . . 'the voice' would be bigger than Coca-Cola's." To bring sincerity, Backer told the New Seekers pop folk group, "to make the arrangement warm and universal. Resist the temptation to editorialize on the idea with an arrangement that is tender or cute." The New Seekers, originally from Australia and making their careers in London, had never done a commercial before; their commercial "purity" both worried and attracted the advertising executives. The first takes in the recording studio sounded contrived and Backer had to convince the group that they were purposely not singing a jingle; they should instead sing a "song-form commercial." "The subject of a jingle is a product: 'Pepsi-Cola Hits the Spot (or Is the Choice of a New Generation)' 'The Heartbeat of America is Today's Chevrolet' 'Coke Is It.'" "I'd Like to Buy the World a Coke" was advertising a much bigger concept, Backer insisted. Or, better understood, it would not work as an advertisement for Coca-Cola unless it sounded sincerely like an advertisement for something bigger than Coca-Cola.[126]

The creative directors decided the song should start with the sweet, clear voice of the female lead vocalist, Eve Graham. The wish at the center of the commercial would seem more sincere and innocent coming from a young woman's voice, they reasoned. "We had realized that what we had was more a woman's wish than a man's . . . when a lovely young blond girl, a total amateur, would lip-sync on film to Eve Graham's voice, the wisdom of our instructions would be appreciated. Eve's was a voice that could wish the world a home, and five hundred million listeners all over the world would know she meant it."[127] As a radio ad, this voice was gendered, and once produced for television, it was young *white* womanhood that became the unifying voice of the song's hopeful wish and the point of reference for coding and managing the racial difference of the "others" who comprised the rest of the group.[128] Reflecting dominant racial and gender ideologies, this central voice and image of white womanhood suggested hope, innocence, and benevolence, implicitly expressing who had the legitimacy to articulate such a call to international cooperation and love, while being unthreateningly palatable and almost maternal in order to mind, manage, and moderate the potentially radically different peoples and demands from the margins.

Coca-Cola spent a record $250,000 on filming the television commercial, "Hilltop." The first attempt to create a utopic visual aesthetic to match the sound took place on the otherworldly English White Cliffs of Dover with a cast of several thousand, but rain soaked the scenery and actors, the footage was dark, and the budget was running out. The producers therefore decided to move the shoot to a hilltop outside of Rome, Italy, where they had heard they could find similarly pastoral, visually denationalized terrain, as well as good weather. As director, they hired Haskell Wexler, no less—fresh from shooting films about the Chicago Democratic National Convention protests, the My Lai massacre, the Brazilian military's torture of radicals, and Chilean socialist president Salvador Allende—to provide a countercultural aesthetic. The cast of sixty-five principals from more than twenty countries were dressed to represent international peoples and called the "First United Chorus of the World." They were backed by twelve hundred lip-syncing Italian teenagers to increase the appearance of the size of the global chorus.

While everything seemed to be in place to portray the utopic vision of global unity, the shooting was almost dystopian. Producers left hundreds of teenage extras shut in buses for four sweltering hours while Wexler and the team filmed the principal cast members. The extras, whom Backer describes as institutionalized "orphans," were hot and angry at the shoot field marshals, who had not explained to them why they were there, and had failed to share with them any of the Coca-Colas from the truck waiting on-site to supply the commercial. When they were finally let off the buses to populate the commercial's final dramatic helicopter shot to evoke the earthly connectedness of humanity, and were handed Coke bottles to hold as symbols of harmonious connection, they more accurately portrayed contemporary youth rebellion, storming up the pristine grassy hillside and hurling the bottles at the helicopter. That is, until they ran out of bottles, at which point they "stampeded" down the hillside to the Coke truck and tried to overturn it. Wexler abandoned the project suddenly, forcing the producers to find Italian filmmakers to reshoot the commercial yet again.[129]

ENVISIONING CAPITALIST
HEGEMONY FROM A HILLTOP

The final commercial plays on the metaphor of the "chorus," in both audio and visual forms, to portray a diverse collective of cultures, together constituting one world, united in voice and consumption of the global commodity, Coke. Only a few years after the "It's the Real Thing" campaign's first racially integrated ads, "Hilltop" endeavored to portray the diversity of the entire world. Graham's voice and the image of the young, white woman on screen leads the commercial and the chorus, with the rest of the group slowly building as the camera pans to take in different members, side by side in long, well-ordered, straight lines (fig. 14). They comprise the "First United Chorus of the World," a tokenist multicultural group of representatives, distinguished by traditional folk costumes, each standing for a people, and together unthreateningly suggesting the possibility of global harmony.

This international assemblage of youth consumers was mirrored by another international group, inscribed in the crawling text at the end of the commercial: Coca-Cola's franchise bottlers.

> On a hilltop in Italy
> We assembled young people
> From all over the world
> To bring you this message
> From Coca-Cola Bottlers
> All over the world
> It's the real thing—Coke.

Visually and sonically, the commercial evoked the countercultural ethos of the day. Shots dissolve into each other, creating a psychedelic panoply of color; lines of brightly dressed multicultural youth lead into a lingering focus on the face of a white woman emphatically singing before dissolving into an ethereal overhead shot of the collective whole (fig. 15). The pop folk-rock style of the song played on the musical authenticity of the moment, while the sing-along lyrics and harmonies of the singers suggested a closeness and intimacy

Quisiera al mundo...

Quisiera al mundo darle hogar
y llenarlo de amor
sembrar mil flores de color
y de felicidad...

Quisiera al mundo yo enseñar
la perfecta armonía
con un abrazo y buen humor
y esta alegre canción...

Con un abrazo y buen humor
y perfecta armonía
el mundo entero ha de cantar
esta alegre canción...

Hay que compartir
el momento feliz
hay que disfrutar
la chispa de la vida...

Quisiera ver por una vez
el mundo en libertad
podemos si queremos ser
felices de verdad...

Ven amigo mío
hay que celebrar
dame tu sonrisa
mi amor es tu hogar...

Podemos con amor y paz
barreras destruir
y ver la gente de un país
pasar a otro país...

Quisiera al mundo darle hogar
y llenarlo de amor
sembrar mil flores de color
y de felicidad.

Su Embotellador
de Coca-Cola

FIGURE 14. "I'd like the world..." Latin American advertisement, 1971.

of community.[130] World peace is never directly mentioned in the text, but implied throughout, most directly through the sonic metaphor in the lyric, "I'd like to teach the world to sing in perfect harmony." This harmonious utopia is set in the pastoral space of the hilltop where political perspectives as radical as racial equality, the distribution of resources, and countercultural utopian communities' codes of generosity, egalitarianism, and earthy simplicity are gestured at, if made palatably vague and consumable.

The commercial and its song struck a chord with a remarkably large audience. The sing-a-long ease of its folksong style invited listeners to join the "First United Chorus of the World." The Coca-Cola Company received the

FIGURE 15. Still from *Hilltop* commercial, 1971.

largest volume of mail it had received on any one subject—more than a hundred thousand letters—from consumers enthusiastically responding to the commercial. People called in to radio and television stations requesting the commercial. Both the New Seekers and a group of studio singers quickly formed by Davis released commercial versions of "I'd Like to Teach the World to Sing," with Coke references removed from the lyrics. They sold a combined one million copies in a year, and the New Seekers' version became a top 10 hit, the other also reaching #13 on the US charts. The song was rerecorded in several languages and amazingly, according to Coca-Cola, sold more sheet music than any song in the previous ten years. Under an agreement with the writers, The Coca-Cola Company donated the first $80,000 in royalties earned from the song to UNICEF.[131] The song was especially popular with churches, schools, and social organizations, which sang the Coke-less version, sincerely wishing for a world in "perfect harmony."

To this day, the "I'd Like to Buy the World a Coke" TV commercial is mentioned as beloved and iconic advertising, with headlines declaring it "the world's most famous ad."[132] Audiences were moved by the commercial's imaginary of world peace, multiracial society, resource-sharing, and collectivity beyond national borders. What was perhaps the Company's most successful advertisement arose from its partial assimilation of the values and styles most closely aligned with its challengers in the period's insurgent social movements and countercultures.

Contemporary viewers can see in the ad the limitations and political problematics of this partial, corporate assimilation. In the ad's representation of racial and international difference and youth counterculture as mere signification, "I'd Like to Buy the World a Coke" symbolically annihilated the politics that was actually bringing together multiracial collectives of young people amid the upheavals of the era. Even the ad's celebration of "harmony," a lack of dissonance despite difference, suggested world peace as the lack of conflict, a post-political project that erased structural power. Instead, the ad's harmony played on the difference of others to suggest their significant similarity: their common thirst for Coca-Cola, "what the world wants today." The commercial mobilized the presence of those that signified youthful insurgency and racial and postcolonial liberation to legitimate the ad's vision of hegemony. "I'd Like to Buy the World a Coke" projected a neoliberal single world order, where diverse peoples could peacefully and freely be sold on, and thus share in, the consumption of Coca-Cola. In the spirit of J. Paul Austin, Coca-Cola consumption was, if only in a commercial, a "new force for peace."

Even historical contemporaries saw in the commercial the representation of a new global capitalist hegemony that would soon be termed neoliberalism. Huey Newton, leader of the Black Panther Party, would comment in the early 1970s that this commercial envisioned a new global development of capitalism, and perhaps even of its challengers, since the global economy united people in exploitation across national borders. "Do you recall the Coca-Cola jingle: 'I'd love [sic] to buy the world a Coke...'?" he asked fellow revolutionary Elaine Brown. "It means that the US capitalists have taken a turn, a right turn. And I think it's affecting the economic structure of the entire world. We're in a brand new game ... we can't define the world anymore as a collection of sovereign states with independent economies. What this bit of advertising bullshit triggered in my mind is that a new economic arrangement has taken hold, one that exists irrespective of language, custom, ideology, flags, and, most of all territory."[133] The result was a "global economic structure" that could only be challenged by "global revolution," Newton concluded.[134]

In the production of "Hilltop," The Coca-Cola Company capitalized on the emerging "new economic arrangement" in the production of its advertising as well as its drinks. The commercial's off-shore filming location contributed to the supranational feel that the commercial's creators desired, but was largely motivated by profit. Coca-Cola and McCann Erickson, which had underwritten some of the commercial's soaring budget, believed that they could recoup production costs by selling it in advertising packages to international bottlers. But the financial structures of the international cul-ture industries provided a hitch: US commercial talent received residual pay-ments every time a commercial aired, even in foreign countries. The Company feared that international bottlers and subsidiaries would be deterred if they were responsible for such payouts to the cast of the United Chorus of the World and their off-screen counterparts every time the commercial aired in their markets. But the unequal political economic playing field of the inter-national culture industries also provided a loophole: European actors and singers did not receive such residuals.[135] So the Company embarked on what would become known as "runaway production," filming outside the US to minimize expense, often with cheaper, nonunionized labor. Thus, in both its imagery and production, "I'd Like to Buy the World a Coke" marked a shift to the era of global advertising campaigns for The Coca-Cola Company; for the first time the Company was internationally producing an ad with an international audience in mind that aimed to represent the international, rather than having it patterned as an afterthought.

But given the televisual form, the high cost of filming, and thus the cen-tralized control of the production of advertising content, this commercial also suggested that more of the visions of the Coca-Cola world would be from the perspective of Atlanta and New York than before. In late 1971, Coca-Cola Export sent "I'd Like to Buy the World a Coke/Hilltop" to inter-national marketing offices along with more than twenty other pattern televi-sion commercials for "The Real Thing" campaign,[136] and by February of 1972 the commercial was airing on radio and television, as well as in movie theat-ers, in "all Zones [Europe, Africa, Latin America, and the 'Far East']."[137] International offices created translated versions of the song for radio and dubbed the existing commercial for television.

Coca-Cola Export discouraged major adaptation of these television com-mercials. Print and even radio ads could be developed and executed centrally, but modified, sometimes significantly, when they traveled to different mar-kets. Images could be redrawn (or reshot if photographic), local music and language rerecorded relatively cheaply—all according to specific directions and subject to central approval, of course. But TV commercials were a differ-ent matter: the audio could easily be changed through dubbing without too much cost, but it was expensive for international offices and bottlers to reshoot film. The result was that in US pattern footage, the people were racially and culturally coded as American. Making the ads appear more overtly foreign, the mouthed words on screen did not synch up with dubbed audio. Coca-Cola Export tried to get around this by producing cartoons or live-action TV spots with no on-screen dialogue to allow for easy dubbing. Later the Company produced different versions of ads for regions defined by the ethno-racial presentation of the actors and image montages to which music and voice-overs could be added later for different markets. Coca-Cola Export initiated a "TV/Cinema Subscription Service" "to illustrate film production 'ideas' and to serve as a 'story-board' guide to aid Advertising Managers responsible for maintaining film quality in those overseas territories where local production may be required."[138] But, given the cost of shooting film, Coca-Cola Export remained concerned that international offices and bottlers could not guarantee the much-guarded quality of the representation of the Coca-Cola brand. Thus, Coca-Cola Export encouraged its international managers to rely on the centrally produced materials rather than produce their own locally. As a 1966 Coca-Cola Export Marketing News Bulletin sent to international marketing managers forcefully argued, it made more financial and creative sense (in their opinion, to ensure "one sight, one sound") to make use of the supplied pattern footage with simple modifications to the soundtrack. In that single year, Coca-Cola Export "shipped film prints and reproduction materials for 244 films" to international offices for their use. It was "wasteful duplication of effort and of expenditure ... [if] each territory produces original films locally," when using the pattern footage saved 80 percent of the cost of producing each film locally. Instead, Coca-Cola Export exhorted, the money saved should be spent buying more airtime and increasing the number of times audiences saw Coca-Cola commercials.

Dubbing "I'd Like to Buy the World a Coke/Hilltop," rather than having international offices produce their own patterned versions was typical of the representational strategies of "the global era of Coca-Cola" advertising.[139] Increasingly over the 1980s and 1990s, The Coca-Cola Company privileged central control of global brand representation over what little local variation was produced by the earlier model of pattern advertising. The commercials for "Coke is It" in the 1980s and "Always Coca-Cola" in the 1990s developed universal themes and generic situations like "young love," "amusement park," "the big game," and "at the beach" in quick montages easily dubbed for different languages. These campaigns assumed that cultural difference could be managed and represented from the center, with a dozen different versions of the same commercial shot all at the same time to ensure consistency, but with different racially coded casts, to be sent to the major regional markets of the world and subsequently dubbed for smaller linguistic markets. This centralization, or consolidation, of the symbolic system of production mirrored the Company's larger strategy of reshaping its material world system, manifested most prominently in the consolidation of its franchise bottling system beginning in the 1980s (in the United States) and in the much of the rest of the world in the 1990s. These two consolidations emerged from the same logic of corporate globalism that imagined one world under Coca-Cola in "I'd Like to Buy the World a Coke."

"I'd Like to Buy the World a Coke" offered a utopic vision of global unity, but one meant to supplant other counterhegemonic social and cultural movements with a good dose of Coca-Cola. Thus, in the succeeding decades, Coca-Cola and McCann Erickson executives would refer to the ad in both visionary and reactionary terms as "captur[ing] the imagination of an entire generation ... as the world was healing from the turbulent 1960s."[140] The Coca-Cola Company asserted itself as a global corporation and a sign of the global, but also assuaged fears—even its own—by suggesting that the world's peoples and "social revolutions" would be appeased by "a new force for peace": a new capitalist hegemony offering the freedom to consume the global brand.

FOUR

Indianize or Quit India

NATIONALIST CHALLENGES TO COCA-COLA
IN POSTCOLONIAL INDIA

ON A HOT SUMMER DAY in the early 1970s, the Indian socialist labor leader and politician George Fernandes was visiting a small village and asked for a glass of water. But the local officials refused to let him drink the village's water—it was not potable, they said—and instead brought him Coca-Cola. "Something is wrong," Fernandes remembers thinking, "thirty years of freedom and planning and we have Coke that has reached the villages, but we do not have drinking water."[1] Several years later in 1977, as the newly elected Janata Party's industry minister, Fernandes would argue that "people need drinking water, not Coca-Cola,"[2] insisting that at a time when 90 percent of Indian villages still lacked access to safe drinking water, money that could be put to ameliorating their dire situation was being sent out of India in profits to The Coca-Cola Company.[3] There was no reason for a multinational corporation to be extracting capital from India in the sale of a high-profit consumer good that did not productively contribute to the Indian economy and stifled indigenous production. Indian industry could produce soft drinks, perhaps even in smaller-scale plants in rural locales, employing people and bringing "development" to "backward" areas.

"The activities of The Coca-Cola Company in India during the last 25 years furnish a classic example of how a multinational corporation operating in a low-priority, high-profit area in a developing country attains runaway growth and, in the absence of alertness on the part of the Government concerned, can stifle the weaker indigenous industry in the process," Fernandes told the Lok Sabha, or lower house of the Indian Parliament.[4] During the Company's time in India, it had remitted far more money back to the United States than it had invested in India, Indian government officials argued. The Indian government decided the Coca-Cola Export Corporation must

"Indianize" ownership of its operations in the country, both in terms of financial equity and manufacturing "know-how," or leave entirely. By the end of 1977, The Coca-Cola Company was no longer in business in India.

The Company's dramatic 1977 exit from India elucidates the forces that drove one of the greatest challenges to the Coca-Cola world system—the threat of nationalization—through an analysis of the Indian state's efforts to address multinational corporations' extraction of profits from its "developing" economy. The Company's departure from India, although with particularities specific to this corporation and national context, was emblematic of broader struggles, debates, and formations of the historical moment. For "developing" countries of the global south, it was the beginning of the end of a period of open questioning of and alternatives to the economic futures laid out by the "developed" north. Out from under the yoke of colonialism, but living with its legacies and facing growing debt and dependency, leaders of a number of nations attempted to chart a course of more equitable relations in an economy increasingly cast as global but still dominated by a few countries. But these politically if not economically independent nations, including India, struggled to define the terms of their development, and the role of multinational corporations like The Coca-Cola Company therein. The Indian postcolonial state succeeded in drawing attention to the structural inequalities of the international regimes of financial and intellectual property. But rather than throwing off their assumptions, it sought to work within them for the benefit of national development, mobilizing a discourse of nationalism to the advantage of a national industrial bourgeoisie and not the Indian people on the whole. This history demonstrates the possibilities—and pitfalls—of nationalist critiques of transnational capitalism, which may use the language of shared national interest to further ingrain the class structure of winners and losers among those of the same nation.

In the late 1970s, The Coca-Cola Company became the most prominent corporation forced to abide by the rules of India's Foreign Exchange Regulation Act (FERA) of 1973. FERA regulated the flow of foreign currency out of India and thus targeted multinational corporations such as Coca-Cola that repatriated their profits to their corporate home countries, draining dollars from Indian foreign-exchange reserves. The Company made these profits through its US-based subsidiary, the Coca-Cola Export Corporation, and its wholly owned Indian subsidiary of the same name, which charged for soft-drink concentrates, equipment and supplies, marketing materials, and sales and technical assistance to Indian franchise bottlers like the Singh family's Pure Drinks company, and then remitted the profits back to the Company and its stockholders.

For decades the Indian government struggled to maintain reserves of foreign currency, especially US dollars, which were used to peg the value of the Indian rupee. The US government had recently unmoored the dollar from the gold standard during its own economic crisis in the early 1970s, a signal moment in neoliberalism, propelling—as David Harvey and others have argued—the financialization of capital through speculation in newly floating currencies.[5] In the global financial system, the Indian government could not influence the rupee's exchange rate without foreign-currency reserves, thus limiting the nation's capacity both to buy foreign technology deemed essential for development and to repay foreign debt, which rapidly increased as the rupee's value fell. When the Indian government invoked FERA in 1977, it demanded that The Coca-Cola Company "Indianize" its business in the country by divesting at least 60 percent of its shares of Coca-Cola Export's Indian subsidiary to Indians. In addition, FERA required that Coca-Cola Export transfer its technology to Indian management, sharing manufacturing "know-how"—and thus the Company's well-guarded "secret formula"—by putting the production of concentrates in Indian hands. With an Indian-owned and -operated subsidiary producing and selling Coca-Cola's soft-drink concentrates, more profits and industry knowledge would remain in the country. And there was no reason for a foreign company to be making such large profits when Indian industry could produce bubbly drinks on its own, the government maintained. If Coca-Cola did not "Indianize," the Company had to leave.

The controversy over Coca-Cola and FERA occupied proceedings of the Lok Sabha, news headlines, advertising, and public debate for several months in 1977, a year of large-scale political upheaval in India that ended a nearly two-year long suspension of democracy and civil liberties known as "the Emergency," bringing the Janata Party to power as the first non-Congress ruling party since Independence. The Coca-Cola Company's departure in response to calls for Indianization marked both a major blow to the Coca-Cola world system and a dramatic moment in the economic history of India. The debates that led to the Company's departure evidenced a complex melding of critiques of US power, theories of the structural inequality of the international economic system, renegotiated socialist plans for the postcolonial state, and deep-seated discourses of economic and cultural nationalism within India. By publicly challenging Coca-Cola, the Indian government targeted a simultaneously symbolic and material manifestation of the capitalist world system, capturing the imaginations of both Indians and members of the international business community alike.

In India in the late 1970s, politicians directly challenged the developmentalist logic The Coca-Cola Company used to forward its business around the world. The Company had long promised that Coca-Cola's production would not only enrich bottling franchise owners, but would also bring needed economic development by providing employment, expanding related industries like bottle manufacturing and refrigeration, and stimulating sales for local shops and food establishments through the promotion of mass consumption of its product. The Company had attempted to discursively as well as materially justify its business through the logic of the franchise, promoting its product as simultaneously global and local and purveying its multinational developmentalism to the developing world. But as the nationalist challenge in India suggests, Coca-Cola's developmentalist self-promotion was not always persuasive.

To Coca-Cola, the calls for Indianization sounded all too familiar. Over the preceding decade, threats to its business had emerged all around the world, including the nationalization of bottling operations in Latin America. The communist "Second World" was already closed to Coke, branded as a US imperialist and capitalist monopoly, and such challenges were now also appearing in nonaligned "Third World" countries, whose potential consumers of its soft drinks were central to the Company's expansion. In the late 1960s, Arab League nations had instituted a boycott of Coca-Cola for doing business in Israel and thus legitimating Zionist settler colonialism. In countries like Egypt, the ban was driven by demands for economic decolonization (which linked Israel to Western imperialism and Coke to both) and by concern over the Company's foreign-exchange depletion.[6] The Arab boycott severely limited the Company's business in the Middle East and Africa, especially affecting its Indian subsidiary, which had been a principal exporter of soft-drink concentrate to the Middle East. After 1974, the drop in such exports resulted in a 30 percent decline in India's foreign-exchange earnings (profits remitted to India in international currencies), one of the few means by which the Company could justify its existence in India to a government concerned about the extraction of foreign corporations' profits.[7] The loss of India, one of the Company's largest prospective markets, was a further blow, but for sixteen years after its exit in 1977, the Company chose to stay out of the country rather than establish a precedent by Indianizing its subsidiary there.

MULTINATIONALS AND CALLS FOR A NEW
INTERNATIONAL ECONOMIC ORDER

The Coca-Cola Company departed India in the context of mounting international and national critiques of multinational corporations in the global economy, especially their neocolonial role in the "developing" countries that constituted the majority world (with most of the world's population but disproportionately little economic power). This growing critique of corporate neocolonialism was articulated in direct policy demands in 1974 when the Group of 77 (G-77) countries from Africa, Asia, and Latin America, including India, proposed a New International Economic Order (NIEO) at the United Nations, beginning a north-south dialogue to facilitate the development of the global south on its own terms. NIEO's tenets prominently included states' rights over global corporations doing business in their countries, confirming their powers in the "regulation and supervision of the activities of transnational corporations by taking measures in the interest of the national economies of the countries where such transnational corporations operate."[8] Broadly, the NIEO attempted to remake the global economic order by confirming developing countries' sovereignty over their natural resources and economic activities, as well as their economic policies, including the interventionist promotion of import substitution, the protection of local firms from large multinationals, and "the right to nationalization or transfer of ownership to its nationals," while also proposing liberal economic exchange in the form of a "just and equitable" relationship between the prices for the raw materials and products exported from the Third World and those imported from the First World. To ensure this, the NIEO was based on the principles of "securing favourable conditions for the transfer of financial resources to developing countries" and "promoting the transfer of technology [from developed economies to developing ones] and the creation of indigenous technology," principles India would attempt to actualize in FERA.[9] As a result of the NIEO's increased attention on the rise of multinational corporations, the UN established both the Commission on Transnational Corporations (CTC) and the Information and Research Centre on Transnational Corporations (IRCTC). The IRCTC was charged with reporting on the effects of the activities of multinational corporations in developing countries, assisting in securing international arrangements that encouraged the "positive contributions" of multinationals to national development and world economic growth while curbing "their negative effects" and strengthening the negotiating capacity of developing countries in their dealings with multinational corporations.[10] The CTC attempted to formulate a "Code of Conduct on Transnational Enterprises" to delineate the responsibilities of multinationals to host economies, raising the ire of corporations and their home nations. Through the 1970s, the role of multinational corporations in the world economy was being openly challenged by a newly powerful bloc of nations from the majority world asserting the power of nation-states to regulate global capital.

But the NIEO also signaled the beginning of the end of such radically alternative thinking about economic futures generated by the 1960s and 1970s social and intellectual movements. Its emphasis on sovereign national interests belied its vulnerability to domination by national bourgeoisies. The NIEO negotiated a socialist rebuttal of global capitalism from the south, with calls from the global south's liberal elites "to realize a long-standing dream of world capitalism: that is, to ensure continuing growth of the system as a whole by better integrating the peripheral countries."[11] It called for economic growth in "developing countries," an expansion of world trade, and increased aid by the "developed countries" of the industrial north, with the simple demand that global south states be able to govern the extension of capitalism. As Gilbert Rist has argued, the model of third-world development proposed by the NIEO and other development-minded liberal global south elites maintained the basic presuppositions of mainstream economics: a privileging of growth and attainment of a northern level of consumption. The underlying aims were modernization and industrialization, increasing economic productivity, capturing foreign markets with exports, instilling bourgeois values of economic rationality and efficiency, all mostly unimpeded by concern with the ecological or cultural consequences of development, or the fact that its benefits were not distributed across classes within a nation.[12] It called for changes to the rules of the game so that elite global south players could start to win, but not an end of the game itself.

Organized resistance from corporations and their home countries stymied proposals for a NIEO, and by the 1980s a changed political-economic environment, including stagflation in the north and the divergent trajectories of global south oil-rich nations from those facing continued poverty and growing indebtedness, had led to a turn to market-led development policies. By the end of the millennium, the United Nations had fundamentally shifted its approach to multinational corporations; whereas the NIEO's code of conduct warned about the "obstacles multinationals might pose to the developmental objectives of states," by the end of the 1990s, the UN collaborated with corporations and states as "equal stakeholders in the search for solutions to the challenges of globalization."[13]

But in the 1970s, key leaders in India, as in many of the newly independent nations of the global south, bristled at the prospect of continuing economic colonialism through its corollary relationships with transnational corporations and economic interests, after having thrown off the yoke of political and military domination. Third World nationalists and socialists were eager to gain some control of the vital resources within their newly sovereign national borders, often with the intent to use them to aid a citizenry clamoring for rights and welfare. In the context of postcolonial assertions of national identity, which had been restrained under colonialism, foreign companies engendered special ire because of their association with former colonial powers, their employment of foreigners in executive positions, their poor treatment of local workers, and their perceived representation of alien cultural values.[14] Extractive transnational corporations were the most blatant agents of neocolonialism, controlling and draining resources from the wealth of the developing world and transferring them to their home countries. But commercial multinationals could also substantially hinder developing economies as materials or fully manufactured products (often produced with the very raw materials extracted from the global south) were imported from abroad and sold in countries like India, draining them of currency and creating dependency on developed economies by purchasing rather than producing such goods for themselves. FERA was a key part of the Indian government's attempt to address the outflow of money from India to the home countries of multinational companies and seize the reins of productive power through technology transfer.

Even before the end of World War II, Indian politicians and industrialists began proposing limits to foreign corporations' influence. The Reconstruction Committee of the Viceroy's Council, formed in 1943 and led by the director of the powerful Indian Tata group of companies, planned a postwar economic program that included government nationalization or regulation of public utilities, railways, and new industries considered vital to development. These pre-Independence leaders thought government regulation of industry could ensure production in high-priority fields, the location of industry in certain areas of the country, fair labor conditions, satisfactory quality without runaway profits, and the retention of profit within national borders.[15] The group feared that foreign capital, especially the "India Ltds," as the growing branches and subsidiaries of British multinational corporations were called, would dominate the new postwar economic opportunities on the subcontinent. But Indian economic leaders also believed that they needed foreign assistance in developing national industries. Thus, the Indian government proposed that foreigners should be limited to owning a minority interest of Indian companies in key sectors (like metals, engineering, machinery, chemicals, fertilizers, and pharmaceuticals). This conflicted with British interests and the 1935 Government of India Act, which provided "'safeguard' conditions for British business," resulting in the British government's rejection of the Indian government's 1945 proposals for industrial policy.[16]

From Independence in 1947, the stated policy of the ruling Congress Party was to limit the role of foreign corporations and to encourage the development of indigenous enterprise, but no specific legislation was introduced to address these goals.[17] Similarly, there were no restrictions on foreign ownership of Indian corporate subsidiaries, although government authorities informally and often inconsistently exerted pressure on foreign companies. A 1948 industrial policy resolution described foreign capital as valuable to the industrialization of the new nation, but outlined that every proposal for a new enterprise that had foreign capital investment and management required review and approval by the central government.[18]

In 1949, after negotiating a World Bank loan, Jawaharlal Nehru's government shifted its policy towards multinationals. A foreign exchange crisis had hit India, leaving the new country with small reserves of foreign currency, a weak rupee abroad and inflation at home. The foreign-exchange crisis threatened India's ability to acquire the foreign capital goods and technologies to enable indigenous development and enact import-substitution policies. In this climate, the government changed its policy; it would tolerate multinational corporations, even those that maintained complete foreign ownership and control, if they brought technology and investment into India. Nehru argued that foreign investment and technological know-how were necessary for India's development. To attract foreign firms, the Indian government announced that regulation of foreign capital would be the same as that of Indian capital and foreign companies would be permitted to repatriate profits to their corporate home countries.[19] In 1957, the Congress government again shifted to a more liberal policy towards foreign enterprises justified by another foreign-exchange crisis. As a result, by 1967, foreign companies controlled one-fifth of India's corporate assets, up from one-tenth in 1957.[20]

By the mid-1960s, wars with China and Pakistan had led to massive increases in defense spending, and two dry monsoon seasons had resulted in drops in agricultural production. Food shortages and the threat of famine led to increased imports (as well as significant foreign assistance), expending India's already drained foreign-exchange reserves. The United States, the World Bank and the IMF wanted India to further liberalize its trade regulations, devalue the rupee, and adopt a new agricultural strategy.[21] India complied, and then with the resulting assistance of foreign aid and participation of multinational corporations, made major state investment in agriculture, launching the so-called Green Revolution.

In the mid-1960s, even after devaluing the rupee and liberalizing trade as global financial institutions insisted, the Indian recession worsened, failing in the objectives of greater global economic integration through increasing exports and attracting foreign capital through now rock-bottom prices for those paying in foreign currency. India was already in debt to the World Bank and seeking more loans for development. Frustration grew over global north nations' restrictions on free trade to protect their own agriculture and industries, thus limiting India's export potential while simultaneously pressuring India to keep its markets open to imports. The country needed foreign-exchange reserves to import technology and goods as well as pay off growing international debts. In the late 1960s, to address the fiscal deficit and crisis of foreign-currency reserves caused by large international capital outflows, the government drastically slashed expenditures, resulting in cuts to the public sector.[22] The devaluation of the rupee had forced up prices of commodities for Indians, and as unemployment grew and food scarcity continued, the deteriorating economic conditions led to mass unrest directed at the failures of capitalist development.[23]

Militant movements of workers, peasants, and students arose over specific issues like higher wages and rights to land, as well as in general opposition to the Congress government and continued social inequities. This explosion of social movements radicalized Indian politics in the late 1960s and early 1970s, and Indira Gandhi's Congress Party could only retain power with the support of the country's communist parties under the campaign slogan *Garibi hatao* ("eliminate poverty"). The new, more radical socialism of the Indian ruling party that emerged from this period brought a series of government regulations of the economy, including a complex system of licensing that limited the scope of foreign companies and large Indian industrial houses to the "core sector" of critical and strategic industries, restricted foreign-exchange outflows, and established a process of review for business ventures, especially those with foreign capital investment, all part of an economic nationalist response.[24] Its critics called this regulatory system the "License Raj." FERA was one of its principal components.

DE-COCA-COLONIZATION: FERA AND
THE INDIAN STATE'S CHALLENGE TO
THE COCA-COLA WORLD SYSTEM

FERA required foreign companies to incorporate subsidiaries in India and dilute their foreign equity share (non-Indian shareholdings) to less than 40 percent. New Indian shareholders would take up the remaining 60 percent of stock, thus Indianizing ownership. Upon completion of the mandated divestiture, these local subsidiaries of foreign corporations would be treated as Indian companies under the law.[25] These new Indianized corporations would pay dividends to Indian shareholders as well as to investors in the metropole. Businesses in core industries, or those that used sophisticated technology, developed trade, skills or infrastructure not indigenously available, or contributed significantly to national exports, would receive exemptions and be allowed to retain a higher foreign equity share. High-profit, low-tech, "non-priority" consumer goods companies like Coca-Cola were especially vulnerable.[26]

FERA was "one of the most controversial controls on foreign investment" in the world, according to a contemporary US business textbook,[27] and it was rapidly changing the international business landscape in India. By the end of 1981, almost 900 companies had applied for permission to operate under FERA, with the Indian government granting approval to nearly 250 of them without dilution of foreign equity (of which around 100 already had less than 40 percent foreign equity), and to approximately 360 after dilution. Of that latter group, 245 companies diluted their foreign equity share to 40 percent or less, while the rest negotiated higher equity holdings based on agreements regarding the terms of their future operation in India. The Indian government directed nearly 100 companies to close their operations in the country or end their nonresident status. Another 14 companies received permission from the Indian government but decided to close their operations and leave India regardless. Finally, more than a dozen companies were either nationalized or compelled to make strategic mergers with other companies.[28]

The Coca-Cola Company was one of the first targets of FERA, and was by far the most significant, in both material and symbolic terms. In 1958, the

Indian government had granted the US-based Coca-Cola Export Corporation permission to set up an Indian subsidiary for the manufacture of concentrates from imported raw materials, "ostensibly for the purpose of saving foreign exchange spent on the import of concentrates" by the then four bottling plants in India. The subsidiary was allowed to manufacture the concentrates so long as production would be limited to the needs of the existing four plants. Instead, "taking advantage of the facts that the manufacture did not require an industrial license and that the Registration Certificate did not stipulate any approved capacity . . . the Company expanded its capacity enormously within the next few years from 3 lakhs to 26 lakhs kg [one lakh = a hundred thousand] of concentrates per annum without seeking any formal approval from the Government," a later, more regulatory Indian government noted in 1997. This increased concentrate production enabled Coca-Cola Export to expand its Indian bottling system, supplying concentrates to fourteen new franchised bottling plants in addition to those run by Pure Drinks, for a total of twenty-two Indian Coca-Cola bottling plants by 1970.[29] The Indian government expressed concern over the Company's foreign-exchange remittances before the 1973 passage of FERA, and after it, the Company encountered frequent difficulties renewing its industrial licenses, even though weak enforcement of the act allowed its ongoing growth. By the early 1970s, Coca-Cola had attained a dominant position in the beverage industry, beating its primary Indian rival, Parle, and was "fast on its way to becoming almost a national drink."[30]

Pursuing The Coca-Cola Company with the terms of FERA, the Indian government alleged that between 1958 and 1974, the Company had invested more than Rs 6 lakhs (660,000 rupees) in cash, plant, and machinery but had remitted about Rs 6.87 crores (68,700,000 rupees) worth of foreign exchange in profits from imports (such as ingredients for concentrates, trademarked materials, machinery) and charges to the United States. Another Rs 3.69 crores (36,900,000 rupees) worth of foreign exchange was awaiting clearance by the Reserve Bank.[31] The government also accused Coca-Cola of selling its concentrates to Indian bottlers at an extraordinarily high profit of "about 400 per cent," generating substantial income that was remitted to the United States, extracting much-needed foreign exchange from India.[32] This was an argument that the US International Cooperation Administration (ICA) had itself made in 1957 when it rejected the Company's application for US government assistance to build Indian concentrate plants.

"Export was stated to be another objective of the Coca-Cola Export Corporation, as its name would imply," George Fernandes wryly commented in his testimony to the Lok Sabha. But, he continued, Coca-Cola Export's export earnings were Rs. 9.92 crores (99,200,000 rupees) over the same 1958–74 period, resulting in a net outflow of foreign exchange. Coca-Cola Export's actual export numbers were being inflated by the addition of goods it had not manufactured, with Coca-Cola functioning as a trading company dealing in Indian commodities to prop up its export revenues and give it cover from the Indian government, Fernandes asserted. When the Indian government decided that it would "take into account only the export of the items manufactured by the Company for the purposes of fixing a ceiling on their imports and other remittances," the equation changed. A government investigation also accused the corporation of manipulating the prices for the import of ingredients and the export of concentrates, since they were both "handled by the different branches of the parent Company" with "the entire operations . . . closely directed by the Head Office of the Company in the USA." "It is thus not surprising that the exports have virtually collapsed and the Company has exported goods worth about Rs 1.84 lakhs only in 1976–1977," Fernandes concluded.[33] Invoking FERA, the Indian government demanded that Coca-Cola Export form an Indian subsidiary and assign 60 percent of its ownership to Indian shareholders so that more of its profits would stay in the country.

Coca-Cola Export agreed to these terms, but qualified its acceptance by proposing that it should be allowed to retain a "quality control and liaison office" to protect its "carefully guarded trade secrets."[34] Fernandes argued that this counterproposal "was not in consonance with the provisions of the FERA" since the proposed Indian company would not actually be taking over Coca-Cola Export's Indian operations, i.e., the production of Coca-Cola's concentrates, but would merely sell them. The concentrates would still be made under the control of the American company, not an Indian one. Thus, "this arrangement would also militate against the guidelines for transfer of technology to India, which provided that the technical know-how should be fully imparted to the Indian company within a fixed time limit," Fernandes said, announcing that the Reserve Bank had, therefore, rejected the proposal.[35]

In demanding the transfer of know-how, or intellectual property, the Indian government was treading on sacred ground: Coca-Cola's "secret formula." Anthony Young, head of Coca-Cola Export's Eastern Division, covering India and Africa, flew in from Kenya to negotiate. Although the Indian government regarded the formula as "technical know-how," Young told the press after frustrating negotiations, "It is actually a proprietary trade secret, and there is a basic difference."[36] From the Company's Atlanta headquarters, a spokesman indicated that negotiations with the Indian government had come down to "control over the company's trade-secret formula," saying: "The Company has not been able to obtain Government agreement to a fundamental policy, which governs the company's operation worldwide. This refers to the company's insistence that it continually control and supervise the manufacturing of Coca-Cola through a local quality-control unit to insure the integrity and unvarying quality of its beverages."[37]

This wrangling cut to the core of the legal property protections that enabled corporate capitalism, and to the very basis upon which The Coca-Cola Company was able to market itself, maintain market dominance, and profit through the logic of the franchise. Young asserted that the "secret formula" was not "technological know-how," meaning that it was not patented intellectual property, which by US law would have a limited term of protection before eventually entering the public domain. As explained in Chapter 1, by keeping the drink a trade secret and not patenting it, The Coca-Cola Company could maintain a monopoly on the secret formula in perpetuity, which was, as discussed in chapter 3, a central part of the cultural construction of Coca-Cola as the authentic, unitary "real thing," in contrast to generics and upstart competitors.

The application of FERA to Coca-Cola's secret formula, perhaps the world's most famous intellectual property, was emblematic of the struggles of the developing world to challenge the hardening international intellectual property regime and demand the worldwide sharing of the full wealth of human knowledge. The application of FERA's technology transfer requirements to Coca-Cola began a public debate on intellectual property. Meanwhile, behind the scenes the Indian government was applying similar pressure to pharmaceutical and computer corporations, whose potential transfer of patents and trade secrets could dramatically reshape north-south relations in those crucial, growing industries. Framing the technology transfer debate in terms of the north "sharing" proprietary knowledge with the south, as many corporations and international organizations did then, made the issue seem like one of generosity and aid, erasing what had historically been a complex flow and often coercive extraction of intellectual (as well as material) goods from south to north. The history of the creation of Coca-Cola's "secret formula" demonstrated that "know-how" was never the product of solitary individual genius alone, but rather built upon previous contributions, multiple sources, and local knowledge, including some appropriated from the global south, as in consumption of coca (leaf) from Latin American and kola (nut) from Africa, used in Coca-Cola and referenced in the Company's very name.

Numerous published letters to the editors of the world's newspapers demonstrate the level of interest and passionate opinions on the subject of technology transfer and Coca-Cola's departure from India. An angry letter to the editor of the *New York Times* from an American focused on the issue of intellectual property, threatening swift reprisals from the international business community:

> A dramatic lesson in governmental narrowmindedness, shortsightedness and retrograde innovation. . . . Apparently the envious members of the present Government feel that the local Indian beverage companies cannot compete with Coke, so instead of trying to develop a home-grown product that tastes as good or better, they're going to steal it from Coca-Cola, albeit "legally." . . . I suggest that, if the Indian Government is really after big game, it no longer recognize foreign patents. It then can let the rest of the world do the inventing and discovering while India reaps the profits by legislative fiat. No doubt Coca-Cola will choose rather to leave India, and what the Indian Government will soon learn is that if you are not willing to protect trade secrets, you will soon have no trade.[38]

An Indian reader of the Calcutta newspaper *The Statesman* took a sarcastic tone, sending up the Company's resistance to Indians being in charge of the production of its concentrates by pretending that soft drinks required more complicated technology than the extraction of oil or the manufacture of computers (at which Indians were proving themselves adept). In Coca-Cola's business, one had to figure out how to extract huge amounts of money from India, persuade politicians not to follow the law, and fool customers: "Imagine the level of technology and sophistication required to be able to repatriate more than Rs 10 crores in foreign exchange on an investment of Rs 6 lakhs. Many Government officials have to be convinced about the desirability of not complying with FERA. Many politicians have to be systematically made to see the advantages of the operations of this multinational, and many gullible consumers have to be convinced that it is a real thing, even though it is not."[39]

The Indian government's threat to The Coca-Cola Company's secret formula was also a challenge to the corporation's discourse of multinational developmentalism, which promoted the Company as modernizing local economies around the world through its franchise bottlers. Countries like

India "must assign higher priority to power, irrigation and other development projects than investments in such items as soft drinks and toothpaste for the manufacture of which indigenous know-how was available," the *Statesman* editorialized. "What India needed was assistance from the USA in projects involving sophisticated technology."[40] *The Times of India* concurred: The Coca-Cola Company was "engaged in a low-priority industry not requiring sophisticated technology and with little export potential."[41] Indian industry could meet any demand for soft drinks through its own production, perhaps with smaller-scale production units in rural areas, thus creating jobs, Indian leaders argued.

Realizing that the offerings of fizzy drinks and consumer capitalism were not enough to convince development-focused Indian politicians, The Coca-Cola Company promised valuable technological know-how in return for permission to continue its low-priority high-profit business as usual. Young told the Indian government that the Company could help India develop its agriculture, a major government goal, and perhaps even help ameliorate the country's shortage of safe drinking water. Coca-Cola had more to offer to India than merely its sodas: "We are the largest growers of citrus, tea and coffee. . . .We have the know-how on agrochemicals and we can give our expertise on desalination of water," he insisted.[42] The Coca-Cola Company was honing this strategy in India and several other global south countries in the 1970s, with Coca-Cola executives acknowledging the need to make economic contributions to developing economies in order to shield their business from nationalist challenges, especially as they sought to grow international markets. As events unfolded in India, one of Coca-Cola's largest markets in the world, Mexico, attempted to institute a new foreign trademark law with the goal of national economic protection from transnational corporations. Coca-Cola President J. Paul Austin immediately flew down to meet with Mexican President Portillo to assert the Company's foreign investment and foreign-exchange contributions to the country: "bottling franchises owned by Mexican capital, growing and exporting lemons to the United States, buying and exporting cotton and sugar to the United States, test marketing of our nutrition drink and last, and of the greatest interest to the President, our completely successful experiment with growing shrimp in raceways on land." The Coca-Cola Company was exempted from the legislation.[43] As Coca-Cola President Austin explained to the board of directors, almost wistfully, "the day when a foreign company can do business in another country without making a substantial contribution to its balance of payments is just about gone."[44]

Economic, political, and cultural nationalism converged in Coca-Cola's eviction from India in the 1970s. "Liquidate the Liquid," a satirical short story by Bachi J. Karkaria published in *The Times of India* in the midst of the controversy, caricatured the interrelated critiques of The Coca-Cola Company in India. Almost thirty years after its political independence, the unnamed nation in which the story is set has finally decided to "cast off the shackles of a subtler imperialism and become truly free." In the basement of an indigenous soft-drink company, leaders hatch the Committee for the Overthrow of Kingsized Empires (C.O.K.E.) to oppose the "anti-national drink, Colacoca." The battle is symbolic as well as material: "What they were fighting against was not merely a bottle of Indian-made foreign non-liquor. They were fighting against what it stood for." In the language of cultural nationalist critiques of the contamination of cultural heritage by Western outside influences and mass consumerism, the leaders complain that "for years this innocuous-looking drink had weaned millions of young men and women away from their glorious heritage of nimbu pani [lemonade]. Colacoca symbolised, like nothing else, everything that decadent western culture stood for." Western cultural imperialism aside, Colacoca "even more directly . . . stood for American neo-colonialism . . . which tried to suppress the aspirations of developing nations everywhere. Every [US] embassy infiltrator, handing out the free booze, magazines, films and cigarettes, murmured enticingly: 'Things go better with you know what,' and passed around a bottle of the bubbling, sparkling drink." Moreover, from a Marxist perspective, "Colacoca also symbolised perfectly the yawning gap between the haves and the have-nots, between exploited workers, and exploiting capitalist, between urban rich and poor, between slick city dwellers and the 70 per cent who lived and toiled in our villages." Updated *swadeshi* (Gandhian self-reliance) rhetoric asserted: "Colacoca was the antithesis of the great Gandhian ideal, for it harboured in its dark and murky depths the hydra-headed, many-subsidiaried, perk-marked monster of multinationalism." Invoking the World War II–era national independence movement that had demanded an end to British rule, C.O.K.E. announces a "new Quit India movement" against Colacoca and launches an Ayurvedic Indian drink to replace it. Finally, facing the demise of his company at the hands of C.O.K.E., Colacoca's CEO recalls the many times in his career he has "been confronted with the nightmare of death and nationalisation. But this time . . . 'It's The Real Thing.'"[45]

As Karkaria's satire suggests, the real-life challenge to The Coca-Cola Company allowed a newly elected and tenuously constructed Indian state to perform a spectacular act of economic and cultural nationalism. The Janata (Public) Party had been elected to power to end the state of emergency, abuses of civil liberties, and persecution of student, peasant, and labor organizations by the outgoing Indira Gandhi–led Congress Party government, a period known simply as "The Emergency," and, for many in the Janata Party, to revive the Indian nation's foundational socialist mandate. It was the first non-Congress, non-Nehru-Gandhi-family government since Independence, signaling a major break with the past and a political and economic moment full of both possibility and uncertainty. But the Janata Party had been hurriedly formed from a mix of leaders representing a broad spectrum of political ideologies to address the political crisis of the Emergency, and from the moment they took power, party leaders had difficulty establishing government policy.

For Coca-Cola, these kinds of dramatic shifts in political power were especially concerning. India's new Prime Minister Morarji Desai took office with talk of instituting a prohibition on alcohol, a potential boon to the Company. But the good news did not last for long. Janata Party leaders, Desai, Jayaprakash Narayan, and others, as well as its various ministers—industry (Fernandes), finance (H.M. Patel), and commerce (Mohan Dharia)—vied for political leadership, and struggled to develop and communicate the next "five-year plan," as was called the state's centralized economic policies to address unemployment, rural poverty, social "backwardness" (in their terms), and the many other challenges of the postcolonial country.[46] But in the short term, they could pursue Coca-Cola's eviction as a political-economic spectacle, a symbolic as much as a material protest of Western cultural imperialism and exploitative multinational capitalism as embodied in a highly visible commodity form. Targeting Coca-Cola was an act of nationalism on which the spectrum of political ideologies in the government could agree, with the hope of uniting the nation after years of crisis and capturing the imaginations of Indians eagerly waiting for economic reform.

The focus on Coca-Cola drew on the legacy of material and symbolic conflicts over commodities in Indian nationalist politics. Such struggles over commodities were central to the Indian independence movement as it applied philosophies of *swaraj* (self-rule), *swadeshi* (indigenous industry), and

Gandhian nonviolence to an economic strategy of challenging British colonialism by boycotting British goods and supporting products and production
techniques "of one's own country." Indian nationalists boycotted Manchester
cloth, which arrived on their shores manufactured from the very cotton grown
and cheaply purchased in colonies like India, but now with the price tags of a
finished imported product. The swadeshi movement promoted the spinning
and weaving of local cotton into *khadi* (homespun cloth) and indigenous
fashions. Mohandas Gandhi's nonviolent civil disobedience movement had
also taken aim at salt, refusing the colonial salt monopoly and tax and advocating free collection of salt. Not only was the salt tax a material target, since it
raised significant revenue for the British Raj and disproportionately affected
the poor, it was symbolically powerful, as a tax on a mineral that was used
daily, freely available from the environment and necessary for life, as if
extracted from the sweat of Indian workers' brows. Gandhian swadeshi, which
he defined as "that spirit in us which restricts us to the use and service of our
immediate surroundings to the exclusion of the more remote,"[47] emphasized
a commitment to the improvement of local conditions through self-sufficiency
and swaraj. Swadeshi had a foundation in the political-economic, emphasizing
a commitment to the improvement of the material conditions of production:
"The aim of 'swadeshi' as such, is a call to the consumer to be aware of the
violence he is causing by supporting those industries that result in poverty,
harm to workers and to humans and other creatures."[48]

Underlying much Indian political and economic nationalisms was a discourse of cultural nationalism with Gandhi and other Indian nationalists
fostering a "positive Orientalism" of essentialized Indian spirituality, forms
of knowledge, and antimaterialism,[49] which emphasized a unique cultural
"Indianness" that became a "fundamental feature of anticolonial nationalisms."[50] Disowning the alienation of mass consumption and production,
Gandhi rejected these forms of Western modernity and modernization later
represented in The Coca-Cola Company's commodities and consumer culture. As Gandhi expressed it: "The tendency of Indian civilization is to ele-
vate the moral being, that of the Western civilization is to propagate immo-
rality. The latter is godless the former is based on a belief in God.... So
understanding and so believing, it behooves every lover of India to cling to
the old Indian civilization even as a child clings to the mother's breast."[51]

Gandhian values of self-rule and ethical consumption met Hindu and caste
interpretations of purity and pollution in critiques of Coca-Cola as a potentially dangerous foreign influence. Purity was both an individual and collective

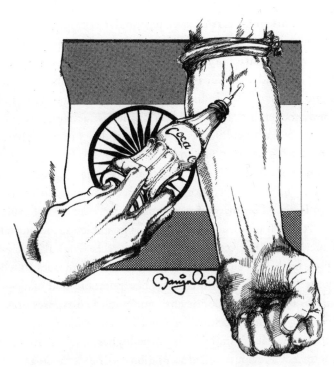

FIGURE 16. Manjula Padmanabhan, "Coca-Cola, 1977," illustration from "The Pop, the Fizz and the Froth," *Times of India*, October 9, 1977, 11.

mandate, which united perfectly in concerns over a product like Coca-Cola, which as a physical drink was corporeally imbibed and as a cultural representation and social practice was widely circulated in public culture. Challenges to Coca-Cola's secret formula were framed in terms, not only of sharing know-how and technology transfer, but of doubts about the health and purity of unknown imported ingredients. "Can you mention the name of a single country where whatever is edible is not subject to scrutiny by the Health Department?" Commerce Minister Dharia asked.[52] Other drinks were comparatively posited as healthy, pure, and intrinsically "Indian," or at least derived from Indian ingredients. The debate over what constituted a "purely" Indian drink took its most striking form when just as Coca-Cola's departure was making headlines, Prime Minister Morarji Desai proclaimed that his exemplary health came from following an Ayurvedic practice of drinking his own urine every day, which both Indian and US newspapers sensationally used as a counterpoint to Coca-Cola.[53]

This bodily discourse carried over to popular critiques of the multiple forms of "dependency" produced by the soft drink company in both the individual and national economic body. (fig. 16). "This firm is only interested in making all Indians Coca-Cola addicts," a member of the Lok Sabha argued in 1975.[54] The Indian state's challenge to Coca-Cola unfolded as part of a broader critique of corporations whose activities were keeping the country in a state of political-economic dependency in the global capitalist system. During the summer and fall of 1977, revelations of corporate avarice, misdoings, and political corruption broke almost weekly, and suggested a deep mistrust of corporations, especially multinationals, doing business in India.[55] Pharmaceutical companies were accused of exploitative practices—selling fraudulent or unproven drugs, remitting too much money to their metropoles, not contributing to local technological development, and keeping medicines out of the hands of the needy through intellectual property law.[56] Newspapers printed lists of corporations that made political contributions to influential politicians[57] and published exposés of multinationals exerting political pressure.[58] A major scandal erupted over the Boeing aircraft company bribing individuals at the highest levels of Indian power to win contracts.[59] Previously veiled accusations of The Coca-Cola Company's own history of political corruption were given more credence in August of 1977, when the Company admitted to paying bribes and kickbacks totaling $1.3 million to foreign political officials in twenty countries since 1971.[60]

US economic and political neocolonialism was also read into the symbol of Coca-Cola, attracting anti-American sentiment. US foreign policies angered Indians and made headlines throughout the 1970s, from military and economic support for neighboring Pakistan as relations on the subcontinent worsened, to the militarization of the Indian Ocean, to US Cold War foreign occupations and policies in the Third World more broadly. As a Lok Sabha member put it, with profits from Indian Coca-Cola purchases being repatriated back to the United States, "Are we not helping arms shipments to Pakistan?"[61] The Coca-Cola Company was easily associated with US political and military power. In news that reached Indian papers, the newly elected US President Jimmy Carter, a former governor of Georgia, brought several Coca-Cola men with him to the White House, even naming former Coca-Cola President Charles Duncan deputy secretary of defense.[62] As *The Hindu* reported, "While campaigning for the Presidency, asked how he could talk with such certitude on foreign policy matters, Mr. Carter quipped: 'I don't need the State Department, I've got Coca-Cola.'"[63] The Carter administration, and President Carter specifically, had a close relationship with Coca-Cola executives, including Company President J. Paul Austin, who not only raised funds for Carter's candidacy, but was committed to giving "all the aid and assistance possible short of going into government." The intimacy was so assumed that Austin had to assure worried Company executives that he would not leave to join the new administration.[64] The relationship between the US government and Coca-Cola went the other way too, with The Coca-Cola Company actively considering hiring former US Secretaries of State Henry Kissinger and Dean Rusk as chairman of Coca-Cola Export to serve in a diplomatic capacity, as James Farley had in previous decades.[65] Even Coca-Cola's Indian bottlers had US political connections, with Daljit Singh (son of Mohan Singh) and head of Pure Drinks traveling to Washington in the 1960s and 1970s, for example, "in connection with some work with the State Department" and claiming Senator Charles H. Percy, chairman of the Senate Foreign Relations Committee, as a personal friend.[66]

"GOING THE INDIAN WAY": ADVERTISING CORPORATE NATIONALISM

The Coca-Cola Company privately negotiated with Indian leaders to try to avoid FERA, but also publicly responded to Indianization by justifying its business in the language of nationalism. Well before late twentieth-century debates about "glocalization" and the commodification of difference within global marketplaces, this history elucidated capital's strategic participation in the construction of nationalist brands, seemingly counter to its own universalizing goals, to defend its interests in postcolonial nations like India. As the Company's possible forced departure headlined newspapers, in their pages corporations advertised their products' links to FERA-related goals and promoted an Indian corporate nationalism. This corporate nationalism suggested that companies and the nation had a shared interest, that their fates were intertwined. What was good for the Indian corporation, or one that could construct itself as Indian, was good for the Indian nation.[67] India's socialist-inflected state capitalism pursued the interests of national companies, which overwhelmingly benefited national elites. Foreign companies marketed their exports and contribution to foreign-exchange reserves, their role in bringing technological know-how to the country, and their long-term

In India Coca-Cola goes the Indian way.

Throughout India 22 companies — wholly Indian-owned, Indian-managed and Indian-staffed — bottle Coca-Cola, India's favourite soft drink — a local business, the way it is in more than 130 other countries. Providing direct employment for 10,000 people and an important source of livelihood for 200,000 more — most of them shopkeepers.

Things really do go better with Coke... like helping to provide a living for more than 200,000 Indian people.

By making it a local business, the Coca-Cola organisation helps to develop other Indian ancillary industries, from bottle and case makers to refrigerator and machinery manufacturers, with annual purchases of their products and services worth more than Rs. 13 crores. The Indian Coca-Cola bottling industry is established with over Rs. 10 crores of investment from Indian entrepreneurs who produce a world-class soft drink of the quality you can trust anywhere, any time.

Enjoy Coca-Cola

issued by the Coca-Cola Bottlers of India.

The Coca-Cola Bottlers of India are registered users of the registered trademarks "Coca-Cola" and "Coke".

FIGURE 17. "Coca-Cola Goes the Indian Way," *Times of India*, April 17, 1972, 4.

commitment to the Indian economy. And Indian companies quickly produced advertising that constructed their national corporate identities to capitalize on their foreign competitors' contrasting vulnerability under FERA.

In the early 1970s, even before FERA's passage, as the Indian government began to show signs of increased concern over The Coca-Cola Company's remittance of profits back to the United States, the Company released a series of ads emphasizing its "Indianness" with the tagline "In India Coca-Cola goes the Indian way," as in figure 17. Like the Latin American ads discussed earlier, these Indian ads asserted the locality of the Coca-Cola bottling industry, stressing the Indian ownership of its bottlers and their employment of local workers in explicitly national terms: "Throughout India 22 companies—

wholly Indian-owned, Indian managed and Indian-staffed—bottle Coca-Cola. India's favourite soft drink—a local business, the way it is in more than 130 other countries. Providing direct employment for 10,000 people and an important source of livelihood for 200,000 more—most of them shopkeepers." Rather than offering evidence of the US-based corporation's foreign direct investment in India, the ads highlighted its Indian bottlers' own financial investment in the industry, citing "over Rs. 10 crores of investments from Indian entrepreneurs," and the benefit of Coca-Cola bottling to related Indian industries: "By making it a local business, the Coca-Cola organization helps to develop other Indian ancillary industries, from bottle and case makers to refrigeration and machinery manufacturers, with annual purchases of their products and services worth more than Rs. 13 crores."[68] Another ad in the series asserted that the Coca-Cola organization in India had generated exports worth Rs. 2.17 crores the preceding year from the export, via Coca-Cola's "world-wide distribution network," of Coca-Cola concentrate to eight countries, mango beverages and tea to the United States, and edible gum and cashew nuts to Europe. "And this is just the beginning," the ad declared. "Our special research and development team is continuously working towards developing new products for export and new overseas markets for India. This is possible because in India, Coca-Cola goes the Indian way."[69] At the most basic level, the Company suggested, its business supported the Indian nation through tax revenue, making the increasing sales of Coke better for India: "The local industry makes an annual contribution of Rs. 10 crores to the national economy through taxes. So the more Coke we produce in India, the more the country's economy benefits."[70]

But the power and authority behind the ads' claims to "Indianness" was expressed through the language of corporate globalism projected by the Company. Although the ads prominently claim to be "Issued by the Coca-Cola bottlers of India," they employed the voice of the multinational corporation, attesting to the fact that "Indian entrepreneurs ... produce a world-class soft drink,"[71] with local quality backed by global standards. One hundred and thirty countries produce and consume Coca-Cola, the ads declare; in other words, one hundred and thirty states allow the successful functioning of the corporation within their nations. That the majority of the list was comprised of global south nations alongside developed European countries suggested global commonality in acceptance of the Company, and thus a legitimation of the local manifestation of its world system in India.[72]

The news that IBM would leave India rather than adhere to FERA requirements, amid charges of price gouging and large remittances to its US headquarters, marked the second most prominent case after The Coca-Cola Company. There was a significant disparity in press coverage, with the application of FERA to Coca-Cola receiving far more public attention than IBM, which could be explained by the fact that in the late 1970s, the world was still at the cusp of the computer age, and IBM's products and business were far less visible to the Indian public than Coca-Cola's bottled drinks, factories, and advertising.[73] But the news of IBM's departure drew concern from India's professional classes, worried that IBM's technology was critical for their businesses and India's economic development.[74] But Indian computer companies hoping to fill the market void left by IBM advertised their "indigenous know-how," and the benefits of their "Indianness," suggesting they were ready to serve the economic and technological needs of the country, and that Indians should unite around import substitution: "If you're using an imported computer today, you're probably worrying your head off about what is going to happen tomorrow. Who will meet your increasing future requirements? Who will give you additional hardware and software compatible with your existing system? . . . relax. We can sort it all out together."[75]

The "public sector venture" Electronics Corporation of India Limited (ECIL), based in Hyderabad, promoted its "indigenous know-how" with ads that invited consumers to participate in the nationalist corporate project, saying, "think of tomorrow. Think indigenously. Come, grow with us." Its advertisements named as clients several high-profile Indian-owned "profit oriented companies," said to be trusted by Indian citizens, linking it to the larger project of national enterprise. The ads drew on references to the uniqueness of Indian culture and knowledge, with images like that of a smiling, barefoot business executive in a modern *achkan* (Nehru jacket) meditating in a yogic sitting position, to even suggest that "indigenous" computers catered to "Indianness." "Every ECIL system is carefully designed to suit Indian needs." In fact, according to the ads, the domestic ECIL systems "have one big advantage over ones made abroad. Appropriate Technology. They're carefully designed to suit Indian conditions best. They're just what you need. No more, no less."[76] "And don't forget," ECIL's ads closed, unlike the multinational IBM, with its vulnerability to FERA, "we're Indian. We're here to stay. We'll always be around when you need us."[77] Likewise, DCM Data Products suggested a reclamation of Indian know-how from the foreign multinational with an image of several smiling people being plucked from the large, otherwise brainless head of the corporation. Indian ex-IBM employees were going to work in their data-processing units: "We've been picking IBM's brains lately. Or, more accurately, IBM's brains have been picking us. A fact we're very pleased about . . . IBM may or may not stay but IBM talent is here to stay."[78] Another ad claimed that "the sensible alternative" to IBM was still foreign, but Soviet rather than American, arguing that the USSR had been the first to bring "the computer age" to India and continued to offer "sophisticated computers known the world over for efficiency and reliability."[79]

Unilever became a rare exception to the "Indianization" of subsidiaries of foreign multinational companies. The Indian affiliate of the company, Hindustan Lever, managed to maintain its majority foreign ownership with skillful bargaining and public relations by its primarily Indian-national executives. As in its negotiations with the government, in a large-scale advertising campaign, Hindustan Lever emphasized its investment in India's core industrial and agricultural sectors through the production of heavy chemicals, as well as its commitment to rural development. This was a change from the corporation's typical brand-specific advertising around the qualities of consumer goods products (soaps, household cleaners, etc.) aimed at the Indian consumer. Instead, this corporate campaign advertised Hindustan Lever as a whole to a broad set of overlapping audiences like consumers, citizens, government regulators, and potential investors. With large newspaper advertisements in the style of a historical scroll, Hindustan Lever proclaimed its importance to national development and the strategic launch of its Hindustan Lever Research Foundation. The Foundation expected to spend Rs. 50 lakhs of Hindustan Lever funds for Indian laboratory research "into problems of national importance." The company's "research in chemical and biological sciences, with special reference to raw materials and products relevant to India" and its "ability to harness the fruits of such research" led it "to believe that there is great scope in India for purposeful research into problems of relevance to our country in agriculture, animal husbandry and industrial chemicals," the advertisement declared.[80]

The Indian state did require Hindustan Lever to divest a minority of its ownership to Indian shareholders, and the company's advertising sought to conscript Indians new to financial investment in a multinational. Hindustan Lever promoted its long-term profitability, while simultaneously justifying its future growth as in the national interest because of its "plan to invest even more in core sector and export-oriented ventures" and the familiarity of its products to Indian households. With the image of a consistently upward trending line chart, it persuasively, if imprecisely, represented its steady rise in India. While it was unclear which values were actually being charted—sales or profit or stock price—the points framed a graphic of a beautiful young South Asian woman in a waterfall surrounding by Lever trademarks, reasserting the message of the ad: rather than being a faceless, maligned multinational company, Hindustan Lever represents a group of familiar household products that make Indians happy, and can make Indian investors happy too. "A company is better known by its products—the performance of its products as seen by the consumer. A company that keeps the consumer happy will keep the investor happy."[81]

Indian soft-drink producers capitalized on the negative publicity around their competitor Coca-Cola, which had dominated the market, and took the opportunity to assert themselves as Indian alternatives. A bottle of Duke's King Kola stood erect and victorious, declaring itself "better than the real thing."[82] State industries that produced competitive drinks like the Uttar Pradesh State Agro Industrial Corporation (Agro) asserted their presence and "purity."[83] Private companies too aligned themselves with official national authorities to promote the "health" of their products for individual and national consumption, like Himalayan Springs bottled water's inauguration by Raj Narain, Union minister for health and family welfare.[84]

Parle, the largest of the Indian soft-drink producers and Coca-Cola's principal rival, stood to gain the most from Coca-Cola's departure. Parle had survived Coca-Cola's post–World War II entrance to India and the loss of its Gluco-Cola drink in a trademark battle with the US brand with the help of the extremely popular Limca, a lemon-lime flavor, and Gold Spot, an orange drink that competed with Coke's Fanta. Representing itself as an Indian multinational worthy of Indian national pride, Parle invested heavily in advertising and bottling plants, expanding both nationally and internationally, and by the late 1970s, its brands were dominant among Indian soft drinks in the image market. Parle spent vastly more on advertising than its Indian competitors (in 1977 Duke and Rogers spent only a few thousand rupees a year, while Parle spent about two and a half million), although not nearly as much as Coca-Cola and its franchisees.[85] The Indian company's concentrate manufacturing plant (Parle Exports Pvt Ltd.) serviced thirty franchises around India and an additional seven in other countries. Parle's corporate future would be inextricably tied to that of The Coca-Cola Company, first as the most prominent beneficiary of Coca-Cola's departure from India in the late 1970s, and later when Parle became the corporate foothold from which Coca-Cola returned to India under market liberalization in the 1990s.

With news of Coca-Cola's imminent departure, Parle flooded the newspapers with ads for its fruit-flavored Gold Spot, Limca, and Maaza drinks. While many of the advertisements stuck with their regular product and brand-specific promotions with slogans like "Gold Spot—The taste goes to your smile," an advertising campaign for Parle as a whole was timed to the news of Coca-Cola's exit, promoting a multinational Indian economic nationalism with taglines like "India exports soft drinks" and "Quality triumphs in India and abroad."[86] The company directly exported its drink concentrates to franchises in Dubai, Kuwait, Mauritius, Bangladesh, East Africa, the Seychelles, and Singapore (a favorite of the ads, which frequently portrayed cartoons of doll-like young East Asian girls drinking Parle products as representations of successful Indian corporate globalization, and perhaps even Indian leadership in Asia),[87] netting foreign exchange of around Rs. 2 crores in the current year. "The future is bright for Indian soft drinks abroad," the advertisements boasted. Parle had "the kind of innovation it takes to adapt a product for competitive foreign markets," it claimed, because it was a large Indian firm.[88] "This achievement took a lot of innovation and dynamism backed up by the experience gained from a network in India—30 bottling plants all over the country. Plus years of research in the technology of developing, formulating, bottling and marketing high-quality soft drinks that can hold their own even in the competitive international marketplace." With Parle, these numerous ads suggested, the country possessed an export-oriented Indian multinational, and Indian consumers could share in the taste of its success: "So the next time you enjoy a Limca or a Gold Spot or a Maaza, you'll know there are millions more enjoying the same drink overseas, thanks to the innovative enterprise of Parles. 30 bottling plants in India. 7 franchises abroad."[89]

The Singh family's Coca-Cola bottling franchise, Pure Drinks, quickly released a new cola product, Campa Cola, to try to replace profits lost along with its Coca-Cola business. In introducing the completely unknown drink brand, Pure Drinks relied on a reference to its famous previous product in its transitional corporate taglines: "A product of Pure Drinks—pioneers in soft drinks and the largest bottlers of Coca Cola [sic] in India,"[90] and "Pure Drinks—The house of quality flavours."[91] Pure Drinks chose a reference to the best-known drink brand to reestablish itself, even though the company no longer produced it. It seems the value of aligning itself with the quality of Coca-Cola outweighed the risk of being associated with the evicted multinational. Pure Drinks' ad closed with a pledge that demonstrated the company's efforts to represent itself as a loyal Indian industry serving the Indian people: "With the introduction of Campa Cola we reaffirm our promise—to provide high quality soft drinks."[92] It was more persuasive than the slogan Pure Drinks used to describe the taste of its new Coca-Cola replacement, Campa-Cola: "The Campa flavour—it grows on you."

On the anniversary of the opening of Coca-Cola's first Indian bottling plant just weeks after the announcement of its departure from the country, Pure Drinks reframed its connection to the multinational corporation by instead focusing on its Indian patriarch as national hero, the "inspired . . . entrepreneur of vision" who had founded the Indian bottling company, Sardar Mohan Singh. In the discourse of national industry, the ad asserted that Pure Drinks not only produced the nation's most popular soft drink (Coca-Cola) but also "pioneered the growth and modernization of the soft drink industry in India, created employment for thousands of people and [was] responsible for the setting up of many small-scale ancillary units," in language that could have come from a policy statement of its nemesis, Industry Minister George Fernandes. The "experience and expertise" Pure Drinks gained, implicitly from its business partnership with the global corporation, would now be applied to its new indigenous products. The company thanked Indian consumers for their "trust and faith . . . [and the] reassuring warmth" with which they had received its new products. And in return, the company reaffirmed its "commitment to bring a little extra joy into your life . . . *that's the real thing* [bold in original]."[93] With this, Pure Drinks semiotically nationalized Coca-Cola's iconic advertising slogan, which had for years helped to promote the multinational corporation in India, deploying it to represent the relationship between Indian industry and consumers in the spirit of corporate nationalism.

While Pure Drinks and its competitors all represented themselves in nationalistic terms, the FERA-related demands on Coca-Cola were only in part a critical response to the foreign power of the transnational corporation, and were to a large degree due to battles over political and corporate power among India's national elite. Newspaper coverage suggests tacit knowledge of "the Government's attitude towards the giant Pure Drinks Company, which manufactures Coca-Cola"[94] as a response to the company's political influence. Charanjit Singh of the Pure Drinks family, publicly stated that the government's treatment of Coca-Cola "smacked of political vendetta." Singh, the *New York Times* noted, "figured prominently as a supporter and financier of the Congress Party, which lost to the Janata Party in the elections in March. Mr. Singh was himself a candidate for Parliament in the elections from a South Delhi constituency."[95] Parle's president, Ramesh Chauhan, was said to be "widely held responsible" for persuading the Janata Party and its ministers to evict Coca-Cola.[96] Critics of Coca-Cola operations charged that with the "connivance of officials the company adopted unfair means to suppress competition and siphon off profits by bypassing Government regulations 'Coca-Cola had always got favored treatment from the Congress Party Government,' said a Janata Party leader.'"[97] Pure Drinks accused Industry Minister George Fernandes of having a personal interest in making a public example of the Company. As a socialist labor leader concerned with unemployment, Fernandes proposed that smaller bottlers would employ more people than monopolies or multinationals. He had previously fought directly with Pure Drinks in a "labor dispute" in Bombay. Pure Drinks' Charanjit Singh deduced: "Fernandes could claim to be George the giant killer and show what a good socialist he was."[98] To draw attention to the loss of employment at Coca-Cola bottling plants and its impact on the national economy, Pure Drinks and its workers' union held a sit-in demonstration in front of Fernandes's house calling for him to act on his commitments to Indian workers by allowing Coca-Cola to be bottled until an alternative drink could be produced in its stead.[99]

The Indian government proposed a plan for the loss of work resulting from the exit of Coca-Cola: an Indian soft-drink concentrate that would be produced for Indian bottlers by state industry. As early as 1973, the Central Food Technological Research Institute received a request from the Union industry minister to develop a substitute for Coca-Cola, and the formula for the beverage became ready for commercial use in 1976.[100] The drink would be an "indigenous substitute for Coca-Cola," it was said. "The flavour blends were mostly indigenous and the final product was good in every respect including stability of flavour and suitability to the Indian market ... [although] a few of the flavours would, however, have to be imported in the beginning."[101] The government even announced a national contest with a significant rupee award for the best name for the drink. The government did not look far for the winner, though: a Lok Sabha member suggested "77" to commemorate "the year of big changes in India—such as the end of the Indira Gandhi Government and the end of Coca-Cola."[102] "We have a national flag, a national anthem, a national bird, a national logo, a national animal and now a national soft drink, christened '77.'"[103] But the release of

Double Seven was repeatedly delayed, and when the drink finally went to market it faced competition from the new colas from Pure Drinks (Campa Cola) and Parle (Thums Up), and eventually faded away.

The nationalistic romanticization of "indigenous" soft drinks requires complication. For the vast majority of Indian people, both rural and urban, regular consumption of bottled beverages was an economic impossibility. Even into the late 1970s, when The Coca-Cola Company departed India, only two billion bottles of sodas were sold each year by the major bottlers, working out to approximately three drinks a person a year,[104] which was not spread out evenly over a population with vast inequalities of access and capital. In addition, corporations like Parle that celebrated their "indigenousness," were not as "pure" as their representations suggested. Parle was also part of a transnational venture, paying foreign exchange to the Italian company Bisleri, which owned the formula and trademark to Limca and an early well-known brand of bottled water, in what was then a very small market for the latter product. Parle held the majority of the shares in Bisleri's Indian subsidiary, Bisleri (India) Ltd., and manufactured and bottled Limca under an agreement with the Italian company, in much the same way that Pure Drinks manufactured Coca-Cola.[105] By the time of Coca-Cola's ousting in 1977, Parle had grown to become a profitable and powerful multinational corporation in its own right, with a concentrate manufacturing plant (Parle Exports Pvt Ltd.) and a bottling plant in Bombay, thirty franchises around India, and an additional seven franchises in other countries. Parle sold over 192 million bottles a year in India, and sold two-thirds of its output abroad, mainly to West Asia and South-East Asia, with exports totaling around Rs. 2 crores.[106] This export orientation brought foreign profits back to India and easily covered the costs of importing ingredients to the country,[107] which no doubt pleased the Indian government with its concerns about foreign-exchange reserves and plans to become a regional economic leader.

Indian capitalists profited from the critiques of the transnational corporation. Parle was best positioned to take over the soft-drink market after Coca-Cola's departure, beating out state industry's efforts to market its own soda. A year after Coca-Cola left, Parle led the Indian soft-drink market with a 33 percent share, which would grow steadily and oligopolistically, until Parle dominated 70 per cent of soft-drink sales by the end of the next decade.[108] Parle's cola, Thums Up, introduced in 1977, would become India's most popular soft-drink brand during Coca-Cola's long absence, and remains the country's most popular cola today.[109]

In 1977, on his first visit to the south of India, the new US ambassador Robert F. Gohee held a press conference to discuss US-Indian relations, most pressingly, the two nations' nuclear policies, US recognition of India's regional power, and the need for independence from Soviet influence. But the press's questions quickly turned to the issue of Coca-Cola, and it became clear that the ambassador was already deeply immersed in the issue. He ominously commented that the government's treatment of Coca-Cola might discourage further American investment in India.[110] But the United States, he said, respected India's desire to become technologically self-sufficient. If the government of India felt it could produce indigenous soft drinks more cheaply than Coca-Cola or could develop an indigenous computer industry, the US government would not stand in its way.[111] There could still be a future for business ties between the two countries, since American businesses were "realistic and would always seize an opportunity to do business and make reasonable profit."[112] But it was his impression "that many American business houses are biding time to see what economic policies the Janata Government is going to make." The "symbolic significance" of the Coca-Cola expulsion could not be overlooked, he asserted.[113]

Over the next few weeks, as one Indian minister after another visited the United States and Europe, they were met by repeated questions about India's policy on foreign investment and multinationals, framed around The Coca-Cola Company. In September 1977, Commerce Minister Mohan Dharia was in the United States to meet with state, business, and financial leaders about the Janata Party government's trade policy. "The Coca-Cola issue was raised repeatedly at the meetings . . . and he was asked whether the policy was conducive to attracting US investments to India."[114] Dharia described as "'malicious propaganda' the impression created by certain quarters that the action taken by the Government of India against the Coca-Cola Company was anti-American. . . . 'It has nothing to do with our friendly, brotherly colleagues in the USA,'" he told a meeting of Indian organizations in the United States.[115] However, he "charged the previous Government with yielding to pressure brought by the Coca-Cola Company and asserted that the present Government would not do so."[116] As multinationals left India, and as pressure from the international business community mounted, the Janata government's public defense of FERA wavered. On Finance Minister H. M. Patel's trip to the United States a month later, when faced with direct questioning on the challenge to Coca-Cola after several months of political pressure from the US government and business interests, he came up with a modified position, saying that "Indianising" foreign companies did not demand them to pass on their know-how.[117]

The Janata Party held power for just three years, quickly collapsing into political fractures that left it ineffective in addressing the major national problems of poverty and inequity. Its goals of creating economic alternatives to multinational corporations, encouraging small-scale industrial development, and investing in clean drinking water to reduce rural poverty went unfulfilled. "Now we have neither drinking water nor Coca-Cola!" a parched villager exclaimed in an editorial cartoon.[118] While Parle's soft drink market share grew, Pure Drinks continued to do a steady business with its Campa Cola brand. But it also expanded into a new business venture that would more materially manifest India's development aspirations.[119] With a new subsidiary, the Singhs launched a joint venture with a leading French hotel group to build the Le Méridien New Delhi hotel, aimed to open in time for India's hosting of the 1982 Asian Games. The hotel was not without controversy, however, since the land acquisition and building permissions were suspected of being influenced by Charanjit Singh's tenure in Congress.[120] Coca-Cola's former president Robert W. Woodruff saw the potential of Singh's political placement, writing to congratulate the family on his election from the perspective of Coca-Cola's return to India: "We are all expecting him to help us get back in proper shape with the Indian government. Mrs. Gandhi's return as Prime Minister is an exciting development."[121] While Coca-Cola was not able to negotiate a quick return, over the 1980s the Congress government began to lay the groundwork by enacting a new five-year plan focused on economic growth and inflation control, cutting public expenditures, requiring greater efficiency from state-owned industries, and stimulating the private sector through deregulation of corporations and capital markets.

The Coca-Cola Company decided to make an example of the nationalist challenge by leaving India rather than setting the precedent of sharing ownership of its subsidiary with Indian investors or its trade secret formula with Indian producers. The Company's annual report made no direct mention of the loss of the huge prospective market in India, but did feature a speech by Executive Vice President Roberto Goizueta, who was being groomed for the presidency and chairmanship. As Goizueta put it, "The expansion of business operations to a full international level offers us the means and the opportunity to improve the world economy by improving local economies, to break down barriers between peoples, ease tensions among countries, and create at least part of a foundation for a lasting peace."[122] This would be accomplished through a focus on four new Company goals, which could have been articulated in India in 1977, but were not representative of its practices there: "Local Ownership," "Transfer of Technology," "Maintain World Perspective," and "International Harmony."[123]

By the end of the 1970s, more large international markets were opening up for Coca-Cola, allowing the Company to refocus its attention away from India. It regained a foothold back in the Middle East and North Africa with a project in Egypt to create a 15,000-acre orange grove in the desert and enable the country to earn much-needed foreign exchange by exporting orange juice.[124] But an even bigger coup was under way at the end of 1978, when a Coca-Cola Company executive made arrangements in Beijing for Coca-Cola's introduction to China, just days before the US State Department normalized relations.[125] By the beginning of the 1980s, the nationalist challenges to The Coca-Cola Company had receded, but new transnational challenges to the Coca-Cola world system were beginning to emerge. In the meantime, The Coca-Cola Company's refusal to abide by the economic nationalism of the Indian state kept the corporation out of India until the country's dramatic neoliberal economic opening in the 1990s, leaving a gaping hole in The Coca-Cola Company's world system for sixteen years.

FIVE

A Man in Every Bottle

LABOR AND NEOLIBERAL VIOLENCE IN
COLOMBIAN COCA-COLA BOTTLING

THERE WAS AN URBAN LEGEND in Colombia at the end of the twentieth century that someone had opened up a bottle of Coca-Cola and found part of a finger—a trade unionist murdered in a bottling plant had somehow gotten into a vat, the *cuento* went. Although surely untrue, and not really meant to be believed, the *cuento*'s spectacular adulteration of the Coca-Cola commodity and brand image was a visceral manifestation of suspicion and disgust about the relationship between global corporate capitalism, workers' lives, and decades of Colombian armed conflict. Indeed, Coca-Cola became a powerfully contested representation of regimes of labor violence in neoliberal Colombia.

Reconstructing Colombian labor history requires a breadth of sources.[1] Workers' history goes undocumented, and workers' experiences of violence, a reality for Colombian trade union leaders, have repeatedly been denied through legal and political impunity for the offenders. The truth is buried beneath decades of cover-ups, or is so complicated by the long, multifaceted history of violence that unionists' testimonies are treated with suspicion, putting them at further risk of becoming targets of accusation or physical threats. In comparison, the corporation's history appears to be documented and objective: company reports, investor profiles, and newspaper articles spell out the history in black and white, with clear dates and actors. But these documents are also the histories of a corporation mythologizing, forgetting, and rewriting its past for a profit-motivated future. In comparison to company documents, workers' memories appear fuzzy and subjective: oral histories, organizing materials, and testimonials can sound like ideological, haphazard narratives colored by doubt. After decades of ethnographic work in Colombia, the anthropologist Michael Taussig suggests that much characterization of the country never gets past portraying it as chaotic, although "the chaos is the everyday, not a deviation from the norm, and in a strategically important political sense is a disordered order no less than it is an ordered disorder."[2] Allowing the chaos produced by the violence to be seen as exceptional, incomprehensible, and random, as the Company and some writers insisted, obscures its targeted application against certain groups and its utility in maintaining systems of power and exploitation. The accounts and actions of working people demonstrate this, as they saw through the construction of chaos and attempted to understand and take back political and economic power from the disordered order imposed on their lives.

Colombian Coca-Cola trade unionists' experience of violence—the precariousness of their lives at the hands of paramilitary forces—was extreme and particular to the Colombian context, but it was interwoven with the precarity produced by The Coca-Cola Company's bottling consolidation and labor restructuring, which was felt by workers across much of its global bottling system. Paramilitary violence against workers abetted Colombian neoliberalism, enabling the Company and its bottlers to impose labor "flexibilization" on quelled, fearful workers. The Company's labor restructuring necessitated opposition, and thus also exacerbated the violence, since labor movements necessarily arose to challenge such policies, they became the targets of violent repression. Whether directly instigated by The Coca-Cola Company and its bottlers, as some Colombian trade unionists maintain, or not, paramilitary violence produced a subdued labor force for Coca-Cola.[3]

As national developmental strategies gave way to neoliberal policies, and corporations pushed for geographic expansion into new markets and new forms of capital accumulation, work at Colombian Coca-Cola bottling plants was dramatically downsized, subcontracted, and casualized (made contingent, short-term and/or part-time), challenging workers' abilities to support themselves and their labor organizations. When the largest union of Colombian Coca-Cola workers, the Sindicato Nacional de Trabajadores del Sistema Agroalimentario (National Union of Food System Workers), or Sinaltrainal, challenged this system with labor actions, it was targeted by paramilitary forces that had risen in the midst of Colombia's ongoing armed conflict between state forces, guerrillas, drug trafficking cartels, and other extra-legal agents of violence. Through threats, kidnappings, assassinations, and the production of an overwhelming culture of fear, paramilitaries served capitalist interests by violently suppressing labor activism. After protracted labor struggles, repeated acts of violence, and loss of membership, trade unionists called for an international campaign against The Coca-Cola Company, accusing it of making their lives precarious through exploitative labor policies and complicity in violence. The outsourcing and "flexibilization" of bottling work in Colombia was an extension of the externalizing dynamics of Coca-Cola's franchise system, which the Company used to evade financial accountability and legal liability, even as its business became more intertwined with that of its "independent" Latin American franchise mega-bottler. The social logic of the franchise meant the Company exerted pressures on its Colombian bottlers doing business in a difficult market and conflict zone, while distancing itself from the repercussions to workers' welfare, both economic and physical. While Coca-Cola framed Colombian Coca-Cola workers as external, peripheral, and exceptional, especially when revelations of the violence emerged, the workers insisted on their centrality to the corporation's system. With international allies, Colombian trade unionists mobilized Coca-Cola's own corporate structure, brand constructions, and relationships with consumers to map an alternative, multinational network of pressure on the Company.

CONSOLIDATING COLOMBIAN COCA-COLA BOTTLING

Under the leadership of Albert H. Staton, Panamerican Beverages Corporation (Panamco) adopted a program of acquisition and expansion in Colombia, Mexico, and Brazil, where it had been doing business since the 1940s. Panamco would not expand across national borders again until the neoliberal 1990s. Through the 1980s, as in other parts of the Coca-Cola world system, such as India, the national developmentalism of the state and the industrial elite led to restrictions on foreign capital and multinational corporations. In this context, Panamco focused on growing its existing subsidiaries in Mexico, Brazil, and Colombia, among the largest Latin American markets. Panamco offered up investment in its subsidiaries to minority shareholders in the nations in which it did business, which "helped the company continue to build its position, despite the recurring waves of political and economic turmoil that affected these markets," and allowed Panamco to claim "close ties to the Latin American community." The Staton family, with their close ties to Coca-Cola, maintained leadership of the corporation (until the early 1980s) and a controlling financial interest (until the 1990s).[4]

Panamco grew its original Colombian subsidiary, Industrial de Gaseosas (INDEGA), from its original Medellín plant to include operations in Bogotá, Buga, Cali, Duitama, Girardot, Ibagué, Neiva, Pasto, Pereira, and Villavicencio. In 1970, Panamco Colombia acquired Embotelladora Román, with its successful regional brand Kola Román and its Barranquilla, Cartagena, Montería, and Valledupar plants on the Atlantic coast, from the large Colombian brewer and bottler, Bavaria S.A. Two years later, it consolidated nearly all Colombian Coca-Cola plants by buying Embotelladoras de Santander, also from Bavaria, along with its plants in the northwest, Bucaramanga, Barrancabermeja, and Cúcuta, on the Venezuelan border, as well as the country's only mineral water plant, Manantial S.A. (with its brands Agua Manantial and Santa Clara). When Panamco acquired these bottlers, it retained use of their names as subsidiaries—Industrial de Gaseosas, Embotelladora Román, Embotelladoras de Santander—in signage, advertising, and company identification, maintaining the public appearance of continuity and masking its expansion. Staton brought employees from the United States, like the son of a family friend, Richard Kirby, who would rise through the management levels of Panamco before succeeding Staton as president of the company. Staton, Kirby, and other investors incorporated the Bebidas y Alimentos plant in 1979 in Carepa in the Urabá banana zone of northern Colombia. They later sold their shares to Kirby, so that Bebidas y Alimentos became one of just three independent franchises in Colombia. In total, Panamco Colombia would grow to own and operate eighteen bottling plants and "produce, distribute, and commercialize 99 percent of the Coca-Cola products consumed in Colombia."[5]

Panamco's corporate growth was motivated by the potential profits from increasing its share of sales through wider distribution, creating economies of scale in production inputs, and leveraging increased clout in dealings with The Coca-Cola Company. But it was also pushed by the consolidation of its primary competition, whose growth had been supported by the Colombian state's promotion of national industries. In the 1960s and 1970s, the Colombian businessman Ardila Lülle oversaw the concentration of the soft-drink industry, acquiring Gaseosas Lux, Gaseosas Posada & Tobón, and Gaseosas Colombianas and merging them into Colombia's largest beverage company, Postobón, which sold a range of popular brands and in 1980 became the franchisee for Pepsi products.[6] Postobón was part of the large, highly diversified corporate conglomerate, the Organización Ardila Lülle, on its way to becoming one of the most influential in Colombia, and it benefited from the vertical integration of factories that produced glass bottles and carbon dioxide, sugar plantations and a sugar mill, and, beginning in the 1970s, the nation's biggest private radio and television networks.

EXPANDING *LA GRAN FAMILIA*

The labor-management relationship in the Colombian bottling plants reflected the influence and ideas of its American ownership. From the 1940s to the 1960s, INDEGA-Panamco had the feel of a family-run company, and Albert Staton was proud of the labor peace and submissiveness he had produced in his plants through corporate paternalism. "For 40 years, I never had a union nor a strike," he wrote to R. W. Woodruff in 1964.[7] This was the era when the "white American managers would walk the shop floor and stop to shake a workingman's hand," an employee from the first decades of Panamco's business nostalgically remembered, in contrast to the management style of the 2000s.[8] One retiree who provided the Staton family's personal security before working as a middle manager in the Medellín plant remembered workers receiving financial assistance from Staton to cover the costs of family illnesses, home repairs, and other hardships. Staton created a foundation to help workers with limited resources pay for housing.[9] "He felt the pain of every one of his workers as if it was his own." But the same retiree related, "Albert H. Staton was very hard, very strict, very reliable himself. He liked it when people worked. With him, there wasn't a problem if you worked. He would have difficulties with his temper when things went bad and people weren't working."[10] But Staton's health was failing by 1972, and his attention, both positive and negative, became less uniform as Panamco consolidated nearly all Colombian Coca-Cola plants.[11]

By the mid 1970s, the next generation of US-born executives were running Panamco, which now had multiple subsidiaries and plants across much of Colombia. The corporation's expansion sought to improve efficiency and stability through scale, but also brought the challenges of managing a large, dispersed workforce. The bottling company strained to extend the sense of being family-run and, more important, paternalistic, even while introducing a new management regime across a now national corporation. The company named a vice president of industrial relations, whose office handled workers' demands and expectations through negotiations with individuals and unions and organized company programs and events in an effort to build a content and pliable workforce. His office produced a new company newsletter entitled *La Chispa de la Vida* ("The Spark of Life"), named for the 1970s Spanish-language slogan of the global "Real Thing" advertising campaign, which, according to its introductory issue, aimed to educate workers about the company and open up lines of communication between management and the recently expanded Panamco workforce. *La Chispa de la Vida* ran articles on the history of INDEGA and The Coca-Cola Company, as well as individual bottling plants, but while it attempted to solidify the allegiances of newly acquired workers, it mystified the company's structure, never referring to the Panamco corporate entity by name, but rather possessively as "our business" or vaguely as "the company and its subsidiaries." The newsletter attempted to embed the company in workers' personal and professional lives, featuring puzzles (with company executives and their families' names as answers), workers' biographies, submissions of cartoons, and news of births, weddings, retirements, and deaths, as well as reporting on company picnics and sporting events like the Albert H. Staton Cup ("La Copa Albert H. Staton") soccer tournament with teams from across Panamco's plants. The publication also reiterated the bottling company's commitment to Colombian identity and industry. The first sentence of the first issue introduced itself by saying: "Who am I? A bulletin printed by offset on 28 lb. bond paper, a raw material produced in Colombia." "What am I for?" the newspaper continued, and provided the answer: "to create direct communication between us [management and workers]. So that we get to know one another and form one *gran familia* (big family)."[12] To this end, the newsletter carried a monthly slate of articles by plant managers and Panamco executives, focusing especially on the joint cooperation of workers and management in the building of a national company. But paternalistic, pedagogical articles on topics ranging from the importance of workers' hygiene and diligence at work to gendered social roles and family responsibility assumed that top-down communication manufactured better, more productive plant workers. Panamco executives were portrayed as generous but authoritative father figures acting for the good of workers in the company's *gran familia*. But everyone had a role to play in honorable, masculine service to the bottling plant, the corporate "family," and Coca-Cola, which depended on each man's hard work. There was "a man in every bottle," *La Chispa de la Vida* asserted, with an illustration of a smiling cartoon worker pressing up against the glass from inside a Coca-Cola emblazoned bottle.[13]

BUILDING WORKER POWER: THE ORIGINS
OF SINALTRAINAL

The *gran familia* was a tenuous construct that existed more comfortably on the pages of the company magazine than in workers' lives. From the late 1970s to the mid-1980s, Colombia entered an economic downturn, a phase of deindustrialization in which manufactured output and wages fell. Coca-Cola workers whose jobs were threatened by lower sales also faced wage stagnation under management requests for the *gran familia* to unite in these economically difficult times. When the economy picked up again in the mid-1980s, workers demanded a place at that family table and increased wages, and management's refusal to meet these demands resulted in strikes in the coastal plants of Barranquilla, Cartagena, Montería, and Valledupar.

Until the 1980s, Coca-Cola workers belonged primarily to small company-specific unions that represented workers in a single plant or across a few Coca-Cola plants, and were heavily influenced by the bottling company. In 1984, after Panamco's consolidation of most of Colombia's Coca-Cola bottling operations, workers saw the necessity of an organization that could encompass Coca-Cola workers from various regions, as well as related bottling workers. They proposed merging their local unions with the workers of Postobón, the largest Colombian soft-drink and juice company and bottlers of Pepsi, into a new union, Sintradingascol. Less than a year into Sintradingascol's organization, workers in the coastal bottling plants were on strike. In Barranquillla, two hundred workers wearing their bright red Coca-Cola uniforms marched through the working-class neighborhood where the bottling plant was located with signs reading: "Sintradingascol Taking a Stand!" "Demand It or They Take It Away!" and "Solution or Strike!" The strike lasted just three days before Panamco increased workers' wages.[14]

At the same time, in other areas of the packaged food and drink industry, an even more militant labor organization was being organized. Workers in the factories of the transnational companies Nestlé and Borden Foods-Cicolac formed Sinaltrainal in 1982 with the aim of becoming an industrywide food and beverage union. The union had an openly Marxist orientation, built an organizing strategy around workers at multinational corporations, and were known for very public displays of protest: "*meetings* [rallies in front of the plants], denunciations, graffiti, and postering."[15] Some of the younger Coca-Cola workers who affiliated with Sintradingascol in this period came of age in the 1970s and 1980s in working-class schools taught by liberation theology priests and participated in Christian Marxist and communist youth groups where they developed critiques of inequality and capitalism in Colombia.[16] They felt held back by the Postobón workers' less radical politics and submissiveness in the face of comparatively worse labor conditions at Postobón plants and were impressed by the growing Sinaltrainal union, and its analysis of the power of multinational corporations and emerging neoliberalism in Colombia. In 1993, the same year the Coca-Cola bottling corporation Panamco went public on the New York Stock Exchange to build capital for international consolidation and in the midst of neoliberal economic and labor deregulation in Colombia, 1,880 Coca-Cola Sintradingascol members attempted to strengthen their union power by joining with Sinaltrainal.[17]

According to Sinaltrainal leader William Mendoza, this is when relations between the union and the Colombian bottler "changed dramatically." No longer a family-owned company, and now beholden to shareholders, including The Coca-Cola Company which bought a major stake in the bottling company, Panamco adopted a new management style. It began a program of expansion and consolidation, and when profits slowed, labor restructuring, including closing warehouses and encouraging "voluntary" retirements of full-time workers. Panamco sent executives to Atlanta to work closely with Coca-Cola: "The policies of Panamco Colombia weren't designed here, they were policies designed in the headquarters of Coca-Cola," Mendoza describes. It also took an adversarial position relative to the oppositional union. Bottling plant managers had warned workers not to affiliate with Sinaltrainal, saying "that it was a mistake, that it was a leftist syndicate, that it was too radical and had ties with the guerrilla" and when they did, the company ran an "anti-union campaign: a campaign that portrayed us as guerrilla members and as monsters against the company," driving several members from the union and making those remaining the targets of paramilitaries.[18] Trade unionists in Coca-Cola plants had faced paramilitary violence and police repression before, but such threats now intensified. Especially as Sinaltrainal unionists contested the downsizing and demanded more of the fruits of their labor from the consolidated bottling company with strikes at Panamco subsidiaries Embotelladoras de Santander in Bucaramanga, Barrancabermeja, and Cúcuta in 1994, and Embotelladora Román in Barranquilla, Cartagena, and Valledupar in 1995, as well as work actions and contentious negotiations at other plants.[19] Their challenge was met with violent repression by paramilitary forces, who facilitated the imposition of a new labor regime in Coca-Cola's Colombian bottling plants.

COLOMBIAN NEOLIBERALISM AND
THE COCA-COLA WORKER

The opening up of Colombia's economy through neoliberal reform rapidly accelerated in these same years after President César Gaviria Trujillo instituted a policy of, literally, *apertura* (opening) in 1990. While Washington consensus institutions pushed structural adjustment measures on debt-burdened countries around the world, Colombia had comparatively little debt. Still, the Gaviria administration agreed to market-liberalization reforms after the United States pledged the bulk of the $2.2 billion Andean Initiative to fight drug trafficking in Colombia.[20] Colombian neoliberal state policies mandated structural adjustment, economic deregulation, opening up to foreign direct investment, trade liberalization, and lower tariff barriers, as well as a new labor code that permitted the "flexibilization" of labor. The government credited the law that created this flexible labor regime, Ley 50 of 1990, with "stimulating employment" by giving Colombian workers and factories a "competitive advantage" in the global market for jobs and investment.[21] Attempting to attract corporations by reducing labor costs, Ley 50 was, according to labor scholars, the most regressive Colombian labor legislation in decades. Yezid García Abello writes:

> Ley 50 included a long list of critical points: it eliminated job security, it reduced the base salary on which social welfare programs could begin, it prolonged the time period for a company to declare a worker's employment [delaying employee labor protections], it established an "integral" salary for those that earned more than ten minimum salaries [a salary tier in which legal benefits are deemed to be included in the salary, which greatly reduces employer contributions to benefits], it eliminated retroactivity of benefits for newly hired workers, introduced private funds to severance pay, accelerated the entry of child labor into the labor market, restricted pay for work at night and on Sundays, reduced union privileges, established a summary judicial procedure to suspend unions from corporate bodies, cut the negotiation period for *pliegos* [lists of union demands], and, above all, slowed and limited the exercise of the right to strike.[22]

Most important for Coca-Cola workers, Ley 50 would lead to a "flexible" labor regime of less job security, fewer benefits, and curtailed union power. "Ten years later [after Ley 50] the market effectively became flexible, but unemployment increased," the Colombian economist Ricardo Bonilla Gonzalez notes.[23] The Spanish word for the result of this deregulation, subcontracting, and flexibilization of the labor market expresses workers' experience far better than any English one: *precarización*. At the same time, the war between guerrillas, paramilitaries, and the state displaced large numbers of people to the cities,[24] contributing to record unemployment rates in the 2000s, and a large contingent and informal workforce, further exacerbating the insecurity of workers, who sensed that they could be easily and cheaply replaced. Increasing worker vulnerability, the social welfare system was put up for neoliberal reform as well, with Ley 100 of 1993 creating a private pension system and further privatizing health care. The Colombian marketplace was further opened up to capitalist expansion with Ley 49, which deregulated trade and removed trade barriers, and Ley 45, which liberalized financial institutions.[25]

These reforms offered Coca-Cola's Colombian bottlers new avenues for profit. Coca-Cola's franchised production, which bottled drinks relatively close to their point of sale, already allowed Coca-Cola to take advantage of low wages in international labor markets. But as a result of this international dispersion of franchises, Coca-Cola bottling was a relatively "sticky" industry geographically, which could not easily relocate production to even cheaper international labor markets as they underwent economic liberalization, as happened with other industries.[26] Bottlers extended the geographical reach of their capital as far as they could, downsizing costly production workforces by converting bottling plants to distribution centers filled with drinks manufactured by more efficient plants in other parts of the country. But where bottlers faced the limits of spatial expansion of their markets, it was possible to expand profits by exploiting the new labor regime to change their relationship with workers and redefine and revalue their work. Panamco began replacing full-time work with "flexible" jobs, characterized by contingent, part-time, and short-term underemployment, outsourcing to employment companies, and reclassifying workers into independent contractors.[27] The Coca-Cola Company's longstanding externalization of production to its franchise system—to avoid costs and liabilities, including the employment of bottling workers—was a strategy now available to those franchises in Colombia, who avoided direct, full-time employment of Coca-Cola workers. Colombian Coca-Cola workers' experience of *precarización* was extreme because it was policed by the threat of paramilitary violence, but precarity was intrinsic to the larger Coca-Cola system's social logic of franchised labor externalization in the context of financialization, corporate consolidation, and labor "flexibilization." And when Coca-Cola workers sought legal recourse, the Company used its corporate externalization of production to evade responsibility for its workers, even as it was becoming ever more financially intertwined with strategically high-priority bottlers.

FINANCE CAPITALISM, CORPORATE CONSOLIDATION, AND LABOR EXPLOITATION

Financialization and the pressure to serve stockholders' interests drove strategies of "globalization," bottler consolidation, and new forms of extraction of surplus value from Coca-Cola's workforce. In the final decades of the twentieth century Coca-Cola's business became increasingly financial. The Coca-Cola Company made key investments in bottlers, which not only allowed for influence over the bottling industry but generated returns from it. The Company also speculated in currency markets by deciding when to repatriate profits from its international business and hedging its international market exposure through various derivative instruments. The Company's international profits were derived not just from the sales of concentrates, but also the licensing of intangible assets (like the use of trademarks, marketing, and business services, for example) to bottlers. The classification and pricing of such assets became a profitable part of the business's immaterial production, as they allowed the Company to elude taxation by transferring profits to subsidiaries in low-tax countries. And, of course, the Company generated capital for itself and shareholders through its stock (issuing and buying back stock and determining dividends), amongst other strategies.

Toward the end of the twentieth century, the US business press paid as much attention to The Coca-Cola Company's financial products—with extensive coverage of the Company's stock price and dividends to shareholders—as it did its soft drinks. This focus on the immaterial production of finance put greater pressure on its material production of soft drink bottling, as the Company attempted to extract greater profits from bottlers through financial investments and cutting costs through consolidation. The Company's seemingly ever-increasing stock price and dividends in the 1980s and 1990s was credited to its "globalization." This term, "globalization," emphasized Coca-Cola's expansion into new markets, but explained little about the practical dynamics of financialization and labor exploitation in the process of investing in and consolidating international bottlers, all with the priority of enriching shareholders.

As executives explained it, Coca-Cola's strategy for global growth hinged on the consolidation of large bottlers, and it proved remarkably profitable for both the Company and its shareholders.[28] Described in a press release, the Company's aim was to "fortify [the] global bottling system" through a "bottling alignment strategy" of "investing aggressively in certain bottling operations around the world" to push mergers and acquisitions of smaller local bottlers, which had flourished under the relatively decentralized bottling system, and facilitate the growth of select, larger bottlers of Coca-Cola's choosing. With the resulting consolidation of giant regional "anchor bottlers," as the Company called them, Coca-Cola could "maximize the strength and efficiency of its production, distribution and marketing systems."[29] CEO Roberto Goizueta, who oversaw the Company's focus on international expansion and strategic investments in bottlers in the 1980s and 1990s, was "revered ... for his relentless focus on shareholder value."[30] And he directly linked the consolidation of bottlers with profits for shareholders: "Our well-established strategy is aligning the purpose, goals and plans of the Company and its bottlers, producing a business system with greater focus and capabilities to capture the immense opportunities for long-term, profitable growth," Goizueta said. "We will relentlessly continue to execute this strategy, as it is an essential component in meeting our objective of maximizing value for our share owners over time."[31]

The Coca-Cola Company's stock—symbol KO—became a fetishized financial commodity, seemingly embodying shareholder value and producing wealth for shareholders.[32] KO was less sexy than technology stocks, but a more stable and reliably profitable player in the dramatic growth in the stock market in the 1990s. If, as Karl Marx theorized, the valuing and exchange of a commodity for money conceals the labor that produced it, with a stock like KO, it was not just the concealment but the actual erasure of labor—of bottling workers under consolidation—that made the financial commodity all the more valuable. KO's reification of the power of growing shareholder value was produced in part by the investor Warren Buffett, who bought $1 billion worth of stock in The Coca-Cola Company in 1988 and continued to invest, making the stock a symbol of his popular investment strategy. The Company's stock had already climbed almost 20 percent a year for eight years, but Buffett believed it to be undervalued, foreseeing a steady rate of future earnings growth for its foreign business on the verge of consolidation. Coca-Cola was a solid investment, he reasoned, because it had an almost unsurpassable competitive advantage in the market: the best-known brand in the world, relatively downturn-proof products, a global production and distribution system, and monopoly power over its bottlers. Because most of Coca-Cola's profits were earned outside the United States, Coca-Cola stock was purchased strategically to diversify investors' stockholdings with international market exposure. The Company did not require vast amounts of capital to be reinvested in its business and more of its profits thus enriched stockholders via dividends and stock repurchases. Buffett became the Company's largest shareholder, with a 9.3 percent stake, valued at $17 billion, and a corporate board member. His public boosterism of Coca-Cola, from the stock to the drink itself, made Buffett a kind of financial mascot of the Company, to the point that his face appeared on Cherry Coke bottles in China in 2017.[33] Whether Buffett inspired anyone to consume Coca-Cola is unclear, but his investment drove many people to buy the Company's stock. Buffett's advocacy of transparency in accounting and corporate governance and his long-term investment style, based on economic fundamentals rather than market valuation alone (as well as his philanthropy) made him an admired investor, perceived to be a positive influence on corporations and markets: a good capitalist. He was also a protagonist in a larger history of the impact of financial capitalism on the behavior of corporations and the effect on workers in their employ. Scrutiny from shareholders and the financial media, and the pressure to show earnings growth, and dividends, demanded that Coca-Cola executives make decisions with the Company's shareholders in mind, even when their interests conflicted with those of managers, workers, consumers, or the social good. Consolidation of bottlers, with the goal of cutting costs for increasing returns to shareholders, came at the expense of international workers.

This bottling consolidation was expected to result not only in increased soft-drink sales, but in increased sales of concentrate, for which the Company planned to raise prices now that its bottlers were operating more efficiently. Under consolidation, a smaller number of larger plants with modernized production lines and workforces sized and managed for efficiency would cut labor costs. The Company could invoke the success of these anchor bottlers to pressure the smaller bottlers in the Coca-Cola system to keep up with their sales or risk becoming targets of acquisition. The anchor bottlers also had their own motivations to grow—to increase returns for their own shareholders and garner greater clout with the Company.

From the Company's perspective, the rewards of its investment in bottling corporations outweighed the risks: not only could it leverage the consolidation of its bottling system to increase concentrate sales, but it made earnings from its investments in the consolidated mega-bottlers. This was true not only of the bottlers that were wholly owned by The Coca-Cola Company, but also of the much larger number in which the Company owned a percentage of stock or had made original capital investments on which the bottlers now had to pay periodic returns. In 1990, the Company held equity positions in bottlers representing less than 40 percent of production worldwide, but just seven years later, in 1997, through "the rapid acceleration in the execution of this strategy," it owned stock in bottlers representing 65 percent of global Coca-Cola production.[34]

Although the Company strategically owned large percentages of shares of its bottlers to influence their businesses, it generally kept that ownership at less than 50 percent. This allowed the Company to keep bottlers' financial performance (especially debt) off its own books for accounting purposes—technically, the bottlers were independent corporations, not subsidiaries—thus inflating its own financial performance and stock price. Distancing itself not only from financial but from legal and social accountability was a strategy that had proven especially profitable in the Company's relationship with bottlers. The Coca-Cola Company let franchises handle the costly business of bottling, exerting pressure on them to grow and expand, sometimes strategically buying up holdings of bottlers so as to consolidate them. The Coca-Cola Company would run these acquired bottlers as subsidiaries, before spinning them off as mega-bottler franchises to avoid the financial risks and debt burdens of bottling, sometimes buying them up again later to repeat the process, with the goal of refranchising them yet again, as it did with its massive North American bottler, Coca-Cola Enterprises. Because of The Coca-Cola Company's multiple forms of power over the bottling industry, financial analysts and corporate accounting critics found the stated structure of independent franchised bottlers disingenuous: as one analyst told the *New York Times* in 1998, "One can't transact business with itself . . . it's not real."[35] Not only was the Company a large shareholder in many of its bottlers, with executives sitting on their boards of directors and overseeing business decisions, its franchise contracts assured influence: the Company required approval of any transactions of bottling plants and orchestrated bottlers' mergers and acquisitions, restricted bottling companies to producing Coca-Cola products, and set the price and terms of payment for the drink concentrates. Not even on paper were the franchises independent.

The consolidation and reconfiguration of Coca-Cola's international bottlers and the resulting growth of large multinational anchor bottlers was enabled by financialization and the neoliberal "aperture" in many economies around the world with the corresponding elimination of restrictions on foreign investments and import controls.[36] Going public on the New York Stock Exchange in 1993, Panamco raised new capital to fund its acquisition of smaller bottlers in other Latin American markets with the aim of creating a larger, more efficient, and more profitable mega-bottler, in the belief that it could shield itself from the vagaries of single "turbulent" markets by "spreading the risk" and expanding internationally. Adding to its already large bottling holdings in Colombia, Mexico and Brazil, Panamco acquired bottlers in Costa Rica, Guatemala, Nicaragua, Panama, and Venezuela, and their rights to produce and distribute Coca-Cola drinks, as well as their other soda, bottled water, and beer brands. This growth was in line with The Coca-Cola Company's "bottling alignment strategy" of boosting efficiency and profits through the merger and acquisition of smaller bottlers and the Company assisted Panamco in these new acquisitions, facilitating negotiations and taking on a larger percentage of investment in the bottling corporation itself. The Coca-Cola Company designated Panamco one of its elite anchor bottlers, and a central player in Coke's corporate global system.[37] Panamco was now not only the largest Latin American Coca-Cola bottler, but also the largest franchise bottler in the world outside of the United States.

Latin America was arguably The Coca-Cola Company's most successful international market, driven by the growth of Panamco and a few bottling companies in the highly lucrative Mexican market. But it was less profitable for the bottling company, which took on large amounts of debt as The Coca-Cola Company encouraged its growth. Coca-Cola's prime international challenger, Pepsi, had started with larger territories and fewer bottlers, which resulted in economies of scale and cheaper prices for the consumer. With pressure to grow and operate more efficiently in order to compete, satisfy The Coca-Cola Company, and maximize returns for shareholders, Panamco expanded more rapidly than its finances could withstand. In the 1990s, it became increasingly difficult to sell more soft drinks in Latin American countries hit hard by lingering recession, currency devaluations, and neoliberal reform. In 1999, Panamco reported a net loss of $60 million—its first. Much of this was due to acquiring bottlers with large debts, like a Venezuelan bottling company sold to it by The Coca-Cola Company itself.[38]

Burdened by debt and now itself a target of corporate acquisition, the *Wall Street Journal* declared Panamco "a victim of rapid consolidation steered during the mid-1990s by Coke."[39] But if Panamco was a "victim" of

Coke's consolidation plans, the pain was primarily felt by its workers. Panamco responded to the financial pressures with cost-cutting; between 1992 and 2002, six thousand seven hundred workers lost their jobs at Colombian Coca-Cola plants.[40] Like Coca-Cola, Panamco credited its success with its decentralized structure of relatively autonomous, country-specific subsidiaries, criticizing other foreign corporations for not having the local knowledge of Latin America necessary for real profit. In 2000, Panamco moved its headquarters from Panama City to Miami, Florida, long a key node in circuits of transnational capitalist exchange with Latin America, as well as the home of Panamco executives executing decisions affecting bottling operations and workers thousands of miles away. From there, management of Panamco acted as a multinational bottling investment company dictating production and financial expectations to local managers who were relatively empowered in the operations of subsidiaries and bottling plants.[41]

Coca-Cola's Colombian plants would be under new distant management within a decade of going public and being tapped as an anchor bottler with investment by The Coca-Cola Company. In 2002, Coca-Cola announced that Coca-Cola FEMSA would buy Panamco. Originating as a brewery in Monterrey, Fomento Económico Mexicano (FEMSA), was a large bottler with popular beer brands and several Coca-Cola plants in Mexico. Its Coca-Cola sales volume was only half the size of Panamco's, but it generated the highest margins of any Coke bottler in the world, was well-capitalized (having gone public on the NYSE at the same time as Panamco), and in the financial position to take on the mega bottler's debt. Coca-Cola had groomed FEMSA for this powerful market position much as it had Panamco, acquiring 30 percent of Coca-Cola FEMSA's stock in 1993.[42] FEMSA, already a powerful Mexican corporation, emerged as a leading transnational corporate actor; the new company was the second largest Coca-Cola bottler in the world, controlling nearly 10 percent of Coca-Cola's worldwide sales.[43] But its take-over of Panamco, and Coca-Cola's large-scale investment in the resulting corporation, reveal interwoven capital and management relationships that belie the Company's insistence of franchise independence. With the deal, the Company increased its voting shares of the new Latin American mega-bottler to 46 percent. The Company was entitled to appoint four of eighteen Coca-Cola FEMSA directors as well as some executive officers and even had the power to veto significant decisions of the bottling company's board of directors. And of course, Coca-Cola retained the rights to unilaterally set the price for its concentrate or refuse to renew bottling contracts.[44] The CEO of the newly transnational Mexican corporation gave requisite praise to Coca-Cola: "The trust of The Coca-Cola Company shown to a Mexican company to let us grow to become the second-largest bottler is very important."[45]

The new FEMSA quickly recommitted itself to the cost-cutting program Panamco had begun. As the Company's annual report informed investors: "In connection with the merger, Coca-Cola FEMSA management initiated steps to streamline and integrate the operations . . . this process included the closing of various distribution centers and manufacturing plants."[46] In 2003, FEMSA's restructuring of the Coca-Cola Colombian bottling system further consolidated operations and restructured the workforce. It closed production lines in eleven of its bottling plants in Colombia, concentrating most manufacturing in five "megaplants" in the larger cities of Bogotá, Barranquilla, Bucaramanga, Medellín, and Cali, downsizing or shuttering other plants or converting them to distribution centers that employed far fewer workers. FEMSA laid off workers, and offered "voluntary" retirement packages for others, cutting its direct workforce by thousands.

Even with such massive restructuring, the work of bottling and distributing Coca-Cola's soft drinks still required people. But any remaining ties to the era of the Coca-Cola *gran familia* were cut by new management, and their strategies of plant closures, outsourcing, and increasing the number of part-time and short-term employees with no benefits. By the mid-2000s, between 75 and 80 percent of the people working in the Coca-Cola industry in Colombia held temporary jobs. These workers received only a quarter of the wages earned by their unionized counterparts and worked in precarious positions without the protection of a union.[47]

WORK AT COLOMBIAN COCA-COLA PLANTS AT THE TURN OF THE TWENTY-FIRST CENTURY

Under neoliberal changes to Colombian labor laws, there were now multiple ways to manipulate cheap labor and undercut union power. Firings, retirements, and the closing of production lines eliminated a large number of unionized jobs, which the unions understandably saw as a direct attack on their members' livelihoods and their ability to organize. Much of the remaining workforce was made contingent and precarious, with workers either ineligible for union representation due to their third party employers or short-term contracts, or so vulnerably employed that they were difficult to organize. These workers were employed by subcontractors, temporary employment agencies, and "cooperatives," which, despite their progressive-sounding name, were outsourcing firms that dispensed short-term subcontracts to do the work previously performed by directly employed workers. Workers involved in the distribution of Coca-Cola products from factories or warehouses to retailers at the point of sale were especially precarious; delivery drivers would have a team of workers contracted by a labor cooperative offering neither benefits nor job security. In a characteristic neoliberal move, the company also convinced a majority of delivery drivers, or "retail sales representatives," to go into business on their own. These new independent contractors were no longer directly employed by the bottler, instead becoming self-employed managers who leased or bought Coca-Cola trucks from FEMSA and hired their own workers.

This neoliberal labor regime devastated the Colombian Coca-Cola unions. By 2005, only 7% of Coca-Cola's Colombian workforce was unionized. Flexible workers, who comprised the majority in Colombian Coca-Cola bottling and distribution operations, had few protections and affiliating with a combative union would mark them for dismissal. Temporary workers were vulnerable to the company's refusal to renew short term contracts of those deemed demanding, and workers subcontracted by employment companies and cooperatives were hired under clauses that limited their right to association. In attempting to organize this new workforce, unions like Sinaltrainal faced vast differences of age, status, and skill. Most of the union leadership had joined in the early 1990s and were older than the newer, younger temporary and subcontracted workers. Many Sinaltrainal members were holdovers from the production line, and they often had more technical training and better paid, secure jobs. As Colombian law dictates, a single plant can have multiple unions, and according to workers, Panamco and later FEMSA fostered the growth of competing *sindicatos amarillos* ("yellow" company unions) to undercut the more militant existing unions. More unions did not increase workers' power, but rather decreased it, since Colombian labor law prohibited minority unions (those not representing the majority of all eligible workers in a plant) from striking. Sinaltrainal was still the largest Coca-Cola union, representing 45% of unionized Coca-Cola workers in Colombia, but it was a minority union in most individual plants, restricting its ability to take legally protected workplace actions. Coca-Cola's labor practices and Colombia's labor laws combined to decimate Sinaltrainal's membership, which fell from 1,400 to 314 members in Coca-Cola plants in 2005, further exacerbated by the physical violence that threatened their lives and stigmatized their organization.[48]

Even in the face of such challenges, Sinaltrainal remained a militant voice not just for its members, but also for broader social and economic justice in Colombia. Sinaltrainal vociferously attacked neoliberal governmental reforms, decrying the resulting *"precarización* and poverty" and drawing attention to the policies' effects on its members' livelihoods and labor organization, while also speaking from their perspective as food and beverage workers to assail these economic shifts as threatening to the physical and ideological sustenance of the Colombian people. Sinaltrainal articulated an analysis of corporate food control and export-oriented agricultural production (in which small farmers are pushed out for the large-scale commercial production of export goods like palm oil) calling for agrarian reform, the nationalization of monopolies, Colombian food sovereignty in basic staples, and a food system motivated by the health of consumers, the well-being and fair employment of agricultural and food workers, and environmental sustainability, rather than profits.[49] Representing workers at multinational food and beverage corporations, including Coca-Cola, Nestlé, Unilever, and Nabisco, which produce some of the most visible and visceral (as commodities physically consumed) global brands, Sinaltrainal leaders saw themselves as crucially positioned for resistance to these shifts. Jobs at Coca-Cola were often seen as setting standards in terms of pay and benefits for similar work. Other Colombian workers felt the effects of neoliberal policies even more severely—including the tens of thousands of public employees who lost their jobs to state privatization—but Sinaltrainal's responses to attacks on its workers were public and high-profile, in large part due to the challenge it represented to highly visible multinationals like The Coca-Cola Company. Sinaltrainal's Marxist orientation led it to create broad alliances with other unions, human rights organizations, *campesino* and displaced persons groups, and advocates for political prisoners and victims of state repression, constituting what in the US context might be called a "social movement unionism," but more accurately, in the broader Latin American political spectrum, constituted a revolutionary class politics, aiming not just for bread-and-butter gains for its members, but large scale social change in Colombia. The union's radical politics, and its public denunciations of The Coca-Cola Company's labor practices in protests and hunger strikes, made its members visible targets for paramilitaries.

Paramilitarism, and the larger violent conflict in Colombia, emerged from a complex history. From 1958 to 1974, Colombia was ruled by the undemocratic centrism of the Frente Nacional, in which, to end the decades-long conflict known as *La Violencia,* elite Liberals and Conservatives traded off political power and the presidency in an alliance based on mutual class interests and shared anti-communism. Political perspectives outside this center were excluded from democratic politics and some radical groups were driven into semi-autonomous rural communist enclaves. Elites pursued a program of capitalist modernization through import substitution and agricultural export, promoting the interests of Colombian industrialists and large landholding agribusinesses. Political and economic alternatives, including the attempts of subaltern classes (workers, *campesinos,* indigenous peoples, Afro-Colombians) to win more power through politics, were effectively foreclosed.[50] Colombian national developmentalism insufficiently addressed the patterns of land colonization and enclosure that had led to vast inequities for these groups, even exacerbating their lack of power by further concentrating land ownership in larger industrial-scale farms, depressing industrial wages as displaced peasants joined the urban workforce, and casting them as backward and premodern and thus excluding them from social rights. From the mid-1960s several revolutionary guerrilla groups, most prominently the Fuerzas Armadas Revolucionarias de Colombia (FARC) and the Ejército de Liberación Nacional (ELN), emerged out of the legacies of restricted democracy and partisan violence of *La Violencia,* as well as ongoing poverty and concentration of land ownership, drawing inspiration from the Cuban Revolution, liberation theology, Marxism-Leninism, and (later) Maoism. Landed elites had been building up their own armed forces; the *autodefensas,* or "self-defense" paramilitary groups that they had formed to protect their interests would become more organized and violent, enforcing the power of landowners, corporations, drug traffickers, and right-wing politicians.

The United States played a significant role in the conflict, with capital flowing to Colombia to ensure the protection of US corporate and geopolitical interests. Colombia was a strategic Cold War political and military ally of the United States in Latin America, and received military aid, financial loans, and political support for its anti-communist policies, as well as advice and training for counterinsurgency campaigns. In later decades, when it became clear that profits from coca cultivation and the cocaine trade financed non-state armed groups on all sides of the armed conflict, this became a new justification for the United States to again extend its influence in Colombia, providing financial and technical assistance under the auspices of the "war on drugs" and what would later be called Plan Colombia (for the eradication of guerrilla groups as well as the coca industry), infusing the Colombian military with billions of dollars, military training, and arms.[51]

In the context of the Colombian state's efforts to exert military control, maintain the appearance of a functioning democracy, and violently subdue guerrilla armies (narrowed down primarily to the FARC and the ELN from a once larger field), a dirty war of extrajudicial killing was outsourced to paramilitary death squads.[52] Elements of the Colombian military and government provided covert and sometimes outright support for armed civilian groups, including coordination with counterinsurgency "self-defense committees" from the late 1960s, cooperation with private militias organized to protect the wealthy from kidnapping and extortion that also acted as political death squads in the 1980s, authorization of a national program of private vigilante "cooperatives" to police guerrilla-occupied zones in the mid-1990s, and the collusion of politicians and paramilitaries revealed in the *parapolítica* (para-politics) scandals of the 2000s. Paramilitarism's power was broad, diffuse, and intertwined with state and capital interests, freeing the Colombian government from accountability for violence and leading to what some have called a "para-state."[53] Paramilitaries defended elite and corporate interests, violently pacified regions for capital expansion, and controlled populations through the production of fear.

In the mid-1980s the FARC adopted a policy of "the combination of all forms of struggle," fighting Colombian capitalism on multiple fronts. Its political wing and party, the Unión Patriótica (Patriotic Union), sought power through official democratic channels, but thousands of party members were assassinated by paramilitaries. The ideologies and initiatives of some unions and social movement organizations on the Left overlapped with those of the guerrillas, although their methods were different. Rightist paramilitaries and their elite enablers, however, targeted them all. "The result was catastrophic: unarmed activists, radicals, and communities were publicly identified as subversives and labeled enemies of the nation and then attacked by heavily armed private armies allied with the security forces."[54]

From the 1980s to the 2000s, more trade unionists were killed in Colombia every year than in all the other countries of the world combined. Nearly

4,000 were murdered between 1986 and 2003. Colombia was deemed the most dangerous country in the world to be a trade unionist, and union organizing was "considered to be the most dangerous work" in the country.[55] Human rights advocates asserted that paramilitary groups waging war on those they regarded as subversive—such as trade unionists—were largely responsible, but few were ever convicted.[56] Paramilitary violence was an effective means of labor management, with selective assassinations, detentions, and anonymous threats against Sinaltrainal limiting the power of Colombian Coca-Cola workers. By 2005, international human rights delegations were reporting that there had been "179 major human rights violations of Coke workers," including nine assassinations, numerous kidnappings, forced detentions, and attacks on Coca-Cola Sinaltrainal unionists, primarily at the Bebidas y Alimentos plant in Carepa and the Panamco (now FEMSA) plants in Barrancabermeja, Barranquilla, Bucaramanga, and Cúcuta. Most of the violations followed a similar pattern of occurring when the union was in conflict with Coca-Cola and its bottlers, such as during strikes, protests, or contract negotiations.[57]

"Paramilitarism was the "midwife of neoliberalism," as anthropologist Leslie Gill has persuasively argued, helping to birth a new era of capital accumulation in Colombia: "Paramilitary violence undergirded the opening of the economy through the repression of working people, labeled 'subversives' for their opposition to neoliberal economic reforms, the theft of their lands, and the assassination of their leaders."[58] Trade unionists, backed by researchers and human rights organizations, have repeatedly asserted the connection between corporate interests and the paramilitaries. Once paramilitaries occupied a region and eradicated the "problematic" members of the local population, corporations followed in their wake, expanding into a subdued area where land was now cheap and labor malleable. Sinaltrainal unionists frequently cited journalist Steven Dudley's book, *Walking Ghosts*, which implicated a number of corporations, including Coca-Cola, in ties with paramilitary groups: "Paramilitary leaders also told me on several occasions that they were protecting business interests in Colombia, including international companies. The AUC [Autodefensas Unidas de Colombia (United Self-Defense Forces of Colombia), a loose national federation of right-wing paramilitary groups in the 1990s and 2000s] had a strong presence near British Petroleum's oil fields . . . where Dole and Chiquita had extensive banana plantations . . . [and] around a coal mine owned by Alabama-based Drummond. Throughout the country, they had established bases near

Coca-Cola bottling factories."[59] The Chiquita claim, at least, proved to be true. In a 2007 plea deal with the US government, Chiquita admitted to paying $1.7 million to AUC paramilitaries in the Urabá region and agreed to a fine of $25 million.[60] The Coca-Cola Bebidas y Alimentos plant in Carepa, Urabá, sits amid the same banana plantations.

Of the paramilitaries' attacks on Sinaltrainal, perhaps the most flagrant was the annihilation of its Carepa union local and the assassination of its president, Isidro Gil, at Bebidas y Alimentos in 1996. According to Sinaltrainal, prior to the killing, the union was pursuing a court order to have one of its leaders reinstated after an unlawful firing, when the plant manager met with a paramilitary commander in the company cafeteria. Workers charge that the manager announced that "he had given an order to the paramilitaries to carry out the task of destroying the union."[61] Threats to workers soon followed, and the union informed both Bebidas y Alimentos and Coca-Cola Colombia of the intimidation. Previous death threats had displaced the union's original board from Carepa, and Isidro Gil stepped in as a new member of the union's governing board amid tense negotiations with the company, presenting a proposed contract for what remained of his union. Less than a week later paramilitaries killed him while he prepared to leave the plant. Two hours later, the paramilitaries made an assassination attempt on another union leader. Later that evening, they broke into the union's office, stole files, then set it on fire. When other union leaders prepared to flee the town, a Bebidas y Alimentos supervisor informed one of them of a meeting with paramilitaries in which they would be given "another chance to keep working in the factory."[62] At the meeting, the paramilitaries presented union leaders with a list of subversives, with each of their names included, and were told that if they intended to keep their jobs, they would have to follow the rule of the paramilitaries, under which there would be no union. Years later, sitting in their still fire-scarred union office in Carepa, workers recounted how on the following day, the paramilitaries occupied the plant and "took possession of the company like it was their own," forcing them to renounce the union by signing resignation letters, printed on company letterhead.[63] With the ongoing threat of violence, a number of the remaining Sinaltrainal leaders fled to Bogotá, where they lodged a complaint with the Ministry of Labor, to no effect.

In the fall of 2008, a local banana plantation and ranch owner admitted to being a paramilitary commander working through the government-sanctioned local security group to counter the growing radical militarism of the banana workers.[64] He confessed to committing assassinations and massacres and extorting or accepting large payments from local landowners and corporations for their security, including Chiquita and Coca-Cola's competitor down the street in Urabá, Postóbon. In one of his first confessions, he said that Coca-Cola also paid the paramilitaries, but later recanted this, saying he was confused. But he did admit to the murder of three union organizers at Coca-Cola in Carepa.[65]

The threats were widespread in paramilitary-occupied areas of the country, producing an encompassing climate of fear for the trade unionists. Sinaltrainal also accused Colombian plant managers of collaboration with local police authorities in the unlawful detentions of their members. Longtime Coca-Cola plant workers pointed out that as the bottling companies consolidated and became publicly traded companies and US owners (like Kirby) of smaller bottlers grew older and were no longer involved in the day-to-day operations, plant management was turned over to Colombians. Sinaltrainal perceived some of these individuals as especially repressive and suspected connections with paramilitaries. After a five-day strike to protest the elimination of employee medical insurance in 1995, the Panamco management in Bucaramanga accused Sinaltrainal members of planting a bomb in the plant. Three of the members were imprisoned for six months on the basis of anonymous witness testimony before the prosecutor concluded that the bomb had never existed. But in the meantime, their families had been thrown into economic crisis and vilified by much of the town. Plant managers stigmatized and threatened remaining Sinaltrainal members: "they invited us to resign from the company, saying that there would be an extensive investigation, they would 'investigate every member, because everyone was a suspect and at risk of going to jail, and the company wouldn't want for 20–50 Coca-Cola workers, Sinaltrainal members, . . . to go to prison for terrorist ties and links to subversion.'" Sinaltrainal membership at the plant dropped from 260 to 50.[66]

Paramilitaries frequently targeted the families of Sinaltrainal members, with nearly every union local having stories of children victimized by paramilitary threats and violence. In Barranquilla, the fifteen-year-old son of union leader Limberto Carranza was kidnapped and brutally beaten, and told that his father was on a list of people to be murdered. At the time, in September 2003, Carranza had been leading the union's challenge to the company's plans to close several plants and force the retirement of workers. During the kidnapping, Carranza received a phone call saying, "Unionist son-of-a-bitch, we are going to kill you . . . and if we can't get you, we'll kill your family."[67]

Sinaltrainal leaders argued that they were not collateral casualties of indiscriminate violence, but rather targets of planned attacks. The violence against their members, they asserted, was aimed at destroying their union. They stress that it was not a coincidence that the incidents occurred when they were challenging Coca-Cola's bottling management. They accuse the bottling companies of hiring former military officers, paramilitaries posing as private security cooperatives, and managers with paramilitary links.[68] Sinaltrainal also publicly criticized the state for its culpability in permitting this violence to occur and for failing to fully prosecute the guilty, while simultaneously persecuting political dissidents. As a result, union leaders took an active role in the Colombian human rights movement—activism that has further made them the targets of radical rightist paramilitaries.

Sinaltrainal's president Javier Correa calls paramilitarism the "hidden arm" of state and capital in Colombia. It effectively repressed challenges to the political and economic order by allowing powerful interests to frame any opposition as a threat linked to the guerrilla, marking opponents for paramilitary violence, and even justifying that violence as necessary. As Correa explains his experience: "They publicly accused me of being a guerrilla . . . it's the way of pointing me out . . . so I've been marked. That's where the work of the paramilitaries comes in. . . . It's the dirty work. The paramilitary arm generates terror, allowing the state, and others that benefit from it, to evade, to not be directly accountable for, or identifiable in, that action."[69] Suggestions that Sinaltrainal members were tied to guerrilla forces not only justified violence against them, further emboldening paramilitary attackers with a degree of impunity, it also eroded public support for the union.

The stigmatization of Sinaltrainal flowed from the highest levels of economic and political power. At the ANDI's Encuentro Internacional de Responsabilidad Social Empresarial (International Meeting of Corporate Social Responsibility) in 2006 the Vice President of Colombia Francisco Santos Calderón made the campaign against Coca-Cola the principal theme of his address, offering thinly veiled accusations of the union's relationship to the guerrillas: "In the case of Coca-Cola today several universities in the world are boycotting the Company. These threats come from radical Colombian sectors that see these types of instruments as an element of ideological war and the destruction of capitalism." He went on to accuse the union of using "its capacity for repercussion in other settings and the lack of responsibility of certain international spaces to *macartizar* [literally, "McCarthyize," or blacklist] and publicly discredit the most important multinational companies that act in our country like Nestlé and Coca-Cola. You know all the drama," he commiserated with Colombia's business elite, radically transposing the experience of blacklists from trade unionists to corporations.[70] This public condemnation from the country's vice president at a conference on corporate social responsibility—where Coca-Cola Colombia had just presented a celebration of its contributions to ameliorating the social costs of the armed conflict—demonstrated the reach of the union's powerful organizing to the highest levels of Colombian government, but also those officials' willingness to recklessly endanger the social and physical lives of trade unionists.

Sinaltrainal *did* organize its members around a radical vision that looked beyond the walls of Coca-Cola plants. The union called for the end to neoliberal globalization and foreign debt; the nationalization of imperialistic multinational corporations and the assertion of national sovereignty; justice against paramilitary repression of the social organizations of indigenous peoples, *campesinos,* and workers; the democratization of the Colombian state; redistribution of wealth; and radical social change that both made its members targets of reactionary forces, and also motivated their continued resistance in the face of such violence.[71]

SINALTRAINAL VERSUS COCA-COLA

The workers of Sinaltrainal and their international allies used the ubiquity of the Coca-Cola brand, its financial relationships, and its bottling business to map an alternative Coca-Cola world system as a way to build solidarity in their struggle against the Company. There was precedent for this kind of multinational organizing in defense of human rights at a Coca-Cola plant. In the 1980s, a Guatemala City Coca-Cola plant experienced aggressive anti-union policies, management collusion with paramilitary forces to quell growing labor radicalism, and the assassination of union leaders. The Guatemalan union's appeals to the International Union of Foodworkers (IUF) began an international boycott and shareholder activist campaign against Coca-Cola, which continued until The Coca-Cola Company in Atlanta intervened and the plant was sold to Panamco, a solution that ultimately served Coca-Cola's interests.[72]

Almost two decades later in Colombia, after years of frustration pursuing justice from the country's national authorities, Sinaltrainal and its US allies launched a US court case and international boycott. In mounting these international campaigns, they hoped to overcome the legal impunity encountered in Colombia by appealing to other authorities. The union was also looking for new strategies for labor activism, seeing globalized free-market capital as the force at work behind the consolidation, financialization, and flexibilization of Coca-Cola bottling. As a result of downsizing, subcontracting, and workers' insecurity and fear, Sinaltrainal was left with only a small membership and limited ability to strike and take direct action against the Company. The union's strategy reflected an emerging analysis that the transnational neoliberal regime in which commodities, corporations, communications, and institutions of governance increasingly crossing national borders could perhaps be used to broaden workers' power beyond withholding their labor. The union and its allies in the United States speculated that legal intervention by international courts or the public attention it attracted might push The Coca-Cola Company to address the conditions of workers and trade unionists in Colombia and even leverage improvements across the Coca-Cola world system.

In 2001, Sinaltrainal, the International Labor Rights Fund (ILRF), and the United Steelworkers of America (USW) filed a lawsuit in federal court in Florida against The Coca-Cola Company, Panamco (about to be acquired by FEMSA), and Bebidas y Alimentos, accusing the three companies of complicity in the unlawful detention, kidnapping, and murder of Sinaltrainal unionists. The USW's attorney, Dan Kovalik, had been looking for legal means to support Sinaltrainal and was inspired by the lawyers of the ILRF, who had just brought a precedent-setting case against the gas company UNOCAL for its collaboration with the Myanmar military in labor and human rights abuses. Like the UNOCAL case, the Coca-Cola lawsuit revived a 200-year-old Alien Tort Statute (ATS) that enabled noncitizens to use US federal courts to prosecute violations of international law committed outside the United States. The USW and ILRF lawyers accused the Coca-Cola defendants of hiring, contracting, and/or directing paramilitaries who perpetrated the violence against Sinaltrainal, alleging that the paramilitaries and managers of the bottling plants acted in concert to terrorize the unionists.

The Coca-Cola Company's defense hinged on the legal implications of its franchise system. Rather than contest the facts of the plaintiffs' case, Company lawyers argued that Coca-Cola was not liable for the activities of the bottling plants in question because it did not directly own or operate them and therefore did not control them.[73] The plaintiffs argued that through the "Bottler's Agreement," the Company's strict contract with bottlers,

Coca-Cola has significant authority over its franchised bottlers, providing the multinational with the power to control "all of the essential production details, including marketing, capitalization, the formula, containers used, requirements for employee qualifications, etc.," and that the bottlers exist only at the service and with the favor of the Company.[74] In 2003, the court agreed with the Company, dismissing it from the case.

While the case against the two bottlers—Panamco and Bebidas y Alimentos—continued, Sinaltrainal's USW and ILRF lawyers appealed to have The Coca-Cola Company reinstated as a defendant, to no avail. The burden was on Sinaltrainal's attorneys to demonstrate that the workers had no means of obtaining justice in Colombia, and that the abuses constituted a violation of international law. In 2006, the court decided that the bottlers could not be held responsible for the violence, because lawyers for the Colombian workers were unable to argue that the paramilitaries had acted as agents of the Colombian state, or that the violence against the unionists constituted war crimes committed by combatants in the course of hostilities, requirements for application of the ATS. And the judge in the 2009 appeal decided that the lawyers had not provided enough evidence to suggest the direct liability of the bottler defendants for actionable torture, deeming alleged conspiracy based on claims of money paid and shared ideology insufficient.[75]

The case against Coca-Cola was one of a number seeking to establish the efficacy of using the ATS to hold corporations liable for their actions internationally.[76] As David Harvey argues, human rights discourse has become the acceptable oppositional culture in neoliberalism, where the most egregious violations of civil and political rights (such as bodily harm) become the focus of legal action, but political struggles and class-based demands for economic justice are comparatively delegitimized.[77] Sinaltrainal's lawsuit was legally limited to individual cases of human rights violations, and not their causes and contexts: social inequality, class struggle, workers' precurity, and anti-union violence exacerbated by neoliberal labor reforms. By treating trade unionists solely as individuals, such human rights cases risked excluding "collective expression of grievances or demands for structural transformation" and shifted power from workers to lawyers as intermediaries of courts and authoritative voices in union campaign strategy. Sinaltrainal recognized the limits of the legal activism, but saw it as a foundation for building strength through international solidarity and a network of pressure on the multinational corporation as paramilitaries hobbled working class and social justice organizations in Colombia.[78]

As both activists and the Company seemed to understand, the real case against Coke would be tried in the court of public opinion, with its effect on the bottom line. While the high-profile case in the US courts was trying to hold the Company in the United States accountable for human rights in Colombia, activists waged a public relations battle against the Company and its brand image to dissuade consumers from buying its products and thus pressure the Company into settling with workers. In the United States, activists from what would be called the "Killer Coke" campaign and student-labor coalitions like United Students Against Sweatshops and Students for Economic Justice were successful in convincing students of the connection between their campus Coca-Cola vending machines and violence at Coke plants in Colombia. In 2007, students at some two hundred colleges and universities in North America and Europe had protested, with forty-five schools severing or refusing to renew contracts with Coca-Cola at least temporarily.[79]

In 2005, *The Nation* called the wave of student mobilizations against The Coca-Cola Company "the largest anti-corporate movement since the campaign against Nike,"[80] alluding to the student activism of the late 1990s that leveraged college and university apparel contracts to target labor abuses at apparel factories. Anti-Coke activists were descendants of the anti-sweatshop movement, benefiting from its legacy both politically and organizationally, with United Students Against Sweatshops prominently articulating a national campaign strategy and mobilizing their campus chapters against the Company. Coca-Cola executives insisted that these student efforts were misguided because of the fundamental difference between the commodity chains of the apparel and soft-drink industries. Whereas the former had brought sweated goods to campuses for sale, the franchised Coca-Cola industry produced and sold drinks by region; Coca-Colas bottled in the anti-union climate in Colombia were sold in Colombia, while those purchased by consumers in the United States and Europe were bottled in those regions, and by "independent" bottling companies, they explained. Therefore, a boycott of Coca-Cola on US campuses would only hurt US bottling workers, not the Colombian bottling company, Coke spokespeople insisted. But student activists were unconvinced, seeing themselves as materially and symbolically connected through the Coca-Cola system: in buying a Coke product they would be supporting a company that profited from violent enforcement of a regime of labor precarity, and buying into the corporation's encoding of

Coca-Cola as happiness while enabling suffering under its brand name. Many students felt themselves compelled to take action in solidarity with workers in distant places or else be complicit with Coca-Cola's global labor practices. More directly, students reasoned that putting economic pressure on the Company by threatening its financial relationships with universities in the global north might elicit a response in corporate behavior in the global south. The anti-sweatshop movement, the anti-apartheid movement, and even activism against Coca-Cola's labor and human rights practices in Guatemala in the 1980s provided historical precedents for the effectiveness of such a strategy. The campaign made critical contemporary links as well, merging with organizing in solidarity with communities struggling against Coca-Cola's water use in India.

In addition to concerns about labor and environmental practices in distant locations, students voiced local critiques from their own position within the Coca-Cola world system. They criticized The Coca-Cola Company's multimillion dollar contracts for "pouring rights," or exclusive soft-drink sales on campuses, and the use of college names and logos in marketing. These financial arrangements were "emblematic of the growing corporatization of education," activists at the University of Illinois at Urbana-Champaign argued.[81] Students at Rutgers University described the way their university's contract with the soft-drink company "delivers corporate gains through the use, branding, and manipulation of a public education institution."[82] Students organized against the Company's contracts on their campuses to simultaneously challenge neoliberalism far and near: regimes of labor insecurity and violence in Colombia, the dispossession and privatization of water in India, and the corporatization of education right where they were.

Much of the US-based activism in support of Sinaltrainal can be credited to the "Killer Coke" campaign spearheaded by Ray Rogers. The "corporate campaign," a strategy he innovated in the 1970s and marketed to labor unions through his Corporate Campaign, Inc., aimed to transform local labor conflicts into large-scale image battles. As such, Killer Coke researched The Coca-Cola Company, identified economically-linked institutions and points of pressure, communicated with the press and potential allies, organized events and maintained a website for blogging news, protests, and exchanges between activists, and produced and hosted a prodigious amount of anti-Coke organizing materials. Rogers was a veteran of US labor struggles who forged his corporate campaign strategy in unionization drives at the anti-union southern textile manufacturer J. P. Stevens in the 1970s and the mid-1980s strike at a Hormel plant in small-town Minnesota portrayed in the documentary *American Dream* (1990). As the documentary shows, Rogers's strategy of the corporate campaign was a product of emerging neoliberalism, union decline, and Reagan-era attacks on workers. Underlying it was the idea that withholding labor power was only one way for unions to fight back, and in fact, that they would have an increasingly hard time winning struggles through striking alone in the face of corporate intransigence, state sanction of union busting, and declining union membership. Rather, unions would need to apply other forms of pressure by generating a public relations challenge for the employer with news stories drawing attention to corporate exploitation and malfeasance. Such campaigns took on issues broader than workers' contractual concerns, using tactics such as attacks on the brand image, consumer boycotts, and leveraging interrelated businesses and investments crucial to the corporation's success.

In the Coca-Cola campaign, Rogers directed efforts at targets such as Sun Trust Bank, the Company's main creditor by exposing the interwoven directorates of the two corporations, and then used the allegations of human rights violations in Colombia to encourage large investors—like labor unions and pension funds—to close their accounts with Sun Trust. He challenged unions in unrelated industries to remove Coke vending machines from their union halls. Most successfully, the Killer Coke campaign mobilized students as consumers concerned with human rights violations, pressuring the Company by threatening its large exclusivity contracts with universities. Often run by staff rather than workers themselves and reliant on the actions and interests of outside groups, corporate campaigns risked producing forms of top-down unionism that could come in conflict with the interests of rank-and-file union members or limit their power by asking little of them in determining their own agency.[83] But they also called on the solidarity of other workers and activists and necessitated their grassroots mobilization to understand and communicate others' issues to build the campaign. In reaction, Coca-Cola tried to produce its own "grassroots" campaign modeled on the strategies of Killer Coke: launching the website cokefacts.com to compete with activists' cokefacts.org, distributing documents and short films on its website, and providing an activist-type e-mail alert from which visitors to its website could send friends "the facts."

Killer Coke faced the political predicaments of consumer campaigns around branded commodities and multinational corporations. The campaign powerfully mobilized the Coca-Cola brand, known to people all over the world, to produce a "critical fetishism," amongst consumers; in other words, to encourage people to look for and evaluate the conditions of a commodity's production and consumption.[84] But the campaign's representational strategies also risked contributing to a refetishization: both the branded commodity imbued with power as the agent of violence and the image of the victimized Colombian worker were packaged to provoke interest and sympathy, concealing the radical critique of the Sinaltrainal unionist. Such activism's attention to hyper-visible branded consumer goods produced by multinationals often overlooks less well-known egregious offenders of environmental or labor standards, as well as those more successfully obscured by complex and long-distance commodity chains of extraction and outsourced production. Corporate campaigns' focus on consumers and corporations, hailing them as agents of incremental social change negotiated between them, also risks marketizing political action, moving it away from the state to the market. The Killer Coke campaign generally neglected to consider the role of states—the role of US power in Colombia, the Colombian state's role in inequality and violence, and the potential role of both states in the protection of labor rights.[85] Consumer campaign strategies that highlight boycotting, or "buycotting"[86] (a vote of support through purchasing), associate political power with the act of consumption, and often no further, to demands for regulations that might positively impact a whole industry's practices, for example. Organizers worried that this form of consumer activism "disenfranchises poorer consumers, often the ones most affected by Coke's actions, by linking political power to purchasing power—one dollar, one vote."[87]

Killer Coke activists also appealed to other empowered agents in the Coca-Cola world system—Coca-Cola shareholders and prospective investors—to pressure the corporation. Much of this was strategic to draw public attention to the violence and perhaps even dissuade investment in the Company in order to pressure Coca-Cola to negotiate with workers. But individuals not directly involved in the campaign, such as liberal investors with commitments to both workers' rights and ongoing profits from a reformed Company, used annual shareholders' meetings to make public statements and offer resolutions about labor rights and organizing, and demand greater transparency and better business practices from the corporation. Drawing on the discourse of socially responsible investing and shareholder activism, they framed their demands with the rationale that the Company's environmental and human rights practices would affect its financial performance (disrupt production, diminish sales, ward off future investors). But these forms of investor activism were even more politically limiting, as only those with shares, for whom the ultimate motivation is profit, get a vote.

While potentially powerful in the short term, these models of social change risked encouraging market solutions like choosing to buy a commodity other than Coke or following a profit-driven ethics of investment where the more "responsible" corporation will make more money for shareholders. Corporations could easily co-opt movements by creating new markets in corporate social responsibility or philanthropy in which to compete for consumer loyalty and profit, discussed in the final chapter of this book. The Killer Coke activist network was in this way emblematic of neoliberal globalization itself, as transnational activists, NGOs, and corporations became central actors in a political sphere that transcended state borders and was increasingly organized through the market in the wake of reduced union power and governmental regulation.

This international solidarity organizing also had a difficult time translating the complexity of the Colombian context and Sinaltrainal's Marxist critiques, instead relying on the discourse and representations of aberrant violations of human rights, perhaps in haste to condemn the violence against the unionists and appeal to a broader political spectrum, but resulting in a simplification and silencing of the workers' own political voices. The campaign encountered the challenge of building solidarity across differences in power and class, as well as disjunctures in the political ideologies and goals of Sinaltrainal workers and their international allies. In the United States, the largest constituency of people who took up the campaign of Colombian workers were students, often white and from middle-class backgrounds, who did not have much previous experience of labor movements. In events on their campuses, US students met Sinaltrainal leaders who had been relocated to the US and Europe for their protection, or been brought on solidarity tours by sponsoring labor and Latin American solidarity groups in order to give them some respite from threats of violence and build the Killer Coke campaign. For some students it was a radicalizing experience that introduced them to labor solidarity and critiques of US empire, even leading them to other social justice work. But to reach a broad constituency of college students, the campaign centered on the act of consuming or abstaining from the product of a bad corporation. In so doing, it privileged the agency of US consumers rather than Colombian workers and even risked validating the market as the primary location for political expression. While powerfully

FIGURE 18. "Colombian Coke Float," www.KillerCoke.org, Concept Joe Pilati. Illustration by Jay Lynch

producing a "liberal anticonsumerism" and critique of corporate malfeasance, the focus on consumption differed dramatically from Sinaltrainal's anti-capitalist politics.[88]

The focus on consumption—or not consuming—was paired with the use of the omnipresent Coca-Cola brand image to make consumers more aware of their consumption of a commodity whose manufacturer was accused of complicity in repression. But these images became the dominant way of understanding the campaign, and they were all about the branded

FIGURE 19. "I Don't Drink Coca-Cola, I Don't Finance Death," Sinaltrainal poster, Fête de l'Humanité, October 16, 2006, Kilobug, Creative Commons Attribution-Share Alike 3.0

commodity, imbuing it with power as an agent of violence—it became a gun, a toxic product, a killer of unionists. This variant of "adbusting" or anti-branding, aimed to make Coke literally, as an early slogan put it, "Unthinkable, Undrinkable" (fig. 18). The most repeated image in the posters and organizing materials of activists was the bloody Coke. Inspired by the red packaging and the dark liquid within it, the activists attempted figuratively to bottle up the violence in Colombia for consumption abroad. The desired effect was repulsion. It worked much like the tales of vermin- or chemical-tainted Cokes promoted by local competitors, communists, and other critics of the drink that circulated in lore and rumor during the Company's mid-century international expansion. The Coke bottle also frequently appeared as a weapon, most often a gun. Here the drink became an actual "Killer Coke." Ironically, in these representations the Coca-Cola product was endowed with more agency than the trade unionists, who often appeared as anonymous, indiscriminately killed victims. The result was a paternalistic victimization, with unionists portrayed as in need of consumers' defense and protection. In contrast, in Sinaltrainal representations, unionists were embodied agents and specifically targeted, like the image of Isidro Segundo Gil in figure 19. Holding and reading the poster written in the first person became a pledge to boycott the drink ("I don't drink Coca-Cola, I don't finance death"), while the memorializing of Gil, invited pride in living and dying *como Isidro.* Similarly, in Sinaltrainal union halls, slain members are celebrated as *los martires,* preparing others to make the sacrifice in the most dangerous nation to be a trade unionist.

This problem of visual representation spoke to the larger challenge of representing Sinaltrainal's struggle in countries like the United States, where the political spectrum was narrow, but solidarity activists hoped to enlist a broad population of consumers in the boycott. In an effort to communicate to US consumers, the campaign frequently deferred to the power of framing Sinaltrainal's struggle in terms of the violation of human rights. Journalistic accounts and organizing materials focused on the unionists' victimhood in the face of paramilitary violence, often erasing the larger context of the economic violence of capitalist exploitation, neoliberal labor reforms, and Sinaltrainal's own trenchant structural analysis. Among activists, especially those within United Students Against Sweatshops and Colombia solidarity networks, there was a highly developed understanding of the trade unionists' experience from solidarity trips to Colombia, contact with the workers themselves, and activists' own class critique. But Killer Coke's broader campaign messaging centered on Colombian workers' victimhood, portraying Sinaltrainal workers' experiences and politics in clear, palatable terms to US audiences.

The language of human rights was more appealing to US audiences than Sinaltrainal's systemic analysis of the relationship of violence to economic conditions of exploitation. By the turn of the twentieth century, class-based and revolutionary movements had fallen further out of favor, replaced by a neoliberal politics of human rights, understood as individual and political freedoms (not at odds with the market), forwarded by international NGOs concerned with human rights violations defined by the most egregious forms of physical violence. Sinaltrainal also laid claim to the discourse and organizations of human rights. But in the Colombian context, human rights grew out of communist organizations and progressives in the Catholic church, and identifying oneself as a human rights activist was a radical act that meant exposure to paramilitary targeting.[89] Colombian Marxists like Sinaltrainal's leaders debated human rights as a bourgeois co-optation of politics that undermined collective action. But as both paramilitary terror and neoliberal labor reforms fragmented social groups and intensified the individualization of harm, human rights became a necessary tool for class struggle in Colombia. It provided new discursive channels for workers to speak to international audiences, even while it narrowed the political language and futures to be expressed and imagined.[90]

As a result, many US activists understood the Killer Coke campaign as a critique of the aberrant human rights abuses of a global corporation, manifest in activists' discomfort with The Coca-Cola Company's "bigness" and international reach and their demand for greater regulatory oversight and corporate reform. Fewer saw workers' experiences in Colombia as Sinaltrainal did, as the inherent production of capitalist exploitation and a symptom of the dispossession and reconfiguration of the working class under neoliberalism. But, as Lesley Gill has pointed out, "anti-corporate" sentiment and "anti-globalization" activism euphemistically stand in for anti-capitalist politics in the United States, where another world does not often seem possible.[91] Given its existing affinities, anti-corporate politics could become the basis for solidarity or a broader class critique. The US side of the Coca-Cola campaign might look different today. Since 2010, the United States has seen large-scale economic crisis, a diverse movement against elite interests—especially corporate and financial capital and their beneficiaries in the richest "1 percent"—and a labor movement that has realized that talking about class, even if in different language (the 1 percent and the 99 percent), has new relevance. Debates about warehousing and automation's downsizing and deskilling of labor, and the experiences of "independent contracting" and forms of casualized and flexibilized labor in various sectors (from Uber drivers to academics), show that US workers have much to learn from Coca-Cola's short-term bottling workers, self-employed delivery truck drivers, and Sinaltrainal. Workers' experiences over the past few years may mean that we may be better able to consider and respond, not just to the most egregious human rights abuses against Colombian workers, but also to the labor injustices that produced their precarity, necessitated their struggle, and made them the targets of violence.

Sinaltrainal leaders took great pride in the success of the international campaign, displaying posters, letters, artwork, pins, and other materials sent to them by solidarity organizations around the world. Several Sinaltrainal unionists credited the international campaign with protecting their lives. Subsequent paramilitary violence against them drew international attention, so while the threats continued, none of their Coca-Cola members were killed during the campaign (not true for members organizing at other companies). Union leaders and even some rank-and-file members expressed validation by the campaign, seeing their work and struggles reflected in the network of activists in the United States, Europe, and India.

And we went along incorporating and incorporating people and groups. And that was the strategy for how we created the web that today permits us to link up with many organizations in the world in favor, not only of the campaign in Colombia, but other affairs of The Coca-Cola Company, like the one in India. And little by little we have been studying other abuses The Coca-Cola Company has committed in other parts of the world. But there are parts of the web that we need to continue weaving. There are a lot of organizations. Imagine! This all came out of the heads of four crazy men in Bogotá, sitting in despair, because we didn't know what to do! We: Edgar Paez, Javier Correa, Dan Kovalik [of United Steelworkers], and William Mendoza.[92]

The campaign's connections with US labor were most powerfully manifested through the legal work of the United Steelworkers of America, but locals in other unions also took up the call to boycott, provide financial assistance to the campaign, and actively lobby their national leadership and government officials about the struggles of Colombian trade unionists. But the leadership of some unions, like the Teamsters, saw a boycott campaign in solidarity with Sinaltrainal, or a corporate campaign that attacked The Coca-Cola Company and its brand image, as a threat to their members' jobs and limited their involvement. Unfortunately, many in the US and European labor movements perceived the campaign as a predominantly legal and corporate one, and neither a real rank-and-file movement nor class-based solidarity fully emerged. The campaign had to build on an uneasy foundation of historical impediments to the formation of transnational solidarities between the Colombian and US labor movements. During the Cold War, the major US labor federation, the AFL-CIO, largely supported US foreign policy towards Latin America and the corporate agenda of expansionism and anti-communism. Many US unions adopted a position of "US exceptionalism" towards the workers of other parts of the world, defining themselves as Americans first, workers second, and not seeing common cause with their international counterparts. Much of this can be blamed on the mid-century McCarthyite anti-communist purges that dramatically stifled leftist union politics in the United States. The AFL-CIO collaborated with the US government to promote anti-communism and a rationalizing and deradicalizing model of labor-management collaboration in Latin America in institutions including the American Institute of Free Labor Development (AIFLD) and the International Confederation of Free Trade Unions (ICFTU). From 1962 to 1968, Coca-Cola Export joined corporations including the Standard and Mobil Oil Companies and the Standard and United Fruit Companies in helping finance the AIFLD to shape Latin American unions in the model of US free trade unions, in which "free" meant not only the freedom to join a union but also freedom from communist influence. The AIFLD offered training in union organizing and management, education and tours in the United States, and loans for the building or purchasing of housing, and emphasized business unionism rather than larger political goals.[93] Not only did the AFL-CIO support this rationalization and deradicalization of Latin American unions, in the 1980s and 1990s economic nationalists in the US labor movement participated in "Buy American" campaigns and generally portrayed workers from other countries as competitors.[94] Despite this, labor internationalists and the labor left in the United States led solidarity campaigns with workers and revolutionary struggles in Cuba, Chile, Nicaragua, South Africa, and elsewhere. Most rank-and-file US union members were generally unaware of the extent of the AFL-CIO's support of US hegemony and anti-communism in Latin America, but they were also often unaccustomed to imagining and practicing transnational solidarity. And, given this history, many Colombian unionists on the Left remained suspicious of US labor representatives in their country and calls for solidarity with US labor.[95]

Notably absent from Sinaltrainal's international solidarity campaign and boycott was the International Union of Foodworkers (IUF), which included a majority of Coca-Cola workers' unions. In the late 1980s, the IUF had played a major role in the international pressure on Coca-Cola in Guatemala—denouncing the violence and employment practices of the franchise owner and even participating in an international boycott of Coca-Cola products. When Sinaltrainal appealed for solidarity, however, the IUF backed the Company, unanimously voting to reject the call for a boycott. The IUF's response demonstrates the complex reticulation of local and global political economic interests in negotiating labor solidarities. The IUF called the boycott campaign's allegations of violence "sweeping [and] unsubstantiated" but its decision seemed ultimately determined by concern about the tactic of a boycott itself, which leaders argued would "do nothing to help the cause of the unions that organize and represent Coca-Cola workers around the world," including the more than 100 Coca-Cola workers' trade unions affiliated with the IUF.[96] The IUF's statement included a thinly veiled critique of Sinaltrainal's independence from the IUF and lack of deference to the US and European-dominated labor federation's authority in deciding on and issuing a call to boycott.[97] Most damaging to Sinaltrainal's efforts at building international solidarity was the IUF's conclusion that Coca-Cola's involvement in the murders was "unsubstantiated," based on statements by two of its affiliate unions Sinaltrainbec, a direct competitor of Sinaltrainal's in Colombian Coca-Cola plants, and Sintrainagro, the large banana workers union operating in the same area of Carepa, which had recently aligned itself with the political right wing in Colombia. The IUF argued that its position was based on the defense of the livelihoods of its Coca-Cola workers around the world, and in so choosing the protection of jobs over solidarity, the IUF echoed The Coca-Cola Company's own statement insisting that a boycott would disrupt plants far from Colombia, putting all of their Coke jobs at risk. The IUF continued that its allegiance would be to its new affiliate in Carepa, SICO, which had emerged after the Sinaltrainal local was destroyed.[98]

The new IUF affiliate in Coca-Cola's Carepa plant had a markedly different orientation from Sinaltrainal, reflecting a business unionism style and less confrontational approach to its employer, as members explained: "The ideology of SICO at the national and international level is to cooperate with the companies and with the work itself . . . work, show respect to your superiors, and 'no patear la lonchera' ['don't kick the lunchbox' similar to 'don't bite the hand that feeds you']."[99]

Indeed, the IUF signed a labor communication agreement with The Coca-Cola Company, with the logic that "engagement will yield better results than confrontation," a strategy mirrored on the Company's side by the newly created position of director of global labor relations.[100] In 2005, the IUF signed a joint statement with the Company acknowledging that "Coca-Cola workers are allowed to exercise rights to union membership and collective bargaining without pressure or interference. Such rights are exercised without fear of retaliation, repression or any other form of discrimination."[101]

The IUF joined with the Company calling for an investigation into the violence against trade unionists by the International Labor Organization (ILO), which activist groups perceived as a strategic move to co-opt international labor organizations in order to clear Coca-Cola's name. They pointed out that Ed Potter, recently hired by the Company as director of global labor relations, had served as the US employer representative to the ILO for the previous fifteen years, and was currently in multiple of positions of significant authority with the organization.[102] Activists argued that Coca-Cola undermined the potential for large-scale solidarity from US labor by such moves. And while a number of US union locals joined the boycott and many more expressed public support for Sinaltrainal, the AFL-CIO's Solidarity

Center, the labor federation's arm for international labor outreach (having replaced the discredited AIFLD), did not. In 2006, the Solidarity Center's assistant director, Stan Gacek, left to work as a consultant for Coke.[103] Working with such labor relations professionals was part of The Coca-Cola Company's strategic deployment of the discourse and practices of global corporate social responsibility, assimilating aspects of the Sinaltrainal and Killer Coke campaign's critiques, namely that workers should not be exposed to the most egregious forms of violence, while continuing to produce labor precarity at its plants.

While recuperating the public image of its labor practices, the Company launched a global corporate advertising campaign, "The Coke Side of Life" in 2006. Coca-Cola chose Colombia, over much larger markets, as the launching ground for the Latin American campaign, which, in a Coca-Cola Colombia executive's words, "invite[d] Colombians to create their own path toward happiness, constantly choosing those positive things in life."[104] But the Company avoided any direct reference to its renewed commitments to labor rights in Colombia as they would have risked acknowledging Coke's association with death rather than life. Instead, one of the campaign's most successful television commercials, "Happiness Factory," produced Coca-Cola as a fantastic commodity fetish, mystifying the actual labor of bottling workers with visions of magical little creatures concealed within vending machines producing each bottle of Coke, and happiness, for the consumer.

But Sinaltrainal's organizing and the visibility of the Killer Coke campaign meant that Coke bottling workers could not be so easily concealed. They successfully brought enough pressure to bear on The Coca-Cola Company that, while denying any responsibility for the violence against trade unionists, Company executives proposed to negotiate a confidential settlement with the Colombian union. In the meantime, Sinaltrainal and Killer Coke would be required to refrain from publicly criticizing the Company. For a year and a half the talks continued, quieting the campaign at a crucial juncture and weakening the union's power in the negotiations. Still, the Company offered a major financial settlement, a massive amount to any Coca-Cola worker but small in comparison to potential awards decided in lawsuits or the money Coca-Cola had already spent on public relations to deal with the controversy in Colombia, and, of course, would require division amongst the several Colombian plaintiffs, Sinaltrainal, and their lawyers. According to journalist Michael Blanding, the terms included language forbidding the union and Killer Coke from making any future denunciations of the Company (an earlier draft, per Blanding, even required the workers to resign from the union in order to receive the settlement and to agree to never campaign against the Company internationally again). And the offer did not address one of the union's primary demands: that the Company end the system of precarious temporary and subcontracted work that was undermining workers livelihoods and collective organizing in Coca-Cola plants. Agreeing to Coca-Cola's terms would have effectively broken the union—impeding its ability to critique its employer and sustain its membership—while offering its members no additional protections, the reason for the lawsuit and campaign in the first place, union leaders believed. They could not take the money from the Company while its labor practices remained the same, that was not their struggle, they argued; the money would not change the structural power in Colombian Coca-Cola plants. In fact, in the context of ongoing violence and impunity in Colombia, the money might increase the targeting of Sinaltrainal members by armed groups. Actual labor reform was not on the table from the Company, and the negotiations broke down.[105]

Sinaltrainal continued to demand "Truth, Justice, and Reparation," and to create a "public audience for human rights abuses denied in Colombia."[106] They called for the Company to enact international labor accords, an ethics code (including independent international third-party reviews of future claims against the Company), and a new labor policy to improve working conditions (like a limit on the flexibilization of jobs at Coca-Cola plants). In Colombia, they broadened their scope to include denunciations of other multinational corporations and the Colombian state, stances that other Colombian unions had criticized the Killer Coke campaign for failing to take. In the face of the Colombian judiciary's perpetuation of impunity, Sinaltrainal helped organize a series of Permanent People's Tribunals composed of international authorities, who acted as alternative judiciaries hearing testimony of Colombians on the activities of multinationals in the country and drawing attention to other labor and popular struggles.

In spite of the financial pressures of the Coca-Cola bottling system, Colombian neoliberal labor policies, and paramilitary violence, the members of Sinaltrainal continue their daily business of making a living, defending the rights of workers against the Company and the Colombian state, and keeping their fellow members alive. Even in the face of these threats, union leaders insist on a vision of a more just and equitable Colombian society and global economy. Their transnational campaign elucidated the ways Coca-Cola capitalized on Colombian paramilitary violence and externalized responsibility for workers to franchise bottlers. And in its ongoing struggle against neoliberal capitalism, Sinaltrainal refuses to have its critique contained by a reforming corporation and be bottled-up by "Killer Coke."

SIX

Water for Life, Not for Coca-Cola

COMMODIFICATION, CONSUMPTION,
AND ENVIRONMENTAL CHALLENGES
IN NEOLIBERAL INDIA

IN 1993, STRATEGICALLY POSED IN AGRA, the site of the iconic Taj Mahal, Coca-Cola's senior vice president (and future CEO), E. Neville Isdell, and his counterparts from corporate partners Parle Exports and Brindavan Agro Industries announced the Company's return to India after a sixteen-year absence. A new television commercial, shot to mark Coke's dramatic return, debuted at the ceremony, with 1,200 extras communicating "a reunion theme" consciously "reminiscent" of "I'd Like to Buy the World a Coke," a Company news release noted, perhaps to help erase the decade and a half in which India had chosen not be a part of that world. When Isdell finished speaking, "a fleet of six-ton delivery trucks bearing new 'image enhanced' graphics on ice, rolled out of the facility," to punctuate Coke's arrival.[1]

From 1977 to 1993 The Coca-Cola Company had been in self-imposed exile, renouncing business in India rather than concede to regulation. But, this was the "sweat belt," as industry executives called the hot, developing countries of the Middle East, Africa, and Asia with large Muslim and/or Hindu populations that generally rejected alcohol consumption, and thus held some of the largest "emerging" soft drink markets, like India.[2] Consumption of carbonated drinks in India was still just a fraction of that in the United States, offering the potential for growth demanded by the Company's shareholders just as Coke's sales had begun to slow in its developed Western markets.[3] Moreover, India was on the verge of opening itself up to foreign corporations, which would continue to push the levers of economic liberalization and deregulation to pry open the barriers to capitalist expansion.

Much would change in India, including George Fernandes's work with the BJP (Bharatiya Janata Party) Coalition to liberalize the Indian economy when it came to power in 1997. But much also stayed the same, including rural villages' lack of access to clean water. These villages, which had endured twenty years of environmental degradation from state-planned development, were also about to face both a strained agricultural system and a state-aided, market-driven rural industrialization program that would threaten common resources and small farmers' livelihoods. Seen through the curvy glass of a Coca-Cola bottle, the Company's history in India—exiled under the national developmentalism of state capitalism in the 1970s, returning in the freer market of the 1990s, and embattled in the 2000s—reveals the transformations and conflicts of a quarter century. For those living it, the Company's reentry made it a highly visible and tangible manifestation of Indian neoliberalism and thus the target of popular frustration with its failings.

When The Coca-Cola Company reentered India in the 1990s, it had to reestablish its brand and bottling system in the country. To do so, the Company engaged in a complex maneuver of corporate globalization: it spent billions of dollars consolidating bottling under US ownership while simultaneously localizing its brands in Indian culture. With Coca-Cola's, quickly ubiquitous presence in the 1990s it became a sign of both the Indian urban middle class's aspiration to global consumerism and the corporate dispossession of rural environmental resources to fuel its consumption. Some Hindu nationalist elements attacked the Company and its material and immaterial products as foreign contamination of traditional Indian culture, values, and bodies, but this response was moderated by the right-wing BJP's active welcoming of multinational corporations. When an Indian environmental NGO discovered *actual* contamination by pesticides in Coca-Cola's bottled drinks, it created an uproar in the mainstream media and the middle class, resulting in a consumerist crisis of confidence in the imagined quality of the commodities produced by global corporations. Contaminated bottles of soda and water encapsulated many of the problems of Indian neoliberalism and its environmental exploitation—the increasingly unrestrained development, lack of regulation of industrial and agricultural pollution and food and water safety, and underinvestment in public water infrastructure—while the middle and upper classes tried to buy their way out of their negative repercussions with privatized, market solutions.

Yet another challenge came from rural peasant communities that now hosted Coca-Cola plants, which protested the corporation's exploitation and pollution of local groundwater as an increasing expanse of the country fell into a crisis of water scarcity. This movement—most notably in Plachimada in the southern state of Kerala, and in the north in Kala Dera, Rajasthan, and

in Mehdiganj, Uttar Pradesh, the latter the primary focus here[4]—powerfully
challenged corporate globalization and privatization, illuminating the dispossession of the environmental resources of the rural poor for the consumption of those on the other side of an increasingly widening economic divide
in India's vaunted new free marketplace. These protests catalyzed an impressive social movement, linking local struggles with others through Coca-
Cola's world system of capital, commodities, and culture. In the 2000s, as
The Coca-Cola Company was localizing the global corporation and commodity in Indian society, Indian activists organizing around Coca-Cola
plants were globalizing their resistance.

NEOLIBERAL INDIA SEEN THROUGH
A BOTTLE OF COKE

The Coca-Cola Company, which had sought for years to reestablish itself in
India, saw an opening with a liberalizing government promoting private sector investments.[5] In 1993, the Company spent $70 million dollars to buy the
brands and bottling network of its one-time competitor Parle, India's largest
soft-drink company. Parle had flourished under the Indian state's import-
substitution policies and restrictions on multinationals resulting in its control of 60 percent of the soft-drink market, but now saw the seeming inevita-
bility of being taken over by the multinational giant. In the deal Coca-Cola
acquired the trademarks and business rights to Parle soft-drink brands—
Thums Up, Limca, Citra, Gold Spot, and Maaza—and its fifty-six owned or
licensed bottling plants. Coca-Cola set up a concentrate-blending plant in
Pune, Maharashtra, to serve its new Indian system of bottlers, and launched
an Indian subsidiary to oversee production and marketing to boost sales.[6]
    While Indian economic liberalization did not happen overnight, major
changes came quickly in the 1990s. In 1991 the government found itself with
rising external debt and depleted foreign-exchange reserves, threatening its
ability both to pay back its debts and to pay for imported technology and
materials perceived necessary for the country's development. The Congress
Party and Finance Minister Manmohan Singh set out to make the Indian
marketplace attractive to and thus lucrative for foreign investors and corporations. In agreement with this new Indian economic program, the International
Monetary Fund intervened in the crisis with loans that came with conditions,
enacted in economic reforms that dramatically opened up India's economy:

fiscal austerity to curb government spending, privatization of state-owned industries, and deregulation and liberalization of the Indian marketplace. With India's membership in the World Trade Organization, the state did away with the regulatory regime known as the "License Raj," reducing tariffs on imports and restrictions on multinational corporations doing business in India (including the Foreign Exchange Regulation Act used to demand Coca-Cola's "Indianization" in the 1970s).[7] India also encouraged foreign direct investment, wooing the return of multinationals like Coca-Cola.

In this context, global brands—Coca-Cola among the most prominent— became evocative representations of India's neoliberal transformation. Members of the mainstream press used Coca-Cola's reentry as a metaphor for neoliberalization in articles with titles like "A Revolution Transforms India: Socialism's Out, Free Market In."[8] The Company's press releases also framed its return as symbolic of India's economic liberalization. "This partnership is a concrete expression of our confidence in the Government of India's meas- ures to liberalize the Indian economy and welcome foreign investment," Isdell said.[9] With more than $1 billion spent on its Indian operations in its first ten years back in the country, Coca-Cola was "one of the country's top international investors."[10]

The Coca-Cola Company not only benefited from Indian neoliberaliza- tion, it actively influenced its terms. Whereas through the 1970s Coca-Coca emphasized "local, independent" Indian bottlers as drivers of national social and economic development, in its second coming to India, the Company imposed direct ownership and control of bottling operations. Upon return in 1993, Coca-Cola launched a subsidiary, Coca-Cola India, to produce concen- trate and market its line of beverages.[11] But its efforts to organize a separate consolidated bottling corporation ran into resistance from the independent bottlers, who refused to merge or sell out to others.[12] Coca-Cola thus decided to control production itself, buying up and building bottling plants that it would own and manage through a new subsidiary, Hindustan Coca-Cola Beverages. The Indian government had allowed this new foreign-owned bot- tling corporation with the stipulation that the Company sell 49 percent of its shares in Hindustan Coca-Cola Beverages, including voting rights, to Indian residents by 2002. The Company agreed, but the Indian business press was skeptical, predicting Coca-Cola's long-term plans to control bottling itself and seeing its acceptance of the condition as a strategy to appease the govern- ment in the wake of public criticism that after taking over Parle, it was now "out to gobble up the 'poor' Indian bottlers."[13] Not surprisingly then, when the time came for the Company to concede the divestment it had delayed until 2003, it was reluctant to sell off its ownership of the stock and deemed giving voting power to Indian shareholders too "'substantive and onerous.'"[14] Analysts further speculated that after heavy outlays in investments in Indian bottling in the preceding years and large losses between 1997 and 2000 stock prices would be low and look like "a distress sale," harming the Company's global brand image and reputation.[15] But government sources spelled out the requirement in no uncertain terms, according to the Indian press, because of the Company's track record of manipulative dealings with government regulation, and it had in this case "resorted to pressure tactics to influence the Government's decision-making process by utilising its clout with the US Commerce Department as well as through the office of the US Ambassador in India in seeking a waiver of the divestment condition itself."[16] The Company, as part of a cohort of nearly two dozen foreign corporations that had been approved to establish themselves in India with the divestment condition, heavily lobbied the Indian government to waive it. But the Indian government was unswayed, and in March 2003, Coca-Cola became the first multinational to divest, albeit reluctantly, to Indian shareholders. To comply with the rules the Company organized a sale of 39 percent of its stock to handpicked private investors and the other 10 percent to its employees' trusts, thus protecting its voting shares.[17] But the Company did not have to abide by these restrictions for long, since by 2005, with the architect of Indian liberalization Manmohan Singh now serving as prime minister, the Indian government further liberalized its policy, allowing 100 percent foreign ownership of business ventures. Hindustan Coca-Cola Beverages promptly bought out its Indian shareholders.[18] Coca-Cola India, and Hindustan Coca-Cola Beverages, the largest Indian bottler that buys concentrates sold by the former, were now both owned by The Coca-Cola Company.

With control over its Indian operations, Coca-Cola set out to double its production capacity through expansion and modernization of its operations, which grew to twenty-five wholly Company-owned bottling plants, another twenty-five franchised plants, and twenty-one contract packers (which manufactured and packaged a range of Company products) in 2009.[19] As a result, the Company controlled 65 percent of production through its bottling plants, including those in Plachimada, Mehdiganj, and Kala Dera, sites of dramatic and persistent resistance to the Company's presence.[20] The Company's control over the Indian bottling industry was consistent with its 1990s and early 2000s strategy of bottling consolidation, but contradicted the terms of the Company's previously celebrated policy of decentralization, making bottling everywhere a local, independent business.

As the material production of The Coca-Cola Company became less Indian with the US corporation's control of the bottling business, advertising conversely attempted to make its brands' representation more local, or "glocal," as advertising executives put it. This strategy was developed in part because of the Company's failure to find quick success in India; its assumptions about the universal applicability of its business model and marketing came up against the demands and desires of Indian consumers and society. Upon arrival in India, the Company began to phase out the country's most popular cola, its newly acquired Thums Up brand, pushing Coca-Cola in its place,[21] much as it had done after acquisitions around the world. Sales of both drink brands suffered, and Pepsi made inroads into the Indian market. Exacerbating matters, in the 1990s, the Company centralized image production much the way it had consolidated bottlers, launching "one-sight one-sell" global campaigns with universal and standardized, if multiculturalist, assertions that it was "Always [time for] Coca-Cola" everywhere in the world. These global advertising campaigns met with limited success in new international markets like India, where viewers found them disconnected and distant from their daily lives.[22]

Such advertising also became cultural evidence of the foreignness of the Company, and fueled critiques by those, especially on the political and religious Right, who saw the Company as contaminating Indian bodies and India's body politic. In the 1990s, Hindu nationalist groups such as the Rashtriya Swayamsevak Sangh (RSS) and Vishva Hindu Parishad (VHP) targeted Coca-Cola—along with Muslim and Christian population growth, communists and other leftists, and any decentering of Hinduism from national identity—calling for protests and boycotts of Coke and Pepsi. Hindu nationalist rhetoric also erupted into direct action, such as in 1998 when the Bajrang Dal (the VHP's youth wing) protested Coca-Cola and Pepsi when the United States imposed nuclear sanctions, using their soft drinks to douse the flames of bonfires of foreign goods. Coca-Cola vans were burned in Gujarat, leading the bottling plant to temporarily suspend distribution.[23] As the BJP and other Hindu nationalist political parties began to champion Indian capitalism and promote the admission of multinational corporations, right-wing communalist rhetoric against Coca-Cola would become less common, but charges of foreignness remained, motivating the Company to further localize its brand in Indian culture.

Such international failures, challenges, and resistances drove a return to the "local" in the Company's broader representational strategy. The "combined approach [of] a centralized management strategy from The Coca-Cola Company, and a consolidated system of larger bottling partners—served our shareowners and us very well," CEO Douglas Daft said in 2000. "During the '80s and well into the '90's we were riding the wave of globalization with extraordinary success. In May of '93, *Fortune*'s cover story called us the world's best brand. Then the world began to change." The Company faced the "second wave of globalization . . . backlash," Daft went on, describing the critiques of multinational corporations recently manifested in locations around the world. To counter them, he adopted a "repositioning strategy" of localizing more of Coke's business decisions and marketing, appropriating the language of the contemporary resistance to assert that the Company would "think locally and act locally," to be a "good neighbor" everywhere, gesturing to the Company's portrayals (if not the reality) of its early internationalization model.[24] This strategy asserted the profitability of local variation, promoting the Company's newly acquired Indian brands like Thums Up, Limca (lemon-lime soda), and Maaza (a mango drink), and pitching the Company's global products in locally produced advertising rather than global campaigns alone. Of course, the structure of the Company and the centrality of the profit motive of its stockholders remained unchanged: most management was centralized, the consolidation of bottlers continued apace, and those that profited remained a tiny, distant group to the vast majority of Indians. But by strategically deploying India's successful soft-drink brands and promoting the "Indianness" of its own global brands, the Company hoped to tread on fewer toes in the country from which it had been so dramatically ejected before.

PRIVATIZING *THANDA* (COLD DRINK)
TO MEAN COCA-COLA

Coca-Cola and McCann Erickson's India office attempted this localization while communicating the universal neoliberal promise of freedom and individual self-betterment through the market. In 2002, the slick ad campaign "Life *ho to aisi*"—"Life as it should be" in Hinglish—placed Coca-Cola in India's global cities and the lives of its aspiring consumer world citizens. The commercials featured the Bollywood star Aishwarya Rai, a "global goddess" symbolizing India's marketability.[25] With Rai singing out from her penthouse apartment to the sleek cityscape all around her, the ads hailed the urban middle class with a celebration of both Coca-Cola and their ability to buy into the global good life of international brands—"life as it should be"—in the new free marketplace of global brands in India.[26]

In its next advertising campaign, The Coca-Cola Company sought to further combat the critical reception of its globality as "foreign" and homogenizing, and also profit, by connecting itself to "Indianness" and perceived authentic Indian popular cultures and identities by "speaking the language of the rural masses and lower socioeconomic class." These rural masses and lower classes comprised the majority of the nation, but with little disposable income, they were infrequent consumers of the Company's products. Drawing on such Indianness was necessary, ad creatives explained, because in India "refreshment was real, earthy and unaffected by global trends." The Company mined popular rural and working-class culture to construct the "localness" of Coca-Cola for its primarily middle- and upper-class consumers in a campaign that saturated media spaces, from building façades to rapidly commercializing television channels, with the slogan "*Thanda matlab* Coca-Cola"—"cold drink means Coca-Cola." The ads tapped the immense popularity of the Bollywood star Aamir Khan. Comically portraying various regional, ethnic, and class "types" of Indian common men, Khan appropriated "local lingo" and "mass sensibilities" to put the commonplace of Indian daily culture to use in the production of Coca-Cola.[27]

The Hindi word *thanda* means "cold," and is colloquially used to mean "cold drink," whether water, soda, *lassi* (a yogurt drink), *nimbu pani* (lemon- or limeade), *nariyal pani* (coconut water), or some other beverage. But the "*Thanda matlab* Coca-Cola" ads aimed to make *thanda* "generic for Coca-Cola."[28] When someone asks for *thanda* they really "mean Coca-Cola"—"*Thanda matlab* Coca-Cola," as the slogan says.[29] To that end, the television commercials progressively resignified *thanda* as Coca-Cola.[30] In the first ad, Aamir Khan's Mumbai street tough explains that when he orders a *thanda* he really means a Coca-Cola. In the second, Khan, now a Hyderabadi shopkeeper, instructs customers to ask for *thanda* to get Coca-Cola. And by the third, when three attractive, urban young women pull in thirsty to a rural village and ask Khan's Punjabi farmer for *thanda pani*, expecting water, he magically pulls up glistening Cokes from his well.

This last commercial unconsciously articulated the hierarchy of rural/extraction and urban/consumption characteristic of Coca-Cola's commodity chain in neoliberal India. In proclaiming that "*Thanda* means Coca-Cola," the Company enclosed a whole symbolic commons of communication and popular drinking culture as its own—what once meant common water now "means" commodified Coke—privatizing this term for the brand. The Indian advertising community declared that it "made the almost universal rural word [*thanda*] . . . a hot catchphrase."[31]

Print advertisements went even further in localization, presenting themselves as photographic evidence of how deeply ingrained Coca-Cola was in local culture, representing the brand sign of global capitalism as an organic and constitutive element of all things *thanda* in the heat of Indian daily life and hybrid modernity (fig. 20). Form meets content in these color "snapshots" which are constructed to look like spontaneous, uncomposed, and authentic representations of the gritty but vibrant Indian quotidian: cooling down an overheating radiator, getting a refreshing bath, freshening up at a barbershop. One has to look twice to identify the Coke bottles decentered and camouflaged through context. In a mediasphere most known for its dream factory productions disconnected from Indian daily life, these images are hyperreal signifiers of reality that make you linger until you see the integration of Coca-Cola's iconic hourglass shape fashioned into a trucker's makeshift coolant applicator, a mother's well decanter, and a barber's spray. The images celebrated the ingenuity of rural and working-class Indians, suggesting a virtuousness born of necessity that would only flourish more with the embrace of multinational goods. The ads seem to undermine advertising conventions intentionally, rather than putting a commercial polish on a product by surrounding it with the aspirational or exceptional, here Cokes are subsumed in the unvarnished Indian everyday. This wink to an audience jaded by advertising's form, as well as the wry play on the slogan (that the *thanda* being offered by Coca-Cola is not from the drink alone), suggests that these ads were intended for a sophisticated, urban population for whom both Coke products and representations of Indian working-class and rural earthiness were offered for consumption.[32] Fully Indianized, and celebrating the opposite of global cultural homogenization, these Coke bottles play a subtle yet constructive cooling role in concert with the agency of India's common people, each bottle dispensing water, but crediting Coca-Cola with its fundamental *thanda*.

But as these commercials went on air and into print, Indian villagers were actively organizing against these symbolic and material enclosures of the system of rural/extraction and urban/consumption of the Coca-Cola commodity, protesting the privatization of their communities' water by Coca-Cola plants. Most of them were not buying Coca-Cola's *thanda* at ten rupees

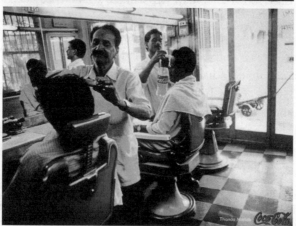

FIGURE 20. "Thanda Matlab Coca-Cola" print ads, 2003–4.

a bottle, the equivalent of a tenth of the average daily salary.[33] Instead, water was extracted out from their communities and sent to the cities where growing middle-class consumerism and its thirst for brands like Coca-Cola was quenched by the natural resources of a rural India already strained by agricultural crisis. But Coca-Cola also inadvertently brought the environmental crisis directly to the consumer class.

KILLER IN THE CORPORATE COMMODITY:
THE CONTROVERSY OVER PESTICIDE
CONTENT IN BOTTLED DRINKS

In 2003, the Centre for Science and Environment (CSE), a respected Delhi-based NGO, revealed that twelve drink brands manufactured by The Coca-Cola Company and PepsiCo and sold around Delhi contained "a deadly cocktail" of pesticide and insecticide residues. In a press conference covered by every national television newscast, the CSE's director announced that "these pesticides include potent chemicals which can cause cancers, damage the nervous and reproductive systems and reduce bone mineral density."[34] Residue levels in all tested samples far exceeded the European Economic Commission (EEC) maximum limit for pesticides in water used as food: Coca-Cola was forty-five times and Pepsi thirty-seven times the EEC limits, with the multinationals' other Indian brands falling between eleven and seventy times higher.[35]

Tainted soft drinks captured the attention of the media and the public, poignantly symbolizing for many middle-class Indians the dark dangers of consumer capitalism and US economic globalization, in addition to highlighting local environmental degradation and the regulatory failings of India's rush into neoliberal modernization. Coca-Cola became a target for protestors from various positions on the broad Indian political spectrum, from pro-environment, anti-capitalist, and anti-imperialist to cultural nationalist. Since the arrival of the US drink brands, Hindu nationalist elements had condemned Coca-Cola as a contaminating "foreign" and "impure" influence on traditional Indian culture and bodies.[36] Now with evidence of the actual contamination of bottled drinks, they attacked Coca-Cola in symbolic acts of rejection, smashing bottles and burning brands in effigy, calling for them to be removed from the market.[37] The United States had just invaded Iraq, and the Company was perceived by many Indians as representative of US soft power abroad, and thus an accessible surrogate target for anger over US imperialism.[38]

Environmentalists argued that the pesticide revelations betrayed the need for greater regulation of agrochemical use, safety standards for food and drinks, and investment in safe and sustainable public water systems. The CSE's report also highlighted the "virtually unregulated" state of the bottled drinks industry: no mandated environmental impact assessments, no regulations on the siting of industry, and no groundwater policy on the safety and sustainability of virtually free water.[39] "Our battle is not with Pepsi or Coca-Cola," the CSE's director told the press, "it is with the Indian government, whose norms are a vague maze of meaningless definitions."[40] But most of the CSE's report and the subsequent public response focused on the products of the global soft-drink giants.

Public-interest groups filed court petitions calling for a nationwide ban of Coca-Cola and Pepsi products. While lawmakers debated a ban on the floor of Parliament, they discontinued the sale of the drinks from their own cafeteria and ordered state governments to launch independent investigations in their regions. As a result, several states banned the sale of Coca-Cola and Pepsi products at schools and public offices, and some state officials even confiscated stocks of them from plants.[41] While the soft-drink giants attempted to quell this outraged response through PR crisis management and a smear campaign against the CSE, a survey conducted in Delhi found that a majority of consumers believed the NGO's report and agreed with the Parliament's move to ban the sale of soft drinks.[42] After 75 percent growth in the previous five years in India, in the weeks following the CSE report, Coca-Cola sales dropped by 30–40 percent.[43]

The revelations that global corporations could be putting consumers at risk of imbibing dangerous pesticides challenged middle-class faith in the multinational corporations taking hold in India. In the 1990s, newly available global brands carried the allure of international popularity and the suggestion of market-proven quality, elements that the Indian middle class felt they had been denied by the state monopolies and closed markets of previous decades.[44] Middle-class consumers' sense of deprivation contributed to their support for neoliberal reforms and gave an air of long-withheld superior quality to the resulting flood of commodities from multinational corporations that they were now entitled and encouraged to consume. This was part of a larger shift in cultural power as India underwent economic reform: the Nehruvian developmentalist state's prioritization of citizen-workers and support for rural poverty reduction was displaced in national discourse by a neoliberal emphasis on the construction of a middle class of urban citizen-consumers.[45] Branded products like Coca-Cola seemed to offer the Indian middle class entrée into global consumption and access to claims of quality and responsibility promised by global corporations. The outcry around the pesticide revelations was a middle-class response to the reality of neoliberalism, an expression of newfound consumer empowerment in the face of the failed promise of global brands and the freer market.

Global brands like Coca-Cola had offered the Indian middle class an opportunity to buy their way out of ongoing problems of postcolonial national development. Those who could purchase one of the Company's several soda, juice, or water brands could both quench their thirst and opt out of the quality, quantity, and sustainability concerns resulting from inadequate investment in public water systems and poorly regulated agricultural and industrial development. That even the products of global corporations were contaminated by pesticides was a perceived betrayal of Indian consumers' confidence in them relative to presumed inferior Indian goods and public water. Before the CSE's report, soft-drink sales had been rapidly rising, with the global brands growing to compete with top Indian labels (Thums Up and Limca, also owned by The Coca-Cola Company). But when the CSE tested Coca-Cola and PepsiCo products from the United States and found them free of pesticides, Indian consumers interpreted this as evidence that a different, lower standard was being applied to products made for the Indian market, and the companies' globality was transformed from an asset into a liability.[46]

Upon its return to India The Coca-Cola Company had introduced its Kinley and Bon Aqua brands, packaging the product most poignantly representative of the commodification of common resources: bottled water. In India, as in many global south countries where governments do not provide safe drinking water, bottled-water companies exploit unpriced, common water resources to cash in on the willingness of the middle and upper classes to pay for private drinking water rather than demand state investment in public water infrastructure. As a CSE publication wryly but concernedly described the construction of a bottled-water market, "India is wholeheartedly disinvesting . . . er, further liberalizing" public water.[47] Before liberalization, Indian bottled-water sales had been miniscule, totaling less than two million cases per year. After liberalization, India was home to the world's fastest-growing market for bottled water. By 2005, water bottlers in India were selling eighty-two million cases annually; Coca-Cola's Kinley water closely rivaled Parle's Bisleri brand for first place, with Pepsi's Aquafina coming third.[48]

The CSE released its 2003 soft-drinks study on the heels of a kindred report on pesticide residues in bottled water. Concerned about agricultural and industrial pollution, the CSE was already monitoring groundwater and municipal water systems, but became increasingly concerned that Indians with the economic means were turning to bottled water as a perceived safer option. Suspicious that the bottled-water industry was unregulated and drawing water for its products from similarly polluted groundwater sources, the CSE conducted tests on seventeen multinational and Indian brands of packaged drinking water. Most bottled water produced in India was contaminated, the report concluded, returning evidence of pesticide residues including lindane, DDT, malathion, and chlorpyrifos, and "should not be considered a sustainable alternative to tap water."[49] The CSE report decried the lack of mandatory regulatory norms for bottled water specifically and bottled drinks generally and argued that the existing regulatory standards were "vague and undefined."[50] Pesticide levels were found to be 14.6 times higher than the European legal maximum in Coca-Cola's Kinley, 79 times higher in Parle's Bisleri, and 104 times higher in Indian brand Aquaplus, which led the list.[51]

The CSE's research was part of an international environmentalist challenge to Coca-Cola's commodification of water and the associated neoliberal logic that private commodities are solutions to public problems. In North America and Europe, where governments have largely succeeded in providing clean and affordable water as a public service, NGOs like the Polaris Institute and Corporate Accountability International led campaigns against the bottled-water industry for its privatization of common water sources, its commodification of a good that is publicly available and safe from the tap, and its needless production of waste and consumption of resources (like plastic bottles and transportation fuel). In fact in North America and Europe, the Company manufactures and bottles the majority of its drinks from the same tap water, bottling up public water. These campaigns thus framed bottled water as the material and symbolic apotheosis of the privatization of an environmental commons. Bottled water not only makes a private commodity out of a common good, it generates suspicion of common sources of water, normalizing their privatization and fostering the conclusion that there are preferred private, market solutions to public needs through which citizens, reconstructed as consumers, can opt out of the public (if they can pay) by purchasing commoditized goods.[52]

Unlike critics of the bottled-water industry in the United States and Europe, however, the CSE called into question the *safety* of commodified water in the context of the failure of the postcolonial Indian state to protect groundwater and provide clean public drinking water. Municipal water systems, even in India's most "developed" cities, have yet to meet citizens' needs, with shortages, contamination, and poor infrastructure especially failing the poor through lack of access, comparative subsidization of wealthier and larger water users (both industrial and individual), and inadequate safety standards. Members of the middle and upper classes deal with their government's failure to provide clean water by purchasing bottled drinks.

It was perhaps a strange choice for an Indian environmental NGO to focus on products that only a limited segment of the population could afford to consume in order to highlight the widespread environmental and public health issue of water insecurity. But by doing so, the CSE's Kushal Yadav explained, the organization crafted a highly visible and tangible representation of the problem, demonstrating the presence of pesticide residues in even the most trusted brand-name commodities.[53] The CSE targeted branded goods to agitate two ascendant powers in liberalizing India—multinational corporations and the middle class that consumes their products—in order to draw attention to widespread environmental concerns.[54] The CSE hoped to arouse middle-class Indians' ire about environmental degradation by demonstrating direct corporeal effects on them as consumers. Even as middle-class consumers turned to the free market to escape India's environmental problems, the goods of that market would be laced with the products of weak governmental regulation and powerful capitalist development.[55] The CSE had been pushing for protection of groundwater for years and feared that middle-class audiences would not register yet another report on that subject. "Since Coke and Pepsi products are perceived as high quality, by analyzing them and demonstrating the presence of contaminants, we could get out the message of widespread contamination effectively and create pressure on the government to act. If we had done the same thing with municipal drinking water, no one would have noticed."[56]

Founded by the celebrated environmentalist Anil Kumar Agarwal in 1980, the CSE was one of the first civil society groups from the development-focused global south to argue for *sustainable* development—the notion that "environmental conservation must go hand in hand with national economic development."[57] Covering a broad range of issues, the CSE emphasized the effects of environmentally destructive development on the lives and livelihoods of India's marginalized peoples, whose concerns had been left out of much middle-class conservationist environmentalism, despite their dependence on the environment for daily survival. In the CSE's words, "the Gross Nature Product is far more important than the Gross National Product. Environmentally destructive economic development will impoverish the poor even further and destroy their livelihood resource base. Therefore, the environmental concern in the developing world must go 'beyond pretty trees and tigers' and must link it with people's lives and protests."[58] The CSE advocated for policies that involved people in natural-resource management and were adapted from traditional community environmental practices, like rainwater harvesting.

Notwithstanding the CSE's concern about global inequality and the effect of environmental degradation on the poor, its criticism of bottled drinks resonated with the Indian middle class's perception of the environment "as yet another consumable" and its sense of entitlement to the quality implied by global brands, anthropologist Neeraj Vedwan has argued.[59] Activists involved in the already year-long protest over Coca-Cola's extraction and pollution of groundwater resources in Plachimada, frustrated with the lack of attention paid to the struggle, noted the contrastingly large media coverage and middle-class reaction to the soft-drink contamination controversy. As the Keralite environmental journalist and activist C. R. Neelakandan remembered: it "sent shockwaves through the minds of the Malayalee [Keralite] middle class. The Malayalee middle class mind needs to be scared to change itself. So they stopped buying Coca-Cola for their kids."[60] The CSE campaign harnessed the middle class's sense of consumer entitlement and vulnerability in the market, taking advantage of its disproportionate purchasing power to make demands of multinational corporations. Rather than challenging the state directly on water insecurity and product safety, in a move now emblematic of neoliberal governance, the NGO's targets were corporations, as entities that could address these issues themselves or demand government regulation to rationalize and stabilize the market.

To respond to the controversy, Coca-Cola launched a marketing counteroffensive featuring its celebrity spokesman Aamir Khan in two health-themed commercials. In addition to his celebrity, Khan brought his reputation as a social justice advocate, having taken a public stand in support of the villagers and activists protesting the damming of the Narmada River. In one ad, the Company mocked consumers concerned by the CSE's pesticide research as dupes of the dogmatic politics of an older, out-of-touch India.

Khan's "Bengali Babu" (a character in the "*Thanda matlab* Coca-Cola" campaign) is a laughably ideological, anti-modern intellectual from communist West Bengal, bespectacled and dressed in traditional white kurta, who doesn't want his family to order Cokes because "they" say the drinks are unsafe. "You heard of the tests, but not of the results . . . you listen to half and understand half," his wife groans. "This is a 100-year old company and people drink Coca-Cola in about 200 countries around the world. How can it be harmful? . . . India, England, the Netherlands—tests have been done in everyone's laboratories. Everyone has said that it's fine." Khan's character thereupon announces his own test, chugging all of the family's Coca-Colas, and elatedly belching out his refreshed results.

Khan even broke from his comic characters to dispel ongoing fears of pesticide contamination, appearing as himself in a 2006 Coca-Cola commercial in which he inspects a bottling plant to ensure that he is endorsing a safe drink. A concerned Khan speaks in serious direct address to the viewer, describing the "400 quality checks" for ingredients, "not one, not two, but a six stage filtration process" for water, and the "special hot-carbon treatment" for sugar, over visuals of Indian Coca-Cola representatives in crisp white lab coats showing him around the shiny, high-tech plant. Coca-Cola is "completely safe," Khan confirms, as the commercial closes with him pulling a fresh bottle directly from the production line and taking a long drink.

Popular culture also revealed traces of the public anxiety about the power of multinationals and the safety of their products. A major feature film set in the Indian soft-drink industry's neoliberal transition, *Corporate* (Madhur Bhandarkar, 2006) tells the story of a young female executive climbing the corporate ladder at a US soft-drink multinational, a thinly-veiled Coca-Cola Company, until her downfall for selling out Indian consumers to bad capitalists and greedy politicians. A melodramatic warning to India's middle class of personal destruction by the corporate system and its toxic commodities, the protagonist ends up mothering a fatherless child while serving a life sentence for helping the company cover up its sales of pesticide-laced drinks. By focusing on corruption, however, rather than on the labor and resource exploitation enriching corporations and impoverishing others, the movie left open the possibility of a reformed, rationalized capitalism, less tainted by manipulations of Indian development.

The movie came quickly on the heels of another CSE report in 2006 revealing ongoing contamination and governmental sluggishness in enforcing limits on pesticide content in soft drinks. The Indian government had agreed as a result of the outcry over the 2003 report to regulate bottled water according to the European Union's maximum limit for pesticide residues, but took almost a year and a half to introduce the new standard. The regulation of soft-drink contamination was proving even more complicated. After over two years of deliberation by representatives of the industry, including Coca-Cola and PepsiCo, with scientific, governmental, and consumer and environmental groups, new limits on pesticide residues in soft drinks had been set by the Bureau of Indian Standards (BIS), but they were voluntary rather than mandatory and were only demanded of companies seeking BIS certification.[61] And when the CSE tested eleven Coca-Cola Company and PepsiCo brands in 2006, all of the results far exceeded the standard, ranging from five to sixty-three times the BIS pesticide limit.[62]

This new CSE report, showing continued pesticide contamination, set off another wave of protests. Piles of Coca-Cola bottles were smashed or burned, several shops where sodas were sold were attacked, billboards of the soft-drink companies were painted over or torn down, and Coca-Cola was poured down the throats of donkeys, in dramatic protests that made for exciting media coverage. Newspapers printed images of cans under headlines like "toxic cocktail."[63] The states of Gujarat, Madhya Pradesh, Punjab, and Rajasthan banned the sale of soft drinks in schools and government offices, and federal lawmakers from the BJP called for a nationwide ban.[64] Protestors exaggeratedly called Coca-Cola's pesticide contamination and environmental degradation around production facilities "a slow Bhopal," likening it to the deadly 1984 toxic gas leak at a Union Carbide plant, which killed an estimated fifteen thousand people and sickened a half a million more, evoking the historical precedent of egregious foreign corporate wrongdoing in India.

From the start of the pesticide controversy, The Coca-Cola Company and PepsiCo, typically highly combative corporate adversaries, had joined forces to fight back. PepsiCo had filed a petition in the New Delhi High Court seeking to block publication of the 2003 CSE report. When that effort failed, the companies attacked the CSE, challenging the scientific legitimacy of the organization's laboratory, suggesting its results were motivated by an anti-capitalist and anti-American agenda, and threatening to sue for libel.[65] The companies commissioned their own independent studies, insisted that the government do so as well, and combatted the CSE's research with their more positive results (although, as journalists would point out, the soft drinks examined in those studies were produced during the monsoon months when chemical concentration would be more diluted by plentiful groundwater.)[66]

Coca-Cola and PepsiCo played on Indian national pride and anxiety over the country's place in the global economy, suggesting that EU standards for food and drink safety were part of a European agenda to restrict Indian agricultural imports.[67] When the CSE released its 2006 report, Coca-Cola again "decided to go on the attack," according to a *New York Times* reporter covering the story, hosting detailed press briefings in which executives questioned the scientific credentials of the CSE, directing reporters to pro-company Internet blogs, and handing out the cellphone number of the director of an organization called the "Center for Sanity and Balance in Public Life," who asserted that one could "drink a can of Coke every day for two years before taking in as much pesticide as you get from two cups of tea."[68]

The corporations also mobilized the support of the US government and Indian industry groups. In the summer of 2006, with the Bush administration preparing to send a large business delegation to India, US Undersecretary for International Trade Franklin Lavin described the bans on the US soft-drink companies' products as "a setback for the Indian economy. . . . In a time when India is working hard to attract and retain foreign investment, it would be unfortunate if the discussion were dominated by those who did not want to treat foreign companies fairly." Leading Indian industry bodies, including the Confederation of Indian Industry and the Indo-American Chamber of Commerce, expressed concern about the bans' potential to harm the image of India as hospitable to foreign investment.[69] Similarly, the industry groups lobbied against adopting EU norms, which they called "arbitrary" and an example of developed countries trying "to create technical barriers to trade," couching their concern in terms of the potential impact on Indian farmers and pushing instead for the adoption of Codex/WHO/WTO norms that do not apply drinking water pesticide residue standards to finished products such as soft drinks.[70]

Coca-Cola India executives read the controversy as a lesson in the need for localization of its image in India. "'The most important [lesson] is that we should project ourselves as an Indian company and not an American multinational,'" according to a "key member" of Coca-Cola's local management. Convinced that they were targeted because of their multinationality, Coca-Cola committed additional efforts to framing the Company as Indian in both advertising and management style.[71] At the same time, while deploying strategic localization to deflect further attacks, executives also sought to leverage the Company's multinationality to underscore their products' superior, globally proven quality compared to local Indian beverages. The companies asserted that their Indian plants adhered to the same processes of filtration as elsewhere in their global systems, telling reporters, "the soft drinks manufactured in India comply with stringent international norms and all applicable national regulations."[72] "The most valuable brand in the world makes no compromises on the quality of beverages it serves Indian consumers," Coca-Cola advertised.[73] While claiming a universalist quality through globality, the multinationals also argued that it was the particularity of the Indian context that was to blame, inasmuch as there was widespread contamination of Indian food and beverages. "This is a classic case of cheap populism which does a disservice to the Indian consumer," an advertising advisor to Coca-Cola India groused. "Most of India's drinking water is unfit for human consumption but the politicians have found it more convenient to go for the global brand names."[74] Common traditional drinks like tea had far more pesticide residues, even mothers' breast milk was tainted by pesticides, the companies argued to the press, summing up their argument for the relative safety of soft drinks with a print advertisement asking the public, "Is there anything safer for you to drink?"[75] Coca-Cola's ads for its Kinley water brand used the Hindi slogan "Boond boond mein vishwas," implying that it was bottling "trust in every drop."[76] The multinational drink companies thus leveraged the crisis into a critique of the broad scale of pesticide contamination in Indian commodities to assert their brands' comparative quality and safety relative to Indian products.

Still, the companies resisted government adoption of a regulatory limit for pesticide residues in their bottled drinks. Coca-Cola and Pepsi tested the quality of the water used in drinks to ensure that contaminants were removed, but were not required to test the finished products for them.[77] India's groundwater is so contaminated that most food products contain some pesticide residue, and one of the soft drinks' principal ingredients, sugar, is difficult to cleanse of pesticide traces. While an Indian parliamentary committee agreed on proposed rules for a test of the final products of the soft-drink manufacturers, Coca-Cola and Pepsi maintained that soft drinks are too complex in their final form to test reliably for pesticide content.[78] In a multi-year campaign that first took shape following the initial controversy, Coca-Cola India actively lobbied Indian regulators, with the Company's internal Global Scientific and Regulatory Affairs department providing "help" to Indian governmental authorities, according to executives. While pushing back against stringent regulation, Coca-Cola executives were eager for a regulatory proposal that met their interests, which might rationalize the market and even give the global soft-drinks giants a competitive advantage, since with their existing quality testing, they might be better equipped than their Indian competitors to meet higher standards.

The CSE-spurred consumerist, middle-class environmental politics was thus difficult to maintain. The Coca-Cola Company and PepsiCo continued to adamantly deny the charges. While admitting that "pesticide residues in traces may get into the source water," Coca-Cola India asserted that the water used in its soft drinks "meets standards which are at par with the most stringent EU norms."[79] The companies could not explain away the continued evidence from multiple laboratories of pesticides in their finished products, but when the Indian government created basic standards for pesticide contamination in water used in bottled drinks, the industry appeared to have been regulated and public protest subsided.

But from the CSE campaign to the movie *Corporate*, representations of the pesticide-laden toxic commodity revealed middle-class frustration over the failed promises of global corporations and neoliberal development in India. Indian consumers' concerns about pesticide contamination encouraged the cognitive mapping of The Coca-Cola Company's systemic threat to and exploitation of the environment. The controversy echoed past politicization elsewhere of the danger of Coca-Cola consumption—French criticism of Coca-Cola's acidity and caffeine content in defense of French wine, threatened by the Company's multinational might, and Colombian rumors of human body parts in bottled drinks that served to evoke the violence of Coca-Cola's labor regime. The persistent presence of pesticides made clear that the urban middle classes would be unable completely to buy their way out of environmental scarcity, pollution, and lack of governmental regulation and investment in public water infrastructure. The trace of pesticides in Coca-Cola was a reminder and a remainder (an immaterial as well as material residue) of the commodity's ties to the uneven development of the Indian countryside, where farmers had little access to clean water and were pumping chemical inputs into their land in the hopes of getting through another season of feeding urban consumers.

MAKING VISIBLE THE SECRET INGREDIENT: CORPORATE EXPLOITATION OF THE WATER COMMONS

While The Coca-Cola Company attempted to localize its products by mining Indian popular language and culture to claim "*Thanda matlab* Coca-Cola,"

FIGURE 21. Sharad Haksar's billboard in Chennai, India, July 14, 2005, © AFP/Getty Images.

and tried to ease middle-class concerns about consuming drinks made from contaminated Indian water and ingredients, Indian villagers were organizing against the symbolic and material enclosures of the Company's practice of rural extraction for urban consumption, protesting the expropriation of their communities' water by Coca-Cola plants. In the midst of the mounting protest, the prize-winning photographer Sharad Haksar offered a competing image, in the oversaturated colors and style of the *Thanda matlab* print ads, using the ubiquitous Coca-Cola advertising as backdrop to a shot of a dry hand pump and a line of empty water pots, which he entitled simply "Thirsty" (fig. 21).

Haksar had not previously been an activist media producer—he had mostly shot ads for "food, fashion and cars" for an agency that Coke itself had used, but he made the image a public act of "iconoclash," as the theorist Bruno Latour terms the uncertain destructive and productive potential of communicating through meaning-rich icons,[80] displaying his photograph on a large billboard in downtown Chennai, notably across from the ritzy Taj hotel in plain view of tourists, international businessmen, and Indian urban professionals. "As a photographer, it is my take on the severe water shortage in the state and across India," he explained. "It is a fact and an irony that there is a shortage of drinking water while Coca-Cola is available everywhere."[81]

The Coca-Cola Company did not appreciate Haksar's use of its brand in such a commentary on ironic realities, and it threatened legal action against him for copyright infringement. But activists put the billboard/photo to work online, in videos, and in organizing materials. The India Resource Center, a San Francisco-based media platform dedicated to building an organizing network in solidarity with Indian communities opposing the environmental practices of multinational corporations, reported it on its website (www.indiaresource.org), to its email list, and in a press release to US, European, and Indian news sources. Major news outlets that picked up the story discovered that Coca-Cola had already served a Keralan newspaper covering the protests with a defamation suit, a "David and Goliath" scenario that aroused public ire, setting up a fight that the Company could not win, regardless of any outcome of a court case (win and look like a bully, lose and set precedent for future attacks on your trademark), and it quickly dropped its legal action. In putting his critique of the dispossession of the water commons on a billboard in a public space made corporate through advertising, Haksar made people see anew the ubiquity of the brand as a commodity claiming ownership of common cultural meanings and spaces (of *thanda* and the public street), a privatization of the symbolic as well as the enclosure of the material commons. Coca-Cola relies on those common meanings and spaces, which makes the Company vulnerable to the power of their constant reproduction by social forces beyond its control.

The image was a product of these social forces, not an artist's individual creation alone: the photo captured a community's everyday defacement and reassemblage of the brand icon for new meaning. Protesting women were regularly placing their plastic pots in front of the Plachimada Coke factory "in mute performance of water scarcity." In repeating it, as Bishnupriya Ghosh describes the reworking of global icons in India: this "semiotic activity turned an ordinary gesture into the kind of expressive ritual that becomes popular culture." The repeating image of the water pot placed in front of Coca-Cola began to "scramble the mass media icon, becoming semiotic acts that were reproduced in news photos and documentary footage." In these accounts, the pot recurs sometimes plastic or earthenware, but "always dry, always empty." When Haksar put up his billboard, the signification of the pots against the Coca-Cola icon had become intelligible to the Indian public, which had learned to read "what they communicate in these daily perform-ances."[82] Thus, the photo not only drew new attention to the growing resist-ance, it captured the already reiterative expressive popular culture of remak-ing the brand image. It thus signaled a fissure in corporate hegemony—the Company was unable "to litigate against temporary, daily, informal perform-ances and communication in those communities" that produced popular meaning, marking "the already begun process of an icon's epistemological crisis" and its reemergence as a volatile signifier, politically potentialized for consumption.[83]

The women who carried these pots were primarily poor farmers, landless agricultural workers, many lower-caste Dalits and indigenous Adivasis. They were protesting various Coca-Cola plants' pollution of surrounding agricul-tural lands by industrial effluent, and more markedly, the Company's extrac-tion of groundwater. The Coca-Cola Company used roughly three liters of water to produce each liter of branded drink it sold. From 100-meter-deep bore wells, each plant extracted hundreds of thousands of liters of water a day to be processed, packaged, and sold as bottled water and soft drinks. During the heavy summer production months, which are also when farmers' lands and wells become parched, extraction could be far higher.[84] Residents and activists called these practices "water mining."

To access reserves of water as well as cheap labor, The Coca-Cola Company located much of its production in rural communities outside of larger metro-politan areas, such as Mehdiganj outside of the city of Varanasi. This was in line with the Indian government's shift from state- to market-led forces to fuel the economic development of rural India, as it disavowed previous rural economic and social welfare policies and overlooked the lack of environmen-tal regulations. In this context, state and local governments compete to attract corporations like Coca-Cola by creating industrial areas, special eco-nomic zones, and financial incentives like tax exemptions to encourage industries to invest in "underdeveloped" or "backward" areas.[85] Here the majority of residents are poor farmers or landless agricultural workers who are under extreme economic and environmental stress, part of what has been called an agrarian crisis in India.[86] The roots of this crisis are deep: beginning in the 1960s the agricultural development of the "Green Revolution" fed India's large population and reduced its vulnerability to famine but also overexploited water and land with intensive irrigation and agrochemical application. Liberalization compounded this environmental toll on rural India, exacerbating disparities in economic and cultural power with the shift from statist development's focus on poverty alleviation in rural India to a market-directed consumerist paradigm catering to the growth of the urban middle and upper classes.[87] Its unrestrained and uneven industrial growth, in a postcolonial context with weak environmental and social protections, wrought "environmental degradation and social dislocation" that disproportionately affected marginalized groups: low-caste Dalits and "backward classes," indigenous Adivasis, and the poor.[88] Higher costs for electricity (to run water pumps), seeds, fertilizers, and pesticides needed to cultivate environmentally degrading land, the deregulation of the banking sector and subsequent credit crunch for farmers seeking loans to pay for these inputs, and the low prices for produced crops have led to extreme indebtedness.[89] Climate change has begun to produce severe droughts and floods as monsoons become more erratic. Changes to the environment, especially those that affect water—a season without a water-recharging monsoon, a corporate neighbor draining groundwater reserves, degrading water quality, or a flood of industrial effluents on farmland—could be a crisis for a farmer. Many small farmers were at the point of severe distress, a fact made dramatically evident in the large number of farmer suicides—between 22,000 and 25,000 by several estimates—in the first decade of the twenty-first century.[90]

These strains were visible in several areas that host Coca-Cola plants, like Mehdiganj in the state of Uttar Pradesh, and contributed to stresses on both water resources and lives in rural India. In Uttar Pradesh, 90 percent of landholding farmers were considered "small and marginal," having on average only a little more than an acre, while over 40 percent of households in the state were in debt.[91] In Mehdiganj, farmers cultivated more water-intensive rice paddy in their search for economically viable crops. With infrequent electricity to the area, farmers ran their water pumps, or rented time on neighbors' pumps, to flood their lands with as much water as possible while the power lasted. As the primary use of land in areas like Mehdiganj, agriculture was the largest use of water, and Coca-Cola executives argued that the farmers were sucking their own wells dry. Behind agriculture, the second source of employment had been sari weaving, an industry that declined dramatically after economic liberalization filled the textile market with imports. At the same time, the area's population increased by almost one third, requiring more groundwater.[92] The further introduction of a heavy industrial water user like Coca-Cola upset an already unstable system. The community reported that since 2000, the number of dry wells increased fivefold compared to the decade before Coca-Cola's arrival.[93]

Coca-Cola plants drew groundwater with little regulation, and at virtually no cost. An archaic Indian law gave landowners private property rights not only to their land but whatever groundwater lies underneath.[94] Few states had enacted and implemented water-resource legislation, even though national and state water policy statements acknowledge ever-increasing water scarcity and disparity in water resources and specify that drinking water and irrigation were higher priorities than hydropower or industrial uses in the planning of water resource management.[95] The Company was not required to assess its plants' potential environmental impact, and its proprietary internal siting studies focused only "on ensuring a sustained supply of water for business operations" and were never made public.[96] The Company needed only to receive permissions from the *panchayat* (elected village council), who were often eager to see Coca-Cola's version of development, associated jobs, and additional tax revenues from a local plant. Local panchayats rarely restricted Coca-Cola's use of groundwater.[97] A tax was collected on water consumed by industry, but the charges were so miniscule that heavy water users like Coca-Cola drew groundwater virtually for free—the Mehdiganj plant paid around $700 for an entire year's water consumption in 2005.[98]

The aquifers that lie under the Coca-Cola plants' as well as neighboring residents' lands are a natural resource commons, essential to life and collectively owned and shared, spanning and disregarding property demarcations. This struggle is biopolitical, over a resource essential to the production of social relationships and forms of life in Mehdiganj.[99] Exploitation or pollution of this shared resource disproportionately hurts the rural poor who rely on it for their lives and livelihoods—for drinking, cooking, bathing, irrigating crops—and their community—for sustaining village life. But this water was increasingly out of their reach as groundwater levels dropped; unlike the Coca-Cola plant's mechanically dug deep bore wells and powerful pumps that can extract water all day long with independent twenty-four-hour supply of electricity from its own generators, the majority of Mehdiganj residents relied on hand pumps, shallow or open wells, and traditional ponds for household water use, which have been dramatically affected by the decline in the water table. To irrigate their fields, poor farmers rented time on electric pumps in the deeper wells of the larger landowners, exacerbating class divisions.[100] Landless agricultural workers were the first to lose work from failed crops. Caste still powerfully organized life in many rural villages in Uttar

Pradesh, like those near the Coca-Cola plant in Mehdiganj, where the Dalit Women in Mehdiganj frequently discussed the gendered effects of water scarcity and contamination on women and girls and their domestic work of water retrieval and cooking, cleaning, and washing. They spent more time traveling longer distances to fetch water, standing in long lines at wells and pumps, which wore down their patience and resulted in "short fuses and quarrels," before they had to arduously carry the water back to their homes. It was even worse when there was not enough water to wash and bathe. Women spoke frankly about the humiliation of not having access to adequate water requiring them to ask for help from neighbors with private bore wells. They were often refused and forced "to swallow their pride and keep going back, and plead for water."[102]

"COCA-COLA, QUIT INDIA"

Within a decade of Coca-Cola's return to India, a half-dozen communities had accused the Company of depleting groundwater through excessive water extraction and polluting reserves and neighboring lands in its disposal of industrial by-product "sludge" material and effluent water. The first of these protest movements to gain public attention emerged in the spring of 2002 when villagers in Plachimada, Kerala, began a permanent sit-in in front of the Coca-Cola plant that abutted their homes. Since it started production in 2000, the plant been drawing up several hundred thousand liters of groundwater a day to be processed, packaged, and sold as bottled water and soft drinks. The plant's surrounding community grew increasingly frustrated watching truck after truck take bottled drinks to be sold across the state, while their fields failed to yield, the water tables dropped in their wells, and the remaining water tasted salty, bitter, and hard. Farmers were forced to shift from their previous water-intensive crops like paddy and coconuts. The Plachimada protesters marched and held an indefinite *dharna* (sit-in) demanding the closure of the plant. The Plachimada protests arose from landless and poor peasants, mostly Adivasis from the Eravalar and Malasar communities. Their movement against the Company had its roots in the decades-long struggles of Adivasis in Kerala for land and self-governance rights, which the state government, and its sometimes Communist Party of India–Marxist leadership, had ignored or suppressed until 2001, when a mass mobilization of Adivasi groups drove the state to recognize these rights in a set of accords that restored some lands to indigenous peoples.[103] In this period of political momentum and consciousness around land as a material essential to their livelihoods, Adivasis in Plachimada identified the change in the quantity and quality of groundwater—another essential resource—with the new Coca-Cola plant in their community. By the spring of 2003, after garnering significant media attention, the villagers swayed the local political leadership to their cause, the panchayat refused to renew Coca-Cola's license, and a year later the plant eventually shut down production. The Company legally challenged the panchayat's authority to limit the rights of private companies to extract local groundwater, winning an appeal, before the case made its way to the Indian Supreme Court.[104]

This first campaign inspired other villages in distant states like Uttar Pradesh to organize against Coca-Cola plants to create multiple points of pressure against the Company and demand a say in the nature of the development in their communities. While Mehdiganj residents remembered a sense of hope about the jobs and development that would come with the arrival of the bottling industry, the relationship between the plant and many segments of the community quickly soured. Almost immediately from its construction in 1996, while still a Parle bottler, the plant encountered resistance from those living closest to its walls.[105] Residents alleged that the plant illegally occupied common land owned by the village, including a local road used by the Kumhar (potter caste) community who live just behind the plant, and the village panchayat sued. The Parle bottler purportedly settled the dispute with political and economic pressure on the village panchayat,[106] who accepted other land in trade.

Agitation emerged from inside the plant as well, as workers pressed for better wages, benefits, and job security, challenging the system of temporary work and labor contracting that often pits one caste against another, and attempting to organize a union, before eventually being replaced with more pliable employees. Several months into the plant's operation, a group of workers began to organize to demand minimum-wage pay and benefits. Inspired by the union at a nearby biscuit factory and armed with the labor code from meetings with the labor office in Varanasi, they argued that the labor contractor who hired (and fired) them was extracting huge percentages of their pay. They won small wage increases from the plant. But they were still dissatisfied with their temporary status and seasonal work, with the Company outsourcing to a labor contractor who only employed workers on a short-term basis, and with poor pay and few benefits. The plant employed around forty permanent workers and two hundred short-term workers, who worked full-time during the summer months of high soft-drink sales, but no more than 120 days a year, and were jobless during the winter, making them ineligible for the rights and benefits of permanent employees.[107] When the workers began to formally organize a union to demand permanent jobs and benefits, its registration was denied by the state, and Coca-Cola fired those making demands. In response, in 2002 a multi-caste group of workers went on strike, effectively shutting down the plant for a week, going back into work after winning a demand from management, then going back out on strike a few months later when demands were not met and leaders laid off. The plant discharged nearly a hundred workers and, according to interviews, used a new contractor to hire replacement workers, overwhelmingly from a single caste, Patel, causing friction in the community and physical altercations between the laid-off workers and the new hires. Coca-Cola responded by hiring new security guards, and the clashes became more violent. Union leaders were charged with assault and violating the peace. Still without a union and subject to the precariousness of short-term work, in 2004, workers were paid only some sixty-six rupees a day (about US$1.65)[108] for 120 days of work. A lot of this money leaves Mehdiganj, according to residents who complain that the labor contractor replaced much of the original local workforce with people from outside the area.[109]

Grassroots efforts around the Mehdiganj plant's environmental impact began around the same time, when farmers and neighboring residents challenged the plant's routine disposal of manufacturing effluent wastewater into a nearby canal. The plant's drainage pipe was disrupted by the construction of the Grand Trunk Road superhighway, a massive post-liberalization modernization project with funding from the World Bank to connect India's four largest cities in a "Golden Quadrilateral" that—conveniently for Coca-Cola trucks—runs alongside the plant. Backed up by the construction, the plant's drain flooded acres of surrounding farmland with effluent wastewater. Many of the farmers' crops were destroyed and other residents complained of skin irritation from contaminated water. In response, they created the Gaon Bachao Sangharsh Samiti (Save the Village Struggle Committee). The group organized a *dharna* with over fifty people sitting in a hunger strike for eight days on the affected land, demanding both compensation from the government for the damaged crops and closure of the plant.[110] Leading Gaon Bachao Sangharsh Samiti were farmers closest to the plant with small to medium-sized holdings (at most a few acres; the leader has three or four acres) closest to the plant who believed that their property was threatened by the plant's environmental practices. Members of the landless Kumhar community joined in the protest, blaming the effluent water for an outbreak of skin problems. As the plant continued operation, a broader swath of the village communities began to complain that the water in their wells had taken on a reddish-yellow hue and tasted bad and, even more distressing, that the water level was visibly dropping.

These more vulnerable members of the villages mobilized against the Company on a larger scale through a local community organization, Lok Samiti, or People's Committee, which counted a few thousand active participants in the villages outside Varanasi. The committee was founded in 1999 by a former child weaver turned young community organizer, Nandlal Master, who by 2009 worked with six full-time organizers to coordinate the group's social work and grassroots organizing from an ashram in Mehdiganj. Master developed strategies for community organizing by assisting Neeti Bhai, a Varanasi-based Catholic priest fighting for a "democratic secular society" and "social as well as structural change in favor of the poor and marginalized" through his community empowerment organization, Lok Chetna Samiti. Soon Lok Samiti took on a range of social projects from education centers for child laborers in the weaving industry, Dalit and women's empowerment groups, dowry-free marriage celebrations, community financial self-help societies, and intercaste programs addressing issues like labor exploitation, political corruption, and gender, caste, and religious discrimination.

Prasad and other organizers were influenced by the thinking of Mohandas Gandhi, socialist Jayaprakash Narayan, and contemporary global south environmentalists.[111] Gandhi's concept of *gram swaraj*, or village self-rule, inspired the group's commitment to promote self-governance, direct democracy, and bottom-up development in village communities. In the 1970s, Narayan would draw on this idea in calling for a "total revolution" of political, economic, and social orders through nonviolent class struggle, participatory democracy, and constructive work by villages through popular movements and committees. Inspired by this idea of a people's committee by and for the village, Prasad decided not to register Lok Samiti as an NGO with the government, he explained, so that its power would not be granted by the state, but instead be derived from the people to hold the state to account. While Prasad and many of the activists of Lok Samiti took inspiration from Gandhi's teachings, they also modified them for the current world of transnational economies and solidarities. Still emphasizing the importance of thinking about the welfare of local communities, the organizers expressed the ideal of *swadeshi* (using domestic not foreign goods), not as economic self-reliance through the privileging of national products, but as "a call to the consumer to be aware of the violence he is causing by supporting those industries that result in poverty, harm to workers and to humans and other creatures,"[112] and thus the valuing of less-exploitative production on a global scale. They were also quick to add, in response to the Company's criticism that they were motivated solely by "anti-globalization" sentiments to target a multinational: "We would protest against any company who is misusing the water," Indian or foreign.[113]

Lok Samiti activists frequently quoted Gandhi—"The earth provides enough to satisfy every man's need, but not any man's greed"—to communicate a materialist environmentalism focused on social justice. The movement in Mehdiganj, in its organizers' own words, rejected the way "water is seen as an asset and a commodity by the Indian government, the international institutions . . . and the multinational corporations." Instead, residents assert that water is "an inalienable right which cannot be sold for profit" and requires the community's say in its "participatory development."[114] So Lok Samiti's work in social and economic justice led to environmental activism, focusing more of its work on advocacy for water rights. They compiled data on the number of dry wells in the area, held conferences on water privatization, dug a community pond for public water use, organized "water stops" to provide free water and information about the struggle at sites like the Varanasi train station where people might otherwise buy Coca-Cola products, and called on the government to provide safe drinking water to the public.

THE ENVIRONMENTALISM OF THE DISPOSSESSED

By challenging Coca-Cola's water use, villagers disputed market and state imposition of rural India's development without their say, contesting the version of industrialization that uses environmental resources to benefit some by negatively impacting others. Their protests against Coca-Cola drew on a history of South Asian environmental politics based on social justice, or as Ramachandra Guha and Joan Martínez-Alier have described it, an "environmentalism of the poor,"[115] in which communities have fought against the depletion and pollution of land, forest, water, and air resources.[116] These movements "powerfully foreground questions of production and distribution within human society . . . [organizing around] 'the use of the environment and who should benefit from it,'" according to Anil Agarwal, the founder of the CSE.[117]

This environmentalism emerged from the "'victims of development,' the poor peasants and tribals who have thus far had to unwillingly make way for the dams, steel mills, and highways that dispossess[ed] them ... intensified social inequalities as well as devastated the natural environment."[118] While these movements in India have challenged both state and private development plans (also frequently the combination of the two), the shift to the free market logic of the past twenty-five years has especially engendered protests against transnational capital and the Indian "urban-industrial complex"[119] as they encroached on the resources of village communities, privatizing and commodifying them for the growing consumer power of the urban middle and upper classes. Thus, the effects of neoliberalism have galvanized a movement that unites an awkward and even sometimes antagonistic[120] coalition of Indian Marxists and environmentalists to fight the inequities exacerbated by environmental exploitation and degradation.

Middle-class conservationism and a market environmentalism exemplified by the promotion of "green" capitalism and lifestyle choices have dominated neoliberal environmental discourse. But the activism of Mehdiganj villagers was part of wave of global south and north environmental movements motivated by social (racial, ethnic, caste, gender) and economic justice, such as fights for the protection of environmental and occupational health, for native land rights, and against the export of environmental hazards to the developing world. Whereas the "environmentalism of affluence" focuses on enhancing the quality of life of the middle and upper classes or derives power from their consumption, as in the concern over pesticide-tainted Cokes, the environmentalism of the poor and dispossessed is oriented towards "confronting structures of political-economic power that lie at the root of the ecological crisis."[121] These movements highlight capitalism's imperative to expand its exploitation and displace resulting ecological damages ("externalities") onto the least powerful members of society.[122] Accruing environmental deterioration and human impact often take place gradually and invisibly, a "slow violence" ignored by mainstream politics because it is unspectacular and wreaks its damage on the marginalized.[123] Unlike organizations that focus on specific environmental problems separate from their larger context, environmentalisms of the dispossessed identify these as the symptoms of the political-economic system that produces them. They have the potential, then, to replace the "not in my backyard" orientation of middle-class environmentalism with "not in anyone's backyard."[124]

It has been difficult to organize across class and caste, in the context of depleting environmental resources in Mehdiganj. Many local elites sided with the Company. Many plant workers, especially those from outside the local villages, did not support the organizing, viewing it as a threat to their jobs. Some workers from the local villages expressed conflicted positions, needing employment at the plant but questioning the cost to their friends and families. Local workers frequently commented that they do not want their work at the plant to hurt their communities. In fact, many workers claim to not care whether the Coca-Cola plant closes: it only employs them for a part of the year, they say, so they have to rely on other work in weaving or agriculture regardless. They would prefer development that considers the villagers' needs, with a local industry that is less water-intensive. People who had protested several times expressed frustration with the Company's intransigence and activists' inability to close the plant, breeding further suspicion of corruption among local leaders and elected officials. Many acknowledged that their water problems are becoming widespread in India with heavy irrigation and chemical application in agriculture drying up and contaminating groundwater reserves. But farmers argued that if education and regulation are necessary to change agricultural use of water to make life in rural India sustainable, so too is a reconsideration of the siting and regulation of a water-intensive industry like Coca-Cola that aggravates water scarcity by drawing up large amounts of water and shipping it as liquid commodities far outside the original watershed.

NETWORKS OF ORGANIZING

Lok Samiti developed its politics on the ground in Mehdiganj and through contact with similar struggles in India. Through their community organizing, its leaders became involved with the National Alliance of People's Movements (NAPM), and the disparate grassroots struggles dedicated to alternative, democratic "people based development," which retained their autonomous organizations and diverse politics, whether Marxist, Gandhian, or Ambedkarian, while mobilizing a national alliance.[125] This movement of tribal, women's, Dalit, minority, workers, and peasant movements arose in the immediate wake of India's economic reforms to make clear the connections between seemingly unrelated local struggles in experiences of national and international systems of privatization and liberalization.[126]

FIGURE 22. Right to Water National Conference and Protest against Coca-Cola, Mehdiganj, Uttar Pradesh, March 30, 2008. Photograph by author.

NAPM's central organizing principle, "the development of a people's democracy based on people's control over resources," called for participatory democracy and the decentralization of political and economic power to transform the nature of politics itself.[127] NAPM's founder Medha Patkar articulated its critique of the collusion of the Indian state and transnational capital (such as multinational corporations and the World Bank) in development that hurt the poor. This thinking emerged from early mobilizations to stop the damming of the Narmada River in central India and Enron's Dabhol Power project in Maharashtra, south of Mumbai, which brought the NAPM to national and international attention. From its founding, NAPM expressed concern about the arrival of soft-drink multinationals and their privatization of water. It called for "a sustained and intense campaign against MNCs with the slogan 'Not Pepsi/Coke—we want water.'"[128] When Plachimada residents began to protest against The Coca-Cola Company several years later, NAPM provided support—organizing marches, with Medha Patkar, who was now famous, crucially drawing media attention and linking the local struggle with similar fights in other parts of India.

Through their involvement with NAPM, members of Lok Samiti connected their own problems of water scarcity and quality to the similar situation in Plachimada and developed a broader political analysis challenging water privatization (fig. 22). Over the course of 2003, Mehdiganj residents, members of Lok Samiti and Gaon Bachao Sangharsh Samiti, and supporters from the NAPM and the socialist Samajwadi Jan Parishad (Socialist People's Council) organized a sit-in, a hunger strike, and a nonviolent march that ended with baton-wielding police arresting seventy-six protestors and wounding several. Protestors dumped sacks full of Coca-Cola's by-product sludge on pollution-control regulators' desks demanding that the plant's license be revoked and that those affected be compensated. In the same year NAPM launched a national march "against globalization and communalism" beginning from the Coca-Cola plant in Plachimada. Lok Samiti sent representatives to Plachimada and organized a protest outside their own plant, linking the two locales in distant parts of the country through their common opposition to Coca-Cola. The 2004 closure of the Plachimada plant buoyed the organizing in Mehdiganj and an increasing number of other communities with Coca-Cola plants. Mehdiganj activists began working with residents angered by the water use of the Coca-Cola plants in their communities of Ballia, Uttar Pradesh, and Kala Dera, Rajasthan—the latter, where the water was so overexploited that the Company was advised to truck water in from outside sources for its bottling or close the plant entirely[129]— and began to create a network of places, concerns, and communities linked by the Company.

These connections through Coca-Cola's capital and commodities were simultaneously local, national, and multinational, like the corporation itself. When residents' persistent protests were met with inaction by local and state governments and faced the multiple scales of Coca-Cola's power at local plants, and national, regional, and global headquarters in Gurgaon, India (the corporate edge city outside Delhi), Hong Kong (a hub of Coca-Cola executives for Asia Pacific operations),[130] and Atlanta, Georgia, the movement reached beyond local elites' traditional control to a likewise national and transnational network of allies and NGOs. Nationally, the NAPM connected the similar struggles in Plachimada and Mehdiganj, across language barriers and a broad geographical distance, and drew international attention to the actions of local activists. Through participation in NAPM and new international venues like the World Social Forum and the People's World Water Forum, activists from Plachimada and Mehdiganj enlisted support from activists and NGOs engaged in related struggles: labor and human rights organizations fighting for Coca-Cola workers' rights in Colombia (the Colombian labor union Sinaltrainal and the US Campaign to Stop Killer Coke), North American environmental NGOs focusing on water privatization (Corporate Accountability International and the Polaris Institute), international social justice groups among the South Asian diaspora (ASHA for Education), and US-based alterglobalization activists concerned with corporate capitalism's effect on the environment in India (the India Resource Center). Two hundred Mehdiganj residents traveled with Lok Samiti to the 2004 World Social Forum in Mumbai, where they met with international allies, other environmental social movements, and NGOs. Many villagers credited their experience of marching in the streets with other water activists at the World Social Forum with animating them to take direct action against the plant back home. Representatives of Lok Samiti met Amit Srivastava of the US-based India Resource Center, as well as trade unionists organizing against the Company in Colombia and their US supporters. Immediately following the World Social Forum, Plachimada hosted a World Water Conference bringing the Indian groups together anti–water privatization activists like Oscar Olivera (Bolivia) and Maude Barlow and Tony Clarke (Canada). North American NGOs like Corporate Accountability International and the Polaris Institute had been campaigning against water privatization, targeting the bottled-water giants' use of water, plastics, and fossil fuels, and calling for boycotts of bottled water and renewed attention to public water systems. Seeing a shared struggle and potential linkages through the signification of the brand, these NGOs began to forward news of the Indian activists to otherwise distant global north media outlets, consumers, and prospective allies.

Drawing on the multinational system of the corporation itself, the India Resource Center became an agent in constructing a transnational network of "counter-power."[131] The founder of the web-based nonprofit and its lone full-time employee, Amit Srivastava, had organized around environmental justice causes in the United States and was researching and publicizing corporations' environmental practices in international contexts for an NGO when he learned about the struggle in Plachimada in 2002.[132] The India Resource Center constructed itself as a "platform" for communicating and representing the Indian movements' news and demands to international media and supporters. It aimed "to mobilize a key constituency in the United States and around the world that will take action in support of movements in India—by applying pressure in the home countries of the corporations where they are more susceptible to public pressure."[133] The India Resource Center epitomized an actor in a transnational advocacy network, as described by Margaret Keck and Kathryn Sikkink: employing the tactics of "information politics," the quick and credible generation of information and testimony and the transferring of it to places where it will have a political impact; "symbolic politics," the mobilization of symbols, actions, or stories that provide a sense of a situation to audiences near and far; "leverage politics," calling powerful actors to take action to affect a situation where distant or weaker members of a network are unable to have influence; and the "accountability politics" of holding powerful actors to their stated policies or principles.[134] Maintaining frequent contact with the local groups and often in India himself, Srivastava represented the Indian movements on the organization's website, in major news sources, and in speaking tours to North American and British activist groups and universities.

College and university students mobilizing to cut their schools' exclusive contracts with Coca-Cola because of abuses in Colombia partnered with those concerned about the dispossession of Indian communities' water. To draw an array of activists to the cause, Srivastava and student organizers emphasized the "broad coalition" of concerns and groups that converged around the issue—South Asian and Latin American students organizations (with interests in India and Colombia), organizations of students of color (concerned about environmental racism), human rights groups (as labor and environmental issues have increasingly been taken up under the rubric of human rights), and women's groups (since women were disproportionately affected), as well as environmental, labor, and broad-based social justice organizations.[135] As a result of student activism, the Company was pressured to submit to an independent assessment of some of its environmental practices at several of its Indian plants. The Company paid for a report by The Energy and Resources Institute (TERI), a New Delhi research institute that had a working relationship with the Company, in the hope that it would clear it of the charges, demonstrate its corporate responsibility, and perhaps also mystify the debate with complex technical details, which in many ways it succeeded in doing. However, TERI's report also made public much of the water-extraction and water-level data for the first time, and went so far as to recommend the shutting of the Coca-Cola plant in Kala Dera because of critically low water levels.[136]

The symbolic capital of the Company's heavily branded products—in 2006, Coca-Cola was the most globally recognized brand, with a value of $67 billion[137]—reflected the Company's ability to endow fizzy drinks with meaning around the world. For activists, this brand value became the means by which they envisioned and represented a common target to fight from their own geographic position in solidarity with struggles in different parts of the world. Student activists redeployed this symbolic capital—Coca-Cola products' ubiquity, iconicity, and intimate corporeality (since it is physically imbibed)—in various forms of culture jamming to subvert brand connotations with new political meanings and get prospective consumers to consider the international struggles. Activists turned vending machines into crime scenes by wrapping them with police CAUTION tape, inflated a giant blow-up Coca-Cola bottle bearing the words "College-Control" to dominate a campus green, performed street theater dressed as "Killer Cokes" or Coca-Cola pinup girls selling water bottled from public fountains, made the advertised image of thirst-quenching bottles of Coke repulsive by adding dripping blood and "Toxic" labels, created images like the radical cartoonist Carlos Latuff's illustration of a Coca-Cola executive sucking water out of an Indian well with a straw, and reproduced "Water for Life, Not for Profit" signs that Indian protestors themselves used to connect their struggles to the global environmental justice movement (fig. 23).

These activists use the brand, known to people all over the world, to create what anthropologist Robert Foster has called a "critical fetishism," in other words, the consideration of the conditions of a commodity's production to incite more ethical consumption.[138] Commodities are vulnerable to this critical fetishism because their meanings are socially produced. As a material product, Coca-Cola is mostly caffeinated sugar water. When consumers purchase it, they are paying as much for the immaterial value of the brand. But this symbolic capital of the Coca-Cola brand is not a product of the Company alone; rather, the brand relies also on consumers' own endowment of it with qualities and associations (happiness, coolness, family, etc.). Accusations that the Company was dispossessing and polluting water resources challenge these meanings of the brand, and thus also the collaborative relationship in this semiotics between consumer and producer.[139] Even more powerfully, activists' production of new meanings and associations for brands can lay bare this system of meaning-making and produce new relationships of solidarity

FIGURE 23. "Coca-Cola Plants' Theft of Indian Water," 2009. Illustration by Carlos Latuff.

among those connected through the corporate brand's own symbols and language. Company executives have a name for this process as well, accusing the India Resource Center, NAPM, and local Indian organizers like Lok Samiti of "brand-jacking." Brand-jacking, as defined by a report by an international business organization of which the Company is one of the most prominent members, is "when a third party hitches a ride on a brand's fame, positioning and slogan" to attract attention to its issues or agenda, "whilst undermining the brand's reputation in the process."[140] In response to this suggestion that the "issues or agenda" are tangential to the brands that are "brand-jacked" to relay them, Indian villagers and activists contend there is nothing more central to the Company's business practices than the sustainability and safety of the resource that is its primary ingredient: water. The corporations' argument about "brand-jacking" is not, however, far from that of this chapter. Activists use the corporation's material and symbolic capital to connect different people, places, and struggles to produce a politics that is at once local and global, much like the multinational itself.

As protests emerged in different parts of North America, Europe, and India, the business press brooded over this multinational network of activists organizing against Coca-Cola's environmental practices in India. On its front page the *Wall Street Journal* portrayed California-based Amit Srivastava as at the center of the movement's communications web, embodying a new kind of challenge to global corporations: mobilizing transnationally through a globally connected network with little organizational structure, threatening the cultural significance of a brand through a communications campaign without the political legitimacy of mainstream media. "That a one-man NGO armed with just a laptop computer, a Web site and a telephone calling card can, with his allies, influence a huge multinational corporation illustrates the role social activists can play in a world that's going increasingly online."[141] While the business press focused on him, overlooking on-the-ground organizers in India, Srivastava consciously identified his role as supportive, as a First World member of a transnational movement, providing a means for the grassroots movements in India to communicate their struggles, while not dictating their direction or putting himself visibly in the forefront.[142] This media attention brought to the fore, not only the difficulties of constructing a movement across the vast differences in power between mobile, multilingual, media-savvy transnational activists and rural peasants, but also the biases of representation when global north audiences assume a lack of agency among social movements in the global south.

Compared with Srivastava, villagers in Mehdiganj were subaltern media activists, using Coca-Cola's brand in powerful, communicative forms of cultural subversion to build their movement locally and create a point of entrance into a broader mediated public that generally neglected them. At protests, female members of Lok Samiti carried earthen water jugs bearing painted slogans attacking Coca-Cola and proclaiming a right to water: "Water is yours and ours"; "Coca-Cola will not work in the country of curd and milk"; "We need water, not Coke"; "Coca-Cola Quit India" (fig. 24). No longer mute water vessels, not solely because of their iconoclash with Coca-Cola, or even their environmental slogans, but because they communicate an alternative to the Coca-Cola commodity, reasserting the symbolic and environmental commons. The pots enacted a sustaining alternative system—dispensing water to anyone thirsty who had joined in their expression of popular discontent, asserting the centrality of common resources to individual and community survival.

Lok Samiti's cultural team created street theater and songs to raise awareness of social issues, and with musicians from Kala Dera, it produced an

FIGURE 24. Right to Water National Conference and Protest against Coca-Cola, Mehdiganj, Uttar Pradesh, March 30, 2008. Photograph by author.

album, *Jahar Ba* ("There Is Poison"), adapting familiar folk tunes to tell of the appropriation and pollution of their communities' water resources. The title song suggests that Coke is dangerous for individuals, referencing the reports of pesticide-laden soft drinks and their relative unhealthiness in comparison to the traditional Indian drinks they are progressively dislodging. But, more metaphorically, the song suggests that Coca-Cola consumption exhausts and pollutes Indian resources and is dangerous to communities. The video accompanying the song enacts a reversal of the Coca-Cola commercial where Aamir Khan's farmer happily provides the city girls with the *thanda* Coca-Cola from his well. Two village men sing the song to two women drinking sodas while directing the refrain to the entire community:

It is India my brothers
Don't make everything so free
Then when foreigners come
They will loot us.

After selling our water
They give us poison
She doesn't know
They are making us fools.

Discharging polluted water
They have made us sick
And have destroyed our wheat,
paddy and entire agriculture.

They make today's new generation sick.
But she doesn't know,
Brother, she doesn't know,
That there is poison in it.[143]

While the *"Thanda matlab* Coca-Cola" ads attempted to "Indianize" Coca-Cola, these texts critically fetishized the commodity by animating the corporate threat in the bottle of Coke and reinserting it back into the global circuits of power that knit Mehdiganj into the Coca-Cola world system. Profits earned from the Mehdiganj plant ended up in the United States, these songs explained. "Coca-Cola came from America and now they have the money of the people of Benares. And the people of Benares are left with both this water problem and a money problem," as one woman put it. Protest signs with the "Coca-Cola Quit India" slogan (in Hindi and English) evoked the "Quit India" movement's call for independence from British rule, and campaigns against salt and Manchester cloth as part of economic systems of colonial power, and alluded to a new colonization by multinational corporations. While swadeshi discourse in the Coca-Cola campaign was sometimes performed through the metaphor of the contaminating foreign commodity that could sound like communalist responses to transnational culture, producing poison in Coca-Cola directly countered the Company's promotion of its commodity as a taste of "life as it should be," as global corporate quality *thanda* over the water commons that was privatized and degraded for its commodification. Company critiques of the movement as "anti-globalization" disregarded that Coca-Cola's very assertions of its globality allowed it to both appropriate and claim to transcend the local environment, meriting a response.[144] In fact, activists avoided the communalist rhetoric of attacks on

Coca-Cola mobilized by the nationalist Right and took great pride in the transnational networks of solidarity that formed around the struggles against the multinational corporation, the globalization of their own movement against corporate development and water dispossession.[145]

While the Company made efforts to appropriate the cool of *thanda* water for its product, the movement against the corporate dispossession of water attempted to globalize its resistance through that very brand commodity. In the semiotic war of positions, the Company's own globalizing and localizing efforts both enabled and demanded a reappropriation of the symbolic as well as the material common resources being privatized by Coke. *Thanda* had come to mean Coca-Cola through these efforts. But for those in the struggle for rural livelihoods and common resources, as graffiti painted on the side of a Mehdiganj farmhouse neighboring the Coca-Cola plant proclaimed to those who passed by: "*Thanda* means toilet cleaner."[146] It was the multinational ubiquity—of Coca-Cola's drinks, brands, bottling plants, and financial networks—that enabled the very transnationally linked activism of its challengers to emerge and express their environmental critique. Lok Samiti's protest song could thus enjoin listeners: "Now come out from the circle of people who speak the language of Coca-Cola. And do something."[147]

In Plachimada, Mehdiganj, and Kala Dera, the continued movement—and water scarcity—pushed The Coca-Cola Company to define new business strategies in India. In 2013, Coca-Cola proposed a $24 million expansion of its Mehdiganj plant, including a new production line that would fill 600 polyethylene terephthalate (PET) bottles a minute, and sought clearances for increased water extraction to serve the planned enlarged production capacity. But protest and political pressure led regulators to delay permits, and in 2014 the Uttar Pradesh Pollution Control board deemed the Mehdiganj plant expansion in breach of its operating license, ordering it closed. The Company was asked to obtain permission from a government agency for its water use, as well as to take measures to dispose of effluent waste and recharge the groundwater level by twice the amount it extracted.[148] An Indian court stayed the closure order but granted Coca-Cola permission to continue to operate its existing returnable glass bottle production line in Mehdiganj.[149] Coca-Cola decided to find a new site elsewhere in water-parched Uttar Pradesh for its planned larger production facility.[150] Production at the Kala Dera plant slowed over several years, and in early 2016, eight years after the TERI study had declared the plant to be "one of the contributors to a worsening water situation and a source of stress to the communities around,"[151] recommending its closure, Hindustan Coca-Cola Beverages finally shuttered its bottling operations there.[152] In 2017, the bottling subsidiary informed the Supreme Court that it did "not intend to operate" the Plachimada bottling plant, resulting in the court's expeditious dismissal of the case with no discussion of its key issues around water rights.[153] But The Coca-Cola Company also did not intend for these challenges to impede its growth over the long term. That same year, in Mumbai, the Company's new CEO, James Quincey, announced plans for deeper localization and address of consumer concerns, with the goal of making India the Company's third-largest market in the world.[154]

As transnational activism targeting the Company's water use in India grew, and the media began to focus on the probability of future water crises around the world, it became evident that the Company's own "sustainability," understood as profitable growth, was vulnerable to both water scarcity and environmental critiques. Even the business press pointed out Coca-Cola's water problem; an *Economist* article entitled "In Hot Water" argued that because water was so essential to its business model, over the long term, Coca-Cola's battle over environmental sustainability would be fiercer than Big Oil's.[155] With a market logic of both ensuring the existence of future exploitable reserves of its primary ingredient and presenting itself as environmentally conscious to concerned consumers, the Company launched a global corporate social responsibility campaign around water, mined from its experience in India.

SEVEN

CSR: Corporate Social Responsibility and Continued Social Resistance

A NONCONCLUSION

THE COCA-COLA COMPANY FACED a "major reputation crisis" in India in the 2000s, with villagers protesting its exploitation of water and consumers angry about pesticides in its soft drinks.[1] The Company responded by making a highly publicized commitment to the sustainability of both its water use and its business in India, proclaiming a global "corporate social responsibility" (CSR) campaign in Hyderabad in 2007. The announcement included a pledge to become "water neutral" in India, as well as, contradictorily, a $250 million expansion of its Indian operations. As part of this new CSR strategy, the Company launched its first corporate, rather than product-oriented, advertising campaign in India: "Little Drops of Joy." Produced especially for the Indian market, the multi-year campaign was "based on insights generated through extensive research and ... designed to connect with various stakeholders."[2] Deflecting criticisms relating to sustainability and safety, the "Little Drops of Joy" campaign promoted the liquid goodness of the Company, vaunting all the "small, but significant steps taken by Coca-Cola India" to "spread joy wherever we go."[3]

"Little Drops of Joy" TV commercials associated Coca-Cola brands with collective happiness—putting them at the center of a family's celebration of the Diwali festival of lights, for example—and cited the Company's good deeds—such as employing the deaf as bottle inspectors, building a rainwater harvesting infrastructure in Hyderabad, and restoring a four-hundred-year-old well in Rajasthan (a contribution to water sustainability that was also "a good reminder of the cultural heritage of India"). The ads thus localized the Company as Indian, even including a specific Indian employee's picture and statement in each print ad. "A mighty ocean we're not. But we are the little drops that make one," the Company insisted. "Because we don't just quench your thirst. We recharge your soul. For one moment. One drop at a time." Like much CSR discourse, "Little Drops of Joy" simultaneously played down the Company's power—a "mighty ocean" it was not—while asserting its contributions to the ethical and good: "little drops" of Coca-Cola recharging not just bodies and watersheds but souls too.

We have been bombarded with such images of CSR as the soul of capitalism, leaving the impression that corporations are as concerned about our welfare as their bottom lines: Walmart is supplying disaster relief, Tata is forging rural development, Bacardi is moderating teen alcohol consumption, Chrysler is driving Detroit back from the brink, Starbucks is energizing fair trade, Pfizer is treating faltering health care systems, Chevron is fueling small business, and BP is pioneering alternative energy. Among them, The Coca-Cola Company has been a leader in seeking to justify itself in terms of CSR (or its variants "corporate citizenship" and "corporate sustainability") through voluntary codes of conduct, social welfare initiatives, and communications campaigns. In addition to the expected chemists and brand managers, the Company employs executives and consultants trained in a range of expertise outside the day-to-day business of soda production—crisis management and public relations, anthropology, labor relations, and environmental, health, and area studies. Working with the senior managers and bottling executives of the Company's aptly named Public Policy and Corporate Reputation Council, they examine risks and opportunities in issues like workers' rights, health, and the environment and strategize whether and how the Company might address them. The Coca-Cola Company claims to have "given back" more than $820 million through CSR initiatives since 1984, and $84.5 million in 2015 alone.[4] CSR proponents have suggested that these corporate social commitments herald a new phase of economic and social relations, "capitalism with a conscience."[5] But CSR did not arise unprompted from the good hearts of corporations. Rather, it is a tool to manage neoliberal globalization's dual production of domination and resistance by containing both the most egregious corporate abuses and the critiques, movements, and regulatory attempts described in this book.[6]

In large part, CSR is a public relations response to what companies see as "reputation crises." Calling attention to the superficiality of many corporate correctives, critics have dismissed it as strategic perception management by improving corporate image through "greenwashing" (association with environmental groups and causes) or "bluewashing" (association with the blue-flagged United Nations). But limiting an analysis of CSR to this point glosses over the complex and subtly insidious logic of the relationship between the economic and the social that undergirds CSR discourses and practices now institutionalized in companies, business schools, NGOs, supranational organizations, and the press. CSR does powerful ideological work, maintaining corporate hegemony against an onslaught of social movements by building popular consent to a perceived kinder, more responsive version of global capitalism. While seemingly constraining corporate freedoms and growth by encouraging the consideration of social as well as economic interests, in fact, CSR demonstrates neoliberal faith in the market's ability to solve the world's problems and ensure social welfare. CSR does not require selfless goodwill but rather self-serving interest, with executives themselves arguing that they have a capitalist responsibility to their businesses, as well as to society, to take up public concerns, because if these go unresolved, profits and the global order will be threatened by social unrest and corresponding state regulation.[7]

Contemporary CSR has become a constitutive element of neoliberalism, which seeks a retrenchment of social welfare states and regulations in favor of the perceived efficiency of the market. The freeing up of international markets and the resulting globalization of capital without corresponding international regulatory regimes made possible rapacious corporate growth. As states lacked the power to deal with corporate exploitation and failed to supply social welfare needs, public protests erupted along corporations' international commodity chains. Citizens found themselves deprived of accountability and corporations of a legitimizing authority to match the international scope of their businesses.[8] Corporations have attempted to fill the governance gap by validating their self-regulation and social welfare initiatives, while continuing to resist state regulation and legal accountability, creating in effect what has been called a "transnational private legitimacy regime."[9] Corporations are thus both empowered and burdened by the freedoms, public expectations, and exploitative practices that are a consequence of their key role in the global economy.[10] As this book has shown, The Coca-Cola Company has been shaped by contestation and resistance, critiques and movements that have exceeded Coca-Cola's capacity to contain them completely. CSR is the Company's current strategy for attempting this containment, and I argue here that the initialism has multiple more accurate expansions than "corporate social responsibility": to name a few, corporations stifling regulation, corporations self-regulating, corporations co-opting social roles, corporate social reputation, and capitalist social realism.

CORPORATIONS STIFLING REGULATION: COUNTERING LEGAL AND REGULATORY ACCOUNTABILITY

In the first decades of the twenty-first century, consumers, communities, workers, and activist groups challenged The Coca-Cola Company's record on workers' rights, environmental sustainability, and the health impact of its products, each resulting in related CSR discourse and initiatives. Most prominently, a Colombian trade union accused the corporation of colluding with paramilitaries to eliminate unionists' lives and livelihoods, drawing attention to forms of labor exploitation and violence in both a court case and a transnational social movement. In India, rural villagers organized against the Company's extraction and dispossession of water resources in the production of its bottled drinks, and groups in North America and Europe attacked the privatization and commodification of bottled water. More recently and potentially even more financially threatening to the Company, nutrition scientists, public health advocates, and consumers have criticized Coca-Cola's products and marketing for contributing to serious health conditions and resulting strains on healthcare systems. Researchers assert that just a single twelve-ounce regular soda a day increases the risk, not just of obesity and type 2 diabetes, but also of coronary heart disease and stroke—concluding that sugary liquids are more dangerous because of the way they are metabolized by the body.[11] Public health advocates call sodas "Liquid Candy" and "Toxi-Colas" and have launched education and social media campaigns to dissuade consumption and sought regulations including the removal of high-calorie soft drinks from public schools, limits on advertising of them to children, rules for health claims and information on package labeling, the implementation of additional taxes on sodas, and caps on product size.[12] In 2016, the World Health Organization recommended that governments around the world tax sugar-sweetened beverages to help reduce obesity.[13] Such taxes have been enacted in thirty countries—including India—and hotly debated in many others—like Colombia—where the soda industry fought fiercely and often dirtily against them.[14]

As part of each of these struggles (labor, environmental, and health), groups of activists and advocacy groups have pursued legal accountability and government regulation where possible as strategies for social protection from corporate abuses. For these attempts at oversight, activists have often had to seek alternative avenues of accountability, racing to compensate for the lag in regulatory governance relative to the speed of global corporate growth.[15] Corporations in response have enacted voluntary, self-policing CSR initiatives to forestall this threat, while also directly challenging efforts at legal and regulatory oversight.

In 2001, in an early example of the application of the Alien Tort Statute (ATS) to corporate actions abroad, labor rights activists brought suit against Coca-Cola for the killings in Colombia. ATS, an archaic law that invests US courts with extraterritorial civil jurisdiction over violations of the law of nations or US treaties, was resurrected by human rights lawyers for use against multinationals' alleged human rights abuses in other countries, becoming one of the most prominent tools in these attempts to elicit legal accountability. The Coca-Cola case represented a remarkably threatening new precedent for multinational corporations: the first time a judge had ordered a US company to stand trial under ATS for alleged human rights violations committed overseas.[16] In response, Coca-Cola and other US corporations aggressively challenged ATS, largely through lobbying and legal argumentation conducted by major US and international business associations,[17] shielding individual corporations from attention by collectively camouflaging their efforts. Their legal briefs argued that the binding norms of ATS would put the United States and US corporations at a competitive disadvantage in the global economy, jeopardize the United States' special strategic, economic, and political (as well as military) relationship with Colombia, and even (somewhat ironically given the just expressed concern with maintaining US corporate power internationally) constitute an imperial extension of the United States' "developed" legal regime to "developing" countries. The cloak of these corporate lobbying groups allowed member companies like Coca-Cola to deploy corporate social responsibility policy statements as their public stance on issues, while fighting precedents like ATS cases that might make them liable for their actions abroad. In the court case, Coca-Cola's defense attorneys argued that even though the US multinational owned a large share of the Colombian Coca-Cola bottlers and exerted significant influence over them through its "bottlers agreement," the Colombian bottlers were independently owned and operated corporate entities whose labor relations were not under Coca-Cola's "explicit control." This was the argument that succeeded in getting Coca-Cola dismissed from the lawsuit.[18]

The threat of legal accountability and regulation as a result of movement demands was also a driving force behind the Company's CSR initiatives in India. Coca-Cola emphasized that its operations complied with existing local Indian laws and thus did not constitute water "overexploitation,"[19] even if regulation was absent (at the time Coca-Cola had an uncontrolled right to groundwater as landowner), taxation negligible, and oversight lax, while water scarcity was dire.[20] When the Plachimada *panchayat* (village council) revoked the plant's licenses, the Company challenged it in court. The resulting lawsuit revolved around two major issues of corporate water use: first, whether private landowners have proprietary rights to extraction of water without limit or permission from the government, or whether overextraction and pollution of groundwater infringes on the right to life and livelihood of others, and the state should thus be empowered and required to protect a public good in public trust; and second, whether the *panchayat* had the authority to preserve water resources in its jurisdiction and thus regulate the use of water on private lands.[21] Awaiting hearing by the Supreme Court after more than ten years, the Company let it be known in 2017 that it no longer intended to restart operations in Plachimada, and the case was dismissed. As a result, the country's highest court did not discuss the case's key legal issues of environmental rights and governance. In the meantime, in 2010, a Keralan government panel constituted to assess the negative socioeconomic impact of the plant recommended compensation of $48 million in damages.[22] The Keralan state assembly passed legislation establishing a tribunal to recover damages from the Company and adjudicate residents' claims for compensation. Coca-Cola asserted that the state assembly lacked "legislative competence," inasmuch as environmental oversight fell under a different authority, and accused it of producing legislation "devoid of facts, scientific data or any input from or consideration given to" the Company.[23] Coca-Cola played on the regulatory power struggles between the Keralan state and the central national government and exerted pressure on the more amenable latter, resulting in the Indian president's rejection of the Keralan bill.[24] The Coca-Cola Company thus subverted the regulatory authority of Indian local and state governments and has thus far avoided precedent for legal challenges to water privatization and compensation for those affected.

The Coca-Cola Company, together with other sellers of sugary beverages, fought hard against attempts at regulation in the interests of public health. Efforts to enact taxes on high-calorie beverages, caps on portion sizes, requirements for nutrition labeling and restrictions on undemonstrated health claims, and limits on advertising to children have met with strong resistance from the beverage industry.[25] The Company has fought these battles through commercial associations and industry-funded "astroturf" (artificial grassroots) front groups. From 2009 to 2015, the American Beverage Association spent over $117 million to fight health-related regulation and taxes. This amount does not include direct payments by soft-drink companies to lobbyists and campaigns, nor "dark money" contributed to political action committees to support candidates and issues that will serve the corporations' financial interests, totaling several million dollars annually in the United States.[26]

In 2016, the Colombian health minister proposed a tax on sweetened beverages to generate $340 million a year for the country's underfunded and strained healthcare system, and raise the cost of the drinks to dissuade purchases. The industry has waged a pitched battle against such taxes in developing countries, which are still growing in both market size and obesity rates (in Colombia, the latter had tripled since 1980 to 19 percent of adults). In Colombia, the Asociación Nacional de Empresarios (ANDI) and the International Council of Beverage Associations partnered with Postobón and Coca-Cola as primary adversaries to the proposal. The soda industry benefited from Postobón being a subsidiary of the massive conglomerate Organización Ardila Lülle, which, in addition to sugarcane growers and sugar mills, owns the country's largest media company, RCN Television, which promoted the anti-tax message. In the rest of the media, the beverage industry fought back against sympathy for the tax proposal. When Colombia's oldest newspaper, *El Espectador*, ran an editorial video "The Sweet Lies of Congressmen," lampooning politicians and the beverage industry for ignoring scientific evidence, a representative from Coca-Cola Colombia reportedly demanded that an image of a Sprite bottle be removed. Other news outlets reported editorial content being challenged by their advertising executives, concerned with maintaining relationships with the soda companies.[27]

Colombian public health NGOs Educar Consumidores and Alianza por la Salud Alimentaria led the charge for a soda tax, producing a dramatic TV ad that dramatically exposed the potential contribution of daily sugar consumption from four sweetened drinks—which amounted to as much as forty-seven teaspoons—to "serious health conditions," represented by an overweight couple, a case of foot gangrene from diabetes, a man having a heart attack, and another in a hospital being treated for cancer.[28] Postobón's lawyer filed a complaint with the consumer protection agency—an agency he had previously headed—claiming that the measurement was imprecise, and that the characterization of all sweetened drinks as unhealthy was unfair. In a sweeping ruling, the consumer protection agency barred the NGOs from speaking publicly about the links between sugar and obesity, in other words, barred them from trying to protect consumers.[29] Employees of the NGOs received threats and believe their communications were under surveillance. While seeming an overreaction, this had happened before: when public health advocates pushed for an increase of the soda tax in 2016 in Mexico, Coca-Cola's biggest consumer market by per capita consumption, military-grade spyware was found on their hacked cellphones.[30]

This is not to accuse The Coca-Cola Company of such wrongdoing. But it should be noted that the Company and its business associations have actively worked to inflame concerns among those with an economic interest in the industry or shared ideological perspectives. To the general public, the Company drew on discourses fostered across decades of promotion, now familiar to the reader of this book, to defend its industry against taxes and regulations like labeling requirements and caps on bottle size. It argued that such actions would limit Coca-Cola's growth, resulting in the loss of jobs for people employed in bottling production and lost revenue for local retailers, as well as infringements on consumers' free choice and individual responsibility at the hands of the "nanny state" (additions for the neoliberal era).[31] In Colombia, at least ninety lobbyists made this case during visits to legislators to push back against the proposed tax on sweetened beverages. Polls showed that 70 percent of Colombians supported the proposed tax, but only 42 of 268 Colombian con-gressional representatives backed it, and the measure was dropped from the larger tax package through a complex procedural maneuver.[32]

CORPORATIONS SELF-REGULATING: VOLUNTARY CODES OF CONDUCT AND CIVIL SOCIETY COLLABORATION

Since the Company's direct challenges to legal and regulatory mechanisms for accountability in the abovementioned cases did little to cleanse the brand image from the tarnish of popular social critique, it simultaneously developed a parallel tactic to its attacks on liability and regulatory accountability: self-regulation. In CSR, corporations construct voluntary self-regulatory mecha-nisms to address issues of public concern, attenuating calls to rein in corporate behavior through legally binding codes and state regulation.[33] As Russell Sparkes, a leader in the field of socially responsible investing, explained in his paradigmatic argument for CSR, these issues of public concern are often the product of private corporate practices that are now borne by the public, inasmuch as "the de-regulation of the 1980s and 1990s enabled profit maximizing companies to pass onto society costs that they were previously forced to internalize." Such social "costs" of capitalism, or systemic negative externalities borne by society, are addressed in one of two ways, he warned companies: either they are corrected via the market or "they can lead to government re-regulation of the economy."[34] Corporate social responsibility is thus a self-regulatory tactic to deflect public critique and state regulation. By self-governing, CSR advocates advised corporations, they could even "immunize" themselves from activist criticism and get out in front of governments' demands.[35] But even further, by asserting the market's ability to provide social protections from its own exploitative practices, corporate social responsibility becomes both a discursive and a practical justification for the privatization of regulatory and social welfare structures.[36] In India, for example, Coca-Cola voluntarily adopted internal water-use standards, and in various locations, when it faced public health criticisms, it changed labels and product sizes, in both cases to legitimize its practices, deflect activist demands, and dissuade regulatory reform and legal accountability. The Coca-Cola Company's recent activities around Colombia demonstrate some of CSR's multiple self-regulatory strategies.

To respond to concerns about labor practices in Colombia, Coca-Cola crafted voluntary self-regulatory codes and assessments of working conditions in collaboration with NGOs and promoted CSR discourse in association with international organizations. In 2005, the Company hired Ed Potter, a longtime labor lawyer and employers' representative with the International Labor Organization (ILO), as director of global labor relations and workplace accountability, a position that had been vacant since 1997 (Potter was the first person hired to fill it since the consumer and labor challenges of the early 1970s). With his leadership, the Company established its Global Workplace Rights Policy for its 93,000 direct employees and a set of Supplier Guiding Principles for the hundreds of thousands more employees working for "direct suppliers" (including franchise bottlers, but not those further down the commodity chain, like producers of sugar, coffee, and aluminum). Framed as international declarations on labor and human rights, the statements cover work hours, wages (to be "competitive . . . with [the] local labor market"), freedom of association, safety, health, security, forced labor, child labor, and discrimination (all in accordance with "applicable laws"). The Company claimed that the Supplier Guiding Principles for the first time provided grounds to terminate the contract of a franchise bottler who could not demonstrate adherence to labor standards, but in reality, it required only the most basic compliance with "applicable local and national" environmental and labor laws.[37]

Both the Supplier Guiding Principles and Global Workplace Rights Policy are internal, self-regulating codes, with adherence accountable only to the Company itself. Such voluntary corporate codes have been shown to have limited effect; research by the United Kingdom's Ethical Trading Initiative found that they "worked only in countries where labour standards (and their enforcement) were higher in the first place."[38] Such codes have also provided cover for commonplace labor exploitation by prohibiting only the most egregious forms of abuse (violence, forced and child labor, etc.). Bottlers' large-scale layoffs, flexibilization, and outsourcing, nearly insurmountable obstacles to union organizing, resulting in economic insecurity, are less articulable in the language of harm to individual human rights and are glossed over by CSR discourse that allows the Company to promote itself as a good global employer for not committing the most extreme forms of abuse.

This CSR self-regulation is legitimized by agencies, NGOs, and other companies, which offer non–legally binding, limited reviews, as with the Company's commissioning of the ILO and a for-profit corporate assessor, Cal Safety Compliance Corporation, to conduct audits of work conditions in Colombian bottling plants. Both reports found only minor issues, but were limited in their investigations to current labor practices (excluding previous charges of violence) and compliance with local labor laws.[39] Activists doubted the credibility of the reports, produced by entities potentially "captured" by industrial influence, especially given that Coca-Cola's director of labor relations had a post with the ILO and the Company was paying for the employment of Cal Safety. And they questioned both Cal Safety's methodology of monitoring (including giving bottlers advance notice of inspections) and its track record of overlooked labor violations.[40]

The Coca-Cola Company promoted CSR's self-regulatory strategy on the world stage, becoming a major proponent of the United Nations Global Compact, "the world's largest corporate responsibility initiative."[41] The Company proclaimed its participation as a victory for "the tenets of corporate social responsibility," since it would improve the UN's ability to promote the initiative to other multinationals.[42] Coca-Cola CEO Neville Isdell, who had been hired in part to clean up the Company's "muddied" corporate name,[43] became one of the most prominent corporate spokespersons for CSR and the Global Compact. Under the auspices of the Compact, signatory corporations agree to pursue general principles in the areas of human rights, labor standards, the environment, and anti-corruption. But as a voluntary, self-reporting, non-binding, and non-monitoring agreement with no enforcement mechanism, sociologist Jennifer Bair calls it "a toothless public relations operation allowing companies the costless benefit of association with the United Nations."[44] To get corporate participation in the Compact, the UN assured corporations that it was not legally-binding and different from "previous attempts to clamp down on global commerce through 'command and control' regulation."[45]

As the preeminent global CSR initiative, the Global Compact demonstrates CSR's constitutive role in the dominant neoliberal paradigm of reliance on the market for development and the provision of social welfare, even at the UN.[46] The Global Compact marked the first time the UN had facilitated agreements between nonstate actors—corporations no less—and in its administration through the Secretary General's office, independent of any intergovernmental body or member states' review of implementation or effectiveness, it bypasses state oversight altogether.[47] This was a stark change from past decades, when in the 1970s, the UN had been the international organization through which countries had called for a New International Economic Order. No longer is the focus on redistributive growth or equitability, but rather on empowering corporate actors and "exhibiting and building the social legitimacy of business and markets."[48] As a result of the past several decades of market-friendly policy aggressively forwarded by international financial institutions, nations around the world privatized state-owned corporations and liberalized trade and investment so that transnational corporations expanded into these new markets, extracting resources and profits in environments of comparative (dis)advantage in regulatory and social standards. Transnational corporate investment was not just a by-product of liberalization but the primary logic of the economic development of poor places, with transnational capital replacing official aid as the strategy for development of the majority world.[49] The Global Compact buttressed this neoliberal framework by keeping activist and regulatory challenges at bay with voluntary codes and affirmations of the market's superiority in improving social welfare around the world, institutionalizing relationships with corporations to address the problems of corporate globalization itself. This was the stated goal of the Compact when Secretary General Kofi Annan proposed the idea at the World Economic Forum in 1999 as a means for corporations to combat the rising "backlash" against economic globalization from human rights, labor, and environmental movements that threatened the openness of the global market with regulatory and protectionist restrictions. Corporations would be forced to achieve "proclaimed standards by other means," either by giving resources and authority to international institutions like the UN or by voluntarily upholding these standards themselves. In return, the UN would "facilitate a dialogue with social groups" and "help make the case for and maintain an environment which favors trade and open markets," Annan assured.[50]

Corporate social responsibility initiatives and frameworks like the Global Compact emphasize partnerships and collaborations with other social actors, including governmental bodies, NGOs, unions, communities, and social movements, hailing them as "stakeholders" in businesses. Activists succeeded in pushing companies to think beyond the interests of their shareholders alone, but as a result, they now face the risk of assimilation and institutionalization of their movements and organizations.[51] Following "stakeholder theory,"[52] a subfield of CSR, corporations are advised to broaden their sense of responsibility from their shareholders to others who can affect or be affected by their actions, its "stakeholders." CSR strategies then conscript activist movements and groups into becoming interested parties—or stakeholders—involuntarily invested in the corporation and its CSR initiatives to get redress of their concerns. The Coca-Cola Company has used its CSR initiatives to encourage communities, organizations, and state authorities to collaborate with rather than confront it. As a Coca-Cola-funded dialogue on CSR in Colombia concluded:

> Civil society organizations will have to consider joining forces with corporations so that different skills and competencies can be shared, despite levels of mistrust built up over decades. Employee organizations like trade unions will have to look afresh at how they can best represent the interests of their members, via confrontation or collaboration. Governments will need to look to their bureaucracies and regulations to see if they are stifling or rewarding social and commercial entrepreneurs.[53]

Since CSR relies on the voluntary actions of companies and often deters regulation, movements must sustain the threat to their corporate bottom lines to insist that they continue to redefine the "social" and recast themselves as "responsible" in new terms, as a form neoliberal corporate governance. This requires a politics of perpetual protest, a difficult condition for movements to maintain once enlisted as stakeholders. Much of the field of stakeholder theory neglects to consider the vast differences in power between corporations and the communities they engage, which have themselves been consciously selected over other, more antagonistic groups.[54] This becomes more overt in literature that refers to this approach as "stakeholder management," suggesting the central power of managers, the management of the interests of such stakeholders, and their instrumental utility to management and the corporation's bottom line in serving as less threatening social regulators as well as legitimizers for the public. Such discourses promote the sense that "it pays to do good unto others": engaging with stakeholders will improve corporate performance, so that the path to goodness can be paved with money.[55] CSR can be understood as part of the larger project of neoliberal privatization of society as it assimilates or corporatizes spheres and activities that were once outside or even challengers to the corporation or capitalism broadly.[56] CSR holds the very real threat of binding together corporate and activist actors in the same neoliberal project of self-regulation and self-governance. As Grahame Thompson puts it, CSR, "'responsibilises' autonomous agents (companies), who increasingly organise their own self-governance, setting themselves targets and standards that they themselves police. Inasmuch as a wide range of organisations— companies, NGOs, governmental and quasi-governmental agencies, individuals, religious organisations, academics—'advocate' corporate social responsibility they are, in effect, enacting and performing such a neo-liberal programme on themselves and others."[57]

The large NGO sector often stands in as the stakeholder on issues of public concern, legitimizing the self-regulatory moves of CSR and thus helping the neoliberal slashing of the welfare state by promoting private-public partnerships to address neglected social issues and the rationalization of social movements into organizations. With the widespread acceptance of CSR, civil society organizations are becoming more corporatized and deradicalized through corporate financing and cooperation. Not surprisingly, the growth of the CSR field has been intertwined with that of corporate-sponsored market-advocating NGOs, or "MaNGOs," which forward corporate solutions to social issues through CSR practices, complementing and validating free-market policies and the neoliberal mode of operation of NGOs and corporate initiatives to fill the void created by governmental retreat from social protections.[58] The International Business Leaders Forum (IBLF), for example, in which Coca-Cola CEO Isdell served as chairman of the Board of Trustees, was founded in 1990 to promote CSR simultaneously along with free markets as multinationals expanded across the majority world and into post-communist states, advocating for voluntary forms of corporate accountability, business "solutions to sustainable development challenges,"[59] and "embedding civil society and enterprise"[60] to "create an 'enabling environment' in which business can have a positive impact on society."[61] These MaNGOs are less identifiably corporate than previous manifestations of corporate performance of "civil society" (like chambers of commerce and associations of manufacturers) and often enjoy treatment as NGOs even though they are distinctly market players, actively shaping the discourses and practices of self-regulation and giving them an aura of legitimacy.[62]

The Coca-Cola Company also engaged amenable labor organizations in nonbinding labor rights pledges as a form of self-regulation that might mend its image as an employer. In CSR discourse, the Company hailed these labor groups as "stakeholders" invested in the economic and social outcomes of its business, emphasizing collaboration over confrontation to effectively deradicalize labor relations. In this vein the Company co-signed a labor rights statement with the International Union of Food, Agricultural, Hotel, Restaurant, Catering, Tobacco and Allied Workers Associations (IUF), the worldwide labor federation that includes the majority of Coca-Cola unions, acknowledging workers' rights to union membership and committing to biannual conversations about labor and human rights.[63] The IUF includes multiple unions that compete with the more confrontational Colombian bottling union, and Coca-Cola touted its relationships with them to suggest that nothing was wrong in its labor relations in Colombia.

While The Coca-Cola Company partnered with international organizations and signed global guiding principles, it also promoted self-regulatory CSR on national and regional levels. In Colombia, Coca-Cola funded CSR conferences partnering with the IBLF, the Colombian NGO Fundación Ideas para la Paz, and the Global Compact, where Coca-Cola's Potter "dialogued" with the leadership of NGOs, unions, and other corporations.[64] The Company, along with Fundación Ideas para la Paz, led a working group of corporations to encourage the adoption of voluntary codes of conduct and collaboration with local NGOs and civil society in Colombia.

In these venues Coca-Cola and CSR proponents mobilized a market logic to motivate self-regulation, arguing that corporations should behave better and address social welfare to protect their bottom lines. The Coca-Cola Company funded a glossy eighty-page report, *Development, Peace and Human Rights in Colombia: A Business Agenda* (2006), that appealed to corporations' enlightened self-interest by emphasizing the costs of Colombia's conflict and societal problems and the commercial incentives for companies to tackle them. Pablo Largacha, a Coca-Cola Colombia executive promoted to the position of director of public affairs and communications in Atlanta in part because of his crisis management of the outcry over violence against Colombian unionists, summarized the report's findings at an ANDI conference on CSR. "Business costs" included security expenses and business development restrained by inability to operate in insecure areas, as well as the scarcity of capable workers and worker inefficiency because of displacement, lack of education, and "delinquency." Most dramatically, violence against trade unionists, and resulting lawsuits, threatened Coke's corporate reputation ("Coca-Cola has been particularly familiar with this ... having been made a defendant by a Colombian union for supposed violations of human rights," Largacha reminded the audience).[65] Accordingly, this representative CSR document transforms Colombia's social and economic issues into a list of commercial incentives for companies to voluntarily address them: CSR "safeguards corporate reputation and brand image; gains competitive advantage; improves recruitment, staff retention and loyalty; fosters greater productivity; secures and maintains a license to operate—including the social license to operate; reduces cost burdens—including security and insurance expenditure; ensures active stakeholder engagement—winning the trust of influential NGOs; meets investor expectations—including those of the growing number of socially responsible investors."[66] As long as the market is the sole motivation for self-regulation, the questions become when (only when a company faces a reputation crisis?) and for how long (until the issue subsides?) a company has to behave itself until the market no longer warrants it doing so.

To reintegrate the poor and ex-combatants into society and the market, The Coca-Cola Company and its bottlers favored educational and training programs in Colombia. Coca-Cola is one of the principal sponsors of the NGO Fundación Colombianitos, which sponsors education, recreation, and physical rehabilitation for vulnerable children. In 2005, Coca-Cola committed $10 million to establish the Fundación Colombia para la Educación y la Oportunidad, which promotes education and employment opportunities in communities that have suffered from violence, including enrolling in technical schools demobilized former combatants and people displaced by violence.[67] Education is a perfect CSR initiative: unthreatening and universally accepted as a social good. It is also representative of a broad shift in the politics of Latin American civil society; as Latin American social movements transformed into more rationally oriented and corporatized NGOs, the goals of large-scale political and economic restructuring and redistribution were replaced with individual and apolitical socioeconomic empowerment by educating and equipping people for survival in the harsh reality of contemporary capitalism.[68] These social welfare initiatives in Colombia exemplify the third element of CSR: corporations co-opting social roles.

CO-OPTING SOCIAL ROLES: CORPORATIONS AS SOCIAL WELFARE PROVIDERS

With CSR, corporations construct themselves as providers of social welfare, offering protection from exploitation by market forces, a role that is always limited and problematic. In India, for example, Coca-Cola's PR department made much of its efforts to "replenish the water [used in the production process] back to communities."[69] It argued its market motivation to equally skeptical shareholders and "stakeholders," explaining that water scarcity had become a business risk: "[W]e are a hydration company. Every product we sell contains water. Without water, we have no business and it is in the long-term interest of our company to be good stewards of our most critical ingredient."[70] The Company began the process of self-regulating: in 2007, it became one of the first to sign a voluntary pledge under the Global Compact to set targets for corporate water conservation and waste-water treatment.[71] It submitted to an independent assessment of a handful of Indian plants by The Energy and Resources Institute (TERI), although critics questioned the independence of the report, given the Company's close relationship with the Institute—more compelling when TERI University announced a new Coca-Cola Department of Regional Water Studies, endowed by its namesake.[72] Internally, Coca-Cola required that all its bottling plants conduct risk assessments to determine vulnerabilities to the quality and quantity of local water—as well as vulnerabilities to "social, environmental and regulatory risks" (i.e., potential resistance) around local water concerns—and meet with civil society groups and governments about source water protection plans.[73] Through reducing and recycling water used at its plants, the Company lowered its 2016 water use ratio to 1.96 liters per 1 liter of product, an impressive 27 percent reduction from 2004, although still using as much water in the production process as fluid content of each bottled drink.[74] But the Company's pledges of reduction in water use ran up against capitalism's imperative to expand. Neglected in the Company's representation of its improved water efficiency was the fact that its global operational water use climbed from 283 billion liters in 2004[75] to 303.65 billion liters of water in 2016.[76] Betraying the limitations of a commitment to sustainability that cannot allow limits to capital accumulation, the Company manufactures more soft drinks every year, adding more water-intensive drinks to its product line, while expanding in water-insecure markets like India.

To make up for the contradiction between corporate expansion and claims of a reduction in water use, the Company attempted to offset its exploitation of water by taking on the role of private protector and provider of water. In 2016, Coca-Cola made the dramatic announcement that it had become "water neutral," returning to communities or watersheds as much water as it sold in bottled drinks that year. To do so, over the previous decade, in partnership with local governments and the World Wildlife Fund (WWF), USAID, CARE, the UN Development Program (UNDP), PlayPumps International, and other NGOs, the Company had launched 250 projects in over seventy countries providing for water protection, conservation, and access to clean water and sanitation.[77] The Company entered into a $20 million partnership with the WWF to conserve seven of the world's most critical freshwater river basins.[78] And it launched the Replenish Africa Initiative (RAIN), a six-year, $30 million commitment to provide access to clean water to over two million people in Africa.[79] Coca-Cola also provided start-up financing for the Global Water Challenge, a coalition of UN agencies, NGOs, and corporations (Cargill, Dow Chemical, and Ford) to support collaboration and investment in community water initiatives and social entrepreneurship, financed through "market-based instruments including loans and guarantees," aimed at the "goal of universal access to clean water and safe sanitation."[80] In India, where the Company faced direct challenges over its water use, it also declared itself water neutral in 2016, having built or maintained hundreds of wells, ponds, dams, rainwater harvesting and recharging systems, and pipelines, and subsidized water-efficient agriculture (drip irrigation, field leveling, etc.) to change local agricultural practices. The scale of the "replenishment" claims is large, and they have been achieved remarkably quickly: in 2011, the Company was "offsetting" 23 percent of its annual sales volume; five years later, it claimed to be returning 133 percent of the water in its bottled drinks.[81]

But environmental activists decried the vagueness of the concepts of "water neutrality," "water balance," and "water offsets," as well as the lack of a workable methodology for measuring their effects,[82] which the Company itself admitted were "questioned," inasmuch as they were "new and developing."[83] The science behind water offsetting is unproven at best (and exists through research and promotion by the likes of The Coca-Cola Company).[84] Unlike carbon offsets, the market-solution environmentalism many corporations have adopted to support clean-air initiatives to subtract from their greenhouse gas emissions, water is naturally renewing, making it difficult to credit in the same way. Similarly, whereas carbon dioxide acts globally on the atmosphere, water scarcity is intensely local.[85] "*Replenish* does not necessarily mean we will balance product water at each plant," the Company acknowledged.[86] A corporation could claim water neutrality by pumping a village aquifer dry in one place while putting the same amount of water back in a far-off rainforest river. The Coca-Cola Company's water offsetting is spread over distant projects, not primarily at the source of extraction, and since putting water in one watershed does nothing to help water scarcity in another, leaves certain bottling-plant communities dry.[87] There has been intense pressure to find water projects to fund in order to claim these replenishment credits; companies involved in such CSR initiatives express concern that "there's not enough water to go around," in other words, not enough viable water conservation efforts to absolve their corporate water consumption elsewhere. As a result, environmentalists allege that the Company has rushed to partner with projects, not fully checking that they are supported by science.[88]

Some critical environmental scientists argue that these "replenishment" claims allow the Company to promote itself as sustainable, while distracting attention from its real environmental impact. The Company's calculations of water neutrality cover little more than its "operational water," considering only water used in the production of bottled drinks at plants—primarily, water that goes into products bottled for sale. They do not include all water used in producing bottled drinks (such as that "returned as wastewater"), and, more important, the vastly larger amounts of water used in its supply chain in the production of agricultural ingredients and packaging materials. The Coca-Cola Company was right about Indian farmers being larger water users than its plants; agriculture has a much larger water footprint. But that is true for The Coca-Cola Company as well, since most of the water that goes into manufacturing a Coke—around 80 percent of its water footprint—is used to produce sugar (e.g., by growing sugar beets). Added to that is the roughly 20 percent of the water that is used to manufacture the soft drink's packaging (e.g., PET bottles). Coca-Cola claims itself to be water neutral by virtue of offsetting a half-liter of water against a half-liter of bottled drink, but according to water footprint assessments at a Coca-Cola plant in Holland, every half-liter bottle of Coke actually requires thirty-five liters of water. Not only do Coca-Cola's claims of water neutrality thus account for only a very small percentage of its total water footprint, more problematically, it has promoted and legitimized a limited environmental accounting framework that inflates the impression of its positive corporate impact.[89]

Still, liberal commentators celebrate CSR's public-private partnership as a new "social compact" setting corporations on track to bring about significant social change. Surely the positive environmental effects of Coca-Cola's large-scale environmental responsibility initiatives are better than irresponsible alternatives. But, in classic neoliberal terms, responsibility for ensuring the security of public water has been turned over to a private corporation, and one that sells that very resource; a privatization of responsibility for public goods. Indian communities wonder what will happen when Coca-Cola no longer deems it necessary or financially justifiable to voluntarily continue these CSR water initiatives. In the meantime, community organizers in Mehndiganj, India, offer a tour of Company water projects in disrepair. And when such projects are working, communities struggle with the dilemma that winning concessions from the Company may result in dependence on the corporation to provide private solutions to public problems. What kinds of solutions arise from The Coca-Cola Company?

In 2013, The Coca-Cola Company pledged to distribute 1,500–2,000 modular kiosks, in the form of modified shipping containers using solar energy to power small water-treatment systems, to rural communities in twenty countries by 2015.[90] Called EKOCENTERs, these kiosks would dispense not only free water but television, electricity for cellphone-charging stations, and Wi-Fi, and even had the potential for vaccine storage in refrigerators offering Coca-Cola products for sale—amounting to a "downtown in a box," as the Company put it. To "jump-start entrepreneurship opportunities and community development," the EKOCENTERs would be run by female entrepreneurs in a Coca-Cola-managed and franchised "micro-business model" to make the distribution of clean water and communications technologies "sustainable" through the sales of snacks and drinks.[91] Critics questioned the motivations of projects that drop such development models in from above without input from communities on their local needs and goals and wondered if the EKOCENTER was actually "a glorified concession stand."[92] The assumption that it could serve as a "downtown in a box" reflects neoliberal governmentality in which, absent state investment, corporations step in to provide services in ways that suit their own needs, while dissuading public accountability and investment. In this case, the project displayed its own limits: only 150 EKOCENTERS had been installed by the end of 2017.[93]

The Company's history also contributes to skepticism about the sustainability of social responsibility and the commitment of corporations to solve societal problems as long as they are motivated by profit. When the Company came under attack from critics in the 1960s and 1970s, CEO J. Paul Austin launched a plan to shield its core industry with other ventures "that would have genuine appeal to idealistically minded but politically potent young people," including buying a water desalination and filtration company, Aqua-Chem in 1970. Austin hoped it would be a "powerful public and government relations tool," creating a "halo-effect" of goodwill around the Company, not just among Coke drinkers, but among environmentalists and in countries seeking to develop clean water projects. Austin explained that Aqua-Chem was, moreover, a good investment: not only would it assist the Company with water filtration for its liquid products, but there were potential profits in the commodification of water, given predicted future problems in water quality and quantity. "Both the benefits and ills of our society are attributed, in the final analysis, to the system itself, i.e., free enterprise," Austin noted in an internal memo. "It is the free enterprise capitalistic feature which has nurtured the industrial complex, and it is the industrial complex which has caused the massive pollution of the natural resources. It also is true that only free private enterprise can eliminate the condition, and free private enterprise will eliminate the condition only if it realizes a profit therefrom."[94] Austin was ahead of his time—water was not yet a super-profitable crisis (just fairly profitable: Aqua-Chem's after-tax earnings were $9 million in 1980).[95] Since Coca-Cola was in it for the money more than the clean water, in 1981 the Company sold off Aqua-Chem.

Functioning at its best, CSR demonstrates the blurring of private-public relations and responsibilities under neoliberalism, and the abdication of the state's responsibility for the public good to a private corporation. Many of the corporations taking up social welfare in CSR are in part to blame for the problems themselves, either due to their business practices or to the gutting of state social services as a result of their push for reductions in taxes and regulations. With business in the role of de facto social welfare provider, the determination of social need and adequate responses is turned over to minimally accountable undemocratic entities.[96] Through the terms of CSR, companies that have contributed to labor, environmental, and health problems now put themselves in charge of solving them: a corporation that profits from extracting and privatizing common water resources makes itself responsible for their conservation and provision to the public. The Coca-Cola Company has indeed committed significant amounts of money (although tiny in comparison to its annual profits) to CSR initiatives for the good of the public. But the Company's larger accounting to the public must also be factored in. As the historian Bartow Elmore has shown, in the United States, Europe, and developed cities, Coca-Cola fills its bottles with taxpayer-funded public water, primarily from municipal systems—accounting for about 50 percent of the Company's global water supply. It has thus outsourced the costs of building, maintenance, and security of water production onto the public. In international contexts where the water infrastructure is lacking or insecure, the Company draws its water from private wells and surface water, making up the other half of the Company's water supply, for which it pays virtually nothing. If you add in the tax breaks that the Company has received for siting plants in particular locales, the accounting looks even more suspect. Elmore concludes that, "considering what many host communities have offered Coke—access to their precious water resources—such donations might more aptly be treated as partial payments for services rendered rather than altruistic do-good handouts."[97]

CSR's potential to improve social welfare is also intrinsically bounded by its limits as a promotional paradigm. Activists have been more successful in pressuring highly visible corporations like Coca-Cola, which sell branded products that depend on consumer goodwill and are publicly traded companies, hence subject to some degree to the ethical standards of their consumers and investors. Less visible, privately held, transitory, or obscure corporations, often the most egregious violators of labor, environmental, and health standards, are rarely discussed in the CSR literature, since they have little to gain from promoting their "responsibility." The burden on CSR initiatives to serve promotional purposes also reveals the limits to what kinds of issues will be addressed. CSR campaigns cannot overcome accusations of egregious corporate wrongdoing, because they would only draw attention to them; any mention of human rights abuses or violence against workers, for example, might repulse viewers rather than creating a positive image of the Company. Advertising "We don't kill workers" would beg the question of a corporation's labor and human rights record rather than assuaging concern. CSR seems only worth committing to, based on Coca-Cola's history, if it improves the corporation's social reputation. Like the sound of a tree that falls in the forest without anyone to hear it, perception is so central to a CSR initiative that it does not exist without promotion. For the corporation, the hope is that the good of CSR extends well beyond any single event, or immediate benefit to the community involved in the program, to produce the desired "halo effect" for a corporation's social reputation.[98] CSR programs, corporations hope, may improve a sullied brand reputation as well as deter or insure against future criticism through innocence by association with positive social contributions.[99]

CORPORATE SOCIAL REPUTATION: BRAND AND MARKET PROMOTION

When The Coca-Cola Company's high-calorie sodas were attacked by public health advocates, it resorted to various "corporate social technologies,"[100] or strategies, to manage its social reputation and relationship with the public. It financed nutrition studies that muddied the accepted health science, made allies of organizations representing health workers and communities of color, created "astroturf" front groups to stir up public anger against regulations and taxation, created advertising to change the perception of its products' relationship to obesity, promoted nutrition and recreation programs to improve its image, and expanded its marketing of products to profit from shifts in public understanding of health, among other strategies.[101] In 2016, leaked emails between Coca-Cola North America's VP for government relations and a Washington, DC, communications consultant revealed a glimpse of these strategies and their goal of "effectively managing the national, state and local public policy issues and strengthening our social license to operate so that business can grow."[102] Central to this was Coca-Cola's reframing of itself as a "hydration company" that fueled active, healthy lives, in a beverage marketplace that was a solution to, not the cause of, public health problems.

The Company strove to improve the reputation of its high-calorie drinks by characterizing obesity as a problem of a lack of "energy balance" between calories consumed and expended, promoting, in the Company's words, "the nutrition principle that all foods and beverages can be part of a balanced, sensible diet, combined with regular physical activity."[103] Coca-Cola and other food and beverage companies "muddied" the scientific discussion linking obesity to the consumption of high-calorie, low-nutrient goods like sugar-sweetened drinks by financing and celebrating certain researchers as "merchants of doubt"—much like the tobacco industry's use of corporate scientists to obfuscate the health risks of smoking several decades earlier. The consensus of non-industry-funded nutrition scientists was that weight gain was primarily determined by caloric intake and the nutritional value of the food and drink those calories came from, not exercise levels.[104] But the Company and its funded "science" argued that the problem was not that consumers were eating and drinking large quantities of sugary foods and drinks that had little nutritional value, especially sodas, but rather that people were not exercising enough to burn off, or "balance" out, those calories. Such studies were promoted by the Company's Beverage Institute for Health and Wellness, which looked like a health NGO purporting to be a legitimate source of scientific information, but solely advanced the Company's position.[105] The Company additionally supported industry front groups like the International Food Information Council and the International Life Sciences Institute to influence public policy on health and nutrition. Even more insidious was the opaquely Company-financed Global Energy Balance Network, since it was fronted by prominent health researchers claiming to be "the voice of science," but promoted the minority scientific opinion that the cause of obesity was a lack of exercise, going so far as to state that "there's really virtually no compelling evidence" that calorie intake was the cause of weight gain. But as the *New York Times* pointed out, such assertions only cited research papers "supported by The Coca-Cola Company."[106] Whether seeking to identify its brands with health or to "capture" groups that might otherwise be outspoken about the potential health repercussions of soda consumption, the Company cultivated strategic relationships with associations of health and medical professionals, including the American Academy of Family Physicians, American Academy of Pediatrics, American Cancer Society, Academy of Nutrition and Dietetics, and Juvenile Diabetes Research Foundation, to name just a few.[107] The Company promoted its "energy balance" perspective in a program called "Exercise Is Medicine" to encourage doctors to prescribe physical activity to patients.[108] After investigative reporting revealed the corporate-funded research, the Company disclosed that between 2010 and 2015 it had spent $132.8 million on scientific research and health partnerships in the United States and Canada alone.[109] As food policy scholar and activist Marion Nestle concluded, Big Soda "uses its links with scientists and officials to distort science, confuse professionals and the public, provoke false debates, and distort reputations."[110]

The Coca-Cola Company was eager to be seen as part of the solution to rather than the cause of the obesity problem. As part of its framing the problem as one of inactivity rather than calorie consumption, it became visibly committed to encouraging exercise by its consumers. By 2014, the Company was funding more than 330 "active, healthy living" programs in 112 markets around the world, and it announced plans to have at least one program in every country in which it did business.[111] In Colombia, Coca-Cola and its bottlers launched nutrition and physical activity programs organized around its questionable "energy balance" theory, bringing its "Apúntate a Jugar" ("Sign Up to Play") and "Hora de Moverse" ("Time to Move") programs to Colombian educators and schoolchildren. As regulatory threats arose around the world, the Company would repeat the model of launching school programs to encourage physical activity (often in cash-strapped public schools), as well as large monetary donations to sites of outdoor activity, children's recreation programs, and the construction of fitness centers.[112] This, after the soda industry had spent years embedding itself in schools, offering school systems facing budget cuts large discretionary funds for exclusive rights to sell its products in their buildings. By 2005, 80 percent of US high schools and nearly 50 percent of elementary schools operated under such contracts.[113] In the face of public criticism, Coca-Cola has recently removed its products from elementary schools and restricted sales of high-calorie sodas in high schools in the United States, Canada, Europe, New Zealand, and Australia, but the Company's "global pledge" states that it will offer a "full range of beverages," including high-calorie as well as healthier drinks, in high schools across the rest of the world.[114] Latin American public health researchers decried these Company initiatives promoting physical activity as "appearing altruistic" when they were really "intended to improve the industry's public image and increase political influence in order to block regulations counter to their interests." They concluded: "If this industry wants to contribute to human well being, as it has publicly stated, it should avoid blocking legislative actions intended to regulate the marketing, advertising and sale of their products."[115]

The Coca-Cola Company's response to the health crisis demonstrates how corporations respond, not just by stifling regulation and provisioning social welfare, but also by capitalizing on new markets through CSR, promoting consumer choice and corporate competition as free market mechanisms for the social good. As The Coca-Cola Company faced growing popular concern about the healthfulness of its principal soda products and a steady decline in sales, it turned aggressively to capturing the market in bottled water, sports drinks, energy drinks, fruit juices, milks, teas, and coffees in the growing field of soda alternatives, buying up competitors in an emerging health market to win over consumers dealing with a surfeit of calories and wanting to consume more healthily (or at least think they were).[116] The Company expanded its "drink portfolio" with these new products and promoted them in CSR-related advertising that emphasized health through consumer choice among the variety of Coke beverage options to suit "active lifestyles." By 2012, the Company boasted that it offered over 800 drink brand options globally and "nearly 25 percent of [its] global portfolio" consisted of "low- or no-calorie options."[117] There was no need for governmental intervention, such corporate repositioning argued; the free market would provide healthy options for consumers.

The Company was now a "hydration company," a producer of liquid refreshment of all kinds, from which the consumer could feel empowered to *choose*. "The choice is yours . . .," the Company's CSR website declared, juxtaposing an image of the colorful spectrum of its brands. In 2006, the Company launched a CSR initiative, "Make Every Drop Count," purporting to combine research, education, and advertising, in order to encourage "awareness among consumers about the benefits of the Company's full product portfolio and to educate them by sharing expertise and information about the roles beverages played in their lives."[118] According to marketers, "for the first time in the company's history, an ad campaign brought together brands within one umbrella campaign" to present the Coca-Cola as offering a range of beverage options.[119] The "Make Every Drop Count" campaign sought to remind "people that for all they expend in their daily lives, The Coca-Cola Company is striving to give those drops back through the benefits of what we sell— whether it is through beverages that deliver hydration, energy, relaxation, nutrition or pure enjoyment."[120] To cement the association with a commitment to health, the Company debuted the ads during the Olympics.

The marketing not only gave consumers a sense of empowered free market choice among brands, but also assigned them individual responsibility for achieving "energy balance." The ads subtly repeated the theme that people do not drink solely to hydrate, but also to "energize, nourish, relax or enjoy" themselves, promoting the "wellness factors of the beverages within the total Coke portfolio." "If you're not in the mood for water, it's okay to reach for something else you enjoy, like tea or a soft drink. Of course water is always the best choice; it's just not the only one."[121] Ads featured active people— swimming, biking, rocking, skating—not drinking anything in the moment, but exuding energy balance and the multicolored drops "of spirit ... of passion ... of drive ... of peace" of the logo. "For every drop of yourself you give ... [you should] get every drop back [by drinking one of several Coca-Cola products]," the legend asserted. Just as it was the consumers' choice to pick more healthful drink options from the Coca-Cola portfolio, it was also their responsibility to choose wisely and to burn off or "balance" out calories through exercise (even as health science suggested that this was impossible). The Company's CSR around health served more to validate consumer choice and justify the rising obesity rates as lack of personal responsibility than to educate consumers about healthy consumption and fitness patterns. A 2013 commercial for Coca-Cola and zero calorie Coke Zero in the United Kingdom used a split screen to argue that it was the difference in lifestyles between grandfather (more active) and grandson (more sedentary) that was unhealthy, not their Coke consumption. If the grandson was not going to get more exercise, as the ad implied, at least he could choose to drink a Coke Zero. These discourses of choice and personal responsibility, so central to the cultures of neoliberalism, benefited the Company in two ways; they could both be used to market products and also be mobilized in arguments against government regulation of the sugar-sweetened-beverage industry—as they were in campaigns against rules for advertising, restrictions on where sodas could be sold (public buildings, schools, etc.), requirements for nutrition labeling, limits to product size, and additional taxes.

The Coca-Cola Company's celebration of consumer choice and free market competition as solutions to societal problems is ironic, given the history of the Company we know from the previous chapters. The Company is in the business of framing consumers' available options and creating demand for its products. For it to celebrate consumer choice as though it existed independently of this advertising-driven demand and suggest that the free market will respond to consumers' needs with a range of competing products is to obscure both the Company's manufacturing of choice and its monopolistic history of buying up and eliminating competitors.

The market's ability to provide healthful products in the interest of citizens has been limited by its self-interest, as becomes clear when one considers the commodification of health by beverage companies. In striving to mark distinctions between brands in the creation of this new market, the Company has inflated health claims. The Company lost a lawsuit over its Glacéau vitaminwater brand's use of the words "defense," "energy," "revive," and "healthy" and the claim to be "vitamins + water + all you need" on its packaging, which a judge found misleading, inasmuch as sugar was one of its principal ingredients and vitaminwater "does not meet required minimum nutritional thresholds."[122] The sense of "choice" itself is constructed by what the market offers to consumers— what it produces for sale and how it positions each product in relation to others. For years the Company worked hard to push consumers away from the free and healthier option of water, not just in marketing and advertising, but also in programs in the 2000s known as "H2NO" and "Cap the Tap," which trained restaurant servers to direct customers to other drinks.[123]

While it promoted its new "healthier" beverage options, The Coca-Cola Company continued to heavily market and defend its signature soda brands where the profit margin for concentrate sales is reliably high. New "health" brands come with higher overhead, and while bottled water sales have increased rapidly in the past two decades, people buy water based on price, without loyalty to specific brands (unlike the fealty of Coca-Cola, Thums Up, or Colombiana drinkers).[124] This is why the Company has invested so much in its soda market internationally and among US communities of color, where soda sales were still growing in this same time period. Proposed taxes would hurt the industry hardest in these markets, as well as hurt these consumers, who on average have lower incomes and are not only unequally burdened by a flat excise tax but also physically burdened by the soda indus-try's targeting of their communities.[125]

CAPITALIST SOCIAL REALISM: CSR AS IDEOLOGICAL JUSTIFICATION FOR CAPITALISM

Why should we give a company a bad time for trying to be good? Because Coca-Cola's CSR doesn't just do good work, it also does ideological work. While some people are coerced into capitalism, the majority of us consent to it, requiring and receiving justifications that the system contributes to the common good.[126] The discourse and practice of CSR in the past fifteen years represents a corporate attempt to assimilate the anti-capitalist critiques of "anti-globalization," labor, environmental, and public health movements, responding with a "capitalism with a conscience" to justify itself to consum-ers, employees, communities, and even some investors.[127] CSR is a product of neoliberalism's celebration and deregulation of the market, produced along-side its less appealing outcomes—rapacious corporate growth, inequality, environmental degradation, deteriorating public health—allowing corporations to contain these negative repercussions as well as the popular resistances that have arisen in their wake. But CSR also attempts to draw on this resistance to create new justifications for capitalism, asserting the market's ability to provide solutions to society's problems, even if it produced them in the first place. Coca-Cola's CSR is part of a larger ideological approach to reaffirming capitalism, as well as a strategy for addressing its ills. This is CSR's "capitalist social realism," which identifies social problems and portrays the corporation as the essential means for their amelioration, asserting that social justice can exist within capitalism as a totalizing system without necessary or even imaginable alternatives.[128] CSR does ideological work for consumers, empowering them with a sense that they are doing social good through their consumption; for workers, who can labor with a sense that their exploitation in service of the company and their own exploitation by the company is for a greater good; for shareholders, promising them a profitably sustainable capitalism; and for "stakeholders," investing them in corporate social welfare and a capitalist future even as it attempts to assimilate and delimit their critiques for its own good.

The rapidly burgeoning discourse and practice of corporate social responsibility attempts to win popular consent to the hegemonic neoliberal logic of recent decades. CSR actions are often the bright public façade of shadier corporate resistance to legally accountable change. CSR buttresses systems of private power (corporations, NGOs, consumers, investors) in relation to the public and the state, with its discourses of individual and corporate responsibility rather than public regulation or investment, and overarching trust in market solutions to resolve the contradictions produced by the capitalist system itself. Even critics of the power of corporations in contemporary society acknowledge that companies "are now often expected to deliver the good, not just the goods; to pursue values, not just value; and to help make the world a better place."[129] Global corporations like Coca-Cola "are increasingly asked to shoulder responsibilities historically expected of governments."[130] Profits and social welfare are often directly opposing goals, however, and CSR initiatives may be limited, ineffective, or never begun at all. "The danger is that a focus on social responsibility will delay or discourage more effective measures to enhance social welfare in those cases where profits and the public good are at odds," as Aneel Karnani argues. "As society looks to companies to address these problems, the real solutions may be ignored."[131]

In addition to supporting investment in the preservation of watersheds and the construction of recreation facilities, Coca-Cola's marketing materials tell consumers that by buying Coca-Cola products, they can help save the polar bears (one of the Company's longtime marketing icons), stave off climate change (with drinks in "Arctic Home" silver cans), and provide technical training to mango farmers in earthquake-ravaged Haiti (to whom 100 percent of the profits from Coca-Cola subsidiary Odwalla's "Haiti Hope Mango Lime-Aid" are promised).[132] "You might not be able to travel to another country to volunteer your time, but you're already helping through your support of Coca-Cola," the Company's "live positively" CSR-themed website explained.[133] In the process, social issues and responsibility themselves have become commodified. In this socially responsible marketplace, Honest Tea, Odwalla, and Innocent Drinks are healthy, environmentally conscious, fair trade, charitable brands that market themselves as alternatives to Big Soda. But check the labels: they are all owned by The Coca-Cola Company. Just as it had bought up smaller competitors when it entered new markets all over the world, Coca-Cola has bought companies marketing "natural" or "ethical" drinks (shuttering some and keeping others) to diversify its brand portfolio and strategically position itself in the market. Thus, in some cases, CSR may not just be a way for corporations to ameliorate problems—the very problems they have produced, the systemic negativities of capitalism—but also a way for them to *profit* from them.[134] Consider Coca-Cola purchasing Honest Tea and selling a fair-trade-certified product to consumers trying to find alternatives to Coca-Cola's exploitative labor system but inadvertently enriching the same company. Corporations should not ignore public critique, but rather consult it to profit, a CSR proponent advises: "Social pressures often indicate the existence of unmet social needs or consumer preferences. Businesses can gain advantage by spotting and supplying these before their competitors do."[135]

This model of harnessing consumer choice and market entrepreneurialism for social change has broad ideological and political ramifications. Social action becomes framed by accumulation and consumption, where social issues are addressed by a corporation motivated by the potential profit of being perceived as socially responsible and consumers choose to buy a certain commodity for its perceived relationship to social change ("buycotting"). As Indian activists in the struggle against Coca-Cola have argued, however, in such strategies political power depends on purchasing and investing power.[136] This "stakeholder democracy" or "market democracy" is not democratic at all: it disenfranchises the poorest while deciding how to address their social ills. CSR advertising campaigns construct what Slavoj Žižek calls "cultural capitalism," offering consumers redemption from their consumerism by buying socially responsible goods: "It's not just what you're buying. It's what you're buying into."[137] Sarah Banet-Weiser and Roopali Mukherjee have described this as "commodity activism." In these "marketized modes of resistance in the neoliberal moment,"[138] citizen-consumers engage in social action through their purchases from and demands on corporations, who are then empowered to respond to those political as well as commercial demands. This is not to negate the possibility of resistance or the formation of critical subjectivities and solidarities through such "commodity activism"—the corporation's failure to fulfill its promises of social change or consumers' realization of its underlying profit motive could contribute to a larger critique for those who participate. But such cultural capitalism frames people's potential power, agency, and citizenship in the terms of capitalism itself.

One of the main arguments of this book is that The Coca-Cola Company's business model is one of interlinked material (bottled drinks) and immaterial production (advertising, brands, business models and investment). Since the late 1970s, financial capital has been a central focus and organizational logic of the Company. As with most other large publicly traded corporations, maximizing returns on stock investment has been of the utmost importance, since it is beholden to investors who hold its stock price, ability to raise capital, and the election of its board of directors in their hands, especially the private equity funds and large institutional investors who have taken large ownership stakes in the Company. Investors see corporations, not as producers of goods, but as collections of assets, which are measured, managed, bought, and sold. This "structuring power of financial hegemony"[139] also drives the motivations and workings of CSR, which offers social reputation and goodwill as another such asset.

Company executives subtly justify CSR initiatives to investors in terms of necessary concessions to capitalist expansion, and thus as an act of enlightened self-interest, arguing that assisting in the social good is an instrumental investment in the long-term profits of the corporation and its shareholders. Reading two sets of reports that the Company produces—its annual financial reporting (to investors and the SEC) and its annual CSR reports—tells the story of the economic motivation of CSR initiatives. Since 2003, the annual 10-K filed with the SEC has identified water quality and quantity, respect for human and workplace rights, obesity and health concerns, and threats to free trade, as "risk factors" that could "materially affect [the Company's] business, financial condition or results of operations in future periods." These have also been the focus of its CSR initiatives, highlighted in the Company's annual CSR reports produced beginning in the early 2000s. "Sustainability" (often phrased as "sustainable growth") became a key word for commitments to CSR, which might reduce shareholders' immediate returns but would lead to long-term gains. The *2002 Annual Report* introduced investors to the idea of social responsibility initiatives in these terms: "Ultimately, the social investment we make in our communities is returned to The Coca-Cola Company through a more prosperous marketplace, greater consumer buying power and increased loyalty"; this is "why enduring economic value is best achieved when we uphold our social values."[140] The Company's 2005 "Manifesto for Growth" recognized the "long-term opportunities" opened up to it by accepting "a renewed responsibility for meeting our short term commitments," identified on the Company's website, and on large placards in its Atlanta headquarters, as People, Planet, Portfolio, Partners, and Profit, the last graphically represented through color and its central position on the chart as primary.[141]

Scholarship on CSR and the popular press celebrate "shareholder democracy" as a form of governance in which stockowners hold corporations to account for their business activities, even pressing for more socially responsible behavior. True, activists have used the Company's annual meetings as public forums for challenging executives about corporate practices (although still private, open only to stockholders). Ray Rogers of Killer Coke owns Coca-Cola stock so that he can attend annual shareholder meetings and gets others to buy or donate single shares so that activists can have a protest presence at one of the few opportunities to be face-to-face with executives and the corporation's board. In 1979, after Coca-Cola managers colluded with paramilitaries to quell labor radicalism in a plant in Guatemala, resulting in the assassination of union leaders, a group of US nuns who held stock in the Company attended annual meetings demanding justice for Coca-Cola workers.[142] But holding investors accountable for regulating corporations' practices is untenable, especially when the vast majority of investors often do not even know they hold Coca-Cola stock in pension or mutual funds and their interest is in maximizing their profit through rising share prices and dividends, which puts them at odds with both activists threatening Company profits and Company executives spending money on CSR initiatives rather than paying it out to shareholders. There are heated debates led by "activist investors" at companies' annual meetings, but these are not small shareholders fighting for social justice, but rather hedge fund managers who pressure corporations to distribute more dividends, be more aggressively oriented toward increasing share price, or even sell parts or all of themselves to another company, with a focus on short-term profit for shareholders.

Ardent neoliberals believe that a corporation's main purpose is to make as much money as possible for its shareholders, limiting the possibility of prioritizing social good. In 1970, in his frankly entitled article "The Social Responsibility of Business Is to Increase Its Profits," Milton Friedman calls CSR a "fundamentally subversive doctrine . . . preaching pure and unadulterated socialism," seeing any corporate action not in the service of maximizing profits, such as CSR, as an imposition of the "political" onto the economic, and "undemocratic" taxation without representation that makes the majority of stockholders pay for the social cause of a minority.[143] CSR's good deeds must be justified as a "means to maximize shareholders' wealth—not as ends in themselves."[144] Some cite an outdated legal doctrine of "shareholder primacy" rooted in the hundred-year-old decision in *Dodge v. Ford Motor Company* (1919) that the corporation is legally obliged to prioritize profits for its shareholders.[145] Corporate executives must, in any event, rationalize CSR initiatives in terms of their long-run profitability for the corporation and its shareholders—social responsibility must be commodified and valued by the market. This puts temporal limits on the effectiveness of CSR—the "business case" for it can only be made after injustice has already been done—and interpretive limits on the struggle of those affected—since CSR obscures the original profit-maximizing imperative that caused the harm in the first place with the post facto appearance of social concern.[146] For example, it is cynically ironic to pledge workplace rights and "citizenship" to employees who have been hired as outsourced, underemployed workers when they have been hired in precarious, benefitless jobs precisely because their lack of real rights makes them more exploitable and disposable, maximizing surplus value.

CSR's most powerful ideological function may be enabling corporate employees and executives to work with a sense that their own exploitation and exploitative actions are for a greater good. For workers who have witnessed the destructive tendencies of capitalism, hear the critiques of social movements, or are just fed up with what feels like the reduction of our daily lives to waged work over which we have little control in the production of private goods that can seem meaningless, the ideological work of CSR can have a "palliative effect" on the alienation felt in the capitalist mode of production.[147] As we wonder what the point of our labors is, and what good they do society, CSR offers a sense of meaning and contributions to a common good. It may thus also make us more pliable employees—and easier for corporations to recruit, retain, and extract the best work from us.[148]

Many advocates of CSR, including Coca-Cola's former CEO Neville Isdell, came of age ideologically in the 1960s and 1970s and are sympathetic to calls for social justice.[149] Some of these children of the long 1960s became businessmen and women who believed they could "teach the world to sing" by linking liberal social values with the profit motives of the corporate world, constructing a discourse and practice of CSR that legitimized the concessions to capitalism made in the process.[150] For these executives, "Nobody Has to Be Vile," as Slavoj Žižek titled his essay on business leaders who propose that they can both "have the global capitalist cake (thrive as entrepreneurs) and eat it (endorse the anti-capitalist causes of social responsibility, ecological concern, etc.)" too. The Coca-Cola investor and philanthropist Warren Buffett and Coca-Cola's recent CEOs promote a kinder, gentler capitalism to both profit and change the world for the better. They tell the public that the market can be used to help "resolve [the] secondary malfunctions of the global system, while reinforcing the system itself. They are in effect "giv[ing] away with one hand what they grabbed with the other."[151]

The capitalist social realism of Coca-Cola's CSR portrays concrete, discrete problems that can be dealt with through private enterprise, assisting the state and public while undermining them, rather than recognizing the structural violence endemic to capitalism itself. There is a focus on shortages of potable water and cases of corporate exploitation of water resources, but not on capitalism's creation of new markets and the privatization of common environmental resources.[152] There is a focus on extreme forms of violence against workers, but not on the everyday violence of precarity that structures neoliberal labor regimes. It is this kind of logic that allows corporate executives to imagine CSR as a "win-win" enterprise, so that multinational capitalism can flourish while addressing specific crises as "externalities" as they emerge.[153] All the while the ideology negates the evidence that such crises are the products of the system itself, instead promoting the market as the means of current solutions and the only possible direction for the future.

The Coca-Cola Company will give rise to new struggles, and people will rise to fight them. The logic of CSR itself admits this. CSR attempts piecemeal corrections to the costs of capitalism—the human exploitation, environmental degradation, and poor consumer health, for example—but it cannot keep up with its ravages. CSR identifies society's problems and admits the necessity of working for the collective good, but is also inherently limited by the impossibility of corporate accountability to a public higher than its investors. By failing to meet social needs, CSR will be unable to contain the critiques of corporate behavior. Inadvertently, then, CSR may lay bare the social ills produced by capitalism and the urgent need for real political intervention. This brings us to the final C-S-R of the contemporary moment, continued social resistance.[154]

Like the challenges to The Coca-Cola Company across its history described in this book, the discourse and practice of corporate social responsibility developed through a process of exploitation, contestation, and assimilation of critique that is never fully resolved. Workers, consumers, government authorities, activists, and cultural producers have repeatedly contested Coca-Cola's business practices and the assumption that the corporation's only motivation should be profit. We clearly want more from our consumer goods and from the system that produces them. We need compelling reasons to justify continuing with this system, and capitalism cannot generate them internally. It finds such values outside itself when we compel it to serve interests other than profit. As shown by the preceding chapters, in the face of public critiques, The Coca-Cola Company has repeatedly sought to legitimize itself in the terms of larger collective projects, defined by their historical moments—with economic modernization, with national development, with freedom and liberation, with labor rights, with environmental sustainability, and with public health. Our drive to contribute positively to society, which makes these justifications hard to resist, will also continue to challenge capitalism and oblige it to adapt to win our consent. In the process, we may more clearly define both the common good that we desire and ways to achieve it that go beyond capitalism's assimilation for its own good.

ABBREVIATIONS

BPP	Biblioteca Público Piloto, Medellín
CE, MPBRSD, LC	Coca-Cola Collection, Creative Exchange, Motion Picture, Broadcasting and Recorded Sound Division, Library of Congress
INDEGA	Industrial de Gaseosas
INDEGA-Panamco	Industria Nacional de Gaseosas, subsidiary of Panamco Colombia
INDEGA-FEMSA	Industria Nacional de Gaseosas, subsidiary of Coca-Cola FEMSA
FEMSA	Fomento Económico Mexicano
Coca-Cola FEMSA	Coca-Cola bottling subsidiary of Fomento Económico Mexicano
MAD, LC	Manuscripts and Archives Division, Library of Congress, Washington, DC
MARBL	Stuart A. Rose Manuscripts, Archives, and Rare Book Library, Emory University
MPBRSD, LC	Motion Picture, Broadcasting and Recorded Sound Division, Library of Congress
NARAII	National Archives and Records Administration II, College Park, MD
Panamco	Panamerican Beverages
Panamco Colombia	Colombian subsidiary of Panamco that owns controlling stakes in INDEGA and other bottling subsidiaries
SINALTRAINAL	Sindicato Nacional de Trabajadores del Sistema Agroalimentario, Colombian National Union

of Food System Workers (formerly Sindicato
Nacional de Trabajadores de la Industria de
Alimentos)

TCCC	The Coca-Cola Company
TCCEC	The Coca-Cola Export Corporation

NOTES

INTRODUCTION

1. Pendergrast, *For God, Country, and Coca-Cola*, 10.
2. Barlow and Clarke, *Blue Gold*, 147.
3. "The 100 Top Brands," *Business Week*, August 1, 2005, 90–94.
4. The Coca-Cola Company (henceforth cited as TCCC), *1995 Annual Report*, 14–16.
5. This book has benefited from the models and historical insights of Mintz, *Sweetness and Power*; Okihiro, *Pineapple Culture*; Beckert, *Empire of Cotton*; and Merleaux, *Sugar and Civilization*, among other studies.
6. TCCC, "The Coca-Cola System."
7. Wallerstein, *Modern World-System*, 229.
8. See Casanova's analysis of the power relations internal to the "global literary space" in *World Republic of Letters*.
9. The production and sourcing of materials for Coca-Cola are also part of the Coca-Cola world system, as are the stores, vendors, and machines that sell Coca-Cola products, as well as the commodity's "afterlives" in waste or reuse. *Counter-Cola* focuses, however, on the material and immaterial production of Coca-Cola soft drinks. For an environmental history of the drink, see Elmore, *Citizen Coke*.
10. MacArthur, "Peter Drucker."
11. Coombe, *Cultural Life of Intellectual Properties*, 56.
12. For this reason, an analysis of Coca-Cola necessitates an approach to the history of capitalism that integrates tools of media and cultural analysis, and *Counter-Cola* has benefited greatly in this respect from Marchand, *Advertising the American Dream* and *Creating the Corporate Soul;* Domosh, *American Commodities;* Frank, *Conquest of Cool;* Klein, *No Logo;* Laird, *Advertising Progress;* Lears, *Fables of Abundance;* McGovern, *Sold American;* Ewen, *Captains of Consciousness;* and Strasser, *Satisfaction Guaranteed*.
13. See Wayne, "How Delaware Thrives."
14. See Esterl and Dulaney, "Coca-Cola Owes $3.3 Billion in Taxes."

15. See Mandel, "Reuters: Tax Experts Closely Watching."

16. Citizens for Tax Justice, "Fortune 500 Companies."

17. Elmore, *Citizen Coke,* 9.

18. See Finan, "10 Years."

19. This book is indebted to critical consumer culture studies such as de Grazia, *Irresistible Empire*; Mazzarella, *Shovelling Smoke;* Milanesio, *Workers Go Shopping in Argentina.*

20. See Featherstone, *Resistance, Space and Political Identities.*

21. "Sun Never Sets on Cacoola," *Time,* May 15, 1950.

22. J. Paul Austin to Charles Malik, October 15, 1970, Charles Malik Papers, MAD, LC.

23. Barlow and Clarke, *Blue Gold,* 147.

24. "Sun Never Sets on Cacoola."

25. Kirsch, *Mining Capitalism,* 3.

26. Boltanski and Chiapello, *New Spirit of Capitalism,* 42.

27. See, e.g., Kirsch, *Mining Capitalism;* Tsing, *Friction;* Welker, *Enacting the Corporation;* Gill, *Century of Violence;* Foster, *Coca-Globalization.*

28. Including LaFeber, *Michael Jordan and the New Global Capitalism;* Chandler and Mazlich, eds., *Leviathans;* Bakan, *Corporation;* Micklethwait and Woolridge, *Company;* Lichtenstein, *Retail Revolution;* Striffler, *In the Shadows of State and Capital;* Moreton, *To Serve God and Wal-Mart.*

29. Felipe Márquez Robledo, Gerente Legal Colombia, Coca-Cola FEMSA, email with author, November 8, 2006.

30. Mark Pendergrast notably left his research to Emory University, which also holds the papers of several Coca-Cola executives.

31. See Jameson's classic theory of the "cultural logic of late capitalism" in *Postmodernism* and Martin, *After Economy?* for an analysis of the "social logic" of a capitalist form, the derivative.

32. TCCC, "The Coca-Cola System—History of Bottling."

33. Joan Martínez-Alier quoted in Guha, *How Much Should a Person Consume?* 59.

34. Harvey, *New Imperialism,* 159.

CHAPTER I. THE COCA-COLA BOTTLING SYSTEM AND
THE LOGICS OF THE FRANCHISE

1. See Elmore, *Citizen Coke.*

2. Coca-Cola syrup and extract label, June 28, 1887; Pendergrast, *For God, Country, and Coca-Cola,* 30–31.

3. Lears, *Fables of Abundance,* 103–4, 146–47.

4. Allen, *Secret Formula,* 17; Pendergrast, *For God, Country, and Coca-Cola,* 110n491.

5. The Coca-Cola Company Archives Department, "International Bottling Operations" (2000), CE, MPBRSD, LC.

6. Harrison, *"Footprints on the Sands of Time,"* 47; Hays, *Real Thing,* 18–22.

7. Rosenberg, *Spreading the American Dream,* 25.

8. Pendergrast, *For God, Country, and Coca-Cola,* 127–128; Wilkins, *Maturing,* 51.

9. Dicke, *Franchising in America,* 1–2.

10. Ibid., 113–14.

11. "Indenture of Agreement between The Coca-Cola Company and Solomon's, Ltd., Burma," May 14, 1927, CE, MPBRSD, LC.

12. Hays, *Real Thing,* 18–22.

13. "Sun Never Sets on Cacoola."

14. Hays, *Real Thing,* 80; "A Brief History of Coca-Cola Overseas," *Coca-Cola Bottler,* April 1959, 182.

15. "Sun Never Sets on Cacoola."

16. "In the last issue of the 'Digest' I mentioned the new training course ...," *T.O. Digest,* January 1948, 5–6.

17. "Sun Never Sets on Cacoola."

18. Nicholson, "The Competitive Ideal."

19. Pendergrast, *For God, Country, and Coca-Cola,* 143–44.

20. As codified in the 1906 Pure Food and Drug Act. Strasser, 52.

21. Strasser, 43.

22. Strasser, 43–44.

23. Strasser, 44–45

24. Pendergrast, *For God, Country, and Coca-Cola,* 102–103; Coombe, 80.

25. Pendergrast, *For God, Country, and Coca-Cola,* 103.

26. Strasser, 43–44.

27. Pendergrast, *For God, Country, and Coca-Cola,* 129–130.

28. *Coca-Cola Co. v. Koke Co.,* 254 US 143, 146, 41 S.Ct. 113, 114, 65 L.Ed. 189 (1920).

29. McCracken, "Overseas Story," 27.

30. Rosenberg, *Spreading the American Dream,* 21; Frundt, *Refreshing Pauses.*

31. "Coca-Cola as Sold throughout the World."

32. Although Americans were the most common foreign factors in international bottling, international bottlers would sometimes expand into neighboring or similar markets. For example, it was a wealthy Greek bottler of Coca-Cola who made major inroads into the Nigerian market.

33. Postobón, "Historia."

34. "Postobón: Un negocio líquido," 100.

35. Both men would play prominent roles in Colombian business and industry. Gabriel Posada, who would serve as treasury minister, invested heavily in the Ferrocarril de Antioquia and the Banco Alemán. Valerio Tobón became linked to the Compañía Suramericana de Seguros and the Compañía Colombiana de Tabaco.

36. Dávila, "Estado de los estudios"; Farnsworth-Alvear, *Dulcinea;* Palacios, *Coffee in Colombia;* Bergquist, *Labor in Latin America;* LeGrand, *Frontier Expansion. and Peasant Protest.*

37. Farnsworth-Alvear, *Dulcinea,* 42–47.

38. Ibid.

39. Ibid., 45–46.

40. McGreevey, *Economic History of Colombia*, 2.

41. Rosenberg, *Spreading the American Dream*, 7.

42. Henderson, *Modernization in Colombia*, xvi.

43. Camacho Arango, "*Respice polum*"; Tickner, "Colombia," 169–70.

44. Henderson, *Modernization in Colombia*, 4

45. Ibid., 108.

46. Ibid., 115.

47. Drake, *Money Doctor*.

48. Ibid., 32–33; Henderson, *Modernization in Colombia*, 115.

49. Drake, "Origins of United States Economic Supremacy in South America," 3.

50. Rosenberg, *Financial Missionaries*, 50.

51. Drake, *Money Doctor*, 30.

52. Ibid., 30–31, Louis Domeratsky to Walter J. Donnelly, April 17, 1929, US Department of Commerce, Bureau of Foreign and Domestic Commerce, Record Group 151, file no. 460, "Colombia."

53. Drake, *Money Doctor*, 74, 30.

54. Henderson, *Modernization in Colombia*, 40, 214.

55. Drake, *Money Doctor*, 33.

56. Ibid., 34; Henderson, *Modernization in Colombia*, 117.

57. Henderson, *Modernization in Colombia*, 120.

58. *Advertisers' Guide to Latin American Markets*.

59. Orlove and Bauer, "Giving Importance to Imports," in *Allure of the Foreign*, ed. Orlove, 8–13.

60. Henderson, *Modernization in Colombia*, 168.

61. *El Heraldo de Antioquia*, January 3, 1928.

62. Ibid., October 27, 1930.

63. Ibid.

64. Ibid., July 14, 1930.

65. Ibid., March 20, 1928.

66. "Coca-Cola as Sold throughout the World."

67. "Your Association," *Coca-Cola Bottler*, September 1927, 49; "Home of Coca-Cola in Medellin, Colombia," ibid., December 1930, 16; "Twenty Years Ago," ibid., August 1948, 48.

68. CE, MPBRSD, LC: photo of man with Coca-Cola carts on Cali streets, W8223; postcard of café in Cali, W8225; photo of a street scene with Coca-Cola sign in Medellín, W8226; photo of horse-drawn cart in front of Café Nacional in Medellín, W8215; photo of cart on a street in Medellín, W8227; postcard of Coca-Cola sign on building opposite railroad station in Medellín, W8219.

69. Photo illustration. "Aspectos de la imponente manifestación de ayer tarde," *El Tiempo*, June 9, 1929, 1.

70. Moreno, "Coca-Cola, US Diplomacy, and the Cold War," in *Beyond the Eagle's Shadow*, ed. Garrard-Burnett et al., 34.

71. Industrial de Gaseosas Ltda. (INDEGA), "Inducción," *La Chispa de la Vida*, no. 9 (October 1976), Hemeroteca, Biblioteca Pública Piloto (BPP), Medellín, Colombia. In Postobón's version, it bottled and distributed Coca-Cola from 1927 to 1936, at which point the Company "decided to officially establish itself in Colombia and Panamá" (Postobón, "Historia").

72. *El Colombiano*, September 30, 1943; "Postobón: Un negocio líquido," *Dinero*, September 17, 2004.

73. Raventós, *Cien años de publicidad colombiana* (sponsored by Coca-Cola, whose trademark is printed on every page of the book), 83.

74. An "Elixir de Kola y Coca" was being sold in Bogotá as early as 1898 (Cadavid, *"Revista Ilustrada"*).

75. Stephen P. Ladas, affidavit, New York, NY, March 31, 1953, in Pendergrast Collection, Emory University, box 15, item 6.

76. Roy D. Stubbs, "Letters from Latin America," in Pendergrast Collection, MARBL, box 3, folder 11.

77. "Medellin, Colombia . . . New Plant for 'Coca-Cola,'" *Red Barrel* (September 1941), 29.

78. Gutiérrez Gómez had been an executive in mining, agricultural credit, and pharmaceutical industries (Saénz Rovner, *Ofensiva empresarial,* 41).

79. Ibid., 33; Farnsworth-Alvear, *Dulcinea*, 210–11; Palacios, *Entre la legitimidad y la violencia,* 174–80.

80. INDEGA, *La Chispa de la Vida*, no. 9 (October 1976), BPP; "Coca-Cola es así," *Bebidas y Manjares*, 13.

81. Armando Grumberg, "Coca-Cola in Colombia," *Coca-Cola Overseas*, February 1959; Al Staton, "Colombia and Coca-Cola," ibid., June 1949; Caballero Truyol and Polo Escalante, "La industria en Barranquilla," 94–95.

82. Wade, "Music, Blackness and National Identity," 10.

83. Interview with retiree, Barranquilla, November 2, 2007.

84. INDEGA, *La Chispa de la Vida*, no. 10 (October 1976), BPP.

85. Ibid.; Albert Staton to R. W. Woodruff, October 1, 1951, R. W. Woodruff Papers, MARBL, Emory University, Collection no. 19, box 301, folder 4; Staton to W. O. Solms, The Coca-Cola Interamerican Corp., ca 1972, in Inge Staton and Luz de Villa, *Unknown Legacy*, 420.

86. Urrutia, *Development of the Colombian Labor Movement*, 81–126.

87. Wilkins, *Maturing*, 223.

88. Stoller, "Alfonso López Pumarejo," 373.

89. Sáenz Rovner, *Ofensiva empresarial,,* 17–18.

90. Farnsworth-Alvear, *Dulcinea,* 210–11; Palacios, *Entre la legitimidad y la violencia,,* 174–80.

91. *El Heraldo de Antioquia*, October 10, 1930.

92. *El Colombiano,* August 3 and 21, 1943.

93. Ibid., July 28 and August 20, 1943.

94. Ibid., July 22 and August 12, 1943.

95. Ibid., August 7 and 27, 1943.

96. Ibid., January 1, 4, and 6, 1944.

97. *ANDI 65 años en imágenes publicitarias*, 86.

98. *Women's Wear*, February 15, 1944, quoted in "At Colombia Exposition," *Red Barrel*, March 1944, 40.

99. INDEGA, *La Chispa de la Vida*, no. 10 (October 1976), (BPP).

100. Ibid.

101. Kist ads from its first week of introduction; *El Colombiano*, September 16, 22, and 27, 1943.

102. The history of the use of nationalism in the selling of commodities is told in Marchand, *Advertising the American Dream;* McGovern, *Sold American;* Mazzarella, *Shovelling Smoke;* and Milanesio, *Workers Go Shopping.*

103. "'KIST,' una nueva bebida," *El Colombiano*, September 24, 1943.

104. Albert Staton to R. W. Woodruff, October 3, 1945, R. W. Woodruff Papers, MARBL, Emory University, Collection no. 19, box 301, folder 4. Raynaud, "La gaseosa KIST no ha muerto."

105. Saénz Rovner, *Ofensiva empresarial,,* 22, 26.

106. Moreno, *Yankee Don't Go Home,* 69; Haines, "Under the Eagle's Wing," 385; "Memorandum to the Under Secretary of State: Project for Increasing Advertising in Friendly Papers and by Radio within the American Republics," Campaign, Office of Inter-American Affairs—General Records—Commercial and Financial Economic Development Advertising, RG 229, NARA II; "Initial Step in the Advertising Project," Advertising in OAR, Office of Inter-American Affairs—General Records—Commercial and Financial Economic Development Advertising, RG 229, NARA II; memo to the Department of Commerce, June 4, 1942, OIAA, General Records, Commercial and Financial Development, Advertising, RG 229, NARA II.

107. Coca-Cola Export Corporation, "Forecast 1943 Foreign Advertising Expense," US Advertising in OAR, Office of Inter-American Affairs—General Records—Commercial and Financial Economic Development Advertising, RG 229, NARA II; J. F. Curtis, Coca-Cola Export Sales Company, to William Phillipson, Office of the Coordinator of Inter-American Affairs, January 7, 1943, US Advertising in OAR, Office of Inter-American Affairs—General Records—Commercial and Financial Economic Development Advertising, RG 229, NARA II.

108. "Forecast 1943 Foreign Advertising Expense."

109. Jaime Garzon to Nelson Rockefeller, April 10, 1944, Information Radio Country files—Colombia, RG 229, NARA II.

110. Moreno, *Yankee Don't Go Home,* 146–47; "La invitación universal . . . tomemos una Coca-Cola!" *Selecciones del Reader's Digest,* December 1944, front interior cover.

111. For more on the history of Coca-Cola's sourcing of sugar and benefiting from state intervention in the market, see Elmore, *Citizen Coke.*

112. Allen, *Secret Formula,* 88–89.

113. Elmore, *Citizen Coke,* 107.

114. Allen, *Secret Formula,* 104.

115. Ibid., 105.

116. Elmore, *Citizen Coke*, 111.

117. Ibid.

118. Roy Jones, "A Brief History of Coca-Cola Overseas," *Coca-Cola Bottler,* April 1959, 182.

119. Elmore, *Citizen Coke*, 110–11.

120. Ibid., 117.

121. Ben Oehlert to A. A. Aicklin, February 5, 1942, quoted in Pendergrast, *For God, Country, and Coca-Cola,* 196. The Company performed an even more dramatic act of national industrial citizenship when it was drafted into a $14 million military contract to build and manage an artillery plant. "Coca-Cola Firm Given Task of Operating Defense Plant," *Atlanta Constitution,* February 21, 1941, 1; "Coca-Cola Plant Finishes Good War Job," ibid., August 19, 1945, 3B; Hymson, "Company That Taught the World to Sing," 64–65.

122. Hostetter, "Sugar Allies," 23.

123. Pendergrast, *For God, Country, and Coca-Cola,* 196–97; Allen, *Secret Formula,* 252; Hostetter, "Sugar Allies," 23–24

124. E. J. Forio, "Out of the Crucible," *Coca-Cola Bottler,* December 1945, 15–16.

125. Hayes was a political insider who had served as private secretary to the US secretary of war during World War I. See "Ralph Hayes: First Director of the New York Community Trust," www.nycommunitytrust.org/Portals/o/Uploads/Documents /BioBrochures/Ralph%20Hayes.pdf (accessed September 13, 2018).

126. Ralph Hayes, "Soft Drink in War," memorandum, September 1941, R. W. Woodruff Collection, MARBL; Hymson "Company That Taught the World to Sing," 76

127. Pendergrast, *For God, Country, and Coca-Cola,* 196.

128. Ibid., 197.

129. TCCC, *The Coca-Cola Company: An Illustrated Profile,* 77.

130. Ben Oehlert to Robert Woodruff, June 13, 1942, Ben H. Oehlert Collection, MARBL.

131. "The Overseas Story," *Coca-Cola Overseas,* June 1948, 4–5.

132. Hunter Bell, "Fifty Fabulous Years of Overseas Growth for Coca-Cola, 1926–1976," *Refresher USA* 8, no. 3 (1976), 5.

133. Pendergrast, *For God, Country, and Coca-Cola,* 198, 512.

134. "Coca-Cola in India," *Red Barrel,* August 1944, 51.

135. *T.O. Digest* was the Company bulletin for TOs stationed around the world. "Sydney W. McCabe—India—October 30, 1944," *E.T.O. Digest* 1, no. 1, MARBL, Pendergrast Papers, Collection no. 741, box 16, folder 2, p. 12.

136. "Turk Beard—New Delhi—June 19, 1945," *T.O. Digest* 1, no. 5, MARBL, Pendergrast Papers, Collection no. 741, box 16, folder 2, p. 4.

137. "It is with the deepest regret . . ." *T.O. Digest* 1, no. 7, MARBL, Pendergrast Papers, Collection no. 741, box 16, folder 2, p. 1.

138. Bell, "Fifty Fabulous Years," 5.

139. "Watt Lovett—Tunis—August 13, 1944," *E.T.O. Digest* 1, no. 1, MARBL, Pendergrast Papers, Collection no. 741, box 16, folder 2, p. 2.

140. "Sam Holden—New Guinea—March 10, 1945," *T.O. Digest* 1, no. 4, MARBL, Pendergrast Papers, Collection no. 741, box 16, folder 2, p. 5.

141. "Paul Madden—New Guinea—April 4, 1945," *T.O. Digest* 1, no. 5, MARBL, Pendergrast Papers, Collection no. 741, box 16, folder 2, p. 4.

142. "Lt. Robert G. Fisher, with the US Armed Forces in India," *Red Barrel,* February 1944, 34.

143. Foster, *Coca-Globalization,* 43; Hymson, "Company That Taught the World to Sing," 109.

144. Wexler, *Tender Violence;* Hymson, "Company That Taught the World to Sing," 121.

145. Hunter Bell, "'It Had to Be Good' to Become the Global Hi-Sign" (n.d.), MARBL, Pendergrast Papers, Collection no. 741, box 16, folder 4.

146. Sforza, *Swing It!* 91; Curtis, "Rum and Coca-Cola."

147. Pendergrast, *For God, Country, and Coca-Cola,* 209.

148. Developmental Programs for Latin America: The Colombia Study (1941), Economic Analysis, Commercial and Financial Country Files: Colombia, RG 229, NARA II.

149. Ibid.

150. INDEGA, *La Chispa de la Vida,* no. 9 (October 1976), BPP.

151. Inge Staton and Luz de Villa, *Unknown Legacy,* 456.

152. "45 Years and 4 Careers," *Coca-Cola Overseas,* April 1969, 33; Coca-Cola Colombia, "Historia," www.cocacola.com/co/asps/e_coca-cola_colombia.asp (accessed June 12, 2006; page discontinued); Van Yoder, "Thirst for Success."

153. INDEGA, *La Chispa de la Vida,* no. 10 (October 1976), BPP.

154. "Luncheon for Staton in Montevideo," *Red Barrel,* August 1947, 35; "New Officers in Export," ibid., July 1947, 42; "Off Duke's Desk," *Coca-Cola Overseas,* June 1948, 30; "Happenings around the World," *Coca-Cola Overseas,* December 1954, 28; "Staton Brothers Honored," *The Refresher,* September–October 1966, 34.

155. INDEGA, *La Chispa de la Vida,* no. 11 (November 1976), BPP.

156. Ibid.

157. Mario B. Adams, "Yo-Yos Catch Fancy in Colombia," *Coca-Cola Overseas,* August 1965.

158. INDEGA, *La Chispa de la Vida,* no. 11 (November 1976), BPP.

159. Staton, "Colombia and Coca-Cola," *Coca-Cola Overseas,* June 1949.

160. INDEGA, *La Chispa de la Vida,* no. 11 (November 1976), BPP.

161. Ibid., no. 10 (October 1976).

162. "José Gutiérrez Gómez," *Semana,* April 1, 2006; Albert Staton to R. W. Woodruff, January 10, 1958, R. W. Woodruff Papers, MARBL, Emory University, Collection no. 19, box 301, folder 4.

163. Albert Staton to R. W. Woodruff, October 30, 1945, MARBL, R. W. Woodruff Papers, Collection no. 19, box 301, folder 4.

CHAPTER 2. MEDIATING COCA-COLONIZATION: NEGOTIATING NATIONAL DEVELOPMENT AND DIFFERENCE IN COCA-COLA'S POSTWAR INTERNATIONALIZATION

1. "Farley Plays Unofficial but Busy Role at Conference," *Baltimore Sun,* July 1, 1945, 11, James Farley Papers, MD, LC, reel 36.

2. Pendergrast, *For God, Country, and Coca-Cola,* 231.

3. "Farley Plays Unofficial but Busy Role at Conference."

4. Pendergrast, *For God, Country, and Coca-Cola,* 231.

5. E.J. Kahn Jr., interview with R.W. Woodruff, Mark Pendergrast Collection, MARBL, Emory University; Hymson, "Company That Taught the World to Sing," 73.

6. President Lyndon Johnson to James Farley, March 2, 1964, Mark Pendergrast Collection, MARBL, Emory University, MSSN741, box 1, folder 18—"Farley."

7. Farley, "Brand Names," in *Vital Speeches,* 475.

8. "Farley Says He Does Not Come on a Mission from Roosevelt," *El Mundo,* San Juan, Puerto Rico, January 14, 1941. James Farley Papers, MD, LC, reel 38. "Farley Going on Long Trip," *Times-Union,* Albany, NY, March 9, 1947, James Farley Papers, MD, LC, reel 36.

9. Untitled cartoon, Ecuador, 1941, James Farley Papers, MD, LC, reel 34.

10. De Grazia, *Irresistible Empire,* 3.

11. J F. Curtis, "The Overseas Story," *Coca-Cola Overseas,* June 1948, 5.

12. "Sun Never Sets on Cacoola."

13. "Coca-Cola as Sold throughout the World."

14. Martin, *Hell or High Water,* 56.

15. "Sun Never Sets on Cacoola."

16. Ibid.

17. Ibid.

18. Ibid.

19. Rist, *History of Development,* 76.

20. Pendergrast, *For God, Country, and Coca-Cola,* 234.

21. Kuisel, *Seducing the French,* 60.

22. Ibid., 52

23. Ibid., 55, citing *L'Humanité,* November 8, 1949; "France: Colonization by Coke," *Newsweek,* December 12, 1949 and other clippings in James Farley Papers, reel 37, MD, LC.

24. Allen, *Secret Formula,* 2.

25. Kuisel, *Seducing the French,* 60.

26. Ibid., quoting the French Ministry of Finance, 57, 55.

27. Ibid., 55, citing Makinsky letter to Ladas, January 23, 1950, in TCCC Archives.

28. Alter, *Truth Well Told,* 102, 108.

29. Allen, *Secret Formula,* 4.

30. Kuisel, *Seducing the French,* 62, 60, 63.

31. Pendergrast, *For God, Country, and Coca-Cola,* 236.

32. Ibid., 237.

33. "Drink and Be Merry," *Times of India,* October 22, 1950, 8; "Más sobre el café," *El Tiempo,* March 22, 1957, 4.

34. Pendergrast, *For God, Country, and Coca-Cola,* 238.

35. Kuisel, *Seducing the French,* 68, citing "Les Etats-Unis, les Américains, et la France, 1945–53," *Sondages,* no. 2 (1953), 46.

36. Kuisel, *Seducing the French,* 68. Coca-Cola's postwar global expansion was such a compelling example of the internationalization of US capitalism, and its contestation that it became fodder for Hollywood treatment. In Billy Wilder's 1961 comedy *One, Two, Three,* James Cagney plays a Coca-Cola executive sent to grow the bottling franchise in West Berlin, and perhaps even get Coca-Cola behind the Iron Curtain. The frenetic pace of the corporate ugly American's fast-talking dialogue satirized the speed, aggression, and even guile of US capitalist expansion. In its lampooning of both American capitalists and Soviet bureaucrats, the film suggests that the polar Cold War ideologies, in practice, manifested ridiculously similar conformity and imperial aspirations.

37. "The Convention," *Coca-Cola Bottler,* April 1948, 20; Pendergrast, *For God, Country, and Coca-Cola,* 232.

38. Pendergrast, *For God, Country, and Coca-Cola,* 232.

39. Ibid., 240.

40. Quoted in Kahn notes, 52; Pendergrast, *For God, Country, and Coca-Cola,* 240.

41. Farley, "Brand Names," 475; see also Farley, "Trademarks" and "Advertising as a World Force."

42. Farley, "Brand Names."

43. Farley, "Influence of Foreign Markets on Your Business."

44. Ibid.

45. Bucheli, *Bananas and Business* 9; Wilkins, *Emergence of Multinational Enterprise,* 157–60.

46. Nicholson, *Host to Thirsty Main Street,* 9.

47. Roy S. Jones, "A Brief History of Coca-Cola Overseas," *Coca-Cola Bottler,* April 1959, 183.

48. Nicholson, "Competitive Ideal."

49. Dicke, *Franchising in America,* 54, 124–26.

50. Rist, *History of Development,* 85, 87.

51. Duffield, "As I Recall," 41.

52. CE, MPBRSD, LC, Egyptian ads (1951), items ES005454 and ES005455.

53. Ibid., Egyptian ads (1950), items ES000332, ES005442, and ES005430.

54. Ibid., Egyptian ad (1951), item ES005452.

55. Ibid., Mexican ads (1953), items ES000865 and ES000857.

56. Ibid., "Un reflejo de unidad industrial: El azúcar" (1953), item ES000855.

57. Ibid., Coca-Cola de México, "Do You Know This Man from Tuxpan?" (1953), item ES000851.

58. Inge Staton and Luz de Villa, *Unknown Legacy*, 132, 135, 128.

59. "Farley Returns from World Tour," *Red Barrel*, February 1947, 36.

60. Duffield, "As I Recall," 43–44.

61. Ibid., 45.

62. Michael James, "Only One Turban Remains at U.N.," *New York Times*, January 27, 1957; Copland, "Master and the Maharajas," 677–78; Khan, *Great Partition*, 137.

63. Duffield, "As I Recall," 47; Frank Harrold to R. W. Woodruff, December 13, 1956, and to his wife, February 10, 1953, both cited in Pendergrast, *For God, Country, and Coca-Cola*, 243–44.

64. Ajit Singh, interview with author, May 1, 2008, New Delhi, India.

65. Mooson Kwauk, "First Coca-Cola Bottling Plant Opened in India—at New Delhi," *Coca-Cola Overseas*, February 1951, 5.

66. Ibid.; Kahn, *Big Drink*, 4.

67. Kwauk, "First Coca-Cola Bottling Plant Opened in India," 5, 4, 8.

68. A. S. Kamm, "Coca-Cola Comes to Bombay," *Coca-Cola Overseas*, August 1951, 14, 11.

69. Pendergrast, *For God, Country, and Coca-Cola*, 244.

70. Kwauk, "First Coca-Cola Bottling Plant," 4–5.

71. Sucheeta Majumdar, "The Pop, the Fizz and the Froth," *Times of India*, October 9, 1977, 11.

72. Ibid.

73. Manuel, "Sosyo: The Forgotten Drink."

74. Roy, "Chhibabhai & Gluco-Cola."

75. "Parle's Present India's First Cola Drink," *Times of India*, March 21, 1949, 1.

76. "A Matter of Taste," *Times of India*, April 4, 1951, 3.

77. "Who Came First!" *Times of India*, March 28, 1951, 3.

78. "Milk and Grow Rich!" *Times of India*, April 11, 1951, 3.

79. "British Counsel Briefed," *Times of India*, December 18, 1952, 3; "Trade Mark of 'GLUCO-COLA' Registration Refused," ibid., February 4, 1954, 3.

80. "We Don't Want to Sell Parle: Chauhan," *Mint*, New Delhi, India, November 28, 2012.

81. Majumdar, "Pop, the Fizz and the Froth," 11.

82. Ospina, *Bogotálogo*, 68.

83. Especially under the administrations of President Alfonso López Pumarejo.

84. Henderson, *Modernization in Colombia*, 336.

85. Sáenz Rovner, *Ofensiva empresarial*, 29.

86. Ibid.; Sáenz Rovner, *Colombia años 50*; Farnsworth-Alvear, *Dulcinea*, 210–11; Palacios, *Entre la legitimidad y la violencia*, 174–80.

87. Bucheli, *Bananas and Business*.

88. Rosenberg, *Spreading the American Dream*.

89. Al Staton, "Colombia and Coca-Cola: Rapid Progress Towards Industrial Future," *Coca-Cola Overseas,* June 1949, 17.

90. Sáenz Rovner, *Ofensiva empresarial,* 28–30.

91. Henderson, *Modernization in Colombia,* xiv.

92. Sáenz Rovner, *Ofensiva empresarial,* 29; Henderson, *Modernization in Colombia,* xiv.

93. Henderson, *Modernization in Colombia,* 329.

94. Ibid., 327.

95. *El Colombiano* (Medellín), 1950, quoted in Roldán, *Blood and Fire,* 21.

96. Henderson, *Modernization in Colombia,* 341

97. Ibid., 389.

98. Ibid., 344.

99. Varhola, *Fire and Ice,* 132–33.

100. Avilés, *Global Capitalism,* 38.

101. Ruiz, *Colombian Civil War,* 104

102. De La Pedraja, *Wars of Latin America,* 47.

103. Ibid.

104. Drexler, *Colombia and the United States,* 74.

105. Henderson, *Modernization in Colombia,* 331.

106. Ibid., 330.

107. Ibid., 391

108. Albert Staton to R. W. Woodruff, September 13, 1947, MARBL R. W. Woodruff Papers, Collection no. 19, box 301, folder 4.

109. Albert Staton to R. W. Woodruff, September 13, 1947, June 4, 1949, and October 1, 1951, MARBL, Emory University, R. W. Woodruff Papers, Collection no. 19, box 301, folder 4.

110. Albert Staton to R. W. Woodruff, September 13, 1947, MARBL, Emory University, R. W. Woodruff Papers, Collection no. 19, box 301, folder 4.

111. Al Staton, "Colombia and Coca-Cola: Rapid Progress Towards Industrial Future," *Coca-Cola Overseas,* June 1949, 28.

112. "Economic Review of Barranquilla Consular District," April 27, 1955, NARA II RG 84, box 242.

113. "Recent Developments: Colombian International Trade Fair, 1955," April 21, 1955, NARA II, RG 84, box 243; ibid., Harold Pease, US consul in Cali, to Ambassador William Tooney, October 5, 1955.

114. "Camera Shots Around the World," *Coca-Cola Overseas,* June 1957, 31.

115. See Ewen, *Captains of Consciousness;* Lears, *Fables of Abundance.*

116. Phillips-Fein, *Invisible Hands,* 32.

117. See also now Gilman, "Modernization Theory," in *Staging Growth,* ed. Engerman et al., 49; Rist, *History of Development,* 94–99.

118. Agnew, "Advertisements for Ourselves," in *Cultures of Commerce,* ed. Brown et al., 345.

119. Farley, "Advertising as a World Force," 49–50.

120. "Speaking of Quality," *Coca-Cola Overseas,* June 1948, 1.

121. Edward S. Rogers, "Democracy and Trademarks," *Coca-Cola Overseas,* June 1948, 7, 22–24.

122. US multinationals' World War II advertising in Mexico projected a US "consumer democracy" (Moreno, *Yankee Don't Go Home,* 146–47).

123. "De Compras con Nancy Sasser," *Selecciones del Reader's Digest,* February 1954, 15.

124. Mintz, *Sweetness and Power,* 196, 180.

125. Ibid., 196; Agnew, "Advertisements for Ourselves," 351.

126. Mintz, *Sweetness and Power,* 196.

127. Lears, *Fables of Abundance,* 10–11.

128. Sáenz Rovner, *Ofensiva empresarial,* 78–79.

129. Ibid.; Bergquist, *Labor in Latin America,* 4–5, 358; id., *Labor and the Course of American Democracy,* 163–70.

130. UAW's Walter Reuther quoted in Agnew, "Advertisements for Ourselves," 348.

131. Farley, "Brand Names" and "Trademarks."

132. "Cartagena Opening Is Tremendous Success," *Coca-Cola Bottler,* June 1947, 24–25.

133. On production-oriented advertising and aesthetics in advertising in the late nineteenth- and early twentieth-century US advertising, see Laird, *Advertising Progress,* and Marchand, *Creating the Corporate Soul,* 255.

134. CE, MPBRSD, LC, international pattern ad prototypes (1954), items 116982, 116983, and 116984.

135. Ibid., Brazilian ad (1955), item ES000292.

136. Ibid., South African ad (1952), item ES002578.

137. Ibid., Cypriot ad (1952), item ES003054.

138. Ibid., Argentinian ad (1948), item ES000708.

139. Ibid., "Pura como la luz del sol" (brochure, ca. 1950), item 056963.

140. "1958 Pattern Book: More Colorful, More Useful Than Ever," *Coca-Cola Overseas,* October, 1957. *Coca-Cola Overseas* notes that ads in the series were also published in *Life International,* the English-language international edition of the magazine.

141. One sign of these publications' impact: soon after the Cuban revolution, the Havana publication *Revista Mella* ("órgano de la Asociación de Jóvenes Rebeldes a principios de los 60s") began including a satirical supplement called *Salaciones del Reader's Indigest.* A Marxist *Mad Magazine,* it featured scathing send-ups of US capitalist culture, including advertising for "Poca-Chola" ("Little-Head" in Cuban slang) that mocked the stupidity of US consumer culture, portraying cartoonish, bathing-suited American teenagers drunkenly stumbling around the setting of a Coca-Cola ad (May 1960).

142. *Selecciones del Reader's Digest,* November 1954, 198–99.

143. Raventós, *Cien años de publicidad colombiana,* 85; the ad is ca. 1955 although this book cites it as 1931.

144. *Selecciones del Reader's Digest,* May 1954, 142–43.

145. *Selecciones del Reader's Digest,* December 1959, back cover.

146. Raventós, *Cien años de publicidad colombiana,* 86 and *Selecciones del Reader's Digest,* September 1954, 178–79.

147. Raventós, *Cien años de publicidad colombiana,* 87.

148. *Selecciones del Reader's Digest,* January 1954, 116–17.

149. Ibid., July 1954, 138–39.

150. Ibid., March 1954, 152–53.

151. Ibid., January 1955, interior back cover.

152. *Life en Español,* January, 28 1957, back cover.

153. *Selecciones del Reader's Digest,* July 1957, interior back cover.

154. Ibid., November 1956, interior back cover.

155. Ibid., May 1956, interior back cover.

156. *Life en Español,* May 20, 1957, back cover.

157. *Selecciones del Reader's Digest,* July 1956, interior back cover.

158. Ibid., 1956; *Life en Español,* back covers 1957.

159. Farley, "Sovereignty and Integrity."

160. *Coca-Cola Bottler,* January 1941, 40; Kwauk, "First Coca-Cola Bottling Plant," 6.

161. *Coca-Cola Bottler,* May 1948, September 1948, January 1949, March 1949, November 1949, October 1950, December 1962, August 1962, and February 1963.

162. *Coca-Cola Bottler,* October 1947, 53; November 1947, 53–54; December 1947, 54; January 1948, 50; February 1948, 55–56; March 1948, 60.

163. INDEGA, *La Chispa de la Vida,* no. 10 (October 1976), BPP; Albert Staton to R. W. Woodruff, October 1, 1951, R. W. Woodruff Papers, MARBL, Emory University, Collection no. 19, box 301, folder 4; Staton to W. O. Solms, The Coca-Cola Interamerican Corp., ca. 1972, in Staton and de Villa, *Unknown Legacy,* 420.

164. US Department of Commerce, Office of International Trade, *Investment in Colombia,* 89, 95.

165. Inge Staton and Luz de Villa, *Unknown Legacy,* xviii, 456–57; Albert Staton to R. W. Woodruff, October 1, 1951, MARBL, R. W. Woodruff Papers, Collection no. 19, box 301, folder 4.

166. Moreno and The Coca-Cola Company, *Centennial of Coca-Cola in Latin America,* 18.

167. Camacho Guizado, *Capital extranjero,* 92. López Arias, *Empresas multinacionales,* 82.

168. Inge Staton and Luz de Villa, *Unknown Legacy,* xvii; "45 Years and 4 Careers," *Coca-Cola Overseas,* April 1969, 33; "Panamerican Beverages," *International Directory of Company Histories,* vol. 47, ed. Jay P. Pederson (Detroit: St. James Press, 2002), 289; Panamerican Beverages, Proxy Statement Pursuant to Section 14(a) of the Securities Exchange Act of 1934, Securities and Exchange Commission, January 30, 2003.

169. José Vales, "Woods Staton, el paisa que entró al club de los más ricos," *ElTiempo.com,* March 11, 2012; Matthew Kirdahy, "McDonald's Back in the Woods in Latin America," *Forbes,* April 23, 2007.

170. "People," *Beverage Digest,* September 13, 2002, 6.

171. Application for Guaranties under the Economic Cooperation Act of 1948, The Coca-Cola Export Corporation, August 16, 1948, Coca-Cola Export Corporation, 1948, Economic Cooperation Administration, Executive Secretariat, General Correspondence (Name Files), 1948–1954, Record Group 469, NARA II. The Company further requested a waiver from having the European governments review such US investment guarantees.

172. Ibid, 3.

173. Ibid.

174. Handwritten notes on ibid., 8.

175. John C. de Wilde to E. T. Dickinson, August 26, 1948, Coca-Cola Export Corporation, 1948, Economic Cooperation Administration, Executive Secretariat, General Correspondence (Name Files), 1948–1954, Record Group 469, NARA II; handwritten notes on Application for Guaranties under the ECA, 7–8.

176. C. L. Terrel to Harper Bowls re: Coca Cola Request, December 10, 1948, Industries—Coca-Cola, Records of US Foreign Assistance Agencies, 1948–1961, Mission to Greece, Construction Division Subject Files, 1947–1953, Record Group 469, NARA II.

177. De Wilde to Dickinson, August 26, 1948.

178. D. A. Fitzgerald, ECA director of food, to John D. Goodloe, The Coca-Cola Company, August 18, 1948, Coca-Cola Export Corporation, 1948, Economic Cooperation Administration, Executive Secretariat, General Correspondence (Name Files), 1948–1954, Record Group 469, NARA II.

179. G. Anton Burgers, investment advisor of the US Technical Cooperation Mission to India to Charles B. Warden, chief of Investment Guaranties Staff of the International Cooperation Administration, October 11, 1957, Coca-Cola Company, US Operations Mission to India, Industry Division Investment Branch, Subject Files, 1953–1960, Record Group 469, NARA II.

180. These were not radical agencies. Joseph M. Stokes, ICA acting deputy director for technical services, made clear his agency's goals of raising "the standard of living of other countries" to "increase our markets and expand our commerce and investment," solidify capitalist allies, and deter communism (Stokes, "The International Cooperation Administration," World Affairs 119, no. 2 [Summer 1956]: 35). The Export Corporation was unable to convince even the ICA, which defined its international assistance as a project of expanding US capitalism.

181. Charles B. Warden, chief of Investment Guaranties Staff of the International Cooperation Administration to G. Anton Burgers, investment advisor of the US Technical Cooperation Mission to India, October 28, 1957, Coca-Cola Company, US Operations Mission to India, Industry Division Investment Branch, Subject Files, 1953–1960, Record Group 469, NARA II.

182. On the role of international imagery in advertising, cf. Domosh, *American Commodities in an Age of Empire.*

183. "All over the world . . . Sign of Good Taste" *National Geographic,* October 1957.

184. Duffield, "As I Recall," 46.
185. Duffield, "As I Recall," 58.
186. Duffield, "As I Recall," 58.
187. Ibid., 58.
188. Ibid., 61, MARBL.
189. Jones, "Brief History," 181.
190. Ibid., 183.

CHAPTER 3. "I'D LIKE TO BUY THE WORLD A COKE": THE
"REAL THING" AND THE REVOLUTIONS OF THE 1960S

1. Alter, *Truth Well Told,* 188.
2. Ibid., 188–89, quoting 1964 McCann Erickson report.
3. "Indenture of Agreement between The Coca-Cola Company and Solomon's, Ltd., Burma," May 14, 1927, CE, MPBRSD, LC.
4. Coombe, *Cultural Life of Intellectual Properties,* 179.
5. Coca-Cola Export Corporation and Jam Handy, *Community of the World* (1961), MPBRSD, LC.
6. Joe Rintelen, "New Ideas: Theme of 1957 Pattern Advertising Campaign," *Coca-Cola Overseas,* October 1956, 18–20.
7. CE, MPBRSD, LC, ads from Australia (1951), item ES005308; Lebanon (1952), item ES002338; and the Congo (1952), item ES003048.
8. Ibid., Egyptian ad (1953), item ES001128.
9. Ibid., Moroccan ad (1952), item ES005075; Colombian ad (1952), item ES005404.
10. Ibid., Egyptian ad (1953), item ES001123.
11. Ibid., Egyptian ad (1953), item ES001122.
12. Ibid., Egyptian ad (1951), item ES002205.
13. Ibid., Egyptian ad (1953), item ES001133.
14. Beyer, *Coca-Cola Girls.*
15. CE, MPBRSD, LC, Egyptian ad (1953), item ES001136.
16. Elspeth Brown, *Corporate Eye.*
17. Rintelen, "New Ideas," 21.
18. Joe Rintelen, "New 1956 Pattern Advertising Campaign Goes All Over the World," *Coca-Cola Overseas,* October 1955, 22.
19. Ibid.
20. CE, MPBRSD, LC, Iraqi ad (ca 1958), item ES005735; Philippine ad (1958), item ES006020; Italian ad (1958), item ES004853.
21. Delony Sledge, "Our 1955 Consumer Advertising," *Coca-Cola Bottler,* February 1955, 23.
22. Cross, *All-Consuming Century*; Spigel, *Make Room for TV.*
23. CE, MPBRSD, LC, "Key Anniversary Dates, 1987–2000."

24. Alter, *Truth Well Told*, 98; Russell McCracken, "The Overseas Story: Part III," *Coca-Cola Overseas*, December 1948, 11.

25. Pendergrast, *For God, Country, and Coca-Cola*, 62.

26. Backer, *Care and Feeding of Ideas*, 112.

27. Attali, *Noise*, 293–98.

28. See Corbett, "I Sing The Body (In)Corporate" (thank you to Van Truong for providing this reference).

29. CE, MPBRSD, LC, Family Size Radio Commercial, Spot TX32SPOT5SL.

30. Coca-Cola Export Corporation and Jam Handy, *Community of the World*.

31. Pendergrast, *For God, Country, and Coca-Cola*, 177.

32. Moye, "Coke Red on the Silver Screen."

33. Henderson, *Modernization in Colombia*, 342.

34. "Camera Shots around the World," *Coca-Cola Overseas*, April 1967, 33.

35. Ospina, *Bogotálogo*, 68–69; "The Cocacolos," *Time*, January 17, 1955, 42; Hozzman, "Sólo para mayores de 40 años"; Borda Carranza, *Cocacolos*.

36. Antonio Cruz Cárdenas, "'Los cocacolos,' muchachos de hoy," *Semana*, 1954, reprinted in Cruz Cárdenas, *Todavía sin final. . .*, 95–96.

37. Sáenz Rovner, *Colombia años 50*, 164–65.

38. Cruz Cárdenas, *Todavía sin final. . .*, 96–97.

39. Ibid., 94.

40. Arango, "Primer Manifiesto Nadaísta," in *Manifiestos Nadaistas*, 54.

41. Henderson, *Modernization in Colombia*, 405.

42. Ibid., 405, 413.

43. Herrera Duque, "De nadaístas, 'cocacolos' y hippies"; Pérez, *Bogotá, epicentro del rock Colombiano*, 51.

44. Farley, "Troubled International Waters."

45. Prebisch, *Economic Development of Latin America*; Gunder Frank, *Latin America*; Fals Borda, *Ciencia propria y colonialism intellectual*; Cardoso and Faletto, *Dependency and Development in Latin America*; Amin, *Unequal Development*.

46. Baran and Sweezy, *Monopoly Capital*.

47. Barnet and Miller, *Global Reach*, 26, 183–84.

48. Newton, *Encyclopedia of Kidnappings*, 55, 115, 154, 167; Purnell and Wainstein, *Problems of U.S. Businesses Operating Abroad in Terrorist Environments*, 64–80.

49. "How Coke Runs a Foreign Empire," *Business Week*, August 25, 1973, 41; "Memorandum of Conversation between American Consul General Goodwin Shapiro and President of Coca-Cola, S.A. Sr. Tomás Ornstein: Information Concerning the Disappearance of Two French Catholic Nuns," January 16, 1978, NSA, Argentina Project, S200000044.

50. Pendergrast, *For God, Country, and Coca-Cola*, 302.

51. "Aid for Migrants Pledged," *Christian Science Monitor*, July 25, 1970, 2.

52. Pendergrast, *For God, Country, and Coca-Cola*, 293.

53. "Ministers Reach Agreement with Coca-Cola Bottling Co.," *Atlanta Daily World*, October 10, 1963, 1; "Selective Buying Said Still on Coke," ibid., September

10, 1963, 2; "Don't Buy Coca-Cola," Operation Breadbasket ad, ibid., September 15, 1963, 5.

54. Allen, *Secret Formula,* 371.

55. Ibid., 356.

56. Ibid.; J. Paul Austin to R. W. Woodruff, November 28, 1969, R. W. Woodruff Papers, box 16, folder 5, J. Paul Austin, 1976–1977, MARBL, Emory University.

57. J. Paul Austin to J. D. Goodloe and G. M. Lawson, November 7, 1969, R. W. Woodruff Papers, box 16, folder 5, J. Paul Austin, 1976–1977, MARBL, Emory University.

58. Austin to Woodruff, November 28, 1969.

59. Frank, *Conquest of Cool,* 10–11.

60. Ibid.

61. Townsend, *Up the Organization,* ibid., 22–23.

62. Miller, "Introduction" in Packard, *Hidden Persuaders* (2007), 10–11.

63. Packard, *Hidden Persuaders* (1959), 31–32.

64. Sledge, "Our 1955 Consumer Advertising," 21.

65. Packard, *Hidden Persuaders* (1959), 114.

66. Sledge, "Our 1955 Consumer Advertising," 23.

67. Packard, *Hidden Persuaders* (1959), 214–15.

68. Frank, *Conquest of Cool,* 23–25.

69. CE, MPBRSD, LC, McGuire Sisters radio spot, "Be Really Refreshed," TX58SPOT3SL (1959).

70. Pendergrast, *For God, Country, and Coca-Cola,* 274.

71. "Motorbike: Pepsi Generation" (ca. 1963–66).

72. Frank, *Conquest of Cool,* 174–176.

73. Ibid., 173.

74. In 1963, the year the "Pepsi Generation" slogan premiered, Bob Dylan had already written "Blowin' in the Wind," and activists for civil and economic rights had organized the March on Washington, signal moments in the emergence of the 1960s that happened without the impetus of Pepsi.

75. Sloan Wilson, *The Man in the Gray Flannel Suit* (New York: Simon & Schuster, 1955). Taylor, *Sounds of Capitalism,* 148.

76. Fox, *Mirror Makers,* 197. Pendergrast, *For God, Country, and Coca-Cola,* 259; Alter, *Truth Well Told,* 145.

77. MPBRSD, LC, "Highlights in the History of Coca-Cola Television Advertising."

78. According to *Sponsor* magazine, cited in Alter, *Truth Well Told,* 144.

79. Alter, *Truth Well Told,* 56–65, 88–93, 153, 184–85.

80. Ibid., 183, 186, 219.

81. Ferguson, *Reorder of Things,* 62.

82. CE, MPBRSD, LC, "International Bottling Operations" (2000).

83. Alter, *Truth Well Told,* 147–50, 162, 196.

84. Ibid., 106, 188–90.

85. O'Barr and Moreira, "Airbrushing of Culture," 3.

86. O'Barr, Lazarus, and Moreira, "Global Advertising."

87. Ferguson, *Reorder of Things,* 64.

88. Ibid.

89. Backer, *Care and Feeding of Ideas,* 56.

90. Taylor, *Sounds of Capitalism,* 150.

91. MPBRSD, LC, "Highlights in the History of Coca-Cola Television Advertising." The "Things go better with Coca-Cola / Things go better with Coke" jingle was also intended to "establish the trademark 'Coke,'," in addition to "Coca-Cola," in markets around the world (ibid., "International Pattern Advertising—Establishing the Trademark Coke," item VRAXX1955KOCCPM06-A, CE, MPBRSD, LC.

92. Backer, *Care and Feeding of Ideas,* 56.

93. Ibid.

94. *Refresher,* March 1982, 19.

95. Frank, *Conquest of Cool,* 60.

96. For years the Company had neglected the African American market, especially relative to Pepsi's efforts at selling to it. See Capparell, *Real Pepsi Challenge.*

97. Pendergrast, *For God, Country, and Coca-Cola,* 279–81.

98. Ibid., 282.

99. Ibid., 281.

100. The Coca-Cola Company, "Boys on a Bench" ad, 1969.

101. Pendergrast, *For God, Country, and Coca-Cola,* 288.

102. TCCC, "James Brown . . . Bring It on Home" (1970).

103. CE, MPBRSD, LC, Indian ad (1971), item 048690.

104. *Marketing Services News Bulletin,* The Coca-Cola Export Corporation, January 1971; Raventós, *Cien años de publicidad colombiana,* 92.

105. Coca-Cola Export Corporation, "'La Chispa de la Vida' a Commercial Record 'Hit' in Argentina," *Marketing Services News Bulletin,* January 1971, 9.

106. Coombe, *Cultural Life of Intellectual Properties,* 56. See inter alia Baudrillard, *Simulations,* Harvey, *Condition of Postmodernity,* and Jameson, *Postmodernism.*

107. Coombe, *Cultural Life of Intellectual Properties,* 56.

108. Ibid., 52, citing McRobbie, *Postmodernism and Popular Culture* (1994).

109. Foster, *Coca-Globalization,* 80; Coombe, *Cultural Life of Intellectual Properties,* 61.

110. Debord and Wolman, "A User's Guide to Détournement"; Klein, *No Logo,* 281.

111. Scott-Heron, "The Revolution Will Not Be Televised."

112. Coombe, *Cultural Life of Intellectual Properties,* 73.

113. *Coca-Cola Co. v. Gemini Rising Inc.* (E.D.N.Y. 1972) described in Coombe, *Cultural Life of Intellectual Properties,* 72.

114. See, e.g., del Carmen Suescun Pozas, "From Reading to Seeing," in *Close Encounters,* ed. Joseph et al., 543.

115. Ibid. With the permission of the artist, pamphlets and T-shirts reproducing Caro's *Colombia* screenprint were given out to protestors supporting the Colombian Coca-Cola workers' trade union, Sinaltrainal, in New York City in 2002. Bob Schweitzer, "Left Matrix—art/politics," www.leftmatrix.com/caroalist.html (accessed September 2008; page discontinued).

116. *Refresher USA,* April 1970, 4.

117. Samuel Gardner to Charles Malik, August 25, 1970, Charles Malik Papers, MAD, LC.

118. Ibid.

119. Ibid.

120. Austin, "New Force for Peace" and "World Marketing as a New Force for Peace."

121. Backer, *Care and Feeding of Ideas,* 46–48.

122. Ibid., 24–25.

123. Ryan, "Making of 'I'd Like to Buy the World a Coke.'"

124. Backer, *Care and Feeding of Ideas,* 31.

125. Ibid., 46–48.

126. Ibid., 48, 51, 56–57.

127. Ibid., 52.

128. The commercial actually begins and ends with close-ups of white women singing.

129. Backer, *Care and Feeding of Ideas,* 52.

130. Attrep, "Sonic Inscription of Identity," 156.

131. Ryan, "Making of 'I'd Like to Buy the World a Coke.'"

132. Andrews and Barbash, "'I'd Like to Buy the World a Coke.'" The ad's reference in the series finale of *Mad Men* (2007–15) suggests its importance in the history of advertising, its continued meaningfulness, and its emblematic representation of advertising's assimilation of 1960s counterculture.

133. Elaine Brown, *Taste of Power,* 277–78.

134. Ibid., 281.

135. Backer, 197.

136. Coca-Cola Export Corporation, "Special Issue: 1972 Preview—1971 Review," *Marketing Services News Bulletin,* February 1972.

137. Coca-Cola Export Corporation, "'I'd Like to Buy the World a Coke'—A Worldwide Success," *Marketing Services News Bulletin,* March 1972.

138. Coca-Cola Export Corporation, *Marketing News Bulletin,* September 7, 1966.

139. O'Barr and Moreira, "Airbrushing of Culture," 4; O'Barr, Lazarus, and Moreira, "Global Advertising."

140. TCCC, "Celebrating Advertising History," www.thecoca-colacompany.com/presscenter/presskit_hilltop_behind_the_scenes.html (accessed January 19, 2008; page discontinued).

CHAPTER 4. INDIANIZE OR QUIT INDIA: NATIONALIST CHALLENGES TO COCA-COLA IN POSTCOLONIAL INDIA

1. "Backwash: Coke Returns from India Exile."
2. Singh, "Coca-Cola Viewpoint," 27.
3. Gargan, "Revolution Transforms India," 1.
4. "Calling Attention to Matter of Urgent Public Importance,"14–15.
5. Harvey, *Brief History of Neoliberalism*, 12.
6. Labelle, "De-coca-colonizing Egypt"; Pendergrast, *For God, Country, and Coca-Cola*, 285.
7. Singh "Coca-Cola Viewpoint," 27.
8. United Nations General Assembly, "Declaration on the Establishment of a New International Economic Order."
9. Ibid.
10. United Nations Conference on Trade and Development, "United Nations Center on Transnational Corporations Origins," http://unctc.unctad.org/aspx /UNCTCOrigins.aspx (page discontinued).
11. Rist, *History of Development*, 150.
12. Ibid., 121.
13. Bair, "From the Politics of Development to the Challenges of Globalization," 487–88.
14. Jones, *Multinationals and Global Capitalism*, 212.
15. Tomlinson, *Economy of Modern India*, 167.
16. Ibid.
17. Ibid.
18. Tomlinson, *Economy of Modern India*, 170.
19. Ibid., 171.
20. United Nations Centre on Transnational Corporations, *Foreign Direct Investment and Technology Transfer in India*, 79.
21. Chandra et al., *India after Independence*, 352.
22. Ibid.
23. Ibid., 222–23.
24. Ibid., 352.
25. Panagariya, *India*, 62.
26. Sydney Schanberg, "Soft-Drink War between Coca-Cola and 'Gold Spot' Bubbles in an Anti-American Atmosphere in India," *New York Times*, August 8, 1971, 13.
27. Gladwin and Walter, *Multinationals under Fire*, 281.
28. Figures from Lok Sabha testimony "Calling Attention to Matter of Urgent Public Importance," 16; similar numbers are cited by Johan Martinusson, quoted in Panagariya, *India*, 62.
29. "Calling Attention to Matter of Urgent Public Importance," 14–15; "Over Production in Coca-Cola Bottling Plants," 12.
30. Schanberg, "Soft-Drink War," 13.

31. "Action against Coca-Cola 'Not Anti-American,'" *The Statesman*, August 27, 1977.

32. "Calling Attention to Matter of Urgent Public Importance," 17.

33. Ibid., 16.

34. Ibid.

35. "Soft Drink Formula Available: George," *Times of India*, August 9, 1977.

36. "India Chooses '77' Name for Its Coke Substitute," *New York Times*, August 25, 1977, 76.

37. "Coca-Cola's Move to Quit India," *The Statesman*, August 12, 1977; Kasturi Rangan, "India Demands 'Know-How' and 60% Share of Coca-Cola Operation," *New York Times*, August 9, 1977.

38. Stephen F. Somerstein, letter to the editor, *New York Times*, August 18, 1977.

39. V. Shanker, "Bidding a Friendly Farewell Letter 3," *The Statesman*, August 21, 1977.

40. "Action against Coca-Cola 'Not Anti-American.'"

41. "Soft Drink Formula Available."

42. "India Stands Firm against Coca-Cola," *New York Times*, September 5 1977.

43. J. Paul Austin to R. W. Woodruff, December 22, 1977, MARBL, Emory University, R. W. Woodruff Papers, Collection no. 19, box 16, folder 5.

44. J. Paul Austin to directors of the Board of The Coca-Cola Company, January 30, 1976, MARBL, Emory University, R. W. Woodruff Papers, Collection no. 19, box 16, folder 5.

45. Bachi J. Karkaria, "Liquidate the Liquid," *Times of India*, August 14, 1977.

46. Throughout these centralized economic development and industrialization efforts, others argued for *panchayati raj,* or village decentralized governance and economic development, an important issue in Indian villagers' struggles over water rights in the face of Coca-Cola industrialization.

47. Gandhi, "Swadeshi Movement," 127.

48. "Gandhi in conversation with Ramachandran."

49. Steger, *Gandhi's Dilemma*, 91–92.

50. Chatterjee, *Nationalist Thought and the Colonial World,* 85.

51. Gandhi and Parel, *Hind Swaraj,* 71–72.

52. "Action against Coca-Cola 'Not Anti-American.'"

53. Dr. Hari Vaishnava, "Urine Therapy," *Times of India*, October 24, 1977.

54. "Over Production in Coca-Cola Bottling Plants," 12.

55. "Disciplining Multinationals," *The Tribune*, September 16, 1977, 4.

56. See B. Chandramohan Rao, "Tonics—'Pep' Only for Manufacturers," *Times of India*, October 22, 1977; C. V. Gopalakrishnan, "What Role for Multinationals?" *The Hindu*, July 23, 1977.

57. "Companies That Spent over Rs. 1 Lakh: Advts.," *Times of India*, September 8, 1977.

58. C. V. Gopalakrishnan, "The Ways of Foreign Firms," *The Hindu*, September 8, 1977.

59. Minaz Merchant, "The Boeing Connection," *Times of India*, October 23, 1977.

60. T. V. Parasuram, "Coca-Cola Admits Pay-Offs in 20 Nations," *Indian Express*, August 12, 1977.

61. "Over Production in Coca-Cola Bottling Plants," 12.

62. Parasuram, "Coca-Cola Admits Pay-Offs"; Pendergrast, *For God, Country, and Coca-Cola*, 310.

63. "Doing without Coke," *The Hindu*, August 8, 1977.

64. Guest list for luncheon honoring former governor of Georgia Jimmy Carter, hosted by J. Paul Austin, Edgar Bronfman, and Henry Ford, July 22, 1976; J. Paul Austin to R. W. Woodruff, November 16, 1976, MARBL, Emory University, R. W. Woodruff Papers, Collection no. 19, box 16, folder 5.

65. J. Paul Austin to R. W. Woodruff, July 12, 1976, folder 5; Charles W. Adams and Alexander Makinsky to Austin, January 10, 1974, folder 4, MARBL, Emory University, R. W. Woodruff Papers, Collection no. 19, box 16.

66. "Telegram from Senator Charles Percy to New Delhi Embassy and Bombay Consulate," July 31, 1979, NARA II RG 59, 1979STATE199107, D790347–0397— Electronic Telegrams, 1979 in the Series: Central Foreign Policy Files, 7/1/1973–12/31/1979; Daljit Singh to R. W. Woodruff, August 1 and 18, 1979, MARBL, Emory University, R. W. Woodruff Papers, Collection no. 19, box 290, folder 6.

67. On the role of nationalism and political language in marketing and advertising imagery in the first half of the twentieth century, see Marchand, *Advertising the American Dream* (1986) and *Creating the Corporate Soul* (1998) and McGovern, *Sold American* (2006).

68. "Coca-Cola Goes the Indian Way," *Times of India*, April 17, 1972, 4.

69. "Coca-Cola Goes the Indian Way," *Times of India*, May 25, 1972, 2.

70. Ibid.

71. "Coca-Cola Goes the Indian Way," *Times of India*, April 17, 1972, 4.

72. "More than 130 Countries" (1972), CE, MPBRSD, LC, item ES003618, and "Just to Mention a Few" (1972), items ES003619–ES003620.

73. B. Chandramohan Rao, "IBM Imported and Sold 'Junk,'" *Times of India*, October 25, 1977.

74. S. S. Gupta, "IBM Machines," *Times of India*, October 21, 1977.

75. Electronics Corporation of India Limited ad, *Times of India*, November 24, 1977, 18.

76. Electronics Corporation of India Limited ad, *Times of India*, December 15, 1977, 18.

77. Electronics Corporation of India Limited ad, *Times of India*, December 12, 1977, 12.

78. DCM Data Products ad, *Times of India*, November 22, 1977, 9.

79. Computronics India ad, *Times of India*, December 14, 1977, 14

80. Hindustan Lever ad, *Times of India*, December 12, 1977, 11.

81. Hindustan Lever ad, *Times of India*, October 23, 1977, 5.

82. Duke's King Kola ad, *Times of India*, November 20, 1977, 7.

83. Agro ad, *Times of India,* August 23, 1977, 7.

84. Himalayan Springs ad, *Times of India,* December 11, 1977, 5.

85. Parle (Exports) Private Ltd. ad, *Times of India,* October 13, 1977, 18.

86. Ibid.; Parle (Exports) Private Ltd. ad, *Times of India,* November 1, 1977.

87. Ibid.; Parle (Exports) Private Ltd. ad, *The Statesman,* September 11, 1977, 4.

88. Parle (Exports) Private Ltd. ad, *The Statesman,* September 11, 1977, 4.

89. Parle (Exports) Private Ltd. ad, *Times of India,* September 18 and 21, 1977, 6, and *The Statesman,* September 18, 1977, 9.

90. Pure Drinks ad, *Times of India,* November 28, 1977, 6.

91. Pure Drinks ad, *Times of India,* October 18, 1977, 6.

92. Ibid.

93. Pure Drinks ad, *Times of India,* October 16, 1977. 5.

94. "Penalized," *The Statesman,* August 29, 1977.

95. "India Stands Firm against Coca-Cola."

96. Ajit Singh; "Coke Swallows Its Pride," *The Independent,* February 15, 1994.

97. Ibid.

98. "India's Cola Conflict," *Atlanta Constitution,* May 30, 1980.

99. "Fernandes Callous, Say Coca-Cola Staff," *Times of India,* September 12, 1977.

100. "Coca-Cola Substitute Passes Tests," *The Statesman,* August 21, 1977.

101. Ibid.

102. "India Chooses '77' Name for Its Coke Substitute."

103. N. N. Sachitanand, "A Tale of a Soft Drink," *The Hindu,* November 3, 1977.

104. Majumdar, "Pop, the Fizz and the Froth," 11.

105. Ibid.

106. Ibid.

107. Singh, "Coca-Cola Viewpoint," 27.

108. Pure Drinks claimed that it had 45 percent of the soft-drink market in India, although politicians suggested it was more. Ibid.

109. Parle's market share peaked at around 70 percent at the end of the 1980s, right before PepsiCo and The Coca-Cola Company returned to India under the country's neoliberal economic reforms. Significantly, Coca-Cola preferred to buy up Parle's business, bottlers, and brands upon its reentry to India rather than compete with it (see chapter 5). See Das Gupta, "How India Became Pepsi's Right Choice"; Biswas and Sen, "Coke vs Pepsi."

110. "US Has Shed Old Notions on India," *The Hindu,* September 11, 1977.

111. Ibid.

112. "Coke, Disincentive to Investor: Envoy," *Times of India,* September 11, 1977.

113. "Us Has Shed Old Notions on India."

114. Sagar, "Dharia Has Talks with Us Officials" *The Hindu,* September 1, 1977; "Action against Coca-Cola 'Not Anti-American.'"

115. Ibid.

116. Ibid.

117. "No Compulsion to Divulge Trade Secrets: Patel," *Times of India,* October 1, 1977.

118. R. K. Laxman, *You Said It* cartoon strip, *Times of India*, October 10, 1977, 1. Laxman had illustrated Parle ads. His series of editorial cartoons on Coca-Cola's ejection targeted Indian political leaders as much as the Company. www .business-standard.com/article/specials/chhibabhai-gluco-cola-197120601032_ 1.html (accessed September 15, 2018).

119. "Sardar Daljit Singh: The Uncrowned King of Country's Cold Drinks Industry."

120. Chawla, "Will Meridien Hotel Turn Out to Be a Pot of Gold for Charanjit Singh?"

121. R. W. Woodruff to Daljit Singh, January 8, 1980, MARBL, Emory University, R. W. Woodruff Papers, Collection no. 19, box 290, folder 6.

122. The Coca-Cola Company, 1978 Annual Report (1979), 21. The 1977 Annual Report made no mention of the loss of the Indian market either.

123. Ibid., 20–21.

124. Pendergrast, *For God, Country, and Coca-Cola*, 543.

125. Ibid., 311.

CHAPTER 5. MAN IN EVERY BOTTLE: LABOR AND NEOLIBERAL VIOLENCE IN COLOMBIAN COCA-COLA BOTTLING

1. This chapter analyzes corporate, activist, legal, journalistic, and academic documents from The Coca-Cola Company, unions, NGOs, activists, the popular press and academia, and archival research in Atlanta, Bogotá and Medellín, as well as interviews with Coca-Cola Colombia executives, plant managers, and Coca-Cola workers in Barrancabermeja, Barranquilla, Bogotá, Bucaramanga, Cali, Carepa, Cartagena, Cúcuta, and Medellín. Because of ongoing threats to members of Sinaltrainal and other unions, I refer to them only as "Coca-Cola workers" unless they have been identified by name in other sources or have given me permission to do so.

2. Taussig, *Nervous System*, 17.

3. Thank you to Lesley Gill for her research, insights, and suggestions, which have greatly influenced this chapter.

4. See "Panamerican Beverages" in *International Directory of Company Histories*; Puertas, "El día que Papá se fue."

5. Coca-Cola FEMSA, "Historia," www.cocacola.com.co/est/lo/conecta_ historia.asp (accessed May 2006; page discontinued); Panamerican Beverages, Form 10-K.

6. See Garay et al., *Colombia: Estructura industrial . . . 1967–1996*.

7. Albert Staton to R. W. Woodruff, December 25, 1964, MARBL, R. W. Woodruff Papers, collection no. 19, box 301, folder 4.

8. Interview with retiree, Barranquilla, November 2, 2006.

9. "Coca-Cola es asi," *Semana*, October 22, 1990.

10. Interview with retiree, Medellín, November 11, 2006.

11. M. H. Farnsworth to J. W. Jones, March 15, 1972, MARBL, R. W. Woodruff Papers, Collection no. 19, box 301, folder 4.

12. *Chispa de la Vida,* no. 1 (January 1976), editorial, 1.

13. *Chispa de la Vida,* no. 9 (October 1976), "La empresa," 3.

14. Interview with Coca-Cola worker, Barranquilla, November 1, 2006.

15. Interview with Coca-Cola worker, Barranquilla, November 3, 2006.

16. Interview with Coca-Cola worker, Barrancabermeja, November 17, 2006.

17. Interview with Coca-Cola worker, Barrancabermeja, November 14, 2006.

18. Interview with William Mendoza, Barrancabermeja, November 17, 2006; Interviews with Coca-Cola workers, Bucaramanga, November 17, 2006, and Bogotá, October 18, 2006.

19. Olaya, "Sinaltrainal."

20. Gill, Century of Violence, 101.

21. "Reforma laboral, exposición de motivos al Congreso por parte de Francisco Posada de la Peña, ministro de trabajo, y Jaime Giraldo Angel, ministro de justicia," in *La revolución pacífica: Modernizacion y apertura de la economia* (Bogotá: Departamento Nacional de Planeación, 1991), 1: 343, as cited in Ahumada, *Modelo neoliberal* (1998), 219–20; Inter-American Development Bank, "Se buscan buenos empleos."

22. García Abello, "Reforma laboral." For more on Colombian neoliberalism, see Arango and López, eds., *Globalización.*

23. Bonilla González, "Empleo y política sectorial," in *Falacia neoliberal,* ed. Restrepo Botero, 218.

24. LeGrand, "Colombian Crisis"; Taussig, *Law in a Lawless Land*; Bergquist, ed., *Violence in Colombia*; Bergquist et al., eds., *Violence in Colombia, 1990–2000*; Palacios and Safford, *Colombia*; Palacios, *Between Legitimacy and Violence*; Gill, "Labor and Human Rights."

25. Gill, *Century of Violence,* 101.

26. See, e.g., Cowie, *Capital Moves.*

27. Bonilla González, "Empleo y política sectorial."

28. Daft, "Globalization."

29. TCCC, "The Coca-Cola Company Continues to Fortify Global Bottling System," News Release, August 8, 1997, CE, MPBRSD, LC.

30. Hays, "Global Crisis for Coca-Cola?"

31. TCCC, "The Coca-Cola Company Continues to Fortify Global Bottling System," News Release, August 8, 1997, CE, MPBRSD, LC.

32. For a history of shareholder value, see Ho, *Liquidated.*

33. "Billionaire Warren Buffett Becomes Face of Cherry Coke in China," *Guardian,* April 5, 2017.

34. TCCC, "The Coca-Cola Company Continues to Fortify Global Bottling System," News Release, August 8, 1997, CE, MPBRSD, LC.

35. Petersen, "Putting Extra Fizz into Profits."

36. For more on The Coca-Cola Company's relationship with its bottlers in the 1980s–2000s, see Hays, *Real Thing.*

37. Huneeus, "Megaembotelladoras."

38. The Venezuelan bottler was a joint venture between Coca-Cola and the powerful Cisneros family, longtime bottlers of Pepsi, effectively taking over Pepsi's largest international market at the time. Hays (2004), 160.

39. McKay and Luhnow, "Coke's Latin Bottlers to Merge."

40. The entry for "Panamerican Beverages" in *The International Directory of Company Histories* describes 3,500 jobs lost in 1999, but workers note that this was just one cost-cutting moment in a longer period of consolidation and restructuring.

41. See "Panamerican Beverages" in *International Directory of Company Histories*.

42. Fomento Económico Mexicano, "Historia Corporativa"; McKay and Luhnow, "Coke's Latin Bottlers to Merge."

43. Fomento Económico Mexicano, "Mexico."

44. Coca-Cola FEMSA, "[2003] Annual Report to US Securities and Exchange Commission, Form 20-F," 8.

45. Malkin, "Latin American Coca-Cola Bottlers"

46. TCCC, "[2004] Annual Report to US Securities and Exchange Commission, Form 10-K," 44.

47. Interview with Coca-Cola worker, Barranquilla, November 3, 2006.

48. Interview with Coca-Cola workers, Barranquilla, November 2, 2006, Bogotá, October 22, 2006, and Cúcuta, November 23, 2006; Gill, "Right There with You," 243; The Company disputed these numbers, as can be seen in the exchange between Ed Potter, director of global labor relations, and Michael Blanding in letters to *The Nation*, May 22, 2006.

49. Sinaltrainal, "Nuestras Propuestas," accessed November 22, 2018, www.sinaltrainal.org/index.php/nuestras-propuestas/propuestas/1469-nuestras-propuestas-propuestas.

50. Palacios, *Between Legitimacy and Violence,* 171–79; Gill, *Century of Violence,* 62–63.

51. LeGrand, "Colombian Crisis"; Palacios, *Between Legitimacy and Violence;* Palacios and Safford, *Colombia.*

52. Gill, Century of Violence, 105.

53. See Civico, *Para-State.*

54. Gill *Century of Violence,* 127.

55. Murillo, *Colombia and the United States,* 133.

56. Gill, "Labor and Human Rights."

57. Blanding, "Case against Coke"; New York City Fact-Finding Delegation, "Investigation of Allegations of Murder and Violence in Coca-Cola's Colombian Plants."

58. Gill, *Century of Violence,* 102.

59. Dudley, *Walking Ghosts,* 201.

60. Chiquita had also previously paid leftist guerrillas $220,000 as *vacuna* (inoculation) to allow the company to operate without the threat of kidnappings. Chiquita's $1.7 million to the paramilitaries, paid from 1996–97, as the AUC began

a national campaign of political assassinations, until 2004, suggests support moving beyond pay for protection to the willful funding of operations of private armed forces that acted as death squads. Pierson, "Chiquita Settles"; Evans, "New Chiquita Papers."

61. Chomsky, *Linked Labor Histories*, 253.

62. New York City Fact-Finding Delegation, "Investigation of Allegations of Murder and Violence in Coca-Cola's Colombian Plants"; Gill, "Labor and Human Rights."

63. Group interview with SICO and former Sinaltrainal members, Carepa, Colombia, November 12, 2006.

64. See Chomsky, *Linked Labor Histories* on the FARC and EPL in Urabá, their struggles between each other and the paramilitaries, and their role among banana workers.

65. "Las confesiones de Hasbún," *Semana*, October 4, 2008.

66. Interviews with Coca-Cola workers, Bucaramanga, November 17, and 18, 2006, and Bogotá, October 18, 2006.

67. Interview with Coca-Cola worker, Barranquilla, November 1, 2007.

68. Interviews with Coca-Cola workers, Barranquilla, November 1, 2006, Bucaramanga, November 17 and 18, 2006.

69. Interview with Javier Correa, Bogotá, October 18, 2006.

70. Santos Calderón, "Palabras."

71. Sinaltrainal, "¡Para que cese la violencia en Colombia!"; "¿Quiénes somos?" and "Modelo de desarrollo democrático"; for more on Sinaltrainal's political orientation and goals, see Olaya, "Sinaltrainal."

72. Frundt, *Refreshing Pauses*; Levenson-Estrada, *Trade Unionists against Terror*.

73. Martin-Ortega, "Deadly Ventures?" 10.

74. International Labor Rights Fund, "Summary of Coca-Cola's Human Rights Violations in Colombia and Turkey."

75. Martin-Ortega, "Deadly Ventures?" 10; Peterson, "Court Cites Iqbal Ruling"; "Eleventh Circuit Dismisses Alien Tort Statute Claims."

76. Using the ATCA, Burmese plaintiffs (represented in part by the ILRF) successfully sued Unocal over labor abuses committed in the construction of an oil pipeline.

77. Harvey, *Brief History of Neoliberalism*, 176–82.

78. Gill, "Limits of Solidarity," 672.

79. Killer Coke, "Colleges, Universities and High Schools Active in the Campaign."

80. Blanding, "Coke: The New Nike."

81. Zafar and Tukdeo, "Coca-Cola Kicked Out."

82. "End Exclusivity Contracts at Rutgers University."

83. Brenner, Brenner, and Winslow, *Rebel Rank and File*.

84. Foster, "Show and Tell," 38.

85. Gill, "Limits of Solidarity," 669.

86. Giridharadas, "Boycotts Minus the Pain."

87. Upadhyaya, "Let Them Drink Coke."

88. Gill "Limits of Solidarity," 673.

89. Gill, "Limits of Solidarity," 674.

90. Gill, *Century of Violence*, 188–89.

91. Gill, "Limits of Solidarity," 669.

92. Interview with William Mendoza, Barrancabermeja, November 17, 2006.

93. Chomsky, *Linked Labor Histories,* 233–38; "Statement by George Meany, President, AFL-CIO, before the Senate Foreign Relations Committee," August 1, 1969, 9 and insert B, NARA II, CIA Records Search Tool (CREST), CIA-RDP71B00364R000200020086–0.

94. Frank, *Buy American.*

95. Chomsky, *Linked Labor Histories*, 233–38;

96. "IUF Coca-Cola Affiliates Reject Call for Global Coca-Cola Boycott,'" www.iuf.org/cgi-bin/dbman/db.cgi?db=default&uid=default&ID=1119& view_records=1&ww=1&en=1. Reproduced on The Coca-Cola Company's website www.thecoca-colacompany.com/presscenter/viewpointscolombian.html (page discontinued).

97. Chomsky, *Linked Labor Histories*, 254.

98. Ibid., 207, 254–55; letter from Ed Potter to *The Nation,* May 22, 2006; Killer Coke, "Another 'Classic Coke' Move" and "Why the IUF Attacks Sinaltrainal"; letter from Javier Correa, national president of Sinaltrainal, to students at McMaster University, May 15, 2006.

99. Group interview with SICO and former Sinaltrainal members, Carepa, Colombia, November 12, 2006.

100. Interview with Ed Potter, director of global labor relations, The Coca-Cola Company, Atlanta, Georgia, July 18, 2006.

101. "Joint Coca-Cola and IUF Statement."

102. Interview with Ed Potter; TCCC, "The Facts."

103. Chomsky, *Linked Labor Histories,* 255.

104. Caraballo Cárdenas, "Colombia el primer país."

105. Blanding, *Coke Machine,* 270–75.

106. Interview with Coca-Cola workers, Barrancabermeja, November 16, 2006.

CHAPTER 6. WATER FOR LIFE, NOT FOR COCA-COLA:
COMMODIFICATION, CONSUMPTION, AND
ENVIRONMENTAL CHALLENGES IN NEOLIBERAL INDIA

1. "Coca-Cola Is Back in India," Coca-Cola Company News Release, October 24, 1993.

2. Mark Pendergrast quoted in Shah, "Coke in Your Faucet?"

3. Sales growth in the US slowed from 5–7 percent annually in the 1980s to only 0.2 percent through the 1990s (Kaye and Argenti, "Coca-Cola India," 2–3).

4. This chapter draws on fieldwork and interviews with residents and activists of Mehdiganj, Kala Dera, and Plachimada, as well as environmentalists and

Coca-Cola executives and bottlers. The history of the Plachimada movement has been well documented; see Ananthakrishnan Aiyer on the context of the larger agrarian crisis; C. R. Bijoy on the role of Adivasis in the struggle; K. Ravi Raman and Sujith Koonan on legal implications of the court case against Coca-Cola; K. R. Ranjith and P. R. Sreemahadevan Pillai for popular and technical studies; business case studies from Terry Halbert and Sridevi Shivarajan (with whom I collaborated on several interviews in Kerala); and the activist literature including Anti-Coca-Cola Peoples Struggle Committee, *Coca-Cola Quit Plachimada, Quit India.*

5. Greising, *I'd Like the World to Buy a Coke,* 282–83.

6. Senadhira and Dawson, "Raising India."

7. Including a law prohibiting multinationals from selling products under internationally known trademarks.

8. Gargan, "Revolution Transforms India."

9. TCCC, "Coca-Cola and Parle Join Hands in India," news release, September 21, 1993, CE, MPBRSD, LC.

10. Kaye and Argenti, "Coca-Cola India," 4; Coca-Cola India, "About Us," accessed January 6, 2009, www.coca-colaindia.com/aboutus/aboutus_ccindia.aspx; page discontinued.

11. Senadhira and Dawson, "Raising India."

12. Blanding, *Coke Machine,* 235.

13. Bannerjee, *Real Thing,* 28.

14. Mukherjee, "To Deny Voting Rights to Indian Shareholders."

15. Bannerjee, *Real Thing,* 29.

16. Mukherjee, "To Deny Voting Rights."

17. Balakrishna and Sidharth, "MNCs"; "Indian Government Allows Coke to Buy Out Shareholders."

18. Ibid.; Mukherjee, "To Deny Voting Rights"; Blanding, *Coke Machine,* 236.

19. Kaye and Argenti, "Coca-Cola India," 4; Coca-Cola India, "About Us."

20. Hindustan Coca-Cola Beverages Pvt. Ltd., "Overview."

21. Bannerjee, *Real Thing,* 43–44.

22. See O'Barr, Lazarus, and Moreira, "Global Advertising"; Mazzarella, *Shoveling Smoke.*

23. Kornberg, "'Good Drinking Water Instead of Coca-Cola,'" 72; Zubrzycki, "Things Go Bitter"; Ganguly, "Saffron Protests"; Cooper, "Hindu Nationalists Target U.S. Products."

24. Daft, "Globalization."

25. Parameswaran, "E-Race-ing Color" in *Circuits of Visibility,* ed. Hedge.

26. Kurian, "Coca-Cola May Dump *Life ho to aisi* Campaign"; Kaye and Argenti, "Coca-Cola India," 6.

27. "Thanda Matlab Solitary EFFIE Gold."

28. Kadri, "Glocal-Cola," 10.

29. Vaid Dixit, "'Thanda III.'"

30. "Coca-Cola India's Thirst for the Rural Market."

31. Dobhal, "Real Thing"; Shukla, "Prasoon Joshi."

32. Kadri, "Glocal-Cola," 12.

33. Kaye and Argenti, "Coca-Cola India," 6.

34. Sunita Narain quoted in Bist, "India's Cola Controversy."

35. Centre for Science and Environment (CSE), *Analysis of Pesticide Residues in Soft Drinks* (2003), 13; CSE, "Colonisation's Dirty Dozen."

36. Vedwan, "Pesticides in Coca-Cola and Pepsi," 674.

37. Bist, "India's Cola Controversy"; "HC Orders Government to Test Pepsi Products"; "India's Cola Crisis Bubbles Up."

38. Kornberg, "'Good Drinking Water Instead of Coca-Cola,'" 72; Ganguly, "Saffron Protests"; Basheer, "Coke, Pepsi Disappear from Kerala Shops."

39. CSE, *Analysis of Pesticide Residues in Soft Drinks* (2003), 5–6; CSE, "Hard Truths."

40. Lakshmi, "Soda Giants Battle Public Panic."

41. Ibid.

42. Hills and Welford, "Case Study," 170.

43. Ibid.; Kaye and Argenti, "Coca-Cola India," 1.

44. Vedwan, "Pesticides in Coca-Cola and Pepsi," 666.

45. Ibid., 679.

46. Ibid., 670.

47. CSE, "Pesticide Residues in Bottled Water."

48. Bushan, "Bottled Loot"; Bannerjee, *Real Thing,* 63; "Water Wars...?"

49. CSE, *Analysis of Pesticide Residues in Bottled Water,* 2.

50. Ibid.; Kaye and Argenti, "Coca-Cola India," 11.

51. CSE, "Pesticide Residues in Bottled Water."

52. Wilk, "Bottled Water."

53. Interview with Kushal Yadav, Centre for Science and Environment, New Delhi, March 25, 2008.

54. Vedwan, "Pesticides in Coca-Cola and Pepsi," 660.

55. Ibid., 662.

56. Ibid., 660. Similar intentions were expressed in the author's interview with Kushal Yadav.

57. CSE, "Timeline," www.cseindia.org/cseaboutus/timeline.htm. Accessed June 3, 2009; page discontinued.

58. Ibid.

59. Vedwan, "Pesticides in Coca-Cola and Pepsi," 679.

60. C.R. Neelakandan quoted in Baburaj and Saratchandran, *1000 Days & a Dream.*

61. CSE, *Analysis of Pesticide Residues in Soft Drinks* (2006), 6.

62. Ibid., 3, 13.

63. Gentleman, "For 2 Giants... a Crisis."

64. Gentleman, "India Widens Ban."

65. Lakshmi, "Soda Giants Battle Public Panic."

66. Bannerjee, *Real Thing,* 96.

67. Ibid., 99, 100.

68. Gentleman, "For 2 Giants. . . a Crisis."

69. Joshi, "Pesticide Row"; Rai, "Move in India to Ban Coke and Pepsi."

70. Bannerjee, *Real Thing*, 242, quoting Federation of Indian Chambers of Commerce and Industry (FICCI) press conference.

71. Ibid., 124.

72. Gentleman, "Coke and Pepsi Try to Reassure."

73. Vedwan, "Pesticides in Coca-Cola and Pepsi," 672.

74. Bannerjee, *Real Thing*, 123–24.

75. Lakshmi "Soda Giants Battle Public Panic"; Gentleman, "For 2 Giants. . . a Crisis."

76. Bannerjee, *Real Thing*, 67.

77. Gentleman, "Coke and Pepsi Try to Reassure."

78. Interviews with Coca-Cola executives Harry Ott, Deepak Jolly, Kamlesh Kumar Sharma, and Dr. MVRL Murtha, Gurgaon, India, April 10, 2008.

79. Coca-Cola India, "Health and Wellness," www.coca-colaindia.com /health_wellness/health_wellness_text.asp#pesticide (accessed August 1, 2008; page discontinued).

80. Bruno Latour, "What Is Iconoclash? Or Is There a World Beyond the Image Wars?" in *Iconoclash: Beyond the Image Wars in Science, Religion and Art,* ed. Latour and Peter Weibel (Cambridge, MA: MIT Press, 2002), as cited in Ghosh, *Global Icons,* 3.

81. Chadha, "Coke Tries to Can Indian Poster."

82. Ghosh, *Global Icons,* 52.

83. Ibid., 51–52.

84. The Energy and Resources Institute, *Independent Third Party Assessment,* 206. Average daily intake for a plant is around 600,000 liters, but the plants have withdrawn as much as 1.5 million liters a day during the summer months.

85. This was true of Plachimada and Kaladera, where new plants were built; the plant at Mehdiganj, Uttar Pradesh, was a brownfield acquisition of Kejriwal Beverages Pvt. Ltd., a Parle franchise bottling plant.

86. Aiyer, "Allure of the Transnational."

87. Vedwan, "Pesticides in Coca-Cola and Pepsi," 661–62.

88. Ibid.

89. Aiyer, "Allure of the Transnational," 650–51.

90. Ibid., 650.

91. Sunil Kumar, "Note on Farm Sector in Uttar Pradesh," 5.

92. The Energy and Resources Institute, *Independent Third Party Assessment,* 205.

93. Chandrika, *To Protect Our Right,* 5–6.

94. See The Energy and Resources Institute, *Independent Third Party Assessment,* 90, on the Easement Act of 1882.

95. Ibid., 220.

96. Ibid., 6.

97. The Mehdiganj plant paid the *gram panchayat* Rs 6,000 ($136.36) in annual taxes and Rs 2,500 ($56.82) in license to operate fees. Ibid., 222.

98. For all the water it withdrew in Mehdiganj during 2005–6, the plant paid a water cess of just Rs. 31,573.00, or US$717.57, with an average exchange rate of around Rs. 44.00/$1.00 in 2005–6. Ibid., 223.

99. Hardt and Negri, *Commonwealth*, viii.

100. Interviews with villagers, Mehdiganj, India, April 2, 2008.

101. Chandrika, *To Protect Our Right.*

102. The Energy and Resources Institute, *Independent Third Party Assessment,* 216. These sentiments were echoed in several interviews by the author.

103. Interviews in 2008 in Kochi, Kerala, with C. Saratchandran (March 19) and C. R. Neelakandan (March 21); and see also Bijoy, "Adivasi Groups vs. Coca-Cola."

104. Twelve years later, the Supreme Court dismissed the case when it was informed that the Company no longer intended to run the plant; see chapter 7.

105. The Parle franchise, Kejriwal Beverages Pvt. Limited, was bought by Hindustan Coca-Cola Beverages Limited in 1999.

106. The Energy and Resources Institute, *Independent Third Party Assessment,* 222; Wolf, "Thanda-Hearted Matlab."

107. Interview with plant management, Mehdiganj, India, April 22, 2008. See also Blanding, *Coke Machine,* 230.

108. Drew, "From the Groundwater Up," 38.

109. Interview with Siaram Yadav, Mehdiganj, India, April 4, 2008. See also Adve, "Coke Lacks Fizz."

110. Interview with Ram Narayan Patel, Mehdiganj, India, April 2, 2008.

111. Interviews with Nandlal (Prasad) Master, Mehdiganj, India, March–April, 2008. For more, see Dana van Breukelen "Marching in the Spirit of Gandhi."

112. "Gandhi in conversation with Ramachandran." See also interviews with Master cited in n. 116 above.

113. Interviews with Master et al. cited in n. 116 above.

114. Chandrika, *To Protect Our Right,* 15–16; interviews with Master cited in n. 116 above.

115. Joan Martínez-Alier quoted in Guha, *How Much Should a Person Consume?,* 59.

116. Guha, *How Much Should a Person Consume?* 57–70. Examples include the struggles of the Chipko forest dwellers against logging, Keralan fisherfolk's challenge to coastal development and unsustainable fishing methods, and the Narmada Bachao Andolan's movement against displacement by the Narmada Dam.

117. Ibid., 59, quoting Agarwal.

118. Ibid., 70.

119. Ibid., 63.

120. Ibid. Interview with C. R. Neelakandan, Ernakulam, India, March 21, 2008.

121. Faber, *Capitalizing on Environmental Injustice,* 237.

122. Ibid., 236.

123. Nixon, *Slow Violence.*

124. Faber, *Capitalizing on Environmental Injustice,* 252.

125. Bhimrao Ramji Ambedkar (1891–1956) was a Dalit Buddhist scholar and political leader who challenged the social discrimination of the caste system.

126. NAPM, "National Alliance of People's Movements."

127. Ibid.; Keating, "Developmental Democracy," 428; Bakshi, "'Development, Not Destruction'," 255.

128. NAPM, "National Alliance of People's Movements."

129. The Energy and Resources Institute, *Independent Third Party Assessment,* 22.

130. Such as Atul Singh, group president of Asia Pacific operations; Bannerjee, *Real Thing,* 94.

131. Castells, "Communication."

132. Stecklow, "Virtual Battle."

133. India Resource Center, "About India Resource Center."

134. Keck and Sikkink, *Activists beyond Borders,* 16–25.

135. Amit Srivastava, interview with Lori Serb, *Prairie Grassroots,* WEFT, November 4, 2005.

136. The Energy and Resources Institute, *Independent Third Party Assessment.*

137. "Best Global Brands 2006."

138. Foster, "Show and Tell."

139. Foster, *Coca-Globalization,* 231.

140. Mitchell, "Brand-Jacking," 5.

141. Stecklow, "Virtual Battle."

142. Interview with Amit Srivastava, Mehdiganj, India, March 29, 2008.

143. Lok Samiti, *Jahar Ba* (ca 2005).

144. Interviews with villagers, Mehdiganj, Uttar Pradesh, March 28 and April 25, 2008.

145. For more on Hindu nationalist responses to the entry of international consumer goods to India, see Kumar, *Gandhi Meets Primetime.*

146. "Thanda matlab toilet cleaner" was popularized by the television yogi Swami Ramdev, who used Coca-Cola's advertising slogan to dissuade his practitioners from consuming soft drinks.

147. Lok Samiti, *Jahar Ba* (ca 2005).

148. "Indian Officials Order Coca-Cola Plant Closed."

149. Coca-Cola India, "Facts and Myths."

150. Chaudhary, "Farmers Fight Coca-Cola."

151. The Energy and Resources Institute, *Independent Third Party Assessment,* Executive Summary, 22.

152. Rana, "Coca-Cola Closes Plant in India."

153. Supreme Court of India, Record of Proceedings in Civil Appeal No. 4033 of 2009, July 13, 2017; Sujith Koonan, email with author, April 26, 2018.

154. "Coca-Cola Wants to Make India."

155. "In Hot Water," *The Economist,* October 6, 2005.

CHAPTER 7. CSR: CORPORATE SOCIAL RESPONSIBILITY OR CONTINUED SOCIAL RESISTANCE? A NONCONCLUSION

1. Business for Social Responsibility, "Drinking It In," 1.
2. Kochhar and Pamula, "Coca-Cola Strengthens Its Bonds with India."
3. Seshan, "Buzz without Fizz."
4. TCCC, "Coca-Cola Foundation."
5. Ira Jackson and Jane Nelson's *Profits with Principles: Seven Strategies for Delivering Value with Values* (New York: Currency/Doubleday, 2004) quoted in Bakan, *The Corporation,* 31–32.
6. Soederberg, "Taming Corporations."
7. Shamir, "Corporate Social Responsibility," in *Law and Globalization from Below,* ed. De Sousa Santos and Rodriguez-Garavito, 95.
8. Vogel, *Market for Virtue,* 8.
9. Haslam, "Is Corporate Social Responsibility a Constructivist Regime?"; Vogel, *Market for Virtue,* 8.
10. Matten, Crane, and Chapple, "Behind the Mask"; Roberts, "Manufacture of Corporate Social Responsibility," 255; Shamir, "Corporate Social Responsibility," 106–7; Raman, "Community–Coca-Cola Interface," 104–5; Brugmann and Prahalad, "Co-creating Business's New Social Compact."
11. Nestle, *Soda Politics,* 48; Moreira, "Soft Drinks as Top Calorie Culprit."
12. Center for Science in the Public Interest, *Liquid Candy.*
13. Guthrie and Esterl, "Soda Sales in Mexico Rise."
14. Jacobs and Richtel, "She Took on Colombia's Soda Industry."
15. Shamir, "Between Self-Regulation and the Alien Tort Claims Act"; id., "De-Radicalization of Corporate Social Responsibility"; id., "Corporate Social Responsibility."
16. Armbruster, "Coke Bottler Faces Death Suit."
17. Including the National Foreign Trade Council, USA*ENGAGE, US and International Chambers of Commerce, the National Association of Manufacturers, the United States Council for International Business, the Organization for International Investment, and the US Business Roundtable. Collingsworth, "'Corporate Social Responsibility,' Unmasked."
18. *Sinaltrainal et al. v. The Coca-Cola Company et al.*
19. TCCC, "India: The Key Facts."
20. Koonan, "Legal Implications of Plachimada."
21. Ibid., 9–10; Raghunandan, "Look at the Legal Issues."
22. Nair, "Coca Cola Must Pay Damages."
23. "Coca-Cola Statement re: Compensation"; "Lawsuits against Coca-Cola Approved in India."
24. Basheer, "Lost Battle"; Faizi, "Why Plachimada?"; Koonan, "Constitutionality of the Plachimada Tribunal Bill"; Shiva, "High Time Plachimada Bill Got Presidential Consent."

25. Ferdman, "Why the Sugar Industry Hates the FDA's New Nutrition Facts Label."

26. Nestle, *Soda Politics,* 325, 383.

27. Jacobs and Richtel, "She Took on Colombia's Soda Industry"; La Pulla, "Dulces mentiras de los congresistas."

28. Alianza por la Salud Alimentaria and Educar Consumidores TV commercial (2017), paid for with funding from Bloomberg Philanthropies, which also provided logistical support for the campaign.

29. Jacobs and Richtel, "She Took on Colombia's Soda Industry"; Ana Marcos, "Un anuncio censurado sobre el riesgo de las bebidas azucaradas podrá volver a emitirse en Colombia," *El País,* April 18, 2017.

30. Nicole Perlroth, "Spyware's Odd Targets: Backers of Mexico's Soda Tax," *The New York Times,* February 11, 2017.

31. Sergio Silva Numa, "Gaseosas: Una pelea gorda," *El Espectador,* November 15, 2015.

32. Jacobs and Richtel, "She Took on Colombia's Soda Industry."

33. Soederberg, "Taming Corporations"; Christian Aid, *Behind the Mask.*

34. Sparkes, "Pragmatic Approach," 8.

35. Mitchell, "Brand-Jacking," 7.

36. Shamir, "Between Self-Regulation and the Alien Tort Claims Act," 660.

37. TCCC, *Workplace Rights Policy* and *Supplier Guiding Principles.*

38. UK Ethical Trading Initiative (www.ethicaltrade.org) cited in Doane, "Alternative Perspective on Brands."

39. California Safety Compliance Corporation, "Workplace Assessments in Colombia"; International Labor Organization, "Report Evaluation Mission Coca-Cola Bottling Plants in Colombia."

40. United Students Against Sweatshops, "Cal-Safety Compliance Corporation Is Not a Credible Monitor."

41. TCCC, "The Coca-Cola Company Joins UN Global Compact."

42. Author interview with Ed Potter, TCCC global labor relations director, Atlanta, Georgia, June 21, 2006.

43. Deutsch, "Coca-Cola Reaches Into Past for New Chief."

44. Bair, "From the Politics of Development to the Challenges of Globalization," 496.

45. Ibid., 496; Hale, "Silent Reform through the Global Compact."

46. World Bank, *Global Development Finance 2006: The Development Potential of Surging Capital Flows* (Washington, D.C., 2006), in Soederberg, "Taming Corporations," 501.

47. Bair, "From the Politics of Development to the Challenges of Globalization," 497.

48. Ibid., 496.

49. Soederberg, "Taming Corporations," 501.

50. Annan, Address to the World Economic Forum. Annan likened the UN Global Compact to the compact capital made with victims of the Great
342 · NOTES TO PAGES 276–282

Depression to create social safety nets restoring "social harmony and political stability."

51. Soederberg, "Taming Corporations," 503.

52. Post et al., *Redefining the Corporation,* 19. The idea that "all company stakeholders—employees, communities, suppliers, shareholders—are 'investors' in the company and deserve to participate in its governance and benefit from its surplus," is articulated in White, "Fade, Integrate or Transform?"

53. International Business Leaders Forum (IBLF), "Dialogue on Business, Peace, Development and Human Rights in Colombia," 2.

54. Fleming and Jones, *End of Corporate Social Responsibility,* 50.

55. Ibid., 53; Freeman, *Strategic Management*; Donaldson and Preston, "Stakeholder Theory."

56. Fleming and Jones, *End of Corporate Social Responsibility,* 6.

57. Thompson, "Responsibility and Neo-Liberalism"; id., "Are We All Neoliberals Now?"

58. Shamir, "Corporate Social Responsibility," 106.

59. International Business Leaders Forum, "Who We Are."

60. Davies, "Making Change Happen."

61. International Business Leaders Forum, "About."

62. Shamir, "Corporate Social Responsibility," 105.

63. "Joint Coca-Cola and IUF Statement."

64. International Business Leaders Forum, Fundación Ideas para la Paz, and United Nations Global Compact. "Dialogue."

65. Largacha, "Los resultados de la investigación."

66. Amis, Hodges, and Jeffery, *Development, Peace and Human Rights,* 27.

67. TCCC, 2006 Corporate Responsibility Review, 19; Guáqueta and Orsini, *Empresarios y reintegración.*

68. Lucy Taylor, "Globalization and Civil Society," cited in Shamir, "Corporate Social Responsibility," 107.

69. TCCC, "Responsible Water Management in India and Beyond."

70. TCCC, "India: The Key Facts."

71. Caring for Climate, "CEO Water Mandate."

72. TCCC, "TERI University and Coke Launch Water Studies Program."

73. TCCC, 2009 Replenish Report.

74. TCCC, "Improving Our Water Efficiency."

75. TCCC, 2004 Citizenship Report, 33.

76. TCCC, "Improving Our Water Efficiency."

77. TCCC, 2009 Replenish Report; TCCC, 2008–9 Sustainability Review: *Live Positively.*

78. TCCC, 2007 Replenish Report: *Achieving Water Balance through Community Water Partnerships*; Isdell, "Remarks at the WWF Annual Conference."

79. TCCC, 2016 Sustainability Report," 10.

80. Global Water Challenge, "Mission" and "New World Program."

81. Pearce, "Greenwash."

82. TCCC, 2009 Replenish Report, 14.

83. Gerbens-Leenes et al., "Water Neutrality."

84. Ibid.

85. TCCC, 2009 Replenish Report.

86. Pearce, "Greenwash."

87. TCCC, 2010–11 Sustainability Report and "Collaborating to Replenish the Water We Use."

88. MacDonald, "Coke Claims."

89. Ibid.

90. TCCC, "Coca-Cola Launches Global EKOCENTER Partnership."

91. Ibid.

92. Walker, "Coke's 'Downtown in a Box.'"

93. TCCC, "EKOCENTER Progress Update."

94. J. Paul Austin to R. W. Woodruff, November 28, 1969, MARBL, R. W. Woodruff Papers, collection no. 19, box 16, folder 5.

95. "Coca-Cola to Sell Aqua-Chem Units," 31.

96. Doane, "Alternative Perspective on Brands," 240.

97. Elmore, *Citizen Coke,* 187.

98. Kytle and Ruggie, "Corporate Social Responsibility as Risk Management."

99. Asongu, "Coca-Cola's Response to HIV/AIDS."

100. Kirsch, *Mining Capitalism,* 160; Rogers, "Materiality of the Corporation."

101. Hamburger and Geiger, "Beverage Industry Douses Tax on Soft Drinks"; Warner, "Soda Tax Wars Are Back."

102. Lappé and Bronsing-Lazalde, "How to Win against Big Soda"; Pfister, "Leaked."

103. TCCC, 2007–8 Sustainability Review, 55.

104. Nestle, *Soda Politics,* 48.

105. Ibid., 335; TCCC, "Continuing Transparency: Evolution of the Beverage Institute of Health and Wellness," www.coca-colacompany.com/our-company /continuing-transparency-evolution-of-the-beverage-institute-of-health-and-wellness (accessed September 18, 2018).

106. O'Connor, "Coca-Cola Funds Scientists."

107. Ibid.; "Coca-Cola Discloses More of Its Funding."

108. O'Connor, "Coca-Cola Funds Scientists."

109. "Coca-Cola Discloses More of Its Funding."

110. Nestle, *Soda Politics,* 266.

111. TCCC, 2014–15 Sustainability Report, 10 and "Active Healthy Living."

112. TCCC, "At Coca-Cola, We Support Physical Activity Programs" and 2007–8 Sustainability Review, 55; Nestle, *Soda Politics,* 238; O'Connor, "Coca-Cola Funds Scientists."

113. Philpott, "80 Percent of Public Schools Have Contracts with Coke and Pepsi."

114. TCCC, "Global School Beverage Guidelines."

115. Gómez et al., "Sponsorship of Physical Activity Programs by the Sweetened Beverages Industry."

116. Bhatnagar, "Coke Slaps On New Tagline"; Sanger-Katz, "Decline of Big Soda."

117. TCCC, 2011–12 Sustainability Report.

118. The Coca-Cola Company, "Coca-Cola North America Marketing and Innovation Focuses on Full Portfolio of Drink Brands," Press Release, February 3, 2006 [Accessed June 21, 2008].

119. Burns Smith, "Make Every Drop Count."

120. TCCC, "Coca-Cola North America Marketing and Innovation."

121. TCCC, "Make Every Drop Count."

122. Gregory, "Is Vitaminwater Really a Healthy Drink?"; Gilbert, "Vitaminwater Label, Name Misleading."

123. Nestle, *Soda Politics*, 309.

124. Ibid., 306.

125. For more on the debate about the excise tax on soda as regressive, that affects poorer consumers more, and how the revenue generated could be used, see Nestle, *Soda Politics*, 361, 382–85 and Mound, "Against the Soda Tax."

126. Boltanski and Chiapello, *New Spirit of Capitalism*, 7–9.

127. Bakan, *The Corporation*, 31, citing Ira Jackson.

128. See the definition of "capitalist realism" in Fisher, *Capitalism Realism*, used by Fleming and Jones, *End of Corporate Social Responsibility*, 2–3.

129. Bakan, *The Corporation*, 31.

130. Weinert, "Can Coke Prevent AIDS?"

131. Karnani, "Case against Corporate Social Responsibility."

132. TCCC, "Haiti Hope Project."

133. TCCC, "Community Water Partnerships."

134. Fleming and Jones, *End of Corporate Social Responsibility*, 5.

135. Ibid., 93.

136. Upadhyaya, "Let Them drink Coke."

137. Žižek, *First as Tragedy, Then as Farce*, 53.

138. Banet-Weiser and Mukherjee, *Commodity Activism*, 4.

139. Fleming and Jones, *End of Corporate Social Responsibility*, 40.

140. TCCC, Annual Report, 2002, 38.

141. TCCC, 2004 Citizenship Report: *Toward Sustainability*, 3. This seems to have been inspired by the "triple bottom line" concept of sustainable business in Elkington, *Cannibals with Forks*.

142. Frundt, *Refreshing Pauses*; Levenson-Estrada, *Trade Unionists against Terror*; Pendergrast, *For God, Country, and Coca-Cola* (2000), 314–315.

143. Friedman, "Social Responsibility of Business."

144. Bakan, *The Corporation*, 34, citing interview with Milton Friedman.

145. Stout, "Why We Should Stop Teaching Dodge v. Ford."

146. Fleming and Jones, *End of Corporate Social Responsibility*, 47.

147. Vogel, *Market for Virtue*, 28.

148. Ibid.

149. Žižek, "Nobody Has to Be Vile."

150. Fleming and Jones, *End of Corporate Social Responsibility*, 47.

151. Žižek, "Nobody Has to Be Vile." As Žižek points out, this is not a new phenomenon: Andrew Carnegie, who used a private army to crush organized labor at his Homestead, Pennsylvania, steel works in 1892, became a leader in educational, cultural, and humanitarian causes.

152. Some organizational behavior research suggests that the goodwill accumulated through CSR initiatives may result in corporations' feeling they've accumulated "moral credits" and are thus entitled to "free passes" to engage in "corporate social irresponsibility" elsewhere in their business (see Ormiston and Wong, "License to Ill").

153. Fleming and Jones, *End of Corporate Social Responsibility*, 71.

154. This book does not conclude with a set of suggestions for The Coca-Cola Company. If you are looking for one, I recommend Nestle, *Soda Politics*.

SELECTED BIBLIOGRAPHY

ARCHIVES

Archivo General de la Nación, Bogotá, Colombia
Archivo Histórico de Medellín, Medellín, Colombia
Atlanta History Center, Atlanta, GA
Biblioteca Luis Angel Arango, Bogotá, Colombia
Biblioteca Público Piloto, Medellín, Colombia
Coca-Cola Collection, Creative Exchange, Motion Picture Broadcasting and
    Recorded Sound Division, Library of Congress, Washington, DC
Communist Party of India–Marxist Archives, New Delhi, India
Manuscripts and Archives Division, Library of Congress, Washington, DC
Motion Picture, Broadcasting and Recorded Sound Division, Library of Congress,
    Washington, DC
National Archives and Records Administration II, College Park, MD
National Archives of India, New Delhi, India
National Security Archive, George Washington University, Washington, DC
Nehru Memorial Library, New Delhi, India
Stuart A. Rose Manuscripts, Archives, and Rare Book Library, Emory University,
    Atlanta, GA

PAPERS AND DOCUMENTS

Ben H. Oehlert Collection, Stuart A. Rose Manuscripts, Archives, and Rare Book
    Library Emory University (MARBL)
Charles Malik Papers, Manuscripts and Archives Division, Library of Congress,
    Washington, DC (MAD, LC)
La Chispa de la Vida (publication of Panamco), Biblioteca Público Piloto, Medellín
    (BPP)

Coca-Cola Collection, Creative Exchange, Motion Picture, Broadcasting and
Recorded Sound Division, Library of Congress (CE, MPBRSD, LC)
Coca-Cola Collection, Stuart A. Rose Manuscripts, Archives, and Rare Book
Library, Emory University (MARBL)
Colombia US Embassy Bogotá General Records 1936–1961, National Archives and
Records Administration II, College Park, MD (NARAII)
Commercial and Financial Country Files: Colombia, National Archives and
Records Administration II, College Park, MD (NARAII)
Economic Cooperation Administration, National Archives and Records Adminis-
tration II, College Park, MD (NARAII)
Electronic Telegrams, 1979 in the Series: Central Foreign Policy Files, National
Archives and Records Administration II, College Park, MD (NARAII)
International Cooperation Administration, National Archives and Records
Administration II, College Park, MD (NARAII)
James Farley Papers, Manuscripts and Archives Division, Library of Congress,
Washington, DC (MAD, LC)
Mark Pendergrast Collection, Stuart A. Rose Manuscripts, Archives, and Rare
Book Library Emory University (MARBL)
Office of Inter-American Affairs, National Archives and Records Administration
II, College Park, MD (NARAII)
Records of US Foreign Assistance Agencies, National Archives and Records Admin-
istration II, College Park, MD (NARAII)
Robert W. Woodruff Papers, Stuart A. Rose Manuscripts, Archives, and Rare Book
Library, Emory University (MARBL)

HISTORICAL PERIODICALS

Advertiser's Digest
Atlanta Constitution
Atlanta Daily World
Bebidas y Manjares (Bogotá)
Beverage Digest
Business Week
Coca-Cola Bottler (TCCC)
Coca-Cola Overseas (TCCEC)
El Colombiano (Medellín)
El Heraldo de Antioquia (Medellín)
El Tiempo (Bogotá)
The Hindu (Chennai)
Illustrated Weekly of India (Mumbai)
Indian Express (Mumbai)
La Chispa de la Vida (publication of Panamco)
La Revista Mella (Havana)

Life
Life en Español
Life International
Lok Sabha Debates (New Delhi)
Marketing Services News Bulletin (TCCC)
National Geographic
New York Times
Printer's Ink
Reader's Digest
Red Barrel (TCCC)
Refresher (TCCC)
Refresher USA (TCCC)
Selecciones del Reader's Digest
Semana(Bogotá)
Statesman (Calcutta, Delhi)
T.O. Digest (TCCC publication for Coca-Cola workers embedded with US troops during World War II)
Time
Times of India (Mumbai)
Tribune (Chandigarh)
Vital Speeches of the Day

WORKS CITED

Adve, Nagraj. "Coke Lacks Fizz for Farmers in Mehdiganj." India Resource Center, October 23, 2004. www.indiaresource.org/campaigns/coke/2004/cokemehdiganj .html. Accessed September 11, 2018.

Advertisers' Guide to Latin American Markets. Chicago: Allied Publishing, 1935.

Agnew, Jean-Christophe. "Advertisements for Ourselves: Being and Time in a Promotional Economy." In *Cultures of Commerce: Representation and American Business Culture, 1877–1960*, ed. Elspeth H. Brown, Catherine Gudis, and Marina Moskowitz, 343–64. New York: Palgrave Macmillan, 2006.

Ahumada, Consuelo. *El modelo neoliberal y su impacto en la sociedad colombiana.* Bogotá: El Ancora Editores, 1996. 2nd ed., 1998.

"Aid for Migrants Pledged." *Christian Science Monitor,* July 25, 1970.

Aiyer, Ananthakrishnan. "The Allure of the Transnational: Notes on Some Aspects of the Political Economy of Water in India." *Cultural Anthropology* 22, no. 4 (2007): 640–58.

Allen, Frederick. *Secret Formula: The Inside Story of How Coca-Cola Became the Best-Known Brand in the World.* New York: Collins Business, 1994.

Alter, Stewart. *Truth Well Told: McCann Erickson and the Pioneering of Global Advertising.* New York: McCann-Erickson Worldwide, 1995.

Amin, Samir. *Unequal Development: An Essay on the Social Formations of Peripheral Capitalism.* New York: Monthly Review Press; Hassocks, England: Harvester Press, 1975.

Amis, Lucy, Adrian Hodges, and Neil Jeffery. *Development, Peace and Human Rights in Colombia: A Business Agenda.* London: International Business Leaders Forum in association with Fundación Ideas para la Paz and the Office of the UN Global Compact, 2006.

ANDI 65 años en imágenes publicitarias de sus empresas. Bogotá: ANDI, 2009.

Andrews, Travis N., and Fred Barbash. "'I'd Like to Buy the World a Coke': The Story Behind the World's Most Famous Ad." *Washington Post,* May 17, 2004. www.washingtonpost.com/news/morning-mix/wp/2016/05/17/id-like-to-buy-the-world-a-coke-the-story-behind-the-worlds-most-famous-ad-whose-creator-has-died-at-89/?utm_term=.3116c2ccoce5. Accessed December 15, 2018.

Annan, Kofi. Address of United Nations Secretary-General to the World Economic Forum. Davos, Switzerland, January 31, 1999. www.un.org/sg/en/content/sg/speeches/1999-02-01/kofi-annans-address-world-economic-forum-davos. Accessed December 2, 2018.

Anti-Coca-Cola Peoples Struggle Committee. *Coca-Cola Quit Plachimada, Quit India: The Story of Anti-Coca-Cola Struggle at Plachimada in Kerala.* Keralam, India, 2004.

Arango, Gonzalo. "Primer Manifiesto Nadaísta." In *Manifiestos Nadaistas,* compiled by Eduardo Escobar, Bogotá: Arango Editores, 1992.

Arango, Luz Gabriela, and Carmen Marina López, eds., *Globalización, apertura económica y relaciones industriales en América Latina.* Santafé de Bogotá: Facultad de Ciencias Humanas, Centro de Estudios Sociales, Universidad Nacional de Colombia, 1999

Armbruster, Stefan. "Coke Bottler Faces Death Suit." BBC News, April 2, 2003. http://news.bbc.co.uk/2/hi/business/2909141.stm. Accessed September 11, 2018.

Asongu, J.J. "Coca-Cola's Response to HIV/AIDS in Africa: A Case Study on Strategic Corporate Social Responsibility." *Journal of Business and Public Policy* 1, no. 1 (2007).

Attali, Jacques. *Noise: The Political Economy of Music.* Minneapolis: University of Minnesota Press, 1985.

Attrep, Kara Ann. "The Sonic Inscription of Identity: Music, Race and Nostalgia in Advertising." PhD diss., University of California–Santa Barbara, 2008.

Austin, J. Paul. "A New Force for Peace." Speech at the International Advertising Association Luncheon, New York, June 10, 1964. *Vital Speeches of the Day* 30, no. 19 (July 15, 1964): 605–8.

———. "World Marketing as a New Force for Peace." *Journal of Marketing* 30, no. 1 (January 1966): 1–3.

Avilés, William. *Global Capitalism, Democracy, and Civil-Military Relations in Colombia.* New York: State University of New York Press, 2007.

Baburaj, P., and C. Saratchandran, dir. *1000 Days & a Dream.* DVD. Third Eye Communications, Thripunithura, India, 2006.

Backer, Bill. *The Care and Feeding of Ideas.* New York: Times Books, 1994.

"Backwash: Coke Returns from India Exile: An Interview with George Fernandes." *Multinational Monitor,* July–August 1995, 32–34.

Bair, Jennifer. "From the Politics of Development to the Challenges of Globalization." *Globalizations* 4, no. 4 (2007): 486–99.

Bakan, Joel. *The Corporation: The Pathological Pursuit of Profit and Power.* New York: Free Press, 2005.

Bakshi, Rajni. "'Development, Not Destruction': Alternative Politics in the Making." *Economic and Political Weekly* 31, no. 5 (February 3, 1996): 255–57.

Balakrishna, P., and B. Sidharth. "MNCs: Not above Flouting Rules." *Hindu Business Line,* April 9, 2003.

Banet-Weiser, Sarah, and Roopali Mukherjee. *Commodity Activism: Cultural Resistance in Neoliberal Times.* New York: New York University Press, 2012.

Bannerjee, Nantoo. *The Real Thing: Coke's Bumpy Ride through India.* Kolkata: Frontpage Publications, 2009.

Baran, Paul A., and Paul M. Sweezy. *Monopoly Capital: An Essay on the American Economic and Social Order.* New York: Monthly Review Press, 1966.

Barlow, Maude, and Tony Clarke. *Blue Gold: The Fight to Stop the Corporate Theft of the World's Water.* New York: New Press, 2002.

Barnet, Richard, and Ronald Miller. *Global Reach: The Power of the Multinational Corporations.* New York: Simon & Schuster, 1974.

Basheer, KPM. "Coke, Pepsi Disappear from Kerala Shops." *The Hindu,* April 12, 2003.

———. "A Lost Battle: Plachimada's Victims May Never Get Coke's Compensation." *The Hindu,* February 7, 2016.

Baudrillard, Jean. *Simulations.* New York: Semiotext(e), 1983.

Beckert, Sven. *Empire of Cotton: A Global History.* New York: Vintage Books, 2014.

Bergquist, Charles. *Labor and the Course of American Democracy: US History in Latin American Perspective.* London: Verso, 1996.

———. *Labor in Latin America: Comparative Essays on Chile, Argentina, Venezuela, and Colombia.* Stanford, CA: Stanford University Press, 1986.

———, ed. *Violence in Colombia: The Contemporary Crisis in Historical Perspective.* Wilmington, DE: SR Books, 1992.

Bergquist, Charles, Ricardo Peñaranda, and Gonzalo Sánchez G., eds. *Violence in Colombia, 1990–2000: Waging War and Negotiating Peace.* Wilmington, DE: SR Books, 2001.

Beyer, Chris H. *Coca-Cola Girls: An Advertising Art History.* Portland, OR: Collectors Press, 2000.

"Best Global Brands 2006: A Ranking by Brand Value." Interbrand and *BusinessWeek.* www.interbrand.com/best-brands/best-global-brands/2006/ranking. Accessed December 15, 2018.

Bhatnagar, Parija. "Coke Slaps On New Tagline." CNNMoney.com, December 8, 2005. https://money.cnn.com/2005/12/08/news/fortune500/coke_meeting/index.htm. Accessed September 11, 2018.

Bushan, Chandra. "Bottled Loot." *Frontline* 23, no. 7, April 8–21, 2006.

Bijoy, C.R. "Kerala's Plachimada Struggle." *Economic and Political Weekly* 41, no. 41 (2006): 4332–33.

———. "Adivasi Groups vs. Coca-Cola." *Ghadar: A Publication of the Forum of Inquilabi Leftists* 10 (September 2006). http://ghadar.insaf.net/September2006 /pdf/Bijoy.pdf. Accessed September 11, 2018.

Bist, Raju. "India's Cola Controversy Widens." *Asia Times,* August 8, 2003.

Biswas, Arijit, and Anindya Sen. "Coke vs Pepsi: Local and Global Strategies." *Economic and Political Weekly* 34, no. 26 (1999): 1704–5.

Blanding, Michael. "The Case against Coke." *The Nation,* May 1, 2006. www.thenation .com/article/case-against-coke. Accessed September 11, 2018.

———. *The Coke Machine: The Dirty Truth Behind the World's Favorite Soft Drink.* New York: Avery, 2010.

———. "Coke: The New Nike." *The Nation,* March 24, 2005. www.thenation.com /article/coke-new-nike. Accessed September 11, 2018.

———. Response to letter to editor from Ed Potter, director Global Labor Relations, The Coca-Cola Company. *The Nation,* May 22, 2006. www.thenation .com/article/letters-133. Accessed September 11, 2018.

Boltanski, Luc, and Eve Chiapello. *The New Spirit of Capitalism.* New York: Verso, 2005.

Bonilla González, Ricardo. "Empleo y política sectorial." In *La falacia neoliberal: crítica y alternativas,* ed. Darío I. Restrepo Botero, 205–30. Bogotá: Universidad Nacional de Colombia, 2003.

Borda Carranza, Alberto. *Cocacolos, ye-yés y go-gós: Recuerdos de una época feliz.* Bogotá: Bitácora, 2014.

Brenner, Aaron, Robert Brenner, and Cal Winslow. *Rebel Rank and File: Labor Militancy and Revolt from Below during the Long 1970s.* New York: Verso, 2010.

Brown, Elaine. *A Taste of Power: A Black Woman's Story.* New York: Anchor Books, 1992.

Brown, Elspeth. *The Corporate Eye: Photography and the Rationalization of American Commercial Culture, 1884–1929.* Baltimore: Johns Hopkins University Press, 2005.

Brugmann, Jeb, and C.K. Prahalad, "Co-creating Business's New Social Compact." *Harvard Business Review,* February 2007, 80–90.

Burns Smith, Amy. "Make Every Drop Count." www.amyburnssmith.com /#!project07/c1208. Accessed September 12, 2018.

Business for Social Responsibility. "Drinking It In: The Evolution of a Global Water Stewardship Program at The Coca-Cola Company." March 2008. www.bsr.org /reports/Coke_Water_Study_March_2008.pdf. Accessed September 11, 2018.

Caballero Truyol, Tomás, and Jhon Polo Escalante, "La industria en Barranquilla: Alimentos y bebidas durante el transcurso de la Segunda Guerra Mundial." Thesis, Universidad del Atlántico, Barranquilla, 2006.

Cadavid, Jorge H. "*Revista Ilustrada* (1898–1899): De la ilustración al Modernismo." *Boletín Cultural y Bibliográfico* 36, no. 31 (1994): 29–43.

"Calling Attention to Matter of Urgent Public Importance." *Lok Sabha Debates* 6, no. 48 (August 8, 1977): 11–26.

California Safety Compliance Corporation. "Workplace Assessments in Colombia." Assessment of Colombian Coca-Cola bottling plants. 2005.

Camacho Arango, Carlos. *"Respice polum:* Las relaciones entre Colombia y Estados Unidos en el siglo XX y los usos (y abusos) de una locución Latina." *Historia y sociedad* 19 (2010): 175–201.

Camacho Guizado, Alvaro. *Capital extranjero: Subdesarollo Colombiano.* Bogotá: Punto de Lanza, 1972.

Capparell, Stephanie. *The Real Pepsi Challenge: The Inspirational Story of Breaking the Color Barrier in American Business.* New York: Wall Street Journal Books, 2007.

Caraballo Cárdenas, Sergio Alberto. "Colombia el primer país de América Latina en lanzar El Lado Coca-Cola de la Vida." RRPPnet.com, August 16, 2006.

Cardoso, Fernando Henrique, and Enzo Faletto. *Dependency and Development in Latin America.* 1969. Berkeley: University of California Press, 1973.

Caring for Climate. "The CEO Water Mandate: An Initiative by Business Leaders in Partnership with the International Community." http://caringforclimate.org /resources/the-ceo-water-mandate-an-initiative-by-business-leaders-in-partner- ship-with-the-international-community. Accessed September 11, 2018.

Casanova, Pascale. *The World Republic of Letters.* Cambridge, MA: Harvard University Press, 2007.

Castells, Manuel. "Communication, Power and Counter-power in the Network Society." *International Journal of Communication* 1 (2007): 238–66.

Center for Science in the Public Interest. *Liquid Candy: How Soft Drinks Are Harming Americans' Health.* Washington, DC, 2005.

Centre for Science and Environment (CSE). *Analysis of Pesticide Residues in Bottled Water.* January 2003. https://cdn.cseindia.org/attachments/0.51403600_ 1499070710_Delhi_uploadfinal_sn.pdf. Accessed August 30, 2018.

———. *Analysis of Pesticide Residues in Soft Drinks.* August 5, 2003. https://cdn. cseindia.org/attachments/0.08790400_1498992534_SOFTDRINK.pdf. Accessed August 30, 2018.

———. *Analysis of Pesticide Residues in Soft Drinks.* August 2, 2006. www .indiaenvironmentportal.org.in/files/labreport2006.pdf. Accessed August 30, 2018.

———. "Colonisation's Dirty Dozen." *Down to Earth,* August 15, 2003, 31–41.

———. "Hard Truths about Soft Drinks." Last updated August 5, 2003. www .cseindia.org/node/507. Accessed September 11, 2018.

———. "Pesticide Residues in Bottled Water." *Down to Earth,* February 15, 2003.

———. "Timeline." www.cseindia.org/cseaboutus/timeline.htm. Accessed April 12, 2008; page discontinued.

Chadha, Monica. "Coke Tries to Can Indian Poster." BBC News, July 17, 2005. http:// news.bbc.co.uk/2/hi/south_asia/4690703.stm. Accessed September 11, 2018.

Chandler, Alfred D., and Bruce Mazlich, eds., *Leviathans: Multinational Corpora- tions and the New Global History.* New York: Cambridge University Press, 2005.

Chandra, Bipan, Mirdula Mukherjee, and Aditya Mukherjee. *India after Independence, 1947–2000.* New Delhi: Penguin Books, 2000.

Chandrika, R. *To Protect Our Right over Our Water.* Lok Samiti (People's Group), 2006.

Chaudhary, Archana. "Farmers Fight Coca-Cola as India's Groundwater Dries Up." Bloomberg.com, October 9, 2014. www.bloomberg.com/news/articles/2014-10-08/farmers-fight-coca-cola-as-india-s-groundwater-dries-up. Accessed December 15, 2018.

Chawla, Prabhu. "Will Meridien Hotel Turn Out to Be a Pot of Gold for Charanjit Singh?" *India Today,* August 5, 2013, updated September 15, 2014. http://indiatoday.intoday.in/story/will-meridien-hotel-turn-out-to-be-a-pot-of-gold-for-charanjit-singh/1/392394.html. Accessed September 11, 2018.

Chatterjee, Partha. *Nationalist Thought and the Colonial World: A Derivative Discourse.* Minneapolis: University of Minnesota Press, 1993.

Chomsky, Aviva. *Linked Labor Histories: New England, Colombia and the Making of a Global Working Class.* Durham, NC: Duke University Press, 2008.

Christian Aid. *Behind the Mask: The Real Face of Corporate Social Responsibility.* January 21, 2004. www.st-andrews.ac.uk/media/csear/app2practice-docs/CSEAR_behind-the-mask.pdf. Accessed September 4, 2018.

Citizens for Tax Justice. "Fortune 500 Companies Hold a Record $2.4 Trillion Offshore." March 3, 2016. http://ctj.org/pdf/pre0316.pdf. Accessed September 13, 2018.

Civico, Aldo. *The Para-State: An Ethnography of Colombia's Death Squads.* Berkeley: University of California Press, 2016.

Coca-Cola Company, The (cited as TCCC). "Active Healthy Living." www.coca-colacompany.com/sustainabilityreport/me/active-healthy-living.html#section-putting-calorie-information-right-up-front. Accessed July 12, 2016; page discontinued.

———. "[2004] Annual Report to U.S. Securities and Exchange Commission, Form 10-K."

———. "At Coca-Cola, We Support Physical Activity Programs." www.coca-colacompany.com/stories/at-coca-cola-we-support-physical-activity-programs. Accessed May 7, 2013; page discontinued.

———. "Celebrating Advertising History." www.thecoca-colacompany.com/presscenter/presskit_hilltop_behind_the_scenes.html. Accessed January 19, 2008; page discontinued.

———. *The Coca-Cola Company: An Illustrated Profile of a Worldwide Company.* The Coca-Cola Company, 1974.

———. "The Coca-Cola Company Joins UN Global Compact." Press Release, March 8, 2006.

———. "The Coca-Cola Foundation." www.coca-colacompany.com/our-company/the-coca-cola-foundation. Accessed September 11, 2018.

———. "Coca-Cola Launches Global EKOCENTER Partnership to Deliver Safe Drinking Water and Basic Necessities to Rural Communities." Press Release. September 24, 2013. www.csrwire.com/press_releases/36151-Coca-Cola-Launches-

Global-EKOCENTER-Partnership-to-Deliver-Safe-Drinking-Water-and-Basic-Necessities-to-Rural-Communities. Accessed September 11, 2018.

———. "Coca-Cola North America Marketing and Innovation Focuses on Full Portfolio of Drink Brands." Press Release. February 3, 2006.

———. "The Coca-Cola System." www.coca-colacompany.com/our-company/the-coca-cola-system. Accessed September 5, 2018.

———. "The Coca-Cola System—History of Bottling." www.coca-colacompany.com/our-company/history-of-bottling. Accessed September 27, 2018.

———. "Collaborating to Replenish the Water We Use." August 29, 2018. www.coca-colacompany.com/stories/collaborating-to-replenish-the-water-we-use. Accessed September 11, 2018.

———. "Community Water Partnerships." www.livepositively.com/#/community_water_partnerships. Accessed August 10, 2010; page discontinued.

———. "EKOCENTER Progress Update." December 6, 2017. www.coca-colacompany.com/stories/infographic-ekocenter-progress-update. Accessed September 11, 2018.

———. "The Facts." www.cokefacts.org/facts/facts_co_fact_sheet.shtml. Accessed May 21, 2006; page discontinued.

———. "Global School Beverage Guidelines." www.coca-colacompany.com/stories/global-school-beverage-guidelines. Accessed September 11, 2018.

———. "Governance and Ethics." www.thecoca-colacompany.com/citizenship/governance_ethics.html. Accessed July 26, 2010; page discontinued.

———. "Haiti Hope Project." www.livepositively.com/#/haitihope. Accessed August 10, 2010; page discontinued.

———. "Improving Our Water Efficiency." August 29, 2018. www.coca-colacompany.com/stories/setting-a-new-goal-for-water-efficiency. Accessed September 11, 2018.

———. "India: The Key Facts." www.cokefacts.org/India/facts_in_keyfacts.shtml. Accessed August 8, 2007; page discontinued.

———. "Make Every Drop Count." www2.coca-cola.com/makeeverydropcount. Accessed October 1, 2007; page discontinued.

———. "Responsible Water Management in India and Beyond." February 15, 2016. www.coca-colacompany.com/stories/responsible-water-management-in-india-and-beyond. Accessed September 11, 2018.

———. "Supplier Guiding Principles." 2007.

———. "TERI University and Coke Launch Water Studies Program." May 13, 2014. www.coca-colacompany.com/stories/teri-university-and-coke-launch-water-studies-program. Accessed September 11, 2018.

———. "Workplace Rights and Coca-Cola in Colombia Update." www.thecoca-colacompany.com/presscenter/viewpointscolombian.html. Accessed August 25, 2007; page discontinued.

———. "Workplace Rights Policy." 2007.

"Coca-Cola as Sold throughout the World." *Red Barrel—Special Overseas Edition,* February 15, 1929. Reprinted in *Coca-Cola Overseas,* February 1954, 3.

"Coca-Cola Discloses More of Its Funding on Health Efforts." *Houston Chronicle,* March 24, 2016. www.houstonchronicle.com/business/article/Coca-Cola-discloses-more-of-its-funding-on-health-7045103.php. Accessed September 11, 2018.

"Coca-Cola es así." *Bebidas y Manjares* (Bogotá) 12 (1985): 11–13.

"Coca-Cola es así." *Semana* (Bogotá), October 22, 1990.

Coca-Cola Export Corporation and Jam Handy. *Community of the World.* Film Strip, 1961. MPBRSD, LC.

———. *Pearl of the Orient.* Film strip, 1954. CE, MPBRSD, LC.

———. *Wonderful World.* 1954. CE, MPBRSD, LC.

Coca-Cola FEMSA. "Historia." www.cocacola.com.co/est/lo/conecta_historia.asp. Accessed May 5, 2006; page discontinued.

———. "[2003] Annual Report to U.S. Securities and Exchange Commission, Form 20-F."

Coca-Cola India. "About Us." www.coca-colaindia.com/aboutus/aboutus_ccindia .aspx. Accessed January 6, 2009; page discontinued.

———. "Facts and Myths About Hindustan Coca-Cola's Varanasi Plant." Accessed. www.coca-colaindia.com/facts-myths/varanasi. Accessed April 20, 2016; page discontinued.

———. "Health and Wellness." www.coca-colaindia.com/health_wellness/health_ wellness_text.asp#pesticide. Accessed August 1, 2008; page discontinued.

"Coca-Cola India's Thirst for the Rural Market." ICMR Center for Management Research. June 18, 2009.

"Coca-Cola to Sell Aqua-Chem Units to Paris Company." *Wall Street Journal,* July 15, 1981.

"Coca-Cola Statement re: Compensation." April 24, 2016. www.business-humanrights.org/en/coca-cola-lawsuit-re-india. Accessed September 11, 2018.

"Coca-Cola Wants to Make India Its Third-Largest Market Globally." *Hindu Business Line,* August 31, 2017.

Collingsworth, Terry. "'Corporate Social Responsibility,' Unmasked." *St. Thomas Law Review* 16, no. 4 (Summer 2004): 669–86.

Coombe, Rosemary. *The Cultural Life of Intellectual Properties: Authorship, Appropriation and the Law.* Durham, NC: Duke University Press, 1998.

Cooper, Kenneth J. "Hindu Nationalists Target U.S. Products." *Washington Post,* June 19, 1998.

Copland, Ian. "The Master and the Maharajas: The Sikh Princes and the East Punjab Massacres of 1947." *Modern Asian Studies* 36. No. 3 (July 2002): 657–704.

Corbett, Martin. "I Sing The Body (In)Corporate: Identity, Displacement and the Radical Priority of Reception." Paper presented to the Critical Management Conference, Lancaster University, July 2003, www.mngt.waikato.ac.nz/ejrot /cmsconference/2003/proceedings/music/corbett.pdf. Accessed September 11, 2018.

Cowie, Jefferson. *Capital Moves: RCA's Seventy-Year Quest for Cheap Labor.* Ithaca, NY: Cornell University, 1999.

Cross, Gary. *All-Consuming Century: Why Commercialism Won in Modern America.* New York: Columbia University Press, 2000.

Cruz Cárdenas, Antonio. *Todavía sin final . . . selección periodística desde 1950*. Bogotá: Universidad Externado de Colombia, 2001.

Curtis, Wayne. "Rum and Coca-Cola: The Murky Derivations of a Sweet Drink and a Sassy World War II Song." *American Scholar* 75, no. 3 (Summer 2006): 64–70.

Daft, Douglas. "Globalization." *Vital Speeches of the Day* 66, no. 19 (July 15, 2000): 606–8.

Das Gupta, Surajeet. "How India Became Pepsi's Right Choice." *Business Standard*, March 27, 2014. www.business-standard.com/article/companies/how-india-became-pepsi-s-right-choice-114032701308_1.html. Accessed September 11, 2018.

Davies, Robert. "Making Change Happen." In *Making Change: Review, 2006–2007*. International Business Leaders Forum, 2007. www.iblf.org/resources/review1.htm. Page discontinued.

Dávila, Carlos. "Estado de los estudios sobre la historia empresarial de Colombia." In *Empresa e historia en América Latina: Un balance historiográfico*, ed. Carlos Dávila, 1–25. Bogotá: Tercer Mundo, S.A., 1996.

Debord, Guy and Gil J. Wolman. "A User's Guide to Détournement." 1956. Translated by Ken Knabb. In *Situationists International Anthology*, 14–20. Berkeley: Bureau of Public Secrets, 2006.

De Grazia, Victoria. *Irresistible Empire: America's Advance through Twentieth-Century Europe*. Cambridge, MA: Harvard University Press, 2005.

De La Pedraja, René. *Wars of Latin America, 1948–1982: The Rise of the Guerrillas*. Jefferson, NC: McFarland, 2013.

del Carmen Suescun Pozas, María. "From Reading to Seeing: Doing and Undoing Imperialism in the Visual Arts." In *Close Encounters of Empire: Writing the Cultural History of U.S.–Latin American Relations*, ed. Gilbert Joseph, Catherine LeGrand, and Ricardo Salvatore, 525–55. Durham, NC: Duke University Press, 1998.

Deutsch, Claudia. "Coca-Cola Reaches into Past for New Chief." *New York Times*, May 5, 2004.

Dicke, Thomas. *Franchising in America: The Development of a Business Method, 1840–1980*. Chapel Hill: University of North Carolina Press, 1992.

Doane, Deborah. "An Alternative Perspective on Brands: Markets and Morals." In *Brands and Branding*, ed. Rita Clifton, 185–98. New York: Bloomberg Press, 2009.

Dobhal, Shailesh. "The Real Thing." *Business Today*, May 23, 2004.

Domosh, Mona. *American Commodities in an Age of Empire*. New York: Routledge, 2006.

Donaldson, Thomas, and Lee E. Preston. "The Stakeholder Theory of the Corporation: Concepts, Evidence, and Implications." *Academy of Management Review* 20, no. 1 (1995): 65–91.

Drake, Paul W. *The Money Doctor in the Andes: The Kemmerer Missions, 1923–1933*. Durham, NC: Duke University Press, 1989.

———. "The Origins of United States Economic Supremacy in South America: Colombia's Dance of the Millions, 1923–33." Washington, DC: Woodrow Wilson International Center for Scholars, Smithsonian Institution, 1979.

Drew, Georgina. "From the Groundwater Up: Asserting Water Rights in India." *Development* 51, no. 1 (2008): 37–41.

Drexler, Robert. *Colombia and the United States: Narcotics Traffic and a Failed Foreign Policy*. Jefferson, NC: McFarland, 1997.

Dudley, Steven. *Walking Ghosts: Murder and Guerrilla Politics in Colombia*. New York: Routledge, 2004.

Duffield, James E. (Ted), Jr. "As I Recall." MS. July 1975. MARBL, Emory University, MSS 10, box 82, folder 3.

"Eleventh Circuit Dismisses Alien Tort Statute Claims Against Coca-Cola Under *Iqbal*'s Plausibility Pleading Standard," *Harvard Law Review* 123 (December 2009): 580–87.

Elkington, John. *Cannibals with Forks: The Triple Bottom Line of 21st Century Business*. Gabriola Island, BC: New Society Publishers, 1998.

Elmore, Bartow J. *Citizen Coke: The Making of Coca-Cola Capitalism*. New York: Norton, 2015.

Energy and Resources Institute, The (TERI). *Independent Third Party Assessment of Coca-Cola Facilities in India*. New Delhi: TERI, 2008.

Esterl, Mike, and Chelsey Dulaney. "Coca-Cola Owes $3.3 Billion in Taxes Over Foreign Transfer Licensing." *Wall Street Journal,* September 18, 2015.

Evans, Michael. "The New Chiquita Papers: Secret Testimony and Internal Records Identify Banana Executives Who Bankrolled Terror in Colombia." NSA. https://nsarchive.gwu.edu/briefing-book/colombia-chiquita-papers/2017-04-24/new-chiquita-papers-secret-testimony-internal-records-identify-banana-executives-who-bankrolled. Accessed November 11, 2018.

Ewen, Stuart. *Captains of Consciousness: Advertising and the Social Roots of Consumer Culture*. New York: Basic Books, 2001.

Faber, Daniel. *Capitalizing on Environmental Injustice: The Polluter-Industrial Complex in the Age of Globalization*. Lanham, MD: Rowman & Littlefield, 2008.

Faizi, S. "Why Plachimada?" *Down to Earth,* July 31, 2015.

Fals Borda, Orlando. *Ciencia propria y colonialism intellectual*. Bogotá: Editorial Oveja Negra, 1971.

Farley, James. "Advertising as a World Force." Speech to the Advertising Club of New York. *Coca-Cola Bottler, July 1949. Advertiser's Digest* 15, no. 9 (September 1950): 1–3. James Farley Papers, MD, LC, reel 37.

———. "Brand Names: A Basis for Unity, Our Greatest Hope of Expanding World Trade." Speech at the Brand Names Foundation, April 16, 1952. James Farley Papers, MD, LC, reel 38. Published in *Vital Speeches of the Day* 18, no. 15 (May 15, 1952): 473–75.

———. "The Influence of Foreign Markets on Your Business: A Major Front in World Power Struggle." Speech to the American Society of Sales Executives, May 7, 1959. *Vital Speeches of the Day* 25, no. 17 (June 15, 1959): 535–37.

———. "Sovereignty and Integrity: Need for a Code of Simple Morality Among Nations." Speech at the National Foreign Trade Convention, November 20, 1957. *Vital Speeches of the Day* 24, no. 6 (January 1, 1958): 172–74.

———. "Trademarks: America's Goodwill Ambassadors." Speech ca. 1952. Mark Pendergrast Manuscript Collection no. 741, Emory University, box 1, folder 18

———. "Troubled International Waters: Some Navigational Lights." Speech to the Executives' Club of Chicago, March 15, 1963. *Vital Speeches of the Day* 29, no. 13 (April 15, 1963): 389–91.

Farnsworth-Alvear, Ann. *Dulcinea in the Factory: Myths, Morals, Men, and Women in Columbia's Industrial Experiment, 1905–1960.* Durham, NC: Duke University Press, 2000.

Featherstone, David. *Resistance, Space and Political Identities: The Making of Counter-Global Networks.* Chichester, England: Wiley-Blackwell, 2008.

Ferdman, Roberto A. "Why the Sugar Industry Hates the FDA's New Nutrition Facts Label." *Washington Post,* May 20, 2016. www.washingtonpost.com/news /wonk/wp/2016/05/20/why-the-sugar-industry-hates-the-fdas-new-nutrition-facts-label. Accessed September 11, 2018.

Fisher, Mark. *Capitalism Realism: Is There No Alternative?* London: Zero Books, 2009.

Fleming, Peter, and Marc T. Jones. *The End of Corporate Social Responsibility: Crisis & Critique.* London: SAGE, 2013.

Fomento Económico Mexicano S.A. de C.V. (FEMSA). "Historia Corporativa." www.femsa.com/es/about/history. Accessed August 11, 2007; page discontinued.

———. "Mexico." www.femsa.com/en/business/coca_cola_femsa/mexico.htm. Accessed August 11, 2007; page discontinued.

Ferguson, Roderick A. *The Reorder of Things: The University and Its Pedagogies of Minority Difference.* Minneapolis: University of Minnesota Press, 2012.

Finan, Irial. "10 Years: Coke's Bottling Investments Group Marks a Milestone." August 11, 2015. www.coca-colacompany.com/coca-cola-unbottled/business /2015/10-years-cokes-bottling-investments-group-marks-a-milestone. Accessed September 11, 2018.

Foster, Robert J. *Coca-Globalization: Following Soft Drinks from New York to New Guinea.* New York: Palgrave Macmillan, 2008.

———. "Show and Tell: Teaching Critical Fetishism with a Bottle of Coke®." *Anthropology News* 49, no. 4 (2008): 38.

Fox, Stephen. *The Mirror Makers: A History of American Advertising and Its Creators.* 1984. Urbana: University of Illinois Press, 1997.

Frank, Dana. *Buy American: The Untold Story of Economic Nationalism.* Boston: Beacon Press, 1999.

Frank, Thomas. *The Conquest of Cool: Business Culture, Counterculture, and the Roots of Hip Consumerism.* Chicago: University of Chicago Press, 1998.

Freeman, R. Edward. *Strategic Management: A Stakeholder Approach.* Boston: Pitman, 1984.

Friedman, Milton. "The Social Responsibility of Business Is to Increase Its Profits." *New York Times Magazine,* September 13, 1970.

Frundt, Henry J. *Refreshing Pauses: Coca-Cola and Human Rights in Guatemala.* New York: Praeger, 1987.

Gandhi, M. K. "Gandhi in conversation with Ramachandran." October 10–11, 1924. www.bombaymuseum.org/ahimsa/sec5/swadeshi.html. Page discontinued.

———. "The Swadeshi Movement." In *Gandhi: Selected Writings*, ed. Ronald Duncan, 127–33. Mineola, NY: Dover, 2005.

Gandhi, M. K., and Anthony Parel. *Hind Swaraj and Other Writings.* Cambridge: Cambridge University Press, 1997.

Ganguly, Dibeyendu. "Saffron Protests Black Out Cola Concerts." *Economic Times,* May 24, 1998.

Garay, Luis Jorge, Luis Felipe Quintero, Jesús Alberto Villamil, Jorge Tovar, Abdul Fatat, Sandra Gómez, Eliana Restrepo, and Beatriz Yemail. *Colombia: Estructura industrial e internacionalización, 1967–1996.* Bogotá: Departamento Nacional de Planeación, 1998.

García AbelloYezid. "La reforma laboral: adecuación de la legislación del trabajo a las políticas neoliberales." *Deslinde,* June–July 1991, 77–91

Gargan, Edward. "A Revolution Transforms India: Socialism's Out, Free Market In." *New York Times,* March 29, 1992, 1.

Gentleman, Amelia. "Coke and Pepsi Try to Reassure India That Drinks Are Safe." *New York Times,* August 6, 2006.

———. "For 2 Giants of Soft Drinks, a Crisis in a Crucial Market." *New York Times,* August 23, 2006.

———. "India Widens Ban on Coke and Pepsi." *New York Times,* August 7, 2006.

Gerbens-Leenes, Winnie, Arjen Hoekstra, Richard Holland, Greg Koch, Jack Moss, Pancho Ndebele, Stuart Orr, Mariska Ronteltap, and Eric de Ruyter van Stevenink. "Water Neutrality: A Concept Paper." November 20, 2007. www.researchgate.net/publication/323150858_Water_neutrality_a_concept_paper. Accessed September 11, 2018.

Ghosh, Bishnupriya. *Global Icons: Apertures to the Popular.* Durham, NC: Duke University Press, 2011.

Gilbert, Sarah. "Vitaminwater Label, Name Misleading, Judge Tells Coca-Cola." DailyFinance.com. July 28, 2010. www.dailyfinance.com/story/company-news/vitaminwater-label-name-misleading-judge-tells-coca-co/19569378. Page discontinued.

Gill, Lesley. *A Century of Violence in a Red City: Popular Struggle, Counterinsurgency, and Human Rights in Colombia.* Durham, NC: University of North Carolina Press, 2016.

———. "Labor and Human Rights: 'The Real Thing' in Colombia." *Transforming Anthropology* 13, no. 2 (October 2005): 110–15.

———. "The Limits of Solidarity: Labor and Transnational Organizing Against Coca-Cola." *American Ethnologist* 36, no. 4 (November 2009): 667–77.

———. "'Right There With You': Coca-Cola, Labor Restructuring, and Political Violence in Colombia." *Critique of Anthropology* 27, no. 3 (2007): 235–60.

Gilman, Nils. "Modernization Theory, The Highest Stage of American Intellectual History." In *Staging Growth: Modernization, Development and the Global Cold*

War,* ed. David C. Engerman, Nils Gilman, Mark H. Haefele, and Michael E. Latham, 47–80. Boston: University of Massachusetts Press, 2003.

Giridharadas, Anand. "Boycotts Minus the Pain." *New York Times,* October 11, 2009.

Gladwin, Thomas N., and Ingo Walter. *Multinationals under Fire: Lessons in the Management of Conflict.* New York: John Wiley & Sons, 1980.

Global Water Challenge. "Mission." www.globalwaterchallenge.org/about-us/our-story.php. Accessed August 12, 2010; page discontinued.

———. "New World Program." www.globalwaterchallenge.org. Accessed September 11, 2018.

Gómez, Luis, Enrique Jacoby, Lorena Ibarra, Diego Lucumí, Alexandra Hernandez, Diana Parra, Alex Florindo, and Pedro Halla. "Sponsorship of Physical Activity Programs by the Sweetened Beverages Industry: Public Health or Public Relations." *Revista de Saúde Pública* 45, no. 2 (2011): 423–27.

Gregory, Sean. "Is Vitaminwater Really a Healthy Drink?" *Time,* July 30, 2010. http://content.time.com/time/business/article/0,8599,2007106,00.html. Accessed September 11, 2018.

Greising, David. *I'd Like the World to Buy a Coke: The Life and Leadership of Roberto Goizueta.* New York: Wiley, 1998.

Guáqueta, Alexandra, and Yadira Orsini, *Empresarios y reintegración: Casos, experiencias y lecciones.* Bogotá: Fundación Ideas Para la Paz, December 2007.

Guha, Ramachandra. *How Much Should a Person Consume? Environmentalism in India and the United States.* Berkeley: University of California Press, 2006.

Fals Frank, André. *Latin America: Underdevelopment or Revolution.* New York: Monthly Review Press, 1969.

Guthrie, Amy and Mike Esterl. "Soda Sales in Mexico Rise Despite Tax." *Wall Street Journal,* May 3, 2016.

Haines, Gerald K. "Under the Eagle's Wing: The Franklin Roosevelt Administration Forges an American Hemisphere." *Diplomatic History* 1, no. 4 (October 1977): 373–88.

Hajoori & Sons. "Company Profile." www.sosyo-thesoftdrink.com/sosyo/products_profile.htm#. Accessed June 27, 2008; page discontinued.

Halbert, Terry. "Coke in Kerala." *Journal of Business Ethics Education*, 3, no. 1 (2006): 119–141.

Hale, Thomas. "Silent Reform through the Global Compact." *UN Chronicle* 44, no. 1 (March 2007): 26–31. https://unchronicle.un.org/article/essay-silent-reform-through-global-compact. Accessed September 4, 2018.

Hamburger, Tom and Kim Geiger. "Beverage Industry Douses Tax on Soft Drinks." *Los Angeles Times,* February 7, 2010.

Hardt, Michael, and Antonio Negri. *Commonwealth.* Cambridge, MA: Harvard University Press, 2009.

Harrison, DeSales. *"Footprints on the Sands of Time": A History of Two Men and the Fulfillment of a Dream.* New York: Newcomen Society in North America, 1969.

Harvey, David. *A Brief History of Neoliberalism*. New York: Oxford University Press, 2005.

———. *The Condition of Postmodernity*. Cambridge: Blackwell, 1989.

———. *The New Imperialism*. Oxford: Oxford University Press, 2003.

Haslam, Paul Alexander. "Is Corporate Social Responsibility a Constructivist Regime? Evidence from Latin America." *Global Society* 21, no. 2 (2007): 269–96.

Hays, Constance L. "Global Crisis for Coca-Cola, or a Pause that Refreshes?" *New York Times,* November 1, 1998.

———. *The Real Thing: Truth and Power at The Coca-Cola Company*. New York: Random House, 2004.

"HC Orders Government to Test Pepsi Products." *Tribune* (Chandigarh), August 12, 2003.

Heller, Steven. "Jack Potter, 74, Illustrator Who Turned to Teaching, Dies." *New York Times,* September 23, 2002.

Henderson, James. *Modernization in Colombia: The Laureano Gomez Years, 1889–1965*. Gainesville: University Press of Florida, 2001.

Herrera Duque, Diego Alexander. "De nadaístas, 'cocacolos' y hippies, expresiones juveniles en la Medellín de los años sesenta." *Alma Mater: Agenda Cultural de la Universidad de Antioquia* 144 (June 2008).

Hills, Jonathan, and Richard Welford. "A Case Study: Coca-Cola and Water in India." *Corporate Social Responsibility and Environmental Management* 12, no. 3 (2005): 168–77.

Hindustan Coca-Cola Beverages Pvt. Ltd. "Overview." www.hindustancoca-cola .com/about_us.aspx. Accessed September 11, 2018.

Hostetter, Christina. "Sugar Allies: How Hershey and Coca-Cola Used Government Contracts and Sugar Exemptions to Elude Sugar Rationing Regulations." Master's Thesis, University of Maryland, 2004.

"How Coke Runs a Foreign Empire." *Business Week,* August 25, 1973.

Hozzman, Edgar. "Sólo para mayores de 40 años: La época de los Cocacolos, camajanes y pandillas." *Ver Bien Magazin,* January 17, 2012.

"The 100 Top Brands." *Business Week,* August 1, 2005, 90–94.

Huneeus, Alejandra. "Megaembotelladoras al ataque." *América Economía,* May 1994.

Hymson, Laura. "The Company That Taught the World to Sing: Coca-Cola, Globalization, and the Cultural Politics of Branding in the Twentieth Century." PhD diss., University of Michigan, 2011.

India Resource Center. "About India Resource Center." www.indiaresource.org /about/index.html. Accessed September 11, 2018.

"India's Cola Crisis Bubbles Up." CNN.com, August 18, 2003. www.cnn.com/2003 /WORLD/asiapcf/south/08/18/india.drinks. Accessed September 11, 2018.

"Indian Government Allows Coke to Buy Out Shareholders in Hindustan Coca-Cola." *Hindu Business Line,* November 25, 2005.

"Indian Officials Order Coca-Cola Plant Closed for Using Too Much Water." Agence France-Presse. *Guardian,* June 18, 2014.

"In Hot Water." *The Economist,* October 6, 2005.

Inter-American Development Bank. "Se buscan buenos empleos: Los mercados laborales en América Latina." Departamento de Investigaciones, Banco Interamericano de Desarrollo, Washington, DC, 2004. https://publications.iadb.org /bitstream/handle/11319/7400/La-Realidad-Social-Una-introduccion-a-los-Problemas-y-Politicas-del-Desarrollo-Social-en-America-Latina-Modulo-V-Se-Buscan-Buenos-Empleos.pdf?sequence=1. Accessed December 10, 2018.

International Business Leaders Forum (IBLF). "About the International Business Leaders Forum." www.iblf.org/whoweare/aboutus.aspx. Accessed September 22, 2010; page discontinued.

———. "Dialogue on Business, Peace, Development and Human Rights in Colombia: A Summary of Contributions from Speakers and Participants at a Meeting in Bogotá, Colombia." July 24, 2006.

———. "Who We Are." www.iblf.org/Default.aspx. Accessed September 22, 2010; page discontinued.

International Business Leaders Forum, Fundación Ideas para la Paz, and United Nations Global Compact. "Dialogue on Business, Peace, Development and Human Rights in Colombia." Bogotá, July 24, 2006.

International Labor Organization. "Report Evaluation Mission Coca-Cola Bottling Plants in Colombia, June 30–July 11, 2008." October 8, 2008. https://laborrights .org/publications/report-evaluation-mission-coca-cola-bottling-plants-colombia. Accessed December 8, 2018.

International Labor Rights Fund. "Summary of Coca-Cola's Human Rights Violations in Colombia and Turkey." 2006.

Isdell, E. Neville. "Remarks at the WWF Annual Conference." Beijing, China, June 5, 2007.

Jacobs, Andrew, and Matt Richtel. "She Took on Colombia's Soda Industry. Then She Was Silenced." *New York Times,* November 13, 2017.

Jameson, Fredric. *Postmodernism, or, The Cultural Logic of Late Capitalism.* London: Verso, 1991.

"Joint Coca-Cola and IUF Statement." March 15, 2005. www.iufdocuments.org /www/documents/coca-cola/jtstate-e.pdf. Accessed September 11, 2018.

Jones, Geoffrey. *Multinationals and Global Capitalism: From the Nineteenth to the Twenty-First Century.* New York: Oxford University Press, 2005.

Joshi, Jitendra. "Pesticide Row May Have Ripple Effect in India." *Independent Online,* August 14, 2006.

Kadri, Meena. "Glocal-Cola: Visual Communications of Coca-Cola in India as a Site of Mediation between Global and Local Factors." *South Asia Journal for Culture* 1 (October 2006).

Kahn, E. J. *The Big Drink: The Story of Coca-Cola.* New York: Random House, 1960.

Karnani, Aneel. "The Case against Corporate Social Responsibility." *Wall Street Journal,* August 23, 2010.

Kaye, Jennifer, and Paul Argenti. "Coca-Cola India." Tuck School of Business at Dartmouth, 2004.

Keating, Christine. "Developmental Democracy and Its Inclusions: Globalization and the Transformation of Participation." *Signs: Journal of Women in Culture and Society* 29, no. 2 (2003): 417–37.

Keck, Margaret E., and Kathryn Sikkink. *Activists beyond Borders: Advocacy Networks in International Politics.* Ithaca, NY: Cornell University Press, 1998.

Khan, Yasmin. *The Great Partition: The Making of India and Pakistan.* New Haven: Yale University Press, 2007.

Killer Coke. "Another 'Classic Coke' Move to Deny and Delay Accountability for Human Rights Violations in Colombia." www.killercoke.org/restciuf.htm. Accessed May 23, 2006; page discontinued.

———. "Colleges, Universities and High Schools Active in the Campaign to Stop Killer Coke." www.killercoke.org/active-in-campaign.htm. Accessed September 21, 2008; page discontinued.

———. "Why the IUF Attacks Sinaltrainal." www.killercoke.org/iufsinal.htm. Accessed February 19, 2006; page discontinued.

Kirdahy, Matthew. "McDonald's Back in the Woods in Latin America." *Forbes,* April 23, 2007.

Kirsch, Stuart. *Mining Capitalism: The Relationship Between Corporations and Their Critics.* Berkeley: University of California Press, 2014.

Klein, Naomi. *No Logo.* New York: Picador, 2000.

Kochhar, Vikas, and Satya Pamula. "Coca-Cola Strengthens Its Bonds with India, Launches 'Little Drops of Joy.'" Coca-Cola India Press Release. August 17, 2007. www.andhranews.net/India/2007/August/17-Coca-Cola-Little-Drops-of-Joy .asp. Accessed September 11, 2018.

Koonan, Sujith. "Constitutionality of the Plachimada Tribunal Bill, 2011: An Assessment." *Law, Environment and Development Journal* 7 no. 2 (2011): 151–63.

———. "Legal Implications of Plachimada." Working Paper of the International Environmental Law Research Centre, May 2007. www.ielrc.org/content/w0705 .pdf. Accessed September 11, 2018.

Kopple, Barbara, dir. *American Dream.* 1990. DVD. Los Angeles: Miramax Home Entertainment, 2012.

Kornberg, Dana Nicole. "'Good Drinking Water Instead of Coca-Cola': Elaborating Ideas of Development through the Case of Coca-Cola Inda." Master's Thesis, University of Texas at Austin, 2007.

Kuisel, Richard F. *Seducing the French: The Dilemma of Americanization.* Berkeley: University of California Press, 1997.

Kumar, Shanti. *Gandhi Meets Primetime: Globalization and Nationalism in Indian Television.* Urbana: University of Illinois Press, 2006.

Kumar, Sunil. "Note on Farm Sector in Uttar Pradesh." Department of Planning, Government of Uttar Pradesh (October 2005).

Kurian, Boby. "Coca-Cola May Dump *Life ho to aisi* Campaign." *Hindu Business Line,* December 19, 2002.

Kytle, Beth, and John Gerard Ruggie. "Corporate Social Responsibility as Risk Management: A Model for Multinationals." Corporate Social Responsibility

Initiative Working Paper No. 10. Cambridge: John F. Kennedy School of Government, Harvard University, 2005.

Labelle, Maurice Jr M. "De-coca-colonizing Egypt: Globalization, Decolonization, and the Egyptian Boycott of Coca-Cola, 1966–1968." *Journal of Global History* 9 (2014): 122–42. doi:10.1017/S1740022813000521.

LaFeber, Walter. *Michael Jordan and the New Global Capitalism.* New York: Norton, 1999.

Laird, Pamela Walker. *Advertising Progress: American Business and the Rise of Consumer Marketing.* Baltimore: Johns Hopkins University Press, 1998.

Lakshmi, Rama. "Soda Giants Battle Public Panic." *Washington Post,* August 10, 2003.

Lappé, Anna, and Christina Bronsing-Lazalde. "How to Win against Big Soda." *New York Times,* October 15, 2017.

La Pulla. "Las dulces mentiras de los congresistas acerca de las bebidas azucaradas." *El Espectador,* December 16, 2016. www.elespectador.com/opinion/opinion/las-dulces-mentiras-de-los-congresistas-acerca-de-las-bebidas-azucaradas-columna-670621. Accessed September 11, 2018.

Largacha, Pablo. "Los resultados de la investigación, 'Desarollo, paz y derechos humanos en Colombia: Una agenda para las empresas.'" Speech, Encuentro Internacional de Responsabilidad Social Empresarial de la Asociación Nacional de Empresarios de Colombia, Cali, Colombia, October 11, 2006.

"Lawsuits against Coca-Cola Approved in India." Associated Press, February 25, 2011. www.business-humanrights.org/en/lawsuits-against-coca-cola-approved-in-india. Accessed September 11, 2018.

Lears, Jackson. *Fables of Abundance: A Cultural History of Advertising in America.* New York: Basic Books, 1995.

LeGrand, Catherine C. "The Colombian Crisis in Historical Perspective." *Canadian Journal of Latin American and Caribbean Studies* 28, nos. 55–56 (2003): 165–209

———. *Frontier Expansion and Peasant Protest in Colombia, 1850–1936.* Albuquerque: University of New Mexico Press, 1986.

Levenson-Estrada, Deborah. *Trade Unionists against Terror: Guatemala City, 1954–1985.* Chapel Hill: University of North Carolina Press, 1994.

Lichtenstein, Nelson. *The Retail Revolution: How Wal-Mart Created a Brave New World of Business.* New York: Picador, 2009.

Lok Samiti. *Jahar Ba* (ca. 2005). Compact disc.

López Arias, César Augusto. *Empresas multinacionales.* Bogotá: Ediciones Tercer Mundo, 1977.

MacArthur, Kate. "Peter Drucker, Father of Modern Management Theory, Had Profound Impact." *Advertising Age,* November 21, 2005.

MacDonald, Christine. "Coke Claims To Give Back As Much Water As It Uses." *The Verge,* May 31, 2018. www.theverge.com/2018/5/31/17377964/coca-cola-water-sustainability-recycling-controversy-investigation. Accessed December 15, 2018.

Majumdar, Sucheeta. "The Pop, the Fizz and the Froth," *Times of India,* October 9, 1977.

Malkin, Elisabeth. "Latin American Coca-Cola Bottlers in Giant Merger." *New York Times,* December 24, 2002.

Mandel, Eric. "Reuters: Tax Experts Closely Watching Coca-Cola's $3.3 Billion Battle with IRS." *Atlanta Business Chronicle,* April 2, 2018.

Marchand, Roland. *Advertising the American Dream: Making Way for Modernity, 1920–1940.* Berkeley: University of California Press, 1986.

———. *Creating the Corporate Soul: The Rise of Public Relations and Corporate Imagery in American Big Business.* Berkeley: University of California Press, 1998.

Marcos, Ana. "Un anuncio censurado sobre el riesgo de las bebidas azucaradas podrá volver a emitirse en Colombia." *El País,* April 18, 2017. https://elpais.com /internacional/2017/04/12/colombia/1492010982_084627.html. Accessed September 11, 2018.

Manuel, Mark. "Sosyo: The Forgotten Drink." *Upper Crust.*www.uppercrustindia .com/oldsite/8crust/eight/feature4.htm. Accessed September 14, 2018.

Martin, Paul. *Hell or High Water: My Life In and Out of Politics.* Toronto: McClelland & Stewart, 2009.

Martin, Randy. "After Economy? Social Logics of the Derivative." *Social Text* 114, no. 1 (Spring 2013): 83–106.

Martin-Ortega, Olga. "Deadly Ventures? Multinational Corporations and Paramilitaries in Colombia." *Revista Electrónica de Estudios Internacionales* no. 16 (December 2008).

Matten, Dirk, Andrew Crane, and Wendy Chapple. "Behind the Mask: Revealing the True Face of Corporate Citizenship." *Journal of Business Ethics* 45, no. 1–2 (June 2003): 109–120.

Mazzarella, William. *Shovelling Smoke: Advertising and Globalization in Contemporary India.* Durham, NC: Duke University Press, 2003.

McCracken, Russell. "The Overseas Story," *Coca-Cola Overseas,* August 1948.

McGovern, Charles. *Sold American: Consumption and Citizenship, 1890–1945.* Chapel Hill: University of North Carolina Press, 2006.

McGreevey, William Paul. *An Economic History of Colombia, 1845–1930.* London: Cambridge University Press, 1971.

McGregor, Douglas. *The Human Side of Enterprise.* New York: McGraw-Hill, 1960.

McKay, Betsy and David Luhnow. "Coke's Latin Bottlers to Merge to Form Powerhouse." *Wall Street Journal,* December 24, 2002.

McRobbie, Angela. *Postmodernism and Popular Culture.* New York: Routledge, 1994.

Meireles, Cildo. *Interções em circuitos ideológicos: Projeto Coca-Cola.* 1970. Tate Collection, London, www.tate.org.uk/servlet/ViewWork?workid = 84302&searchid = 19774&tabview = text. Page discontinued.

Merleaux, April. *Sugar and Civilization: American Empire and the Cultural Politics of Sweetness.* Chapel Hill: University of North Carolina Press, 2015.

Micklethwait, John, and Adrian Woolridge. *The Company: A Short History of a Revolutionary Idea.* New York: Modern Library, 2003.

Milanesio, Natalia. *Workers Go Shopping in Argentina: The Rise of Popular Consumer Culture.* Albuquerque: University of New Mexico Press, 2013.

Miller, Mark Crispin. Introduction to *The Hidden Persuaders,* by Vance Packard, 9–30. Brooklyn, NY: Ig, 2007.

Mintz, Sidney. *Sweetness and Power: The Place of Sugar in Modern History.* New York: Penguin Books, 1986.

Mitchell, Alan. "Brand-Jacking and How To Avoid It." *Issues: A Publication for Brand and Identity Decision Makers* (Enterprise IG in collaboration with the International Business Leaders Forum), October 11, 2004.

Mora, Frank, and Jeanne Hey, eds. *Latin American and Caribbean Foreign Policy.* Lanham, MD: Rowman & Littlefield, 2003.

Moreira, Naila. "Soft Drinks as Top Calorie Culprit." *ScienceNews,* June 17, 2005. www.sciencenews.org/blog/food-thought/soft-drinks-top-calorie-culprit. Accessed September 11, 2018.

Moreno, Julio. "Coca-Cola, US Diplomacy, and the Cold War in America's Backyard." In *Beyond the Eagle's Shadow: New Histories of Latin America's Cold War,* ed.Virginia Garrard-Burnett, Mark A. Lawrence, and Julio Moreno, 21–50. Albuquerque: University of New Mexico Press, 2013.

———. *Yankee Don't Go Home: Mexican Nationalism, American Business Culture, and the Shaping of Modern Mexico, 1920–1950.* Durham, NC: University of North Carolina Press, 2003.

Moreno, Julio, and The Coca-Cola Company. *The Centennial of Coca-Cola in Latin America.* Atlanta: The Coca-Cola Company, 2006.

Moreton, Bethany. *To Serve God and Wal-Mart: The Making of Christian Free Enterprise.* Cambridge, MA: Harvard University Press, 2010.

Motion Picture Broadcasting and Recorded Sound Division, Library of Congress. "Highlights in the History of Coca-Cola Television Advertising." http://memory.loc .gov/ammem/ccmphtml/colahist.html. Accessed May 12, 2009; page discontinued.

Mound, Josh. "Against the Soda Tax." *Jacobin,* June 21, 2016.

Moye, Jay. "Coke Red on the Silver Screen: Exploring the Brand's Role in Movies." February 28, 2014. www.coca-colacompany.com/history/coke-red-on-the-silver-screen-exploring-the-brands-role-in-movies. Accessed September 11, 2018.

Mukherjee, Ambarish. "To Deny Voting Rights to Indian Shareholders." *Hindu Business Line,* January 30, 2003.

Murillo, Mario. *Colombia and the United States: War, Terrorism, and Destabilization.* New York: Seven Stories Press, 2004.

Nair, C. Gouridasan. "Coca Cola Must Pay Damages, Says Panel." *The Hindu,* March 15, 2010.

National Alliance of People's Movements (NAPM). "National Alliance of People's Movements." December 1996. www.proxsa.org/politics/napm.html. Accessed September 11, 2018.

"Un negocio líquido." *Dinero* (Bogotá, Colombia), September 17, 2004.

Nestle, Marion. *Soda Politics: Taking on Big Soda (and Winning).* New York: Oxford University Press, 2015.

Newton, Michael. *The Encyclopedia of Kidnappings.* New York: Facts on File, 2002.

New York City Fact-Finding Delegation on Coca-Cola in Colombia. "An Investigation of Allegations of Murder and Violence in Coca-Cola's Colombian Pants." April 2004.

Nicholson, H.B. "The Competitive Ideal: The Economic Route to Friendship." Speech to the New York Herald Tribune Forum, October 20, 1952.

———. *Host to Thirsty Main Street.* New York: Newcomen Society, 1953.

Nixon, Rob. *Slow Violence and the Environmentalism of the Poor.* Cambridge, MA: Harvard University Press, 2013.

O'Barr, William and Marcio Moreira. "The Airbrushing of Culture: An Insider Looks At Global Advertising." *Public Culture* 2, no. 1 (1989): 1–19.

O'Barr, William, Shelly Lazarus, and Marcio Moreira. "Global Advertising." Project Muse. *Advertising & Society Review* 9, no. 4 (2008).

O'Connor, Anahad. "Coca-Cola Funds Scientists Who Shift Blame for Obesity Away from Bad Diets." *New York Times.* August 9, 2015. https://well.blogs.nytimes.com/2015/08/09/coca-cola-funds-scientists-who-shift-blame-for-obesity-away-from-bad-diets. Accessed September 11, 2018.

Okihiro, Gary. *Pineapple Culture: A History of the Tropical and Temperate Zones.* Berkeley: University of California Press, 2010.

Olaya, Carlos. "Sinaltrainal: Transforming the Workers' Movement in Colombia." In *The Class Strikes Back: Self-Organised Workers' Struggles in the Twenty-First Century,* ed. Dario Azzellini and Michael G. Kraft, 176–94. Leiden: Brill, 2018.

Orlove, Benjamin, and Arnold J. Bauer. "Giving Importance to Imports." In *The Allure of the Foreign: Imported Goods in Postcolonial Latin America,* ed. Benjamin Orlove, 1–30. Ann Arbor: University of Michigan Press, 1997.

Ormiston, Margaret E., and Elaine M. Wong. "License to Ill: The Effects of Corporate Social Responsibility and CEO Moral Identity on Corporate Social Irresponsibility." *Personnel Psychology* 66, no. 4 (2013).

Ospina, Andrés. *Bogotálogo: Usos, desusos y abusos del español hablado en Bogotá.* Bogotá: Instituto Distrital de Patrimonio Cultural, 2012.

"Over Production in Coca-Cola Bottling Plants." *Lok Sabha Debates* 13, no. 5 (March 5, 1975): 2–14.

Packard, Vance. *The Hidden Persuaders.* 1957. New York: Pocket Books, 1959.

Palacios, Marco. *Between Legitimacy and Violence: A History of Colombia, 1875–2002.* Translated by Richard Stoller. Durham, NC: Duke University Press, 2006.

———. *Coffee in Colombia, 1850–1970: An Economic, Social and Political History.* Cambridge: Cambridge University Press, 1980.

———. *Entre la legitimidad y la violencia: Colombia, 1875–1944.* Bogotá: Norma, 1995. 2nd ed., 2003.

Palacios, Mark, and Frank Safford. *Colombia: Fragmented Land, Divided Society.* New York: Oxford University Press, 2002.

Panagariya, Arvind. *India: The Emerging Giant.* New York: Oxford University Press, 2008.

"Panamerican Beverages." Funding Universe. www.fundinguniverse.com/company-histories/Panamerican-Beverages-Inc-Company-History.html. Accessed September 11, 2018.

"Panamerican Beverages." In *International Directory of Company Histories,* vol. 47, ed. Jay P. Pederson, 289–91. Detroit: St. James Press, 2006. www.encyclopedia.com

/books/politics-and-business-magazines/panamerican-beverages-inc. Accessed September 11, 2018.

Panamerican Beverages. Proxy Statement Pursuant to Section 14(a) of the Securities Exchange Act of 1934, Securities and Exchange Commission. Filed January 30, 2003. www.sec.gov/Archives/edgar/data/911360/000095012303002921/g81191prpreri14a .htm. Accessed September 11, 2018.

Parameswaran, Radhika. "E-Race-ing Color: Gender and Transnational Visual Economies of Beauty in India." In *Circuits of Visibility: Gender and Transnational Media Cultures,* ed. Radha S. Hedge, 68–87. New York: New York University Press, 2011.

Pearce, Fred. "Greenwash: Are Coke's Green Claims The Real Thing?" *Guardian,* December 4, 2008.

Pendergrast, Mark. *For God, Country, and Coca-Cola: The Definitive History of the Great American Soft Drink and the Company That Makes It.* New York: Basic Books, 2000.

"People." *Beverage Digest,* September 13, 2002.

Pérez, Umberto. *Bogotá, epicentro del rock Colombiano entre 1957 y 1975. Una manifestación social, cultural, nacional y juvenile.* Bogotá: Secretaría Distrital de Cultura, Recreación y Deporte–Observatorio de Culturas, 2007.

Perlroth, Nicole. "Spyware's Odd Targets: Backers of Mexico's Soda Tax." *New York Times,* February 11, 2017.

Petersen, Melody. "Putting Extra Fizz Into Profits." *New York Times,* August 4, 1998.

Peterson, Kristina. "Court Cites Iqbal Ruling to Dismiss Coca-Cola Case." *Wall Street Journal,* August 14, 2009.

Pfister, Kyle. "Leaked: Coca-Cola's Worldwide Political Strategy to Kill Soda Taxes." October 14, 2016. https://medium.com/cokeleak/leaked-coca-colas-worldwide-political-strategy-to-kill-soda-taxes-9717f361fb04. Accessed September 11, 2018.

Phillips-Fein, Kim. *Invisible Hands: The Businessmen's Crusade against the New Deal.* New York: Norton, 2009.

Philpott, Tom. "80 Percent of Public Schools Have Contracts with Coke and Pepsi." *Mother Jones,* August 15, 2012.

Pierson, Brenda. "Chiquita Settles with Families of US Victims of FARC." Reuters, February 5, 2018. www.reuters.com/article/us-usa-court-chiquita/chiquita-settles-with-families-of-u-s-victims-of-colombias-farc-idUSKBN1FP2VX. Accessed November 12, 2018.

Pillai, P. R. Sreemahadevan. *The Saga of Plachimada.* Mumbai: Vikas Adhyayan Kendra, 2008.

Post, James E., Lee E. Preston, and Sybille Sachs. *Redefining the Corporation: Stakeholder Management and Organizational Wealth.* Stanford, CA: Stanford University Press, 2002.

Postobón. "Historia." www.postobon.com/la-compania/la-historia. Accessed September 11, 2018.

Potter, Ed (director Global Labor Relations, The Coca-Cola Company). Letter to the editor. *The Nation,* May 22, 2006. www.thenation.com/article/letters-133. Accessed September 11, 2018.

Prebisch, Raúl. *The Economic Development of Latin America and Its Principal Problems.* New York: United Nations, 1950.

Puertas, Antonio. "El día que papá se fue." *Expansión,* September 20, 2011. https://expansion.mx/expansion/2011/09/14/el-da-que-pap-se-fue. Accessed September 11, 2018.

Purnell, Susanna, and Eleanor Wainstein. *The Problems of U.S. Businesses Operating Abroad in Terrorist Environments.* Santa Monica, CA: Rand Corporation, 1981.

Raghunandan, Gayatri. "A Look at the Legal Issues Plachimada's Struggle for Water against Coca-Cola Has Brought Up." *The Wire,* August 20, 2017.

Rai, Saritha. "Move in India to Ban Coke and Pepsi Worries Industry." *New York Times,* August 15, 2006.

Raman, K Ravi. "Community–Coca-Cola Interface: Political-Anthropological Concerns on Corporate Social Responsibility." *Social Analysis* 15, no. 3 (Winter 2007): 103–20.

Rana, Preetika. "Coca-Cola Closes Plant in India." *Wall Street Journal,* February 10, 2016. www.wsj.com/articles/coca-cola-closes-plant-in-india-1455122537. Accessed September 11, 2018.

Ranjith, K. R. *Holy Water from the West.* Thrissur: Altermedia, 2004.

Raventós, José M. *Cien años de publicidad colombiana, 1904–2004.* Bogotá: Centro del Pensamiento Creativo, 2004.

Raynaud, Gerard. "La gaseosa KIST no ha muerto." *La Opinion,* February 15, 2015.

Rist, Gilbert. *The History of Development: From Western Origins to Global Faith.* London: Zed Books, 2014.

Roberts, John. "The Manufacture of Corporate Social Responsibility." *Organization* 10, no. 2 (2003): 249–65.

Rogers, Douglas. "The Materiality of the Corporation: Oil, Gas, and Corporate Social Technologies in the Remaking of a Russian Region." *American Ethnologist* 39, no. 2: 284–96.

Roldán, Mary. *Blood and Fire: La Violencia in Antioquia, Colombia, 1946–1953.* Durham, N.C.: Duke University Press, 2002.

Rosenberg, Emily S. *Financial Missionaries to the World: The Politics and Culture of Dollar Diplomacy, 1900–1930.* Cambridge, MA: Harvard University Press, 1999.

———. *Spreading the American Dream: American Economic and Cultural Expansion, 1890–1945.* New York: Hill & Wang, 1982.

Rostow, Walt W. *The Stages of Economic Growth: A Non-Communist Manifesto.* Cambridge: Cambridge University Press, 1960.

Roy, Nilanjana S. "Chhibabhai & Gluco-Cola." *Business Standard,* January 27, 2013. www.business-standard.com/article/specials/chhibabhai-gluco-cola-197120601032_1.html. Accessed September 11, 2018.

Ruiz, Bert. *The Colombian Civil War.* Jefferson, NC: McFarland, 2001.

Ryan, Ted. "The Making of 'I'd Like to Buy the World a Coke.'" January 1, 2012. www.coca-colacompany.com/stories/coke-lore-hilltop-story. Accessed September 11, 2018.Saénz Rovner, Eduardo. *Colombia años 50: Industriales, política y diplomacia*. Bogotá: Universidad Nacional de Colombia, 2002.

———. *La ofensiva empresarial: Industriales, politicos y violencia en los años 40 en Colombia*. Bogotá: Tercer Mundo Editores, 1992.

Sanger-Katz, Margot. "The Decline of Big Soda." *New York Times*, October 2, 2015.

Santos Calderón, Francisco. "Palabras del vicepresidente de la República, Francisco Santos Calderón, en el Encuentro Internacional de Responsabilidad Social Empresarial de la Asociación Nacional de Empresarios de Colombia." Speech, Cali, Colombia, October 12, 2006.

"Sardar Daljit Singh: The Uncrowned King of Country's Cold Drinks Industry." *National Investment and Finance Weekly*, July 4, 1982, 839.

Scott-Heron, Gil. "The Revolution Will Not Be Televised." *Small Talk at 125th and Lenox*. Compact disc. Originally released in 1970. BMG, 1988.

Senadhira, Sugeeswara, and Havis Dawson. "Raising India: Coca-Cola Company Re-Enters Indian Market." *Beverage World*, February 1, 1994.

Seshan, Govindkrishna. "The Buzz without Fizz." September 11, 2007. www.rediff.com/money/2007/sep/11cola.htm. Accessed September 11, 2018.

Sforza, John. *Swing It! The Andrews Sisters Story*. Lexington: University Press of Kentucky, 2004.

Shah, Sonia. "Coke in Your Faucet?" *The Progressive*, August 2001.

Shamir, Ronen. "Between Self-Regulation and the Alien Tort Claims Act: On the Contested Concept of Corporate Social Responsibility." *Law & Society Review* 38, no. 4 (December 2004): 635–63.

———. "Corporate Social Responsibility: A Case of Hegemony and Counter-Hegemony." In *Law and Globalization from Below: Towards a Cosmopolitan Legality*, ed. Bonaventura De Sousa Santos and César A. Rodriguez-Garavito, 92–117. New York: Cambridge University Press, 2005.

———. "The De-Radicalization of Corporate Social Responsibility." *Critical Sociology* 30, no. 3 (2004): 669–89.

Shiva, Vandana. "High Time Plachimada Bill Got Presidential Consent." *Mathrubhumi*, May 15, 2016.

Shivarajan, Sridevi. "Dynamic Networks and Successful Social Action: A Theoretical Framework to Examine the Coca-Cola Controversy in Kerala, India." In *Enhancing Global Competitiveness Through Sustainable Environmental Stewardship*, ed. Subhash C. Jain and Ben L. Kedia, 184–206. Northampton, MA: Edward Elgar Publishing, 2011.

Shukla, Gouri. "Prasoon Joshi: The 'Thanda Matlab Coca-Cola' Man." *Business Standard*, May 5, 2003.

Silva Numa, Sergio. "Gaseosas: Una pelea gorda." *El Espectador*, November 15, 2015.

Sinaltrainal. "Modelo de desarrollo democratico." www.sinaltrainal.org. Accessed April 10, 2005; page discontinued.

———. "Nuestras Propuestas." www.sinaltrainal.org/index.php/nuestras-propuestas/propuestas/1469-nuestras-propuestas-propuestas. Accessed November 25, 2018.

———. "¡Para que cese la violencia en Colombia!" www.sinaltrainal.org/Textos/boikot/noconsumo.html. Accessed April 10, 2005; page discontinued.

———. "¿Quienes somos?" www.sinaltrainal.org. Accessed April 10, 2005; page discontinued.

Sinaltrainal v. The Coca-Cola Co., 256 F. Supp. 2d 1345 (S.D. Fla. 2003).

Sinaltrainal et al. v. The Coca-Cola Company et al., No. 06–15851, 2009 WL 2431463 (11th Cir. Aug. 11, 2009).

Singh, Prabha K. "The Coca-Cola Viewpoint." *Illustrated Weekly of India,* September 25, 1977.

Soederberg, Susanne. "Taming Corporations or Buttressing Market-Led Development? A Critical Assessment of the Global Compact." *Globalizations* 4, no. 4 (December 2007): 500–513.

Sparkes, Russell. "A Pragmatic Approach to Corporate Social Responsibility." Address Given to the School of Management, London School of Economics. May 19, 2003.

Spigel, Lynn. *Make Room for TV: Television and the Family Ideal in Postwar America.* Chicago: University of Chicago Press, 1992.

Srivastava, Amit. Interview with Lori Serb. *Prairie Grassroots.* WEFT, November 4, 2005.

Staton, Inge, and Ofelia Luz de Villa. *The Unknown Legacy of Albert H. Staton.* Amherst, MA: White Poppy Press, 2015.

Stecklow, Steve. "Virtual Battle: How a Global Web of Activists Gives Coke Problems in India." *Wall Street Journal,* June 7, 2005.

Steger, Manfred. *Gandhi's Dilemma: Nonviolent Principles and Nationalist Power.* New York: St. Martin's Press, 2000.

Stokes, Joseph M. "The International Cooperation Administration," *World Affairs* 119, no. 2 (Summer 1956): 35–37.

Stoller, Richard. "Alfonso López Pumarejo and Liberal Radicalism in 1930s Colombia," *Journal of Latin American Studies* 27, no. 2 (May 1995): 367–97.

Stout, Lynn A. "Why We Should Stop Teaching Dodge v. Ford." *Virginia Law & Business Review* 3, no. 1 (Spring 2008): 164–90.

Strasser, Susan. *Satisfaction Guaranteed: The Making of the American Mass Market.* Washington, DC: Smithsonian Books, 2004.

Striffler, Steve. *In the Shadows of State and Capital: The United Fruit Company, Popular Struggle and Agrarian Restructuring in Ecuador, 1900–1995.* Durham, NC: Duke University Press, 2001.

"The Sun Never Sets on Cacoola." *Time,* May 15, 1950.

Taussig, Michael. *Law in a Lawless Land: Diary of a Limpieza.* Chicago: University of Chicago Press, 2003.

———. *The Nervous System.* New York: Routledge, 1992.

Taylor, Lucy. "Globalization and Civil Society Continuities, Ambiguities and Realities in Latin America." *Indiana Journal of Global Legal Issues* 7, no. 1 (Fall 1999): 269–95

Taylor, Timothy D. *The Sounds of Capitalism: Advertising, Music, and the Conquest of Culture*. Chicago: University of Chicago, 2012.

"Thanda Matlab Solitary EFFIE Gold: EFFIE Awards 2003." Indiantelevision.com, August 22, 2003.

Thompson, Grahame. "Are We All Neoliberals Now? 'Responsibility' and Corporations." *Soundings* 39 (Summer 2007). www.lwbooks.co.uk/soundings/39/are-we-all-neoliberals-now-responsibility-and-corporations. Acccessed September 11, 2018.

———. "Responsibility and Neo-Liberalism." *OpenDemocracy*, July 31, 2007. www.opendemocracy.net/article/responsibility_and_neo_liberalism. Acccessed September 11, 2018.

Tomlinson, B. R. *The Economy of Modern India, 1860–1970*. New York: Cambridge University Press, 1993.

Townsend, Robert. *Up the Organization: How to Stop the Corporation from Stifling People and Strangling Profits*. New York: Knopf, 1970.

Tsing, Anna Lowenhaupt. *Friction: An Ethnography of Global Connection*. Princeton, NJ: Princeton University Press, 2005.

United Nations Centre on Transnational Corporations. *Foreign Direct Investment and Technology Transfer in India*. New York: United Nations, 1992.

United Nations Conference on Trade and Development. "United Nations Center on Transnational Corporations Origins." http://unctc.unctad.org/aspx/UNCTCOrigins.aspx. Accessed May 12, 2014; page discontinued.

United Nations General Assembly. Declaration on the Establishment of a New International Economic Order, May 1, 1974. Resolution 3201 (S-VI).

United States. Department of Commerce Office of International Trade. *Investment in Colombia: Conditions and Outlook for United States Investors*. Washington, DC: GPO, 1953.

United Students Against Sweatshops. "Cal-Safety Compliance Corporation is Not a Credible Monitor for Coca-Cola's Labor Practices." April 15, 2005.

Upadhyaya, Himanshu. "Let Them Drink Coke: The Commodification of Thirst and the Monopolization of Hydration." *Ghadar: A Publication of the Forum of Inquilabi Leftists* 10 (November 2006). http://ghadar.insaf.net/September2006/MainPages/editorial.htm. Accessed September 11, 2018.

Urrutia, Miguel. *The Development of the Colombian Labor Movement*. New Haven, CT: Yale University Press, 1969).

Vaid Dixit, Sumita. "'Thanda III'—Coke Scores on Naturalness." AgencyFAQs, September 30, 2002. www.afaqs.com/news/story/4958_Thanda-III---Coke-scores-on-naturalness. Accessed December 8, 2018.

Vales, José. "Woods Staton, el paisa que entró al club de los más ricos." *ElTiempo.com*, March 11, 2012.

van Breukelen, Dana. "Marching in the Spirit of Gandhi: A Case-Study into Gandhian Elements of the Lok Samiti Movement in Mehediganj, India." Master's Thesis, Vrije Universiteit Amsterdam, 2006.

Van Yoder, Steven. "Thirst for Success—Panamco, the Giant Latin American Bottler and Distributor, Thrives Despite Erratic Markets." *IndustryWeek,* May 15, 2000.

Varhola, Michael. *Fire and Ice: The Korean War, 1950–1953.* New York: Basic Books, 2000.

Vedwan, Neeraj. "Pesticides in Coca-Cola and Pepsi: Consumerism, Brand Image, and Public Interest in a Globalizing India." *Cultural Anthropology* 22, no. 4 (November 2007): 659–84.

Vogel, David. *The Market for Virtue: The Potential and Limits of Corporate Social Responsibility.* Washington, DC: Brookings Institution Press, 2006.

Wade, Peter. "Music, Blackness and National Identity: Three Moments in Colombian History." *Popular Music* 17, no. 1 (January 1998): 1–19.

Walker, Alissa. "Coke's 'Downtown in a Box' Delivers Clean Water and Wi-Fi to Africa." Gizmodo, October 10, 2013. https://gizmodo.com/cokes-downtown-in-a-box-delivers-clean-water-and-wi-1443039556. Accessed September 11, 2018.

Wallerstein, Immanuel. *The Modern World-System: Capitalist Agriculture and the Origins of the European World-Economy in the Sixteenth Century.* New York: Academic Press, 1976.

Warner, Melanie. "The Soda Tax Wars Are Back: Brace Yourself." BNet.com, March 25, 2010. http://industry.bnet.com/food/10001789/beverage-lobbyists-load-the-canon-for-round-two-on-soda-taxes/?tag = content;selector-perfector. Accessed September 11, 2018.

"Water Wars: Has Coke's Kinley Overtaken Bisleri?" *Financial Express,* September 24, 2002. www.financialexpress.com/news/water-wars-has-cokes-kinley-overtaken-bisleri/59318/2. Accessed September 11, 2018.

Wayne, Leslie. "How Delaware Thrives as a Corporate Tax Haven." *New York Times,* June 30, 2012.

Weinert, Lisa. "Can Coke Prevent AIDS?" *The Nation,* October 24, 2002.

Welker, Marina. *Enacting the Corporation: An American Mining Firm in Post-Authoritarian Indonesia.* Berkeley: University of California Press, 2014.

White, Allen L. "Fade, Integrate or Transform? The Future of CSR." Business for Social Responsibility, August 2005.

Wilder, Billy, dir. *One, Two, Three.* 1961. DVD. MGM Home Entertainment, 2003.

Wilk, Richard. "Bottled Water: The Pure Commodity in the Age of Branding." *Journal of Consumer Culture* 6, no. 3 (2006): 303–25.

Wilkins, Mira. *The Emergence of Multinational Enterprise: American Business Abroad from the Colonial Era to 1914.* Cambridge, MA: Harvard University Press, 1970.

"We Don't Want to Sell Parle: Chauhan." *Mint,* November 28, 2012.

Wexler, Laura. *Tender Violence: Domestic Visions in an Age of US Imperialism.* Durham, NC: University of North Carolina Press, 2000.

Wilkins, Mira. *The Maturing of Multinational Enterprise: American Business Abroad from 1914 to 1970.* Cambridge, MA: Harvard University Press, 1974.

Wolf, Shira. "Thanda-Hearted Matlab, Coca Cola in India: A Case Study in Mehandiganj Village of Environmental and Community Impact of the Grassroots Movement." Thesis, University of Wisconsin, 2004.

Zafar, Faiza, and Shivali Tukdeo. "Coca-Cola Kicked Out of University of Illinois." http://caccuc.blogspot.com. Last updated August 6, 2007. Accessed September 11, 2018.

Žižek, Slavoj. *First as Tragedy, Then as Farce.* London: Verso, 2009.

———. "'Nobody Has to Be Vile.'" *London Review of Books* 28, no. 7 (2006).

Zubrzycki, John. "Things Go Bitter about Coca-Cola." *The Australian,* June 2, 1998.

INDEX

accountability: Corporate Accountability International, 240, 262; CSR and, 273, 274–78; distancing from, 197, 210–11; financial accountability, 186; of investors, 301–2; legal accountability, 274–86; regulatory accountability, 220, 274–86

acquisitions/mergers: of bottlers, 5, 195–200, 197, 198; consolidation and, 24; control through, 30; in India, 229, 232, 338n85; in Latin America, 42, 186, 195–200; of Parle's trademark, 229; of sugar, 49; of technology, 158

activism/activists: AFL-CIO and, 223–24; Alien Tort Statute (ATS), 210–11, 275; anti-Coke activists, 212; anti-corporate movements, 212, 220; anti-globalization activism, 220; anti-water privatization, 262; challenges from, 274; in Colombia, 204, 208; consumer activism, 215; CSR and, 279, 291; documentations from, 331n1; environmentalism of the dispossessed, 257–59; in India, 229, 256–57, 259–63, 260fig.22, 261, 335n4; investor activism, 215–16; Killer Coke campaign, 212–24; legal accountability issues, 274–78; Lok Samiti (People's Committee), 256–57, 259, 262, 265, 266–67, 269; market democracy and, 190–91, 299; networks of organizing, 259–63, 260fig.22; Plachimada movement, 242, 256, 335n4; self-regulation and, 280; shareholder activism, 215–16, 301–2;

student mobilizations, 263; US based activism, 212–13, 220, 324n74; on water offsetting, 287–88. *See also* Sinaltrainal (National Union of Workers of the Agri-Food System)

Adivasis, 250, 251, 253–54

advertising: activism and, 324n74; advertising difference, 125–29; African American market, 123, 325n96; "All over the World Coca-Cola Brings Refreshment" (1947 advertisement), 7fig1; anti-Coke ads, 340n146; bottling plants in, 91–92, 92fig.9; broadcasting modern consumption, 113–16; capitalist modernity in, 45, 321n180; Coca-Cola Export/Panamco collaboration, 58; coca-colonization and, 93–95; in Colombia, 34–41, 44, 93–95; as commodity, 5; consumption as modernization, 89; corporate advertising campaigns, 271–72; corporate nationalism in India and, 171–82, 172fig.17; countercultural values in, 125; country-specific advertising campaigns, 106; creation of market-specific targeted advertising, 110; critiques of, 124–25; CSR advertising campaigns, 299–300; in Cuba, 319n141; decentralization, 65; domesticity images, 53; economic growth and, 88; effects of, 81; in Egypt, 73–74; focus on national development in Latin America, 93–95; in France, 68; global advertising strategies, 105, 148, 232; global postwar period, 86–87,

advertising: activism *(continued)*
87fig.8; hospitality themed, 107, 109;
"I'd Like to Buy the World a Coke"
campaign, 140–50, 303, 326n132; images
of corporate globalism, 101–3; imports
of, 42, 57; INDEGA and, 59; in India,
78, 171–82, 232, 271–72; international
pattern advertising, 68, 106–9; jingles,
114–15, 116, 129, 132; in Latin America,
47, 133fig.12, 134; limits on, 274, 276–
77; local advertising companies, 106;
localization in, 234–35; manufacturing
market expansion, 64; market segmentation, 44; mass consumption and, 88;
McCann-Erickson advertising agency,
68, 106–7, 127–29, 132, 140, 147, 150; in
Mexico, 74; multinational advertising
agencies, 106; multiracial casting, 105;
national corporatism and, 171–82;
national development contributions in,
92fig.9, 93–95; OIAA incentives for, 47;
One Sight/One Sound concept, 128;
Parle attacks in, 80; patterning, 109–13,
319n140; Postobón, 34–38, 40; print
ads, 125; product marketing and, 88;
prototype ads, 107–9; radio advertising,
113–14, 115, 125, 127; social justification
in, 73; song-form commercials, 129–30;
sports-themed ads, 110; success and, 65;
"*Thanda matlab* Coca-Cola" campaign,
234–35, 236fig.20; trademarks, 325n91;
translations issues, 39; universal appeal,
47, 53–55, 54fig.6; US capitalism and,
321n180; wartime advertising, 47, 52–53,
319n122; whitewashing, 109, 326n128
The Affluent Society (Galbraith), 124
AFL-CIO, 221
Africa: Congo, 109; Group of 77 (G-77),
155; Replenish Africa Initiative (RAIN),
287; soft-drink market, 51, 227; South
Africa, 222. *See also* Egypt
African American market, 123, 131, 141,
325n96
Agarwal, Anil Kumar, 241, 257
agricultural issues: agrarian reform, 120,
201, 250–51; agricultural commodities,
88; Green Revolution in India, 159;
rural industrialization in India, 228

Agro Industrial Corporation (Agro), 176
Agua Cristal, 31
Agua Manantial, 187
AIFLD (American Institute of Free Labor
Development), 221–22, 224
alcohol consumption, 118, 167, 227
Alianza por la Salud Alimentaria,
277–78
Alien Tort Statute (ATS), 210–11, 275
Allen, Frederick, 10
Alliance for Progress in Latin America, 85
"All over the World Coca-Cola Brings
Refreshment" ad, 7fig1
alternative systems, 259, 266
"Always Coca-Cola" campaign, 149
American Beverage Association, 277
American Century, 13, 55, 64, 66, 101
American Dream (1990 documentary)
(Kopple), 214
American Institute of Free Labor Develop-
ment (AIFLD), 221–22, 224
Americanization, 67, 69, 117, 138–39
Amin, Samir, 121
Anand, Dev, 133
anchor bottlers, 12, 195, 196, 197–98, 199.
See also FEMSA (Fomento Económico
Mexicano); Panamco
Andean Initiative, 192
ANDI (Asociación Nacional de
Industriales; later Asociación
Nacional de Empresarios), 46, 82, 84,
208, 277
Annan, Kofi, 281
anti-apartheid movement, 213
anti-capitalist politics, 217–18, 220, 297
anticocacolista, 119
anticolonialism, 79, 168
anti-communist ideology: AFL-CIO and,
222; in Colombia, 83, 84, 90, 203; of
Farley, 121; of Makinsky, 68; US foreign
policy and, 221
anticonsumerism, 217–18
anti-corporate movements, 212, 220
anti-globalization activism, 6, 220, 257,
268–69, 297
Antioquia, Colombia, 34, 41, 309n35. *See
also* Medellín
anti-sweatshop movement, 212–13

BJP (Bharatiya Janata Party), 227, 228, 232, 244

blacklisting (McCarthyize) (*macartizar*), 208–9, 221

Blanding, Michael, 10, 225, 333n48

bluewashing, 272

Bogotá, Colombia: Colombian International Trade Fair (1955), 86; documentations from, 331n1; historical photos from 1920s, 39; INDEGA in, 41–42, 59, 187; megaplants in, 200; Postobón plant in, 30; radio broadcast advertising in, 47; Sinaltrainal leaders in, 206, 221; student protest in, 119

Boltanski, Luc, 8

Bombay: Pure Drinks bottling plant in, 77–78, 81, 179, 180; soft-drink companies in, 78, 79, 80, 81. *See also* Mumbai

Bon Aqua, 239

Bonilla Gonzalez, Ricardo, 192

Borden Foods-Cicolac, 190

bottled water industry: Bisleri (India) Ltd., 180; boycotts, 262; commodification of, 239–40, 274; critiques of, 241; Manantial S.A. (Agua Manantial and Santa Clara), 187; Panamco, 198; pesticide residues, 240, 244; privatization of, 274; public health issues and, 176, 240, 294, 297; regulations and, 244; rural extraction and, 250, 253

bottlers: overview, 3, 4, 12–13; anchor bottlers, 12, 195, 196, 197–98, 199; Coca-Cola Enterprises, 197; Coca-Cola FEMSA, 9–10, 199–200; in Colombia, 12–13, 58, 118, 187; consolidation and financial investment in, 194–220; in France, 20; INDEGA, 57–60, 62, 83; in India, 12–13, 152–53, 171, 230; local, independent bottling, 60; locally sourcing, 95; mega-bottler franchises, 9, 12, 15, 186, 197–200; Panamerican Beverages/Panamco, 57–60, 98, 186–88; portrayal of, 94; Posada y Tobón, 29; tributary industries, 94–95, 97, 99, 102; US power assertions and, 57; work at, 188–89, 200–202. *See also* FEMSA (Fomento Económico Mexicano); *specific bottlers*

Bottler's Agreement, 210–11, 275

Bottlers' Association, 39

bottles: activism and, 137–38, 137fig.13, 237, 244, 264; as advertising image, 86, 89, 90, 105, 109–10, 111fig.10, 143, 235, 236fig.20; bottle cap promotions, 58–59, 277; caps on size, 274, 276, 277, 278; difficulties of getting, 85; environmental issues, 123, 240; expense of, 98; iconic shape of, 235; import of, 42, 97; polyethylene terephthalate (PET) bottles, 269, 288; production of, 44, 51, 102, 188; shipment of, 21, 30, 240

bottling contracts: advertising and, 45; Bottler's Agreement, 210–11, 275; challenges to, 30; CSR and, 280; Embotelladora Tropical Ltda., 42; with FEMSA, 199–200; in France, 68–69; INDEGA, 44; local monopolies and, 123; modifications to, 48; negotiations, 59; political corruption and, 170; Postobón, 30; renewals of, 199; restrictions of, 4, 5; rights granted under, 23–24; shareholders and, 197; with US corporations, 29

bottling machinery, 98; in advertising, 91, 93; import of, 42, 57, 161; imports of, 96–97; Indianization of, 173; investment in, 161; startup services and, 25

bottling plants: in Africa, 51; in Asia, 20, 51; in Colombia, 91–92, 205; early international, 20; in Europe, 20; in India, 51, 229, 269–70; in Latin America, 20; opening events, 91–92, 92fig.9; in Pacific, 20; US government subsidizing of during WWII, 51–52; wartime Indian plants, 51. *See also specific plants*

bounty programs, 48

boycotts: Arab Boycott, 122; corporate campaign strategies and, 215; of foreign-made goods, 79, 166, 167–68; in Guatemala, 209; in India, 232; IUF and, 222–23; Killer Coke campaign, 212–13; Operation Breadbasket, 123; Sinaltrainal and, 209–10; union leadership and, 221

"Boys on a Bench" ad, 131

brand images, 114–15, 248fig.21; overview, 8; consumer demand and, 87; critiques

and, 278; as iconoclash, 248–50; Killer
Coke campaign and, 217–18, 217fig.18,
218fig.19
branding: Hollywood brand references,
116–17; multinational brand, 86–93;
origins of advertising brands, 134; social
production of brands and revaluing
Coca-Cola's symbolic capital, 264–66
brand-name system: overview, 5; brand-
jacking, 263–65; brand loyalty, 50–51;
brand promotion, 292–97; brand value,
2–3, 264–66; capitalist democracy and,
70; capitalist values and, 70; changing
signification in, 116–20; coca-colonization and, 86–93; as commodity, 5;
consumer campaigns and, 214–15;
consumption and, 88; diversification
in, 299; expansion of, 127; in India, 77;
Killer Coke campaign, 212–24, 212–26,
217fig.18, 218fig.19; promotion of, 134;
reestablishment of, 228; threats to, 70
Brandon (Indian soft drink company), 80
Brazil: corporate expansion and acquisition
in, 186; cultural integration in, 65;
franchises in, 58; international markets
in, 101; Meireles, Cildo, 137–38,
137fig.13; Panamco bottling holdings in,
198; pattern advertising and, 108; radio
programming, 114; Staton in, 58, 97–98;
subsidiary discounts in, 5; US companies servicing franchises in, 96
breweries, 29, 31, 42, 187, 199
Brindavan Agro Industries, 227
British Guiana, 65
broadcast media: bottling plant opening
events, 91; in Colombia, 188, 277;
expansion of, 127; in India, 237; magazine advertising model, 116; McGuire
Sisters, 115; transitions in, 113, 116, 128;
universal appeal, 107, 127–29; youth
culture and, 116, 125–26. *See also* radio
advertising; radio programming; television advertising
Bronfman, Edgar, 329n64
Bucaramanga, Colombia, 187, 191, 200, 205,
207, 331n1
"Buena Compañía" ("Good Company"),
35–36

Buffett, Warren, 195–96, 303
Buga, Colombia, 187
Bureau of Indian Standards (BIS), 244
Burma, 20, 334n76
"Buy American" campaigns, 222
buycotts, 215, 299

Café Cola, 41
Calcutta, India, 51, 74, 80, 81, 164
Cali, Colombia, 39, 59, 118, 187, 200, 331n1
Cal Safety Compliance Corporation, 280
Camilo Torres Restrepo, 120
Campa Cola, 177–78, 180, 182
capitalism: overview, 7, 8–9, 12; advertising,
321n180; coffee capitalism, 29–34, 31,
34, 81, 86, 120; Colombian critiques of,
120; consumption and, 87; CSR and,
272–73, 297–303; culture and, 65, 134;
finance capitalism, 194–200; franchise
capitalism, 20–23, 65, 69–74; long term
protection for, 56; Marchand and,
307n12; market control and, 121; multinational developmentalism, 69–71, 73;
postwar internationalization of, 120,
316n36; revaluing of, 264–66; rise of in
Third World, 66; social costs of, 279;
social revolution threats to, 138–39;
universal appeal, 101; US capitalist
expansion, 316n36
capitalist democracy, 47, 69, 70, 88
capitalist expansion: in Colombia, 193;
concessions to, 300; critiques of, 65;
domesticity images and, 53; global
appeal of, 102; Hollywood portrayal of,
316n36; in India, 227
capitalist modernity: abundance, 48; in
advertising, 34–39, 44, 113, 114–15, 116;
expansion of, 83; franchise bottlers and,
60; Postobón and, 40–41; promotion
of, 48, 53–55; representational politics
and, 34–41
capitalist social realism, 273, 297–303
carbonic gas, 42, 44, 59, 85, 97
Cardoso, Fernando Henrique, 121
CARE, 287
Carepa, Colombia, 187, 205, 206, 207, 223,
331n1
Cargill, 287

discontents of, 66–69; Indian critiques of, 77; mid-century corporate globalism, 101–3; multinational developmentalism, 69–71, 95–101; national development, 71–74, 86–93; in postcolonial India, 74–81. *See also* national development; postwar internationalization

cocacolo subculture, 118–19

codes of conduct, 278–86

coffee capitalism, 31, 34, 81, 86, 120

coffee industry, 31, 43, 57, 81–86, 86, 120

cokefacts.com website, 214

cokefacts.org website, 214

"Coke in your home" marketing, 89, 109, 115

"Coke is It" campaign, 149

"The Coke Side of Life" campaign, 224

cola (term), 41

Cola-Champaña, 31

Cold War era, 67, 84, 121, 130, 139, 154, 170, 203, 221, 316n36. *See also* Third World

Colombia: overview, 6–7, 184–85, 184–86; armed groups, 82, 185, 191, 203–9, 212–24; banking system, 33–34; *cocacolo* subculture, 118–19; coffee industry, 81–86; economic decline in, 120; economic growth in, 118; economic nationalism of, 81–86; economic reliance on coffee, 31; Escuela de Lanceros, 85; expropriation threats, 43; import-substitution industrialization, 83, 120; industrial elites, 82, 84, 97; interviews in, 331n1; labor-management relationships, 188–89; labor movement in, 81; labor rights in, 7; labor unions in, 81; manufacturing sector expansion, 56; marketplace control, 82; military forces, 84–85; *Nadaísmo* (Nothing-ism) literary movement, 119–20; national developmentalism in, 81–86; national development of, 85; National Front, 120; national identity of, 81; neoliberalism in, 192–94; neoliberalism of, 185, 192–94; Panama, loss of, 32, 34, 53; Plan Colombia, 204; political/military dictatorships, 82; Postobón (previously Posada y Tobón), 29, 30, 86, 187, 190,

207, 311n71; postwar economic policies, 83; self-regulation in, 279, 284; Sinaltrainal origins, 190–91; state promotion of national industry in, 83, 187; sugar-sweetened beverage tax debate, 274, 277; US companies servicing franchises in, 96; US government ties to, 84; *La Violencia* conflict, 82, 83–85, 119, 203; youth consumer group in, 118. *See also* labor issues

Colombia (Caro), 137, 326n115

Colombiana, 40, 297

Colombian Coca-Cola bottling: in 21st century, 200–202; 21st century workers, 200–202; overview, 184–85, 224–26; advertising in, 34–41, 92fig.9, 93–95; Alien Tort Statute (ATS), 210–11, 275; Bottler's Agreement, 275; branding battles, 212–24; brand signification in, 116; Cisneros family and, 333n38; Coca-Cola and Colombian economic nationalism, 81–86; Coca-Cola intellectual property claims in, 40; Coca-Cola's entrance into, 31; competing drink brands in, 40; consolidation, 333n40; consolidation of bottling, 186–88; consumption increases in, 84; corporate consolidation, 194–200; corporate expansion and acquisition in, 186; CSR and, 17, 282; Elixir de Kola y Coca, 311n74; energy balance programs, 294; export markets, 57; finance capitalism, 194–200; franchise bottlers in, 58; global growth strategies in, 195; government interventions in, 84; *gran familia* expansion in, 188–89; importation difficulties, 85; INDEGA-Panamco *gran familia*, 188–89; indirect control methods in, 82; interviews in, 331n1; Killer Coke campaign, 212–24; labor exploitation, 194–200; machinery imports, 96; Panamco bottling holdings in, 198; paramilitary violence, 333n60; Postobón (previously Posada y Tobón), 29, 30, 311n71; Sinaltrainal and, 209–11; Staton and, 30, 58, 97–98; US machinery in, 96. *See also* Coca-Cola FEMSA; paramilitary violence; Sinaltrainal

"Colombian Coke Float" protest poster, 217fig.18, 218

Colombian International Trade Fair (1955), 86

Colón, Panamá, 42

colonialism: in India, 78–79, 157, 268; Rostow on, 87–88

Commission on Transnational Corporations (CTC), 155–56

commodification: overview, 227–29, 266–70; average daily intake for plants, 338n84; of bottled water, 239–40, 274; branding ethical commodities, 215–16, 264, 291, 299; caste system challenges over social discrimination, 340n125; Chipko forest dwellers, 339n116; Coca-Cola Company's influence on in India, 229–33; Coca-Cola stock and, 195; commodity fetishism, 195, 224; corporate exploitation of the water commons, 239, 247–53; critical fetishism, 264; of cultural representation, 134; environmentalism of the dispossessed, 257–59, 268; Gandhi's rejection of, 168; in India, 258, 335n4; Keralan fisherfolks coastal development challenges and unsustainable fishing methods, 339n116; legal issues, 339n104; Mehdiganj plant and, 339nn97–98; multinational brand, 86–93; Narmada Dam displacement movement, 339n116; networks of organizing, 218, 259–63; origins of advertising brands, 134; Parle franchise, 339n105; pesticide residues, 237–47; privatization, 233–37; protest movements in India, 253–57; revaluing Coca-Cola's symbolic capital, 264–66; social production of brands and revaluing Coca-Cola's symbolic capital, 264–66; Warhol and, 136; of water resources, 240; of the world, 64

commodification of culture. See cultural commodification

commodity market: commodity chain, 212, 215, 234, 273; effects on franchise model of globalization, 48

commonality, 140

communism: anti-communism, 45, 68–70, 83–84, 90, 203, 208, 221–22; brands combatting, 70; capitalist strategies against, 69–70; Chinese Communist Party, 66; in Colombia, 43, 82, 120, 190–91, 219; communist parties, 66; deterring of in Colombia, 85; in France, 67, 68, 69; in India, 159; social revolution threats and, 121; against TCCC in Second World countries, 154; US fight against, 84

Community of the World (1961 TCCC film), 107

Compañía Colombiana de Tabaco, 309n35

Compañía Suramericana de Seguros, 309n35

concentrates: Coca-Cola India, 230, 231; Colombian concentrate factory, 85–86; concentrate manufacture in India, 176, 179, 180; concentrate plant proposal in India, 100–101; consolidation and, 196; dependence on, 96; difficulties of getting, 85; FEMSA and, 199–200; FERA and, 153; franchising and, 12; high profits on, 161; imports of, 42, 57; imports of in India, 77; manufacture in India, 161, 162, 229; Parle export of, 177; production of, 27, 98

Confederation of Indian Industry, 245

Congress of Racial Equality, 123

The Conquest of Cool (Frank), 126

Conservative Party, in Colombia, 83, 120, 203

consumer capitalism: appeal and adaptability of, 101; critiques of, 121, 123, 139; effects of, 64; modernity and, 89; pattern advertising and, 109; questioning of, 134–35; universal appeal of, 55; virtuous cycle model, 86–87

consumer confidence, reduction of, 46

consumer culture: economic balance and, 90; Gandhi's rejection of, 168; in India, 258; Youth Market marketing, 107, 115, 118, 125, 129–30

consumer democracy, 88–89

consumer demographics: African Americans and Latina/os, 129; minority demographic, 130–31; postwar baby boomer consumer demographic, 129–38; youth consumer group, 125–27, 129–30

consumerism, cultural capitalism and, 299–300

consumer markets: advertising constructed, 115; expansion of, 83

consumers: overview, 4; African American market, 131; bottled drink safety in India, 274; challenges by, 274; in Colombia, 82; Colombian consumer market, 56; consumer campaigns, 214–15; consumer concerns, 270; consumer goodwill, 27; crisis of confidence, 228; Cuban critiques of US consumer culture, 319n141; development of strategies and promoting product to, 19–20; excise tax on soda as regressive; gendered responsibility of, 89; global consumers, 139; Indian urban middle class, 242, 258; Indian urban middle class as, 234–35, 238–39; Killer Coke campaign, 214; liberal anticonsumerism, 217–18; projected US consumer democracy, 319n122; US servicemen as, 30; wartime, 53; youth consumer group, 105, 125–27, 129–30

consumption: overview, 227–29, 266–70; average daily intake for plants, 338n84; broadcasting modern consumption, 113–16; buycotts, 215–16, 299; capitalism and, 87–88; capitalist modernity and, 48; caste system challenges over social discrimination, 340n125; Chipko forest dwellers, 339n116; Coca-Cola Company's influence on in India, 229–33; consumer segmentation, 115; corporate exploitation of the water commons, 247–53; creating consumer demand, 86–93; developing world increase in, 70; development as increase in, 66; effects of, 267; environmentalism of the dispossessed, 257–59; ethical consumption, 168, 215–16, 264, 291, 299; in global south, 156; health issues and sugary drinks, 274; increases in Colombia, 84; in India, 168–69, 335n4; Keralan fisherfolks coastal development challenges and unsustainable fishing methods, 339n116; labor negotiations and, 90; in Latin America, 47; legal issues, 339n104; liberal anticonsumerism, 217–18; Mehdiganj plant and, 339nn97–

98; Narmada Dam displacement movement, 339n116; as national civil duty, 46; national development and, 86–93; networks of organizing, 259–63; Parle franchise, 339n105; pesticide residues, 237–47; in postwar advertising, 86–87, 87fig.8; privatization, 233–37; protest movements in India, 253–57; revaluing Coca-Cola's symbolic capital, 264–66; social action and, 299; social production of brands and revaluing Coca-Cola's symbolic capital, 264–66; universality of, 102–3; US multinationals and, 70

contracts: overview, 5; Bottler's Agreement, 210–11, 275; contract manufacturing, 12; indirect control through, 82, 210–11; modifications to, 48; university contracts, 213

copyrights, 4

Corporate (2006 film) (Bhandarkar), 243, 247

Corporate Accountability International, 240, 262

corporate advertising campaigns, 271–72

Corporate Campaign, Inc., 213–14

corporate campaign strategy, 213–15, 221

corporate capitalism: in Colombia, 184–85; counterculture critique of, 121; universal appeal of, 55; in US, 220; US based activism, 262; US government promotion of, 47

corporate citizenship, 272. *See also* corporate social responsibility (CSR)

corporate consolidation: in Colombia, 191, 194–200, 207; FEMSA and, 200; in India, 231

corporate expansion: in Colombia, 185, 191; in India, 271; in Latin America, 186; negotiation with national developmentalists in Third World, 66; role of the state in, 48; water use reduction and, 287

corporate exploitation: in Colombia, 214, 219, 220; CSR and, 273, 279, 286–87, 299, 302–3; in India, 167, 170, 247–53, 271; state regulations and, 273; of the water commons in India, 247–53; of water resources, 228–29, 247–53, 261, 271, 276, 287, 303

Eliécer Gaitán, Jorge, 82
elites: in Colombia, 82, 97, 203, 209; in US,
    220
Elixir de Kola y Coca, 311n74
Elmore, Bartow, 5, 10, 291
ELN (Ejército de Liberación Nacional),
    120, 203–4
Embotelladora Román, 187, 191
Embotelladoras de Santander, 187, 191
Embotelladora Tropical Ltda., 42, 85
emergent development paradigm, 73
employment, 73, 73–74, 192. *See also* labor
    issues; workers
"Employment for Thousands of Egyptians"
    ad, 73
Encuentro Internacional de Responsabili-
    dad Social Empresarial (International
    Meeting of Corporate Social Responsi-
    bility), 208–9
energy balance programs, 292–94
England, 96
"Enjoy Cocaine" posters (Gemini Rising),
    136
Enron, 260
environmental challenges: overview, 16,
    227–28, 266–70; average daily intake
    for plants, 338n84; caste system chal-
    lenges over social discrimination,
    340n125; Chipko forest dwellers,
    339n116; Coca-Cola Company's influ-
    ence on in India, 229–33; corporate
    exploitation of the water commons,
    247–53; environmental costs, 3; envi-
    ronmentalism of the dispossessed,
    257–59; in India, 335n4; Keralan fisher-
    folks coastal development challenges
    and unsustainable fishing methods,
    339n116; legal issues, 339n104; Mehdi-
    ganj plant and, 339nn97–98; Narmada
    Dam displacement movement, 339n116;
    networks of organizing, 259–63; Parle
    franchise, 339n105; pesticide residues,
    237–47; privatization, 233–37; protest
    movements in India, 253–57; revaluing
    Coca-Cola's symbolic capital, 264–66
environmental issues: overview, 227–29; Big
    Soda alternatives, 299; commodification
    of water, 240; conservationist environ-

mentalism, 242; CSE and, 238, 247;
    dispossession, 257–59; environmental
    degradation, 228, 251, 297; environmental
    impact, 5; environmentalism of the
    dispossessed, 257–59; environmentalists,
    335n4; environmental movement, 123;
    environmental resources, 228, 229; green-
    washing, 272; lack of regulations, 250–51;
    natural resource management, 242;
    pesticide content in bottled drinks, 228,
    237, 238; rights and governance in, 276;
    state-planned development, 228; sustain-
    ability, 241, 270; sustainability challenges,
    274; sustainability efforts, 201; unsustain-
    able fishing methods, 339n116; water
    rights struggles (*panchayati raj*) (village
    decentralized governance), 213
Escuela de Lanceros, 85
Ethical Trading Initiative, 280
ethics, 225, 280
ethnocentrism, 117
Europe: bottling ventures in, 20; European
    Economic Commission (EEC), 237;
    European economies, 71; EU standards,
    245; neoliberal globalization in, 139;
    opposition in postwar period, 66;
    postwar economic recovery plan,
    98–99; protests over bottled water, 274
exclusivity/inclusivity, 5, 112–13
expansionism. *See* corporate expansion
exports: Colombian economy and, 43, 46,
    81–86; European recovery and, 100;
    export markets, 57; FERA and, 160;
    foreign exchange situation, 161–62;
    foreign markets and, 156; from India,
    159; of Indian soft drinks, 177
expropriation, 83
externalization, 5

fair trade products, 299
FAL (Fuerzas Armadas de Liberación), 122
Falangism, 84
"Family Size" marketing, 93, 107, 115, 125
Fanta, 176
FARC (Fuerzas Armadas Revolucionarias
    de Colombia), 120, 203–4
Farley, James Aloysius "Jim," 61–62, 68,
    70–71, 75, 88, 90–91, 96, 121, 171

free trade: coffee capitalism and, 81; in
Colombia, 43, 83, 192; global north
restrictions on, 159; ideology of, 31; US
economic assistance programs and, 67
Freskola/Popular, 31, 40, 41
"Friendly Hospitality" campaign, 109
Fuerzas Armadas de Liberación (FAL), 122
Fuerzas Armadas Revolucionarias de
Colombia (FARC), 120, 203–4
Fundación Colombianitos, 285
Fundación Colombia para la Educación y la
Oportunidad, 285
Fundación Ideas para la Paz, 284

G-77 (Group of 77), 155
Gacek, Stan, 224
Galbraith, John K., 124
Gámez, Rubén, 136–37
Gandhi, Indira, 159, 167, 179, 182
Gandhi, Mohandas, 79, 124, 167–68, 168,
256, 257
Gandhian values, 166, 168–69, 259
Gaon Bachao Sangharsh Samiti (Save the
Village Struggle Committee), 255–56,
261
García Abello, Yezid, 192
Gaseosas Colombianas, 31, 187
Gaseosas Lux, 31, 187
Gaviria Trujillo, César, 192
Gemini Rising, 136
Germany, 108
Ghosh, Bishnupriya, 249
Gil, Isidro, 206
Gil, Isidro Segundo, 218–19, 218fig.19
Gill, Leslie, 205, 220
Girardot, Colombia, 187
Glacéau vitaminwater brand, 296–97
global advertising strategies, 105
global capitalism, 1, 3, 8, 71
Global Compact, UN, 280–82, 284, 286,
342n50
global consumerism, 228, 234
global depressions, 43, 71
Global Energy Balance Network, 293
global financial system, 153
global growth, 72, 195
globalization: corporate globalism, 101–3;
financialization and, 194; franchise

model of, 48, 103–4; globalization icon,
1; images of, 53–55, 54fig.6; international
pattern advertising, 106–9; pattern
advertising and, 109; patterning sameness, managing difference, 109–13;
protests against, 261; second wave of, 62;
second wave of? 56–60; stocks and
dividends increase and, 194
global north: free trade restrictions by, 159;
India Resource Center and, 262; intellectual property transfers, 162–64;
movement leveraging economic pressure
on, 213; NIEO and, 155–57; raw resource
extraction of global south by, 71; stagflation in, 156
Global Reach (Barnet and Miller), 122
global south: bottled water in, 239; consumption increase in, 70; dependency
theory and, 121; economic exploitation
of, 122; environmentalism of, 256;
exploitation of, 122; global capitalism
and, 71; industrialization of, 71; industrialization of by corporate investment,
73; intellectual property transfers,
162–64; nationalization threats, 121;
neocolonialism of, 71; NIEO and,
155–57; oil-rich nations, 156; opposition
in postwar period, 66; postcolonial
nationalisms, 72; potential markets in,
70; role of multinationals in, 152; small,
local companies of, 139; sweat belt, 227.
See also specific countries
Global Water Challenge, 287
Global Workplace Rights Policy, 279–80
Gluco-Cola, 79–80, 176
Godard, Jean-Luc, 129
Gohee, Robert F., 181
Goizueta, Roberto, 1, 182–83, 195
Gold Spot, 176, 177, 229
Gómez, Laureano, 84
Good Neighbor policy, 56, 62
goodwill, 72, 273, 290
government interventions: in Colombia,
84, 85–86; Farley and, 70; government-
planned economies, 71; government
reforms, 81; government restrictions,
85; in the market, calls for, 72; negative
effects of, 48; US multinationals and,

imperialism: comparisons to, 64; decentralization and, 65; domesticity images and, 53; franchise ownership and, 29; imperial expansion, US, 121

imperialism, US: anger over, 238; criticism of, 139; Mexico and, 136–37; questioning of, 134–35

imperialism, Western, 154

"Importance of the Rest-Pause in Maximum War Effort" pamphlet, 50

imports: in Colombia, 46, 57, 83; dependence on, 57; dependency and, 73; developing world lack of money to buy, 70; elimination of restrictions on, 198; government interventions, 71; government substitution of, 66; high cost of, 71; import duties, 85–86; import-substitution industrialization, 70; INDEGA and, 42, 85; in India, 159, 161, 180, 230; limitations on in Colombia, 82, 85; World War II and, 43

import-substitution industrialization, 66, 70; in Colombia, 81, 120; in India, 158, 229; postwar period, 72; as product replacement, 73; state promotion of in Colombia, 83; US multinationals and, 71

INDEGA (Industrial de Gaseosas Ltda.), 41–42, 187; advertising, 44; Colombian International Trade Fair (1955), 86; distribution systems and, 59; franchise and, 57; government protectionism and, 85; INDEGA-Panamco, 42–43, 62, 83, 188–89; Kist brand, 45–46; local industry promotion by, 45–46; as Panamco subsidiary, 187; Staton and, 58, 97; wartime economy and, 45. See also Gutiérrez Gómez, José; Staton, Albert H.

independent contractor status, 193, 200, 220

independent franchises, 29, 187, 199–200

India: overview, 6–7, 227–29, 266–70; acquisitions in, 232; advertising corporate nationalism in, 171–82, 172fig.17; average daily intake for plants, 338n84; bottling plants in, 81; brand signification in, 116; caste system challenges over social discrimination, 340n125; Chipko forest dwellers, 339n116; civil disobedience movement, 168; "Coca-Cola, Quit India" campaign, 253–57; Coca-Cola eviction pursuit, 166–71; Coca-Cola's departure from, 152, 174–83, 227; Coca-Cola's return to, 227–28; corporate advertising campaigns in, 271–72; corporate exploitation of the water commons, 247–53; critiques of coca-colonization, 77; critiques of multinationals, 170; CSR initiatives and moral credits, 17; cultural nationalism, 168; defense spending increases, 159; divestment conditions, 230–31; economic nationalism, 168; economic recovery plans, 229–30; economic reforms, 259; The Emergency, 167; environmental challenges in, 335n4; environmentalism of the dispossessed, 257–59; expansion in New Delhi, 77; FERA and, 160–65, 174; foreign corporation limitations, 158; foreign-exchange reserves, 159; global consumerism in, 228, 234; Green Revolution, 159; Group of 77 (G-77), 155; Hindi advertisement, 132fig.11, 133; ICA application, 100–101; import increases, 159; Independence, 167; independence movements, 167–68, 268; Indian bottling franchises, 96, 161; Indian urban middle class, 247, 258; indigenous soft drinks, 180, 181; international markets in, 101; interviews in, 335n4, 336n4; Keralan fisherfolks coastal development challenges and unsustainable fishing methods, 339n116; machinery imports, 96; Mehdiganj plant and, 339nn97–98; militarization of Indian Ocean, 170; military-soda industrial complex and, 51–52; multinational policies, 158; Narmada Dam displacement movement, 339n116; national identity of, 79; nationalization threats, 121; networks of organizing, 259–63; NIEO and, 155–60; Parle franchise, 339n105; pesticide residues, 237–47; political nationalism, 168; postcolonial, coca-colonization in,

74–81; privatization in, 7, 230, 233–37; protest movements, 253–57; public health concerns, 169, 169fig.16; Pure Drinks, 76–77; Pure Drinks' soft-drink market in, 330n108; replenishment claims in, 287–88; revaluing Coca-Cola's symbolic capital, 264–66; rural industrialization, 228; sectarian violence in, 75; self-regulation in, 279; soft-drink market in, 80, 180, 227; sugar-sweetened beverage tax, 274; Supreme Court dismissed case against plant, 339n104; TCCC's influence on, 229–33; TOs (Technical Observers) in, 75; US foreign-policies and, 170; US-Pakistan relations and, 170

Indianization: calls for, 154; defined, 15; FERA and, 152, 153, 160, 160–65, 230; water rights and, 328n46

Indian market, 51, 74

"Indianness," in advertising, 234

Indian Ocean, 170

India Resource Center, 249, 262, 263, 265

indigenous know-how, 174

indigenous soft drinks, 180, 181

indirect control, 82

Indo-American Chamber of Commerce, 245

Industrial de Gaseosas Ltda. (INDEGA). See INDEGA (Industrial de Gaseosas Ltda.)

industrial elites, 46, 82, 186

industrialization, 156; in Colombia, 57; by corporate investment, 73; import-substitution industrialization, 70, 120; in India, 182; Rostow on, 88

industrializing economies, 70

industrial management, 50, 188–89

Industria Nacional de Gaseosas. See INDEGA-FEMSA; INDEGA-Panamco

inequality, 121, 156, 242, 297; income inequality, 120

inflation, 120, 158

Information and Research Centre on Transnational Corporations (IRCTC), 155–56

information commercialization, 65. See also knowledge commercialization

infrastructure, 228

Innocent Drinks, 299

intangible assets, 4

integration, 131

intellectual property, 3, 26–27, 65, 162–64

"Interções em circuitos ideológicos: Projeto Coca-Cola" ("Insertions into Ideological Circuits: Coca-Cola Project" (visual/performance art) (Meireles), 137–38, 137fig.13

international advertising, 127–29

international bottling system, 48, 96–97, 309n32

International Business Leaders Forum (IBLF), 283–84

International Confederation of Free Trade Unions (ICFTU), 221

international consumer markets, 56

international conventions, 69

International Cooperation Administration (ICA), 100–101, 161

International Council of Beverage Associations, 277

international debts, 71

international economic development, 71–74, 86–93, 100–101

international economic order, 121, 155–60

international expansion: franchise system and, 12–13; negative response to, 66; US military and, 29–30, 46, 51–52. See also Coca-Cola Overseas (Company magazine)

international harmony goal, 183

internationalization, 63, 63fig.7, 64–65, 316n36

international labor markets, 193

International Labor Organization (ILO), 223, 279, 280

International Labor Rights Fund (ILRF), 210–11, 334n76

international lending authorities, 85

international marketing, 44–45, 62, 101, 148, 183

International Meeting of Corporate Social Responsibility (Encuentro Internacional de Responsabilidad Social Empresarial), 208–9

International Monetary Fund (IMF), 229

international pattern advertising, 106–9, 133–34
international subsidiaries, 106–7
international trade, 70, 88
International Union of Food, Agricultural, Hotel, Restaurant, Catering, Tobacco and Allied Workers Associations (or International Union of Foodworkers), 209, 222–23, 284
interventionism, 81
investments: overview, 3; activism and, 215–16; bottler development and, 30; as commodity, 5; of foreign bottlers, 29; in foreign capital and technology, 73; in India, 181; interventionist monetary policies to stimulate, 81; review of, 321n180; socially responsible, 278; strategic investments, 4
investors: accountability of, 301–2; benefits to, 343n52; Colombian investors, 57; Gutiérrez Gómez as, 82; in India, 102
Iraq, 112
IRCTC (Information and Research Centre on Transnational Corporations), 155–56
Ireland, 5
IRS, 4–5
Isdell, E. Neville, 227, 280, 283, 303
Israel, 122, 154
Italy, 20, 101, 108, 112, 122, 180
IUF (International Union of Foodworkers). *See* International Union of Food, Agricultural, Hotel, Restaurant, Catering, Tobacco and Allied Workers Associations (or International Union of Food

Jahar Ba ("There is Poison") (Lok Samiti), 266–68, 269
jal-jeera (cumin-spiced lemonade) shops, 78
Janata Party (JNP), 151, 153, 167, 179, 181–82
Japan, 101, 139
jingles, 114–15, 116, 125, 129, 132, 138
Jones, Roy S., 103–4
J. P. Stevens, 213
Juventud Comunista Colombiana, 191
Juventud Trabajadora Colombiana, 191

Kala Dera, Rajasthan, 228, 231, 261, 263, 269, 269–70, 335n4

Kali (Indian soft drink company), 80
Karkaria, Bachi J., 166–67
Karnani, Aneel, 298
Keck, Margaret, 263
Kejriwal Beverages Pvt. Limited, 339n105
Kemmerer, Edward, 32
Kerala, India, 276
Keralan fisherfolks, 339n116
Keynesian economic policies, 66, 72, 83, 87, 90
Khan, Aamir, 234, 242–43, 267
Killer Coke campaign, 212–24, 217fig.18, 218fig.19, 264, 301
King, Martin Luther, Jr., 124
King Cola, 40, 41
King Kola, 176
Kinkola, 41
Kinley, 239, 240, 246
Kirby, Richard, 187, 207
Kissinger, Henry, 171
Kist brand, 45–46, 58
knowledge commercialization, 3
Ko-Kana, 44
kola nuts, 40
Kola Román, 187
Kol-Cana, 40
kolkanitas, 118
Korean War, 67, 84
Kovalik, Dan, 210, 221
Kumhar community, 255–56
Kuwait, 177

labeling, 44, 70, 277, 278
labor: overview, 184–85, 224–26; advertising for labor class in Colombia, 89–90; branding battles, 212–24; building labor power: the origins of SINAL-TRAINAL, 190–91; Burmese plaintiffs sue Unocal over labor abuses committed in construction of an oil pipeline, 334n76; Carnegie handling of organized labor, 346n151; Coca-Cola workers and paramilitary violence, 203–9, 209–11; Colombian neoliberalism and the Coca-Cola worker, 192–94; consolidating Colombian Coca-Cola bottling and, 186–88; finance capitalism, corporate consolidation, labor exploitation,

194–200; interviews and, 331n1; job loss in 1999, cost-cutting methods during period of consolidation and restructuring, 333n40; Killer Coke campaign, 212–24; labor abuses, 334n76; labor activism, 185, 210; labor costs, 196; labor discipline, 90; labor legislation, 43, 192–93, 200; labor-management relationships in Colombia, 188–89; *la gran familia* expansion, 188–89; numbers dispute, 333n48; payments to leftist guerillas to avoid kidnappings, 333n60; strikes, 190; at the turn of the 21st century, 200–202; Venezuelan bottler joint venture between Coca-Cola and Cisneros family, 333n38

labor exploitation, 166, 186, 193, 194–200, 220, 256–57, 274, 280, 298, 302

labor flexibilization, 186, 192–93, 220, 225

labor management: AFL-CIO and, 221; in Colombia, 188–89, 191, 205

labor market, *precarización* (precariousness) of, 193

labor militancy, battling, 122

labor movements: in Colombia, 46, 81, 185; in US, 122–23, 220, 222

labor negotiations, consumption and, 90

labor organizations: AFL-CIO, 222–24; in Colombia, 185, 190, 223; global labor relations and, 223, 279; ILO, 223, 279; IUF, 209, 222–23; SICO, 223. *See also* Sinaltrainal

labor precarization (*precarización*), 192–93, 212–13, 220, 224, 225. *See also* labor flexibilization

labor reform, in Colombia, 219, 225

labor restructuring: in Colombia, 191; in US, 220

labor rights: in Colombia, 7–8, 120, 184–85; labor injustices and, 220

labor unions: AFL-CIO, 221; in Colombia, 43, 82, 190; corporate campaign strategy, 213–14; establishment of in Colombia, 81; in Guatemala, 209. *See also* Sinaltrainal

Ladas, Stephen, 40

La Fabrica de Cerveza de San Miguel, 29

La fórmula secreta, o Coca-Cola en la sangre (*The Secret Formula, or Coca-Cola in the Blood*) (1964 fim) (Gámez), 136–37

la gran familia Panamco expansion, 188–89

laissez-faire tenets, 31

Largacha, Pablo, 285

Latin America: advertising in, 93–95, 133fig.12, 134; advertising representations of, 53–54, 54fig.6, 89–90; AFL-CIO and, 221; bottling ventures in, 20; broadcast media in, 127; capitalism in, 32; concentrates, 42; development in, 30; dictators in, 84; films, 136–37; franchise mega-bottler in, 186; Group of 77 (G-77), 155; as international market, 198; modernization of economies of, 83; national development of, 56; radio advertising in, 47, 114; Refrescos, S.A., 57; Staton in, 30; trademark issues in, 40–41. *See also specific countries*

Latour, Bruno, 248

Latuff, Carlos, 264, 265fig.23

Lavin, Franklin, 245

Laxman, 331n118

Lears, Jackson, 90

Lebanon, 109

Ledo, Assam, India, 51

leftists: in Argentina, 122; in Colombia, 43, 204, 222; Colombian repression of, 82; in France, 67; in India, 232; McCarthyize (*macartizar*) (blacklisting) and, 208–9, 221; New Left, 123; opposition in postwar period, 66, 69; postwar struggles in global south, 72; Sinaltrainal and, 191; in Uruguay, 122

legal issues: accountability and, 278; activism, 123, 209–11; bottling contract modifications and, 48; Burmese plaintiffs sue Unocal over labor abuses committed in construction of an oil pipeline, 334n76; case dismissal, 339n104; copyright infringement, 249; CSE report, 244; *Dodge v. Ford Motor Company*, 302; exemptions, 96; exemptions in Mexico, 165; expropriation legislation, 81; financial settlement, 224–25; in France, 68; Glacéau vitaminwater brand, 296–97; groundwater issues, 254;

299; market growth, 60; marketing materials, 3; marketing power, 72; marketing strategies, 115; market-liberalization reforms, 192; market promotion, 292–97; market research, 65; market segmentation, 44; market share, 330n109; polar bear icon, 299; profits from licensing of, 194; promotional campaigns, 58–59; socially responsible marketplace, 299; uniformity in, 108; "Work Refreshed" marketing, 49–50, 89–90, 115

Marshall Plan, 98–99

Martínez-Alier, Joan, 257

Marx, Karl, 195

Marxism, 121–22, 129, 190–91, 201, 203, 216, 219, 253, 258, 259

Masculin féminin (1966 film) (Godard), 129

massification of culture, 134–35

mass production/mass consumption model, 86–87, 113–16, 120, 168

Master, Nandlal (Prasad), 256–57

material production: overview, 2–3; externalization of, 64–65; financial investments and, 194; structure of, 12; US corporate control of, 232

materials: dependence on, 96; production/sourcing/waste/reuse of, 307n9; US production of, 96

Mauritius, 177

McCabe, Sydney W., 51

McCann-Erickson advertising agency, 68, 106–7, 127–29, 132, 140, 147, 150, 233; radio advertising, 106, 127, 127–29; television advertising, 106, 127, 127–29

McCarthyize (*macartizar*) (blacklisting), 208–9, 221

McDonald's, 98

McGovern, George, 123

McGregor, Douglas, 124

McGuire Sisters, 115, 116, 126

Medellín, Colombia, 40, 42, 59; daily newspapers in, 34; documentations from, 331n1; Exposición Nacional de Medellín, 45; historical photos on 1920s, 39; INDEGA in, 41, 187; INDEGA-Panamco plant in, 188; interviews in, 331n1; megaplants in, 200; Postobón plant in, 30–31; Staton,

Woods W., 98; Staton in, 58; textile manufacturers in, 82

mega-bottler franchises, 9, 12, 15, 186, 197–200. *See also* FEMSA (Fomento Económico Mexicano); Panamco

Mehdiganj, Uttar Pradesh, 229, 231, 250, 251, 253–55, 259, 262, 269

Mehdiganj movement, 257, 258, 261

Mehdiganj plant, 229, 252, 255, 268, 269, 335n4

Meireles, Cildo, 137–38, 137fig.13

Mejía, Alberto, 41

Mendes, Gilberto, 138

Mendoza, William, 191, 221

merchandizing, training methods, 108–9

Mexico: bottling companies in, 198; bottling ventures in, 20, 58, 60, 198; corporate expansion and acquisition in, 186, 199–200; FEMSA, 29, 199–200; films, 136–37; foreign trademark law in, 165; franchises in, 29; international markets in, 101; Panamco bottling holdings in, 198; pattern advertising and, 108; radio programming, 114; reframing advertising in, 74; social revolution threats in, 122; soda tax, 278; Staton in, 58, 97–98; subsidiary discounts in, 5; television commercials, 116; US companies servicing franchises in, 96

Miami, Florida, 199

micro-business model franchises, 289–90

Middle East: Arab Boycott, 122, 154; cultural integration in, 65; Indian exports to, 177; markets in, 183; soft-drink market in, 227

Miller, Ronald, 122

mineral water plants, 187

minority demographic, 129, 130–31

Mintz, Sidney, 89

Mobil Oil Company, 221–22

"Modern Egypt" ad, 74

modernity: advertising and, 117; broadcasting modern consumption, 113–16; capitalist modernity, 34–41; consumer capitalism and, 89; Gandhi's rejection of, 168; local modernity, 41–46; modern consumer culture, 53–55; portrayal of, 47; radio advertising and, 115; solutions to modernity gap, 76 modernization, 156; criticism of, 64; development as, 66; Gandhi's rejection of, 168; in India, 255; of Latin American economies, 83; US capitalist development and, 88

Mohan Singh, Sardar, 76–77, 171, 178

Monopoly Capital (Baran and Sweezy), 121

monopoly capitalism: colonial salt monopoly, 168; condemnation of in Colombia, 82; indirect control through, 82; monopolization concerns, 72–73, 123; monopoly power, 5, 42, 196; multinationals and, 88; Staton and, 59

Montería, Colombia, 187, 190

Monterrey, Mexico, 199

Montoneros, 122

Mora, Jesús, 41

moral values, 168, 346n152

motivation research, 124–25

Mukherjee, Roopali, 300

multinational corporations, 238; BJP and, 228; and calls for new international economic order, 155–60; Colombian national developmentalism and, 81–86; critiques of, 233; critiques of in Colombia, 81; cultural power of, 72; distrust of, 170; economic power of, 72; as force of peace, 139; government interventions and, 70; in India, 158, 170, 186; law prohibiting selling of products under internationally known trademarks by, 336n7; monopolization concerns and, 88; political power of, 72; power of in Colombia, 191; WWII advertising of, 319n122

multinational developmentalism: overview, 6–7, 103–4; challenges to, 164–65; ECA application for, 99; franchising the essence of capitalism, 69–71; limits to, 95–101; multinational brand for national development, 86–93; national economic development, 71–74; profit motives and, 65; promotion of, 66; restriction of growth of, 96; strategies of promoting, 66

Mumbai, 262, 270. *See also* Bombay

musicians, 130

Muslim countries/populations, 110, 227, 232

Nabisco, 201

Nadaísmo (Nothing-ism) literary movement, 119–20

Nader, Ralph, 123

NAPM (National Alliance of People's Movements), 259–61, 265

Narain, Raj, 176

Narayan, Jayaprakash, 167, 256

Narmada Bachao Andolan, displacement movement against Narmada Dam, 339n116

Narmada Dam, displacement movement against, 339n116

Narmada Dam displacement movement, 260

Nasser, Gamel Abdel, 64

National Alliance of People's Movements (NAPM), 259–61, 265

national developmentalism: overview, 61–66; in advertising, 93–95; coca-colonization and, 86–93; in Colombia, 81; Colombian, 57, 185; in India, 186, 228; limits to multinational developmentalism, 95–101; multinational brand for, 86–93; threats from, 82; turn to, 66

national economic development, 66, 67, 68, 71–74, 91, 92fig.9

National Foreign Trade Convention, 96

National Front, 120

National Geographic (periodical), 53–54, 54fig.6, 101

national identities: of Colombia, 81; of India, 79

national industrialization, 56, 72, 83, 96, 313n121

nationalism: overview, 14–15, 151–54; advertising corporate nationalism, 171–82; in Colombia, 43; in Colombian marketing, 40; de-coca-colonization, 160–65, 182–83; developmentalism and, 88; in India, 152, 154, 228; Indian market and, 79, 330n108, 330n109, 331n118, 331n122; international economic order, 155–60; postcolonial nationalisms, 66, 72; water rights and, 328n46

nationalization: of CC plants, 121; in
Egypt, 73; franchise ownership and, 29;
in India, 152; of industries, 96; in Latin
America, 154; national market protections, 72

National Syndicate of Workers of the
Agri-Food System (Sindicato Nacional
de Trabajadores de la Industria de
Alimentos). *See* Sindicato Nacional de
Trabajadores de la Industria de
Alimentos

National Union of Food Agri-Food System
Workers (Sindicato Nacional de Trabajadores del Sistema Agroalimentario)
(previously Sindicato Nacional de
Trabajadores de la Industria de Alimentos). *See* SINALTRAINAL (National
Union of Food System Workers)

NATO, 67

Neelakandan, C. R., 242

negotiations, 191

Nehru, Jawaharlal, 77, 158, 238

Neiva, Colombia, 187

neocolonialism: anti-American sentiment
and, 170; "Coca-Cola, Quit India"
campaign, 266, 267fig.24, 268; critiques
of, 154; dependency theorists and, 121;
of global economy, 71; postwar period,
72; TCCC as exemplar of, 121; US
intervention as, 81

neoliberal India: overview, 227–29, 266–
70; corporate exploitation, 247–53;
environmental issues, 257–59, 335n4,
338n84, 339n116; Mehdiganj plant,
339n97, 339n98, 339n104; Narmada
Dam displacement movement, 339n116;
networks of organizing, 259–63; pesticide content in bottled drinks, 237–47;
privatization, 233–37; protest movements, 253–57; revaluing Coca-Cola's
symbolic capital, 264–66; social discrimination, 340n125

neoliberalism: overview, 17, 227–29; in
Colombia, 185, 191, 192, 192–94, 200,
201; contaminated bottled drinks and,
228; CSR and, 272, 273; global economic restructuring and, 147; global
emergence of, 139; in India, 183, 228,

229–33, 230–31, 237; Indian urban
middle class and, 238–39; influences in
India, 229–33; Killer Coke campaign
and, 216; labor reform, 219, 225; paramilitarism and, 205; US economic crisis
and, 153

neoliberal violence: overview, 184–85,
224–26; branding battles, 212–24;
building labor power: the origins of
SINALTRAINAL, 190–91; Burmese
plaintiffs sue Unocal over labor abuses
committed in construction of an oil
pipeline, 334n76; Colombian neoliberalism and the Coca-Cola worker, 192–
94; consolidating Colombian Coca-
Cola bottling and, 186–88; finance
capitalism, corporate consolidation,
labor exploitation, 194–200; interviews
and, 331n1; job loss in 1999, cost-cutting
methods during period of consolidation
and restructuring, 333n40; Killer Coke
campaign, 212–24; numbers dispute,
333n48; paramilitary violence against
Coca-Cola workers, 203–9, 209–11;
payments to leftist guerillas to avoid
kidnappings, 333n60; at the turn of the
21st century, 200–202; Venezuelan
bottler joint venture between Coca-
Cola and Cisneros family, 333n38

Nestlé, 190, 201, 209

Nestle, Marion, 293

New Delhi, India, 77, 81, 182

New Guinea, 52

New International Economic Order
(NIEO), 155, 155–57, 281

Newton, Huey, 147

New York, 106, 108, 129

New Zealand, 96

NGOs (non-governmental organizations),
216, 219, 238, 240, 261, 262, 262–63, 266,
283–84, 287; Alianza por la Salud
Alimentaria, 277–78; in Colombia,
284; CSE, 237–45, 242; CSR and, 273;
documentations from, 331n1; Educar
Consumidores, 277–78; Fundación
Colombianitos, 285; Fundación Ideas
para la Paz, 284

Nicaragua, 98, 198, 222

pattern books, 107, 108, 109, 111, 112, 319n140

Pearl of the Orient (1954 promotional film), 102

Peláez, Daniel, 41, 57, 58, 59

Pemberton, John, 19, 78

Pendergrast, Mark, 10, 308n30

people of color/communities of color, 122, 297

People's World Water Forum, 261

Pepsi-Cola Co., 24, 41, 86, 126, 237, 238; African American market efforts by, 325n96; Aquafina sales, 240; as challenger in India, 232; in India, 246; as international challenger, 198; Pepsi Generation slogan, 324n74; pesticide content in bottled drinks, 244–45; return to India after neoliberal economic reforms, 330n109; Venezuelan bottler joint venture between Coca-Cola and Cisneros family, 333n38

Percy, Charles H., 171

Pereira, Colombia, 30, 59, 187

Permanent People's Tribunals, 225

pesticide residues, 16, 237–47, 267, 271

PET (polyethylene terephthalate) bottles, 269, 288

Pfizer, 272

philanthrophy, 216

Philippines, 20, 29, 30, 91, 102, 108, 112

photography, 110–11, 111fig.10

Pignatari, Décio, 138

Plachimada, India, 231, 262, 269, 270, 276

Plachimada movement, 228, 249–50, 253–54, 260–61, 262, 335–36n4, 335n4

Plan Colombia, 204

planned economy movement, 71–72

Playpumps International, 287

"Poca-Chola" ("Little Head") Cuban satirical ad, 319n141

Polaris Institute, 240, 262

political issues: Colombian political reform, 43; political assassinations campaign, 333n60; political corruption, 170; political nationalism, 168; political neocolonialism, US, 170; postwar political power, 72

polyethylene terephthalate (PET) bottles, 269, 288

populism, 43, 82

Posada, Gabriel, 309n35

Posada y Tobón, 29, 30, 187. *See also* Postobón (previously Posada y Tobón)

Postobón (previously Posada y Tobón), 30, 86, 190, 207, 311n71; Coca-Cola advertisements, 34–40; control of bottled drink business in Colombia, 42; Kist brand, 58; labor unions and, 190–91; Lülle and, 187–88; price setting, 45; sugar-sweetened beverage tax debate, 277–78; US government report on, 57

Posto-Kola, 41

postwar baby boomer consumer demographic, 129–38

postwar internationalization: overview, 13–14, 61–66, 103–4; advertising and, 93–95; coca-colonization, 66–69; Colombian economic nationalism and, 81–86; corporate globalism and, 101–3; franchise as mode of capitalist internationalization, 65; French resistance to, 67–69; as internationalization of US capitalism, 316n36; limits to multinational developmentalism and, 95–101; multinational brand for national development, 86–93; multinational developmentalism, 69–71, 95–101; national economic development, 71–74; in postcolonial India, 74–81; of US capitalism, 316n36

postwar period: advertising for the working class, 89–90; baby boom generation, 115; CC rhetoric in, 69; cultural projections during, 55, 113; currency stabilization, 71; ECA application, 98–99; economic recovery plans in India, 157–58; employment during, 88; free trade in, 83; global advertising strategies, 86–87; major expansion during, 127; negative response to international expansion in, 66; neocolonialism during, 72; opposition during, 66; power assertions, 101; prosperity of, 123–24

Potter, Ed, 223, 279; removable, 333n48

poverty: in global south, 156; in India, 159, 239; US loans to ease, 85

poverty reduction, in Colombia, 120

power assertions, 3; in advertising, 53–55; consumption and, 215; criticism of, 139; CSR and, 298; franchise bottlers and, 57; over franchises, 29; over intellectual property, 26; pattern advertising and, 106; postwar period, 61, 101; US in Colombian marketplace as, 34

Prebisch, Raúl, 121

precarización (labor precarization), 186, 192–93, 200, 201, 212–13, 220, 224, 225

Premier (Indian soft drink company), 80

price controls, wartime, 48

price setting: overview, 3; wartime economy and, 45

print ads, pattern-advertising strategy transitions, 47

private investment, 88, 96, 229

privatization: of bottled water, 274; in Colombia, 201; in India, 230, 235, 258, 259; organizing against, 262

privatization of water resources, 16, 229, 233–37, 240, 260, 262, 268

production: as a commodity, 91, 92fig.9; control of in India, 231; in direct control of, 82; externalization of, 194; full production, 86–93; outsourcing of, 65; production control, 3; production increases, 66; production machinery, 42; production models, 65; production monopolization, 72; production of materials, 307n9; production standardization, 86–87, 87fig.8; productive capacity, 121; product marketing, 88; product replacement, 73; standards of, 91–93

profits, 6; from bottling industry investments, 194; Colombian reforms and, 193, 195; hiding of, 4; from licensing to bottlers, 194; from Mehdiganj plant, 268; offshore profits, 5; profit-extractive business model, 67; retention of, 157, 180; for shareholders, 196–97, 302

Progressive Era reformers, 27

promotional campaigns, 102; bottle cap promotions, 58–59; Coca-Cola Export/ Panamco collaboration, 58–59

proprietary history, 9–10

prosperidad al debe (debt prosperity), 33

protectionism: in Colombia, 43, 46, 81–86; Farley on, 96; Ko-Kana and, 44; policies of, 96; shift to, 60

protections: for foreign capital investments, 96; protectionism in Colombia, 43, 46, 81–86; from taxation, 194; unions and, 200

protests: in Colombia, 190; *Colombia* (Caro) reproductions and, 326n115; commodity chains and, 273; in France, 67–68; Gaon Bachao Sangharsh Samiti (Save the Village Struggle Committee), 255–56; in India, 213, 237, 260fig.22; Killer Coke campaign, 212; Mehdiganj movement, 261; of Mehdiganj plant expansion, 269; Plachimada movement, 253–54, 260–61, 261; supporting SIN-ALTRAINAL, 326n115

prototype ads, 107–9, 110–11, 111fig.10, 128–29

public health issues, 67–68, 78; bottled water industry and, 176; consumer protection reforms, 70; deterioration of, 297; energy balance programs, 292–94; food and drink safety, 245; healthcare, 274, 276–78; healthcare issues, 274; health claims, 50; health costs, 3; impacts of, 274; in India, 274; obesity, 274, 277, 278, 292–94; pollution of water resources, 228; public drinking water in India, 241; public health movements, 297; regulation of, 276–77; secret formulas, 169, 169fig.16; sugar-sweetened beverages and, 49, 274, 276–78, 297

Public Policy and Corporate Reputation Council, 272

public relations, 271; "The Coke Side of Life" campaign, 224; corporate social reputation, 292–97; CSE report and, 238; CSR and, 272; Farley and, 61–62; in India, 286; Killer Coke campaign, 212–24; minor visible adjustments to business practices as, 8; sugar inventory sales, 49

Puerto Rico: bottling ventures in, 20; Sparks Milling Company, 29

risk minimization, 3
Rist, Gilbert, 156
Robinson, Frank, 30
Robinson, William E., 127
Rockefeller, Nelson, 47
Rogers, Henry, 78
Rogers, Ray, 213–14, 301
Rogers company, 78–79, 176
Rojas Pinilla, Gustavo, 84, 119
Roldán, Mary, 83–84
Roosevelt administration, 49
Rostow, W. W., 87–88
royalties, 73
RSS (Rashtriya Swayamsevak Sangh), 232
"Rum and Coca-Cola" (song), 55
rural environmental resources, 228, 229
rural extraction, 235, 248, 248fig.21, 250–51, 274, 276
rural industrialization, 228
Rusk, Dean, 171
Rutgers University, 213

sales growth, 335n3
Sales Shelf, 108
sales training, 65
salt, 268
Samajwadi Jan Parishad (Socialist People's Council), 261
Santa Clara, 187
Santa Marta, 34
Santos Calderón, Francisco, 208–9
The Saturday Evening Post (periodical), 101
school contracts, 294
Scott-Heron, Gil, 134–35
Second World, 154. *See also* Soviet bloc countries
secret formulas, 65; FERA and, 153, 162–64; Indian substitutes for, 179–80; public health concerns, 169, 169fig.16; regulatory issues and, 67–68
secret ingredients, 66, 69, 247–53
segregation, 131
Select Committee on Nutrition and Human Needs, 123
self-regulation, 273, 278–86
self-rule (*swaraj*), 167, 168
sexualization, 110, 116
Seychelles, 177

shareholders: consolidation and, 195–96; in India, 231, 286; in Latin America, 186, 191, 194; shareholder activism, 215–16; shareholder democracy, 301–2; shareholder value, 195
SICO, 223
signifiers, 116–20, 116–23
"Sign of Good Taste" campaign, 101
Sikkink, Kathryn, 263
Sinaltrainal (National Union of Workers of the Agri-Food System): overview, 185, 209, 224–26; Coca-Cola versus, 209–11; IUF and, 222–23; Killer Coke campaign, 220–21; labor exploitation and, 274; Marxist critiques, 216; membership decline, 200–201, 207, 210; NYC protests supporting, 326n115; origins of, 190–91; paramilitary attacks on, 206; paramilitary violence and, 207–8; threats against, 205; visual representations, 218–19, 218fig.19
Sindicato Nacional de Trabajadores del Sistema Agroalimentario (previously Sindicato Nacional de Trabajadores de la Industria de Alimentos). *See* Sinaltrainal (National Union of Workers of the Agri-Food System)
sindicatos amarillos ("yellow" company unions), 200
Singapore, 177
Singh, Charanjit, 76, 178–79, 182
Singh, Daljit, 76, 171
Singh family, 76, 81, 153, 171, 177, 182
Sintradingascol, 190, 191
socialism: CSR and, 302; in India, 153, 156, 159, 167, 230, 261; socialist governments, 121; socialist measures, 70; socialist parties, 81–82
social issues: social and cultural logics of the franchise, 23–29; social associations, 4; social costs, 3; social discrimination, 340n125; social values impact, 67–68. *See also* corporate social responsibility (CSR); social resistance; social revolution threats
social justice: in advertising, 73; CSR and, 303; environmental politics and, 257–59; South Asian diaspora and, 262

social logic (of the franchise), 60, 65, 186

social movements: in Colombia, 201; in India, 159; popular discontent and, 134

social reform, in Colombia, 43

social resistance: overview, 271–73, 303–4; Alianza por la Salud Alimentaria and Educar Consumidores TV commercial (2017), 342n28; Annan on UN Global Compact, 342n50; brand and market promotion, 292–97; corporations as social welfare providers, 286–92; CSR and, 297–303; investors and governance and benefits from surplus, 343n52; legal/regulatory accountability, 274–78; voluntary codes of conduct and civil society collaboration, 278–86

social revolution threats, 83; 1960s activism, 121–23, 324n74; overview, 14, 105; advertising difference, 125–29; broadcasting modern consumption, 113–16; in Colombia, 118–20; conferences on, 138–39; globalization patterns: international pattern advertising, 106–9; hegemonic counterculture, 123–25; "I'd Like to Buy the World a Coke," 140–50; in Mexico, 122; new force for peace/target of new social revolutions, 138–40; patterning sameness, managing difference, 109–13; postwar baby boomer consumer demographic, 129–38; prevention of, 56; sticky signifiers: the capital of American culture at mid-century, 123–25

"The Social Responsibility of Business Is to Increase Its Profits" (Friedman), 302

social unrest in Colombia, La Violencia conflict, 82, 83–85, 119, 203

social welfare initiatives, 56, 273, 286–92

soda tax, 49, 274, 276–78, 297

"Soft Drinks in War" memo, 49–50

solidarity: brand value and, 264–65; Indian activism and, 249, 269; Killer Coke campaign and, 213, 214; Sinaltrainal and, 209, 211, 216, 219–23; Solidarity Center, 223–24; US-based activists, 15

song-form commercials, 129–30

Soviet bloc countries, 66, 139, 154, 175, 181, 316n36

Spain, 20

Sparkes, Russell, 278

Sparks Milling Company, 29

Spencer (Indian soft drink company), 80

Srivastava, Amit, 262–63, 266

Stages of Economic Growth (Rostow), 87–88

stagnation, 121, 156

stakeholder theory, 157, 175, 198, 271, 282–86, 298–300, 343n52

Standard Fruit Company, 221–22

standardization of production, 86–87, 87fig.8, 90, 134

Standard Oil Company, 29, 221–22

Starbucks, 272

Staton, Albert H., 30, 57–60, 62, 74–75, 83, 85, 96–97, 97–98, 186–87, 188

Staton, Albert, Jr., 97

Staton, John, 30, 58, 97

Staton, Woods, 97

Staton, Woods W., 98

Staton family, 186

stocks and dividends: as financial commodity, 195–96; generating capital from, 194; strategic buying of, 5

strikes: American Dream (1990 documentary) (Kopple), 214; in Colombia, 190, 191, 207, 210; Gaon Bachao Sangharsh Samiti (Save the Village Struggle Committee) hunger strike, 255–56; at Hormel, 214; in India, 255; Mehdiganj movement, 261

structural adjustment measures, 192

Stubbs, Roy, 41

student mobilizations, 212, 214, 216, 232, 263

Students for Economic Justice, 212

subcontracting: overview, 3; in Colombia, 15, 185, 200, 210; franchising and, 22; Killer Coke campaign and, 225; labor contractors, 254–55; as outsourcing, 201

subliminal messages, 125

subsidiaries: in Brazil, 186; Coca-Cola India, 230, 231; in Colombia, 186–87, 188, 191, 197; Hindustan Coca-Cola Beverages Limited, 230–31, 270, 339n105; in India, 153, 154, 158, 160, 162, 229, 270; in Latin America, 186; in Mexico, 186; as non-local producers, 96;

subsidiaries *(continued)*
of Panamco, 199; pattern advertising and, 106–7; profit transfers to, 194; subsidiary discounts, 5. *See also* INDEGA (Industrial de Gaseosas Ltda.); Panamco
substitution, import-substitution industrialization, 70, 73, 83, 120
sugar, 59, 98; bottling contract modifications and, 48; bounty programs, 48; in Colombia, 42; Colombian, 44; difficulties of getting, 85; externalization of cost of, 48; lack of vertical integration of, 5; price controls, 49; public health and sugar-sweetened beverages, 49, 274, 276–78, 297; wartime rationing, 49–50; World War II and, 46; World War I rationing of, 48
sugarless concentrate, 49
sugar-rationing, 48–49, 50, 62
Sun Trust Bank, 214
Supplier Guiding Principles, 279–80
sustainability: challenges, 274; commitment to, 271; CSE and, 241; CSR and, 301; in India, 274
swadeshi (foreign-made goods boycott), 79, 166, 167–68, 256–57, 268
Swami Ramdev, 340n146
swaraj (self-rule), 167, 168
Swaziland, 5
Sweezy, Paul, 121–22
syrups, 48, 57, 85–86, 98–99

"Tanda matlab toilet cleaner," 340n146
tariffs: Colombian tariff policies, 85, 192; high tariffs on cheaper priced goods, 82; imports and, 57; reduction of, 43, 230; tariff protection, 48; tariff protection on sugar, 49; tariff protections, 81; on US imports into Colombia, 83
Tata group, 157, 272
Taussig, Michael, 184–85
taxation: colonial salt tax, 168; exemptions, 96; on intangible assets, 4; national soft drink tax, 49; protections from, 194; on sugar-sweetened beverages, 274, 276–77, 297; tax havens, 4–5; use of, 96
Teamsters Union, 221

Technical Observers (TOs), 51–52, 55, 56, 75
technical services, 99; overview, 3
technological advances, Rostow on, 88
technological experience, 72, 160; Indian self-sufficiency, 181; indirect control through, 82; modern workers/consumers and, 90
technological knowledge, in India, 158, 165, 182
technology: acquisition of, 158; for development, 153; transfer of, 157, 163, 183
television advertising: Colombian soda tax ad, 277; global advertising strategies, 105; "Happiness Factory" (commercial), 224; "Hilltop" (1971 commercial), 143–49; "I'd Like to Buy the World a Coke" commercial, 141, 146, 227; in India, 227, 234, 340n146; integration in, 131; international campaigns, 14; international markets and, 148–49; jingles, 114–15; "Little Drops of Joy" campaign, 271–72; "Little Drops of Joy" commercials, 271; McCann-Erickson advertising agency, 106, 127, 127–29; McGuire Sisters, 115, 126; parodies of, 136; pattern advertising and, 116, 148; Pepsi-Cola Co., 126; "Real Thing" campaign, 140, 143, 148; subliminal messages, 125; transition to, 113; youth culture, 116, 126–27
"Tens of Thousands of Egyptian Dealers" ad, 73
TERI (The Energy and Resources Institute), 263, 269–70, 286
thanda drinks, 267
"*Thanda matlab* Coca-Cola" campaign, 234–35, 236fig.20, 248, 268
The Coca-Cola Bottler (Company publication), 26, 39
The Coca-Cola Company (TCCC) executives: Austin, 123, 165, 290; Daft, 233; Goizueta, 1, 182–83, 195; Isdell, 227, 280, 283, 303; Quincey, 233; Woodruff, Ernest, 48; Woodruff, Robert W., 50, 61, 69, 85, 182, 188
The Coca-Cola Company (TCCC) history, 6–9, 11–12
The Coca-Cola Company (TCCC) periodicals, 26, 55, 56, 189

The Coca-Cola Export Corporation
(TCCEC), 25, 28, 40, 74, 80, 103, 110,
121, 151–52, 161
"The Coca-Cola Signature" (waltz), 113–14
The Energy and Resources Institute
(TERI), 263, 269–70, 286
The Real Thing advertising campaign, 1,
105, 130–34
The Red Barrel (Company publication), 26,
39, 52
The Refresher (Company publication), 26
"The Sun Never Sets on Cacoola," 63–65,
66
"The Universal Invitation . . . Let's Have a
Coke" advertisement, 47
"Things go better with Coca-Cola/Things
go better with Coke" campaign, 129–30,
325n91
Third World, 66, 87, 154, 155, 156, 157, 170
"This is How a New Business is Born"
ad, 94
Thompson, Grahame, 283
Thums Up, 180, 229, 232, 233, 239
Time (periodical), 66
Time (periodical), 63–65, 63fig.7, 77
Tobón, Olarte Valerio, 30
Tobón, Valerio, 309n35
T. O. Digest (Company publication), 26, 56.
See also Coca-Cola Overseas (Company
publication)
TOs (Technical Observers), 51–52, 55, 56, 75
Townsend, Robert, 124
trademarks: acquisition of Parle's, 229;
Coke trademark, 325n91; democracy
and, 88; as intangible assets, 4; as intellectual property, 3, 26–27; laws regarding use of, 336n7; legal aspects of, 27–28;
personification of, 63fig.7, 77; in print
advertising, 114; profits from licensing
of, 65, 194; protections, 40; trademark
infringement cases, 40–41, 80, 136, 176;
use of, 3
trade unionists: assassinations of, 209,
220–21; blacklisting of, 209; ILO and,
223; lawsuit over, 210–11; paternalistic
victimization of, 218, 219; representations of, 217fig.18, 218–19, 218fig.19;
solidarity with, 216

trade unions: AFL-CIO and, 221–22;
AIFLD and, 221–22; in Colombia, 274;
Colombian repression of, 82, 184–85,
191, 204–5; financial settlement and,
225; paramilitary attacks on, 206–7;
SICO, 223; trade negotiations, 83; trade
policies, 81; trade regulations, 159. *See
also* Sinaltrainal; trade unionists
traditional drinks, 67, 69, 78, 267
training, 25, 108
transnationals: critiques of foreign power
of, 178, 180; in Latin America, 29, 190;
protests against capital of, 258, 260;
transnational activism, 216, 221, 222,
226, 263, 269, 270; transnational social
movements, 274
transparency, 215
transportation, 59, 85
Treasure Chest, 108
tributary industries: in Colombia, 94–95,
97; in Philippines, 102; promotion of,
99
Trinidad, 96
Tropical Oil Company, 34
Tunis, Egypt, 52
Turf (Indian soft drink company), 80

UN (United Nations). *See* United Nations
(UN)
underemployment, 193
UNDP (United Nations Development
Program), 287
unemployment, 121, 193
UNICEF, 146
uniformity, 108
Unilever, 175, 201
Unión Patriótica (Patriotic Union), 204
unions: Colombian repression of, 82;
documentations from, 331n1; in India,
254–55; undercutting power of, 200. *See
also* Sinaltrainal; trade unions
United Fruit Company, 29, 34, 82, 221–22
United Nations (UN), 61, 76, 155, 156–57,
272, 287
United Nations Development Program
(UNDP), 287
United Nations Global Compact, 280–82,
284, 286, 342n50

United Self-Defense Forces of Colombia (Autodefensas Unidas de Colombia) (AUC), 205

United Steelworkers of America (USW), 210–11, 221

United Students Against Sweatshops, 212, 219

"United today. United Always-" tagline, 47

universality, 47, 53–55, 54fig.6, 101–3, 102–3, 106–9, 115, 128–29, 149

University of Illinois at Urbana-Champaign, 213

UNOCAL, 210, 334n76

Up the Organization (Townsend), 124

urbanization: in Colombia, 84, 90, 118; consumption and, 235; in India, 258

Urrutia, Miguel, 83

Uruguay, 122

USAID, 287

US economic aid, 67, 84

US exceptionalism, 221

US government: Bush administration, 245; Carter administration, 170–71; Colombian development and, 56; Colombian economic development and, 83; ECA application, 98–99; foreign-aid assistance, 71; foreign policy in Latin America, 221; market interventions, 71; Plan Colombia, 204; price controls, 48, 49; push to open national markets, 72; support of, 245; Truman administration, 73, 88

US hegemony: AFL-CIO and, 222; CC as symbol of, 67; in Colombia, 85; differences and, 101–2; national market protections against, 72; reestablishment of, 8; rise of in Third World, 66

US military: advertising universal appeal and, 53–55; aid to Colombia, 84, 85; association with, 170; globalization and, 51–52; interventions/occupations, 29–30, 34, 84; military contracts, 313n121; military-soda industrial complex, 51; strategic bases in Asia, 67; sugar exemption and, 50; wartime collaboration with, 62

USW (United Steelworkers of America), 210–11, 221

Uttar Pradesh, India, 251, 252–54, 261

Uttar Pradesh Pollution Control, 269

Valledupar, Colombia, 187, 190, 191

Varanasi, India, 250, 254, 256, 257. *See also* Benares, India

Vedwan, Neeraj, 242

Venezuela, 20, 96, 98, 198, 333n38

vertical integration, 5, 82, 187

VHP (Vishva Hindu Parishad), 232

Villa, Gabriel Posada, 30

Villavicencio, Colombia, 187

Vincent (Indian soft drink company), 80

La Violencia conflict, 82, 83–85, 119, 203

virtuous cycle model, 86–87

Vishva Hindu Parishad (VHP), 232

Walking Ghosts (Dudley), 205

Walmart, 272

warehousing, 220

Warhol, Andy, 136

waste/reuse: of materials, 307n9; waste production, 240; wastewater disposal, 255; water recycling, 286

water resources: access to, 228, 291; CSR initiatives and moral credits, 17; Department of Regional Water Studies, 286; exploitation of, 239; in India, 165, 182, 274; liberalization of, 239; pollution of, 16, 228, 267; privatization of, 16, 240, 252, 268; rural access to, 228; self-regulations in India, 279

water rights issues, 328n46; overview, 227–29; corporate exploitation of the water commons, 247–53, 248fig.21; plant closures over, 269–70; solidarity with, 213; transnational activism over, 270; water privatization, 7–8

water scarcity, 249–51, 252–53, 259, 269, 276; vulnerability to, 270

water sustainability: CSR campaign and, 271; NGOS and, 287

water use: corporate water use in India, 276; EKOCENTERs, 289–90; lack of vertical integration of, 5; sustainability efforts, 271; water extraction, 263, 269; water neutrality, 271, 287–89; water offsetting, 287–88; water use reduction, 286–87

Welles, Sumner, 56
Wexler, Haskell, 143–44
white supremacism, 117
whitewashing, 92fig.9, 93, 101, 102, 109
WHO (World Health Organization), 245, 274
Whyte, William, 124
Wilder, Billy, 316n36
Wilson, Sloan, 126
Wonderful World (1959 TCCC-promotional film), 102–3
Woodruff, Ernest, 48
Woodruff, Robert W., 50, 61–62, 69, 85, 182, 188
workers: advertising for, 89–90; in Colombia, 82, 184–85, 186, 192–94, 200–209; in Egypt, 73–74; flexibilization and *precarización* (labor precarization), 186, 192–93, 200, 201, 212–13, 220, 224, 225; independent contractor status, 193, 200, 201; in India, 159; labor exploitation, 166, 186, 193, 194–200, 220, 256–57, 274, 280, 298, 302; labor-management relationships in Colombia, 188–89; in Mehdiganj bottling plant, 254–55; in Mexico, 74; outsourcing and, 193; paramilitary violence and, 203–9; postwar period advertising and, 89–90; reclassification, 193; recognition of, 124; strikes, 190, 210; surplus value extraction from, 194; temporary workers, 3; underemployment, 193; virtuous cycle model, 86–87; workers' rights challenges, 274. *See also* downsizing; human rights violations; labor unions; outsourcing; Sinaltrainal; subcontracting; unions

"Work Refreshed" marketing, 49–50, 89–90, 115
World Bank, 85, 158, 159, 255, 260
World Economic Forum, 281–82
World Health Organization (WHO), 245, 274
World's Fair (1964), 103
World Social Forum (WSF), 261, 262
World Trade Organization (WTO), 230, 245
World War II: bottling operations in India during, 75; Colombia and, 43, 46; economic challenges of, 62; government spending, 71; international expansion during, 46–56; national independence movement, 166; sugar-rationing, 48–49, 50, 62; TOs (Technical Observers), 51–52; US military collaboration during, 50–51; wartime advertising, 47
World Water Conference, 262
World Wildlife Fund (WWF), 287
WTO (World Trade Organization), 230, 245

Yadav, Kushal, 241
Yadavindra Singh, Maharaja, 76
Young, Anthony, 162–63, 165
Young, Robert W., 42, 58
youth culture: advertising and, 116, 125–29, 133–34; broadcast media and, 116, 125–26; in Colombia, 118–20; conferences on, 138–39; critiques by, 121; youth consumer group, 105, 125–27, 129–30
Youth Market marketing, 107, 115, 118, 125, 129–30
yo-yo promotion, 58–59

Žižek, Slavoj, 299–300, 346n151